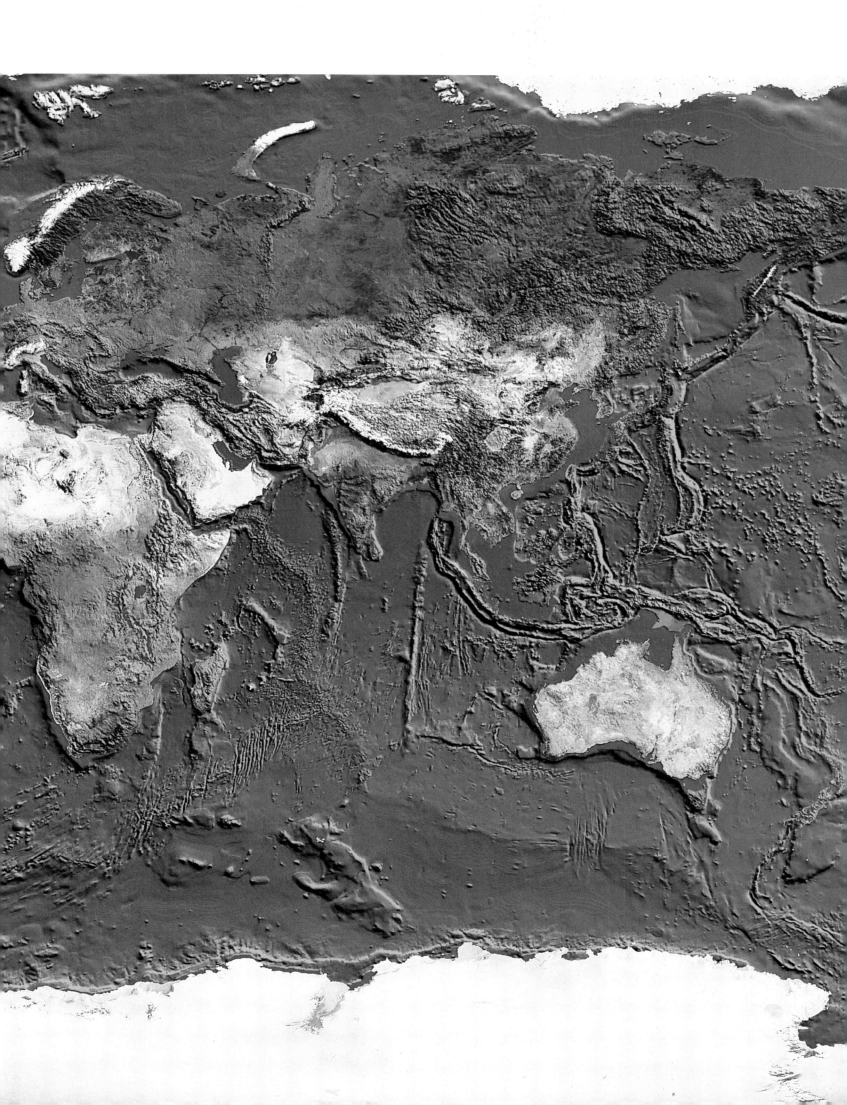

THE CARTOGRAPHIC
Satellite Atlas
OF THE
WORLD

Credits

The Cartographic Satellite Atlas of the World
English Language Edition

Publisher
AND Cartographic Publishers Ltd., Finchampstead, United Kingdom

Consultants
Simon Butler
Menno-Jan Kraak
Peter Sackett
Robert Stacey
Emery Miller
Edith Stacey

Production of satellite imagery
Robert Stacey, WorldSat International Inc., Mississauga, Ontario, Canada;
Jim Knighton

Satellite Data NOAA
Ocean Floor Bathymetry by NOAA courtesy of USGS
Images on pages 26, 27, 36, 37, 38 and 39 based on the Resurs imagert, provided by SSC/Satellitbild
of Kiruna, Sweden
Digital Image processed on a Silicon Graphics workstation using PCI EASI/PACE software

Cartographic Design, Layout and Production
AND Map Graphics Ltd., Finchampstead, United Kingdom
Production Director - Alan Horsfield
Cartographers - Chris Hulford, Adam Meara, Mark Lewis, Ian Dewsbery, Tom Carlin
Editorial - John Watkins, Peter Butler
Reprographics - Jon Pattingale

Cover and preliminary section
Research - Professor Menno-Jan Kraak, TU; Delft, The Netherlands
Design - Designers and Partners, Oxford, United Kingdom

Printing and binding
Editoriale Libraria, Trieste, Italy

© *1998 WorldSat International Inc., Ontario, Canada*
© *1998 ROBAS BV, Weesp, The Netherlands*
© *1998 AND Cartographic Publishers Ltd., Finchampstead, United Kingdom*
© *1996 SPOT Image, Toulouse, France*

ISBN: 9 072770 76 5

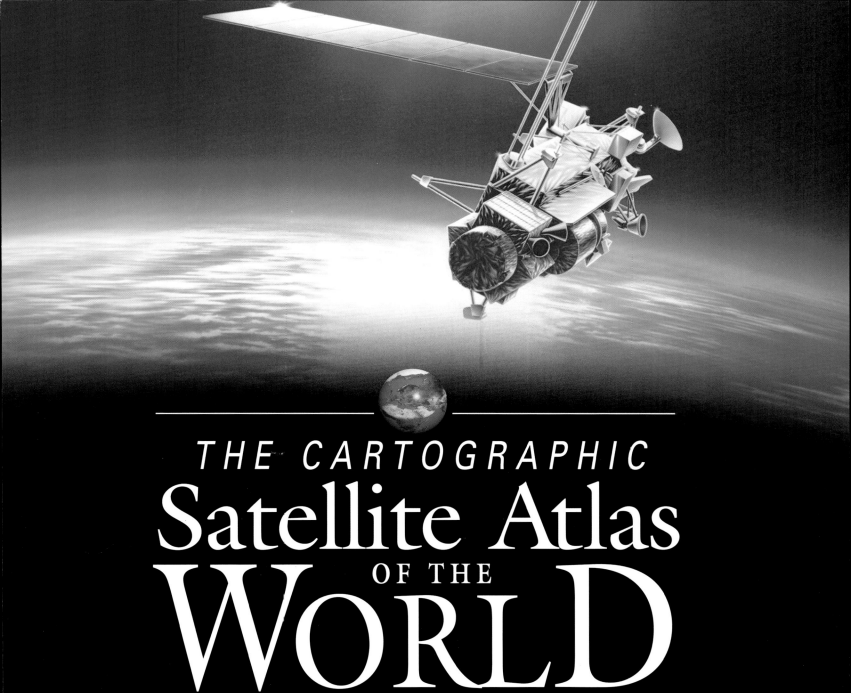

THE CARTOGRAPHIC
Satellite Atlas
OF THE
WORLD

Foreword

The advancing world of technology has done wonders for the armchair traveller as mankind's perspective on the world has brought ever more exciting outlooks on our surroundings. We have moved from the era of climbing the nearest hill to see what we could see on the other side of the mountain, to the first tentative ventures in hot air balloons, to aircraft and cameras and fully on into space through the eyes of the astronauts and the ever circling surveillance satellites that constantly monitor our earth today.

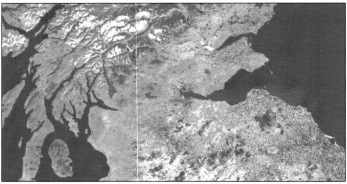

Central Scotland

The Changing Perspective

It is important to recognise the very significant advances that both aerial photography and satellite imagery have brought to the process of mapping. In the case of aerial photography man was finally able to see the reality of vast areas of land, not as interpreted by random sampling or a particular individual's perspective, but as it actually was. In addition to this "perfect" view, aerial photography was also able, using two photographs taken from different angles, to calculate the variations or undulation inherent in the changing elevations of the rolling hills, mountains and valleys of the world. It brought the flat earth into the third dimension.

Not only did satellites add a new viewpoint from which to observe the world they also added a new point of view from which to assess our geography and vegetation or lack thereof. The viewpoint of earth from space allowed mankind to see vast geological and biological features of the earth that were not visible in the relative close-up views from aircraft. Such views resulted in the discovery of the "overthrust" belt in North America from which followed the strike of vast oil reserves buried thousands of metres below existing wells. It lead to views of depletion of the Amazon and other tropical rain forests that were not previously suspected and it allowed us economic access to regions of the world such as the Arctic and Antarctic that were not viable using traditional methodologies.

Equally important, the satellite added a new point of view from which to look at the world. One which used highly accurate colour information collected by the satellite in both the visible and near infra red regions of the electromagnetic spectrum to "see" things that would normally be invisible to the naked eye. It could detect stress in vegetation before it became visible, it could distinguish different species of trees and vegetation from each other from space and it could detect anomalies in vegetation, water and bare earth. Added to this new perspective was the fact that the data, or imagery, existed as digital data - not as film. This meant that images could be compared to each other electronically and added to or subtracted from one another. Detecting and mapping change was now an order of magnitude easier and the prospect of "looking at" and mapping continuous and subtle changes in vegetation over large areas became a reality.

The new Perspective

While it is true that public sector surveillance satellites have been around since the early '70s it is only recently that space based composites of the entire earth have been available. The first of these are based on the NOAA (National Oceanic and Atmospheric Administration) series of satellites designed specifically to monitor and forecast weather around the world. Of all of the satellites launched by mankind the weather satellites have done more to benefit mankind than any of the others, having saved untold thousands of lives through their ability to see cloud patterns and movements in relation to the land masses and to predict major catastrophes, forever changing man's approach to the weather. It seems somehow fitting that the first, ironically cloud-free, composite images of the Earth should be based on this data.

The result is a view of our world as it would appear from 800 kilometres in space and devoid of any cloud cover. For the first time mankind can now gaze down at a realistic miniature of his home in the confidence that this is the reality. The distribution of continents are not presumed or calculated; they are "photographed". The distribution of vegetation, deserts, water and perpetual snow and ice are presented in the comfort that this is "the truth" and, as this is similar to what we have been taught in the past, we can now go to sleep in the comfort that history has not lied to us and the future has dawned as it should.

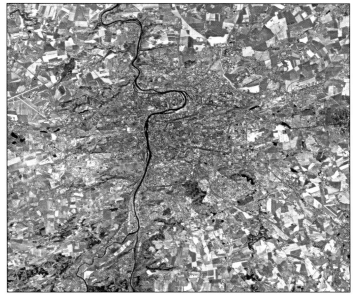

Prague

The Atlas

The production of this Atlas brings a new era in map reproduction to the world. An era where we can not only look at the boundaries that are delineated by the cartographer but also the underlying reality. In the process of creating this reality it was necessary to further enhance the imagery that went into the construction of the atlas. We matched elevation data for the entire earth to the space imagery and generated shaded relief which imparts a sense of the third dimension to the final maps. We incorporated relief data on the ocean floor so that you could peer through the water with your "X-ray eyes" and study the variations in terrain (or elevation) that exist under our vast oceans. This in deference to the "other" two-thirds of our world. Finally, we have incorporated the traditional cartography, delineating the non-visible components (the ether - so to speak) of our World, such as political boundaries, as well as putting place names to towns and regions to provide an all-encompassing perspective of our new earth as it moves us inexorably into our next millennium.

And Finally

This "Space-Based" Atlas certainly opens mother earth's kimono with all of its flaws and in all of its beauty. The scars in the rain forests of South America and the Pacific nations can no longer hide under a surface of clouds or in inaccessibility any more than the scars of logging in western Canada or the dumping of pollutants in our vast and heretofore remote oceans can hide from the prying eyes of the ever-vigilant satellites.

Many would say that we have not treated our home very well. From the dawning of the industrial revolution through the technological revolution and on into the information age we have treated mother earth with disdain and indifference. Would we be so callus and unconcerned if this same book had been published in 1896? Would the comparative differences shock and dismay us? Will the 2096 edition give us pause to reflect? Will we congratulate ourselves on a job well done or will we just wonder where the time went? The publishers of this book hope that this will be the first step in opening our eyes, to presenting an image of the world that will stand as reference to future generations and a guide to the new mappers of our world. As we approach the frontiers of a new millennium it would seem an appropriate time to adjust our view of the world, to embrace the technologies that will improve our understanding of our home and provide that 21st century perspective and outlook to our world. We hope that you enjoy this atlas as much in the reading as we did in its compilation.

Start the fire, curl up in that chair, journey and enjoy.

Emery Miller
WorldSat International Inc.

Contents

Key to Symbols and Images

This section helps you to find your way around this atlas quickly, to check the page location and scale of each of the maps and to familiarise yourself with the symbols, abbreviations and typography used throughout

Satellite Mapping

In order that you can fully understand the complex process by which the satellite maps featured in this atlas are brought to you, this section provides both a simple introduction to satellite mapping and some additional facts for the technically minded.

Satellite Images of the World

A seven page selection of stunning satellite images featuring major cities and contrasting geographical habitats from around the world.
These "zoomed in" images of earth are breath-takingly detailed and provide another perspective of our natural and man-made world.

Maps of the World

This major section of brand-new mapping boasts three unique features:

The first ever satellite cartography at a 1 kilometre resolution, making this the most realistic view of earth ever made and so instantly outdating every other world atlas produced.

The most up-to-date ground elevation data ever produced, copyrighted by the producers of this atlas and exactly matching the satellite imagery thus creating an enhanced three dimensional effect that gives this atlas its so-realistic view from space.

An unprecedented clarity of both legend and image achieved, for the first time, by reversing the map lettering out of the colourful map relief backgrounds.

The maps are presented by continent, beginning with Europe. Each section starts with a double page spread featuring the continent in question, followed by larger scale maps of individual countries.

Europe

Middle East

Key to Symbols and Images

Whether you are searching specifically for a geographic location or for statistical information or just browsing idly through this atlas, an understanding of the symbols and images employed will help you get the most enjoyment and use from *The Cartographic Satellite Atlas of the World*

Time spent studying the pointer labels and tables alongside will be time well spent.

The map shown here depicts different aspects of the information presented in this atlas, allowing you to get a feel for the symbols, abbreviations and type styles used throughout.

Finally, a comprehensive table appears under the map that covers every symbol, abbreviation and type style used in this atlas.

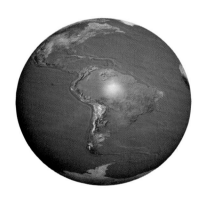

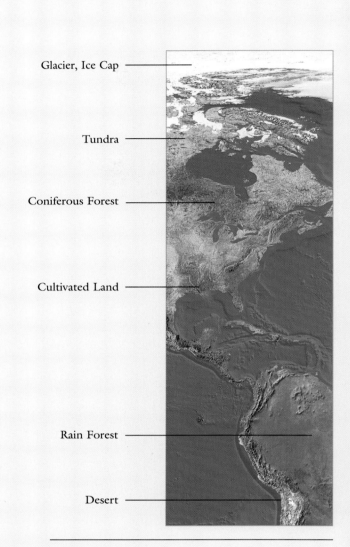

Glacier, Ice Cap

Tundra

Coniferous Forest

Cultivated Land

Rain Forest

Desert

Scale

A scale of 1:12 000 000 means that the distance on the map is 12 Million times smaller than the actual distance measured at the Earth's surface; e.g. 1 centimetre on the map represents 12 Million centimetres or 120 kilometres in reality.

Graticule

Lines of Longitude and Latitude provide a co-ordinate system that allows the user to pin-point the exact location of any feature on the Earth's surface. Latitudes are measured in terms of degrees(°), minutes(') and seconds("), North and South of the Equator, while Longitudes are measured West and East of Greenwich. This would be typically expressed in the following manner;
e.g. 35° 20' 30"N 20° 35' 20"W

Page Title

Country Name

Latitude

Location Map

Gulf or Bay Name

Longitude

Grid Reference
used in the Index

Canada

State Boundary

Mountain Peak

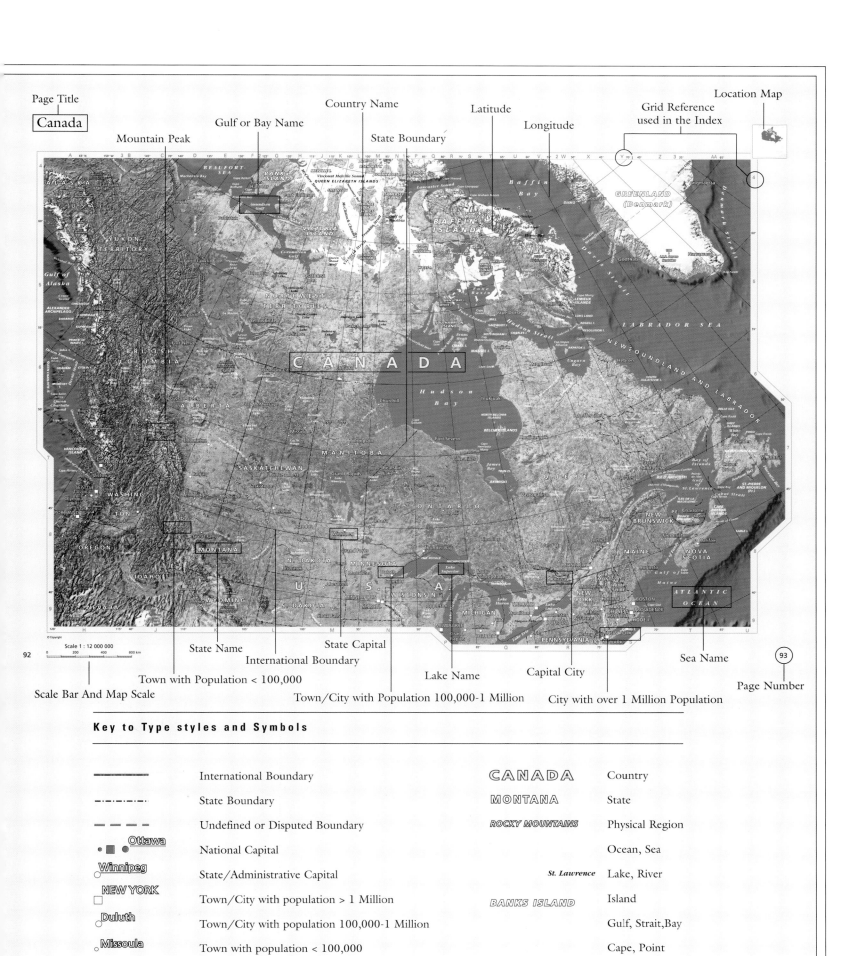

State Name

State Capital

Sea Name

International Boundary

Town with Population < 100,000

Lake Name

Capital City

Page Number

Scale Bar And Map Scale

Town/City with Population 100,000-1 Million

City with over 1 Million Population

92

93

Key to Type styles and Symbols

International Boundary	CANADA	Country
State Boundary	MONTANA	State
Undefined or Disputed Boundary	ROCKY MOUNTAINS	Physical Region
Ottawa — National Capital		Ocean, Sea
Winnipeg — State/Administrative Capital	St. Lawrence — Lake, River
NEW YORK — Town/City with population > 1 Million	BANKS ISLAND — Island
Duluth — Town/City with population 100,000-1 Million	Gulf, Strait, Bay
Missoula — Town with population < 100,000	Cape, Point
3954 △ Mt. Robson — Mountain Peak with height in metres		

Index to Map Pages

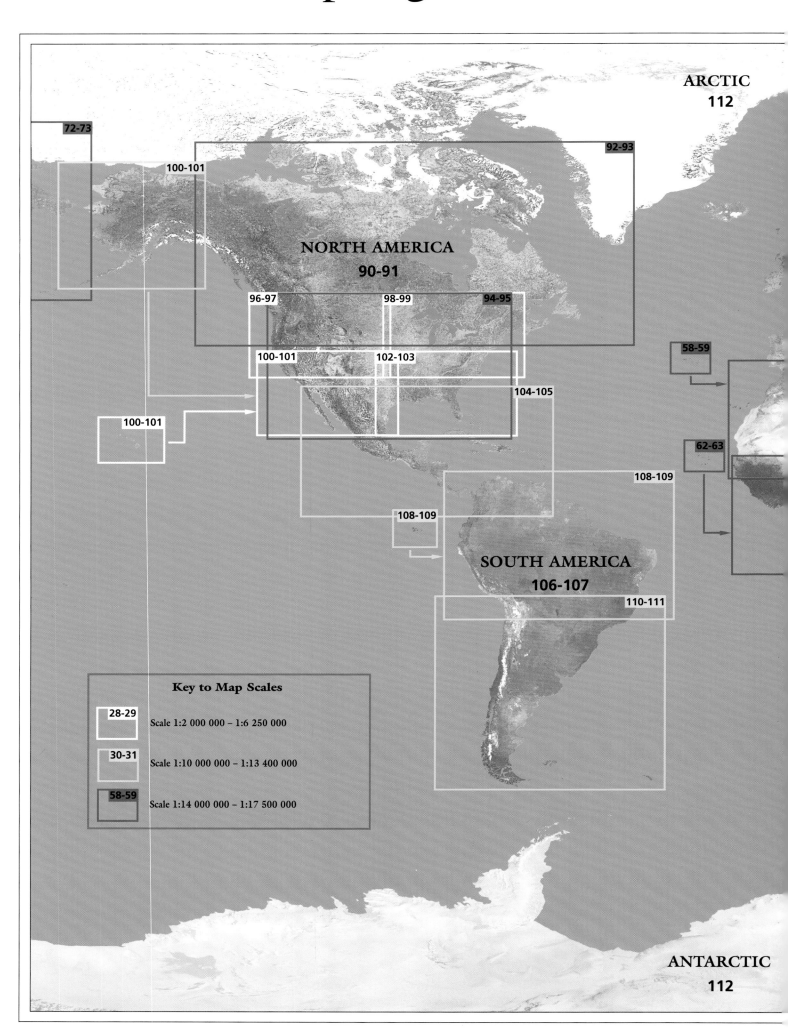

ARCTIC
112

72-73

100-101

92-93

NORTH AMERICA
90-91

96-97

98-99

94-95

58-59

100-101

102-103

104-105

100-101

62-63

108-109

108-109

SOUTH AMERICA
106-107

110-111

Key to Map Scales

28-29   Scale 1:2 000 000 – 1:6 250 000

30-31   Scale 1:10 000 000 – 1:13 400 000

58-59   Scale 1:14 000 000 – 1:17 500 000

ANTARCTIC
112

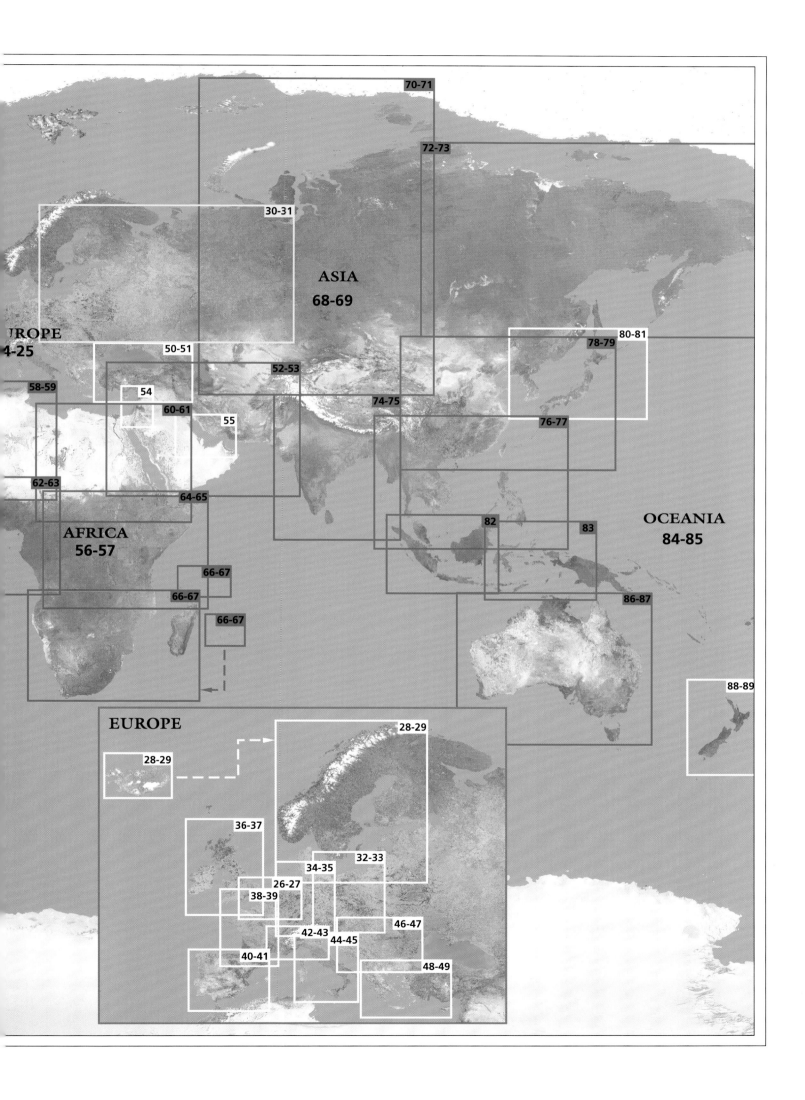

70-71

72-73

30-31

ASIA
68-69

UROPE
4-25

50-51

80-81
78-79

52-53

54

74-75

58-59

60-61

55

76-77

62-63

64-65

OCEANIA
84-85

AFRICA
56-57

82

83

66-67

66-67

86-87

66-67

88-89

EUROPE

28-29

28-29

36-37

32-33

34-35

26-27

38-39

46-47

42-43

44-45

40-41

48-49

Satellite Mapping

The images in this Atlas have been created by processing signals gathered in space by satellites circling the Earth in near polar orbits.

Sensors on the satellite register different kinds of electromagnetic energy emitted or reflected from the Earth's surface. This data is collected digitally and transmitted to ground stations where it is compiled into digital images. These images can then be used to create products such as the pictorial images in this Atlas, or to produce digital data sets used in Geographic Information Systems (GIS), or the data may be analysed using special computer software to extract information such as environmental conditions on the Earth's surface or to detect stress and/or vigour in vegetation, to mention but a few of the possible applications of this technology.

Image Processing and Analysis:

The raw data received from the satellite includes a number of serious distortions induced by pertebations in the satellite's platform and orbit, the Earth's atmosphere, irregularities in the sensor and many other factors. Image processing removes these distortions and provides an output that is spectrally and geographically accurate.

Image analysis is the process of looking into the spectral content of the data to extract information that is not otherwise obvious. Some of the areas where these techniques are used is in the detection of stress in vegetation before it is otherwise visible, in automatically discriminating and mapping different classes of ground cover and in the detection of pollutants in surface water and underground creep.

Maps as Interpreted Images of Earth:
Satellite imagery and image analysis provides the ability to extract many different data sets from a single source. Not only can it be used in the generation of maps as seen in traditional atlases or as combined imagery and cartography, as seen in this atlas, but it can also be used to extract vegetation and land cover information. Such information would include discrimination of forests, pastures, agriculture lands, swamps, deserts, stress in the vegetation, pollutants in the ground and water, used in creating land use and "thematic" maps (thematic maps being maps that present geographic information of a specific "theme", such as land use, mapping vegetation stress or geological structures).

The Final Touches:
The ultimate differences in maps derived from the same source can be found in the "artistic license" that is applied by the cartographer. This encompass such issues as whether or not to apply shaded relief, highlighting terrain variations and imparting a sense of 3-D to the image - as was done in the case of this atlas selecting the size and orientation of the text used on the map, selecting background colours, which can range anywhere from none to actual satellite images as seen in this atlas, and the representation of the water regions which, again, can cover a broad spectrum of choices. In the case of this atlas we chose to apply ocean floor relief (derived from NOAA's ETOPO-5 files) allowing us to view through the water and visualise the continuous geological structures of our Earth. The artistic license applied in this atlas is "reality", bringing the reader closer to a true view of our planet.

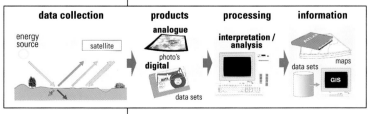

The American Landsat satellites (left) were the first satellites to make space imagery available to the general public. These satellites are based on one of two specific instruments, respectively referred to as the "MSS" (Multi-Spectral Scanner) and "TM" (Thematic Mapper) imagers. The MSS scanner collects data in 4 bands (or regions) of the electromagnetic spectrum and the TM imager expands this capability by acquiring data in 7 bands.

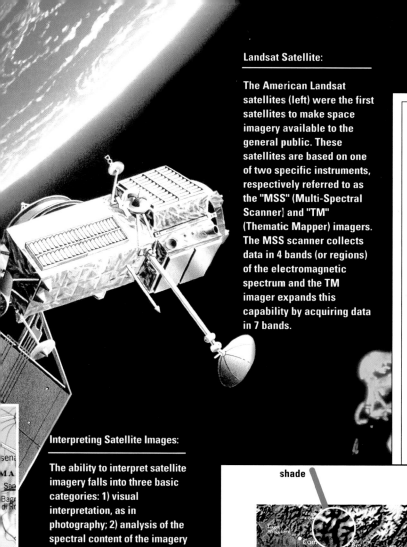

Interpreting Satellite Images:

The ability to interpret satellite imagery falls into three basic categories: 1) visual interpretation, as in photography; 2) analysis of the spectral content of the imagery as noted under "image analysis" and 3) texture and pattern analysis. Texture and pattern analysis is relatively new and promises to significantly enhance the capabilities of the whole "image analysis" process.

The ability to extract specific information is dependent on the particular characteristics of the satellite. Each type of satellite is configured differently and each configuration has strengths that will determine the specific application for which the satellite is best suited.

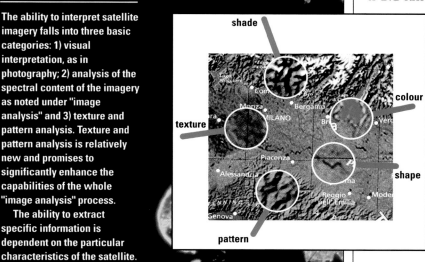

shade
colour
texture
shape
pattern

The Orbit and Sensor Characteristics of NOAA's AVHRR:

The Advanced Very High Resolution Radiometer (AVHRR) refers to the specific sensor aboard the National Oceanographic and Atmospheric Administration's (NOAA) polar orbiting environmental satellites (as different from the GOES - Geostationary Orbiting Environmental Satellites). The AVHRR based satellites are primarily designed for monitoring and forecasting weather, following a sun-synchronys orbit at a height of 833 kilometres and circling the Earth 14 times a day (102 minutes/orbit). During each passage the imager picks up a ground track that is 2399 km wide (see diagram) and registers pixels that are 1.1 km x 1.1 km.

altitude 833 km
orbit period 102 minutes

SATELLITE ORBIT
GROUND TRACK

band	wavelength in µm	applications
1	0.58 - 0.68	cloud (day) / surface mapping
2	1.725 - 1.10	surface water delineation, ice and snow melt
3	3.55 - 3.93	sea surface temperature, night-time cloud mapping
4	10.30 - 11.30	sea surface temperature, cloud mapping (day and night)
5	11.50 - 12.50	sea surface temperature, cloud mapping (day and night)

The AVHRR imager collects data in 5 electromagnetic bands as indicated in the above diagram.

Satellite Imagery for the Technically Minded

The Electromagnetic Spectrum:

The Electromagnetic Spectrum encompasses that set of energy that we define as radio, light, x-rays and gamma rays. The survellience type satellites used in the collection of the type of imagery seen in this atlas sense energy that exists in and near the "visible light" portion of the electromagnetic spectrum (visible light, infra-red and thermal energy - see diagram).

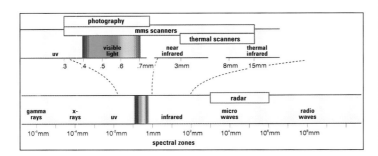

There are two basic types of sensors - passive and active. Passive sensors like the AVHRR detect naturally emitted or reflected energy (such as the emitted temperature of vegetation or reflected light of the sun). Active sensors create and emit signals, measuring the changes to, or timing of, the return signals. Radar is an example of an active sensor.

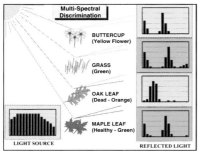

The Nature of Analysis:

While there are many approaches to analysing satellite imagery, the fundamental process underlying satellite image discrimination is based on the different way in which light reflects off of all objects. For example: when sunlight reflects off vegetation it reflects light that is representative of the colours we see. In addition, the water content of the vegetation will absorb light in the infrared region reducing reflectance in this portion of the electromagnetic spectrum. If the light were reflecting off of a painted picture of the same vegetation the visible colours would look the same, however, there would be much greater reflectance of infrared due to the lack of water absorption. In simple terms, it is the analysis and assessment of this type of difference in the reflected electromagnetic spectrum that forms the basis for analysis of satellite imagery (see diagram). In recent years differences in patterns and texture of the imagery have also been applied in refining the analytical process.

The specific process of discrimination is somewhat more complex as atmospheric absorption of portions of the electromagnetic spectrum (see diagram) have to be dealt with and the actual spectral differences between different species of vegetation or land cover can be very minute. In order to improve the discrimination capability of the satellite, the satellites "sight" is limited to very specific portions of the electromagnetic spectrum that optomize this process of discrimination. If the satellite were to view the entire spectrum the "noise" of the rest of the spectrum would hide or confuse the signal that is so critical in the discrimination process.

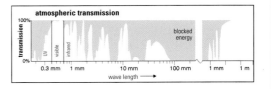

The Landsat Satellite Scanner

Two principle imaging systems are the scanning and the pushbroom imager. The American Landsat satellites use an across-track scanning system which consists of a rotating mirror which moves along a line perpendicular to the satellite's path of movement constantly registering a strip (scan-line) of the earth.

The electromagnetic energy that enters the sensor is spilt into several spectral components. The visible light and the reflective infra red is separated from the thermal infra red. The first component is further split into bands or channels which represent their different wavelength zones.

Measuring Resolution in "Pixels"

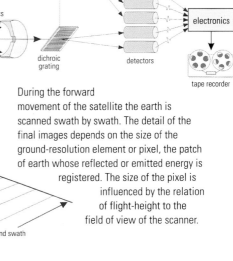

During the forward movement of the satellite the earth is scanned swath by swath. The detail of the final images depends on the size of the ground-resolution element or pixel, the patch of earth whose reflected or emitted energy is registered. The size of the pixel is influenced by the relation of flight-height to the field of view of the scanner.

Satellite Images OF THE World

A seven page selection of stunning satellite images featuring major cities and contrasting geographical habitats from around the world.
These "zoomed in" images of earth are breath-takingly detailed and provide another perspective of our natural and man-made world.

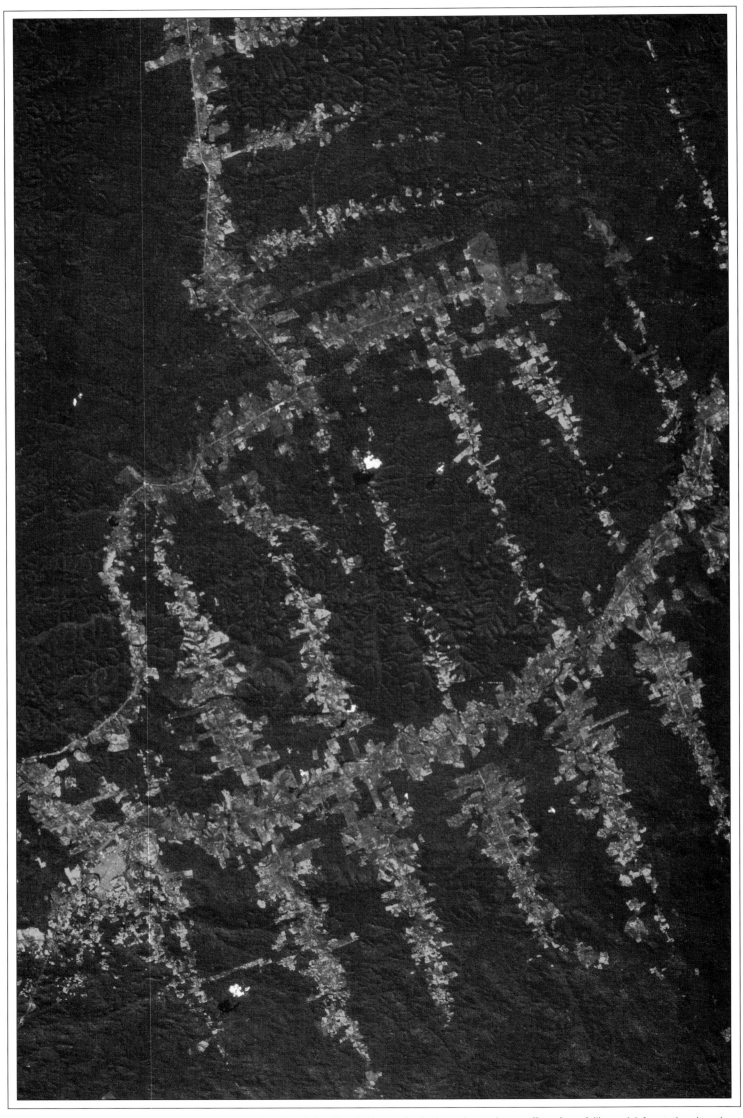

The Amazon forest of Brazil, the green heart of the earth. This French Spot Satellite image clearly shows the continuous effect of tree-felling and deforestation along the arteries of new roads deep into the forest.

A very detailed infra red image of the metropolis of New York, taken by the French Spot 1 satellite. The resolution of the data is so good that roads, residential blocks and features in the harbour area may be seen. This Spot image has a resolution of 20 metres.

Another view of London. This infra red image taken by the French Spot II satellite from an altitude of 833km shows the infrustructure of the city radiating out from the River Thames. The red areas depict areas of open land, fields and parkland.

Beijing , a "full-scene" image spreading over 60 x 60km of one of the largest cities in the world. The capital of China has a population of over 9 million inhabitants of which over 5 million people inhabit the central area. At the centre of the image you can clearly see the Forbidden City, which to the south opens onto the vastness of Tian'anmen Square.

A spectacular view of Istanbul and the Bosporus created from a mosaic of 4 French Spot II images which are simulated in Natural Colour. This highly detailed image shows the spectacular growth of the city either side of the Isthmus.

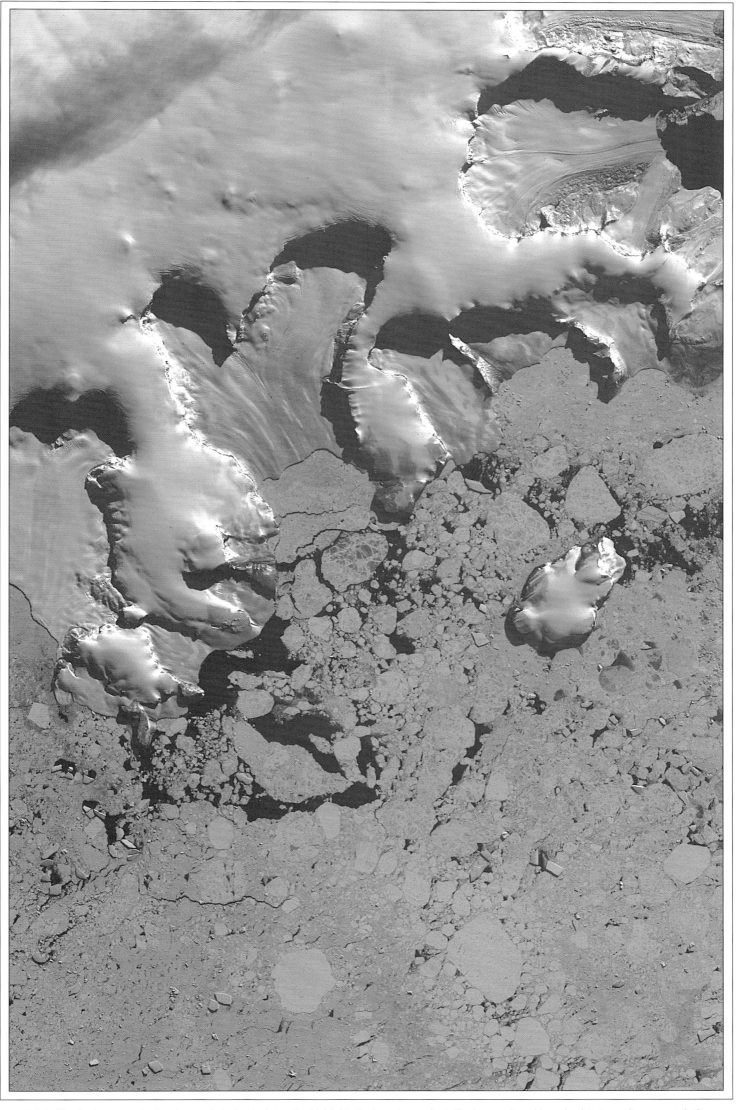

This brilliantly clear natural colour image of glaciers in Antarctica highlights the importance of satellite images. It enables scientists to monitor accurately the depleating ice flows and the movement of sheet ice.

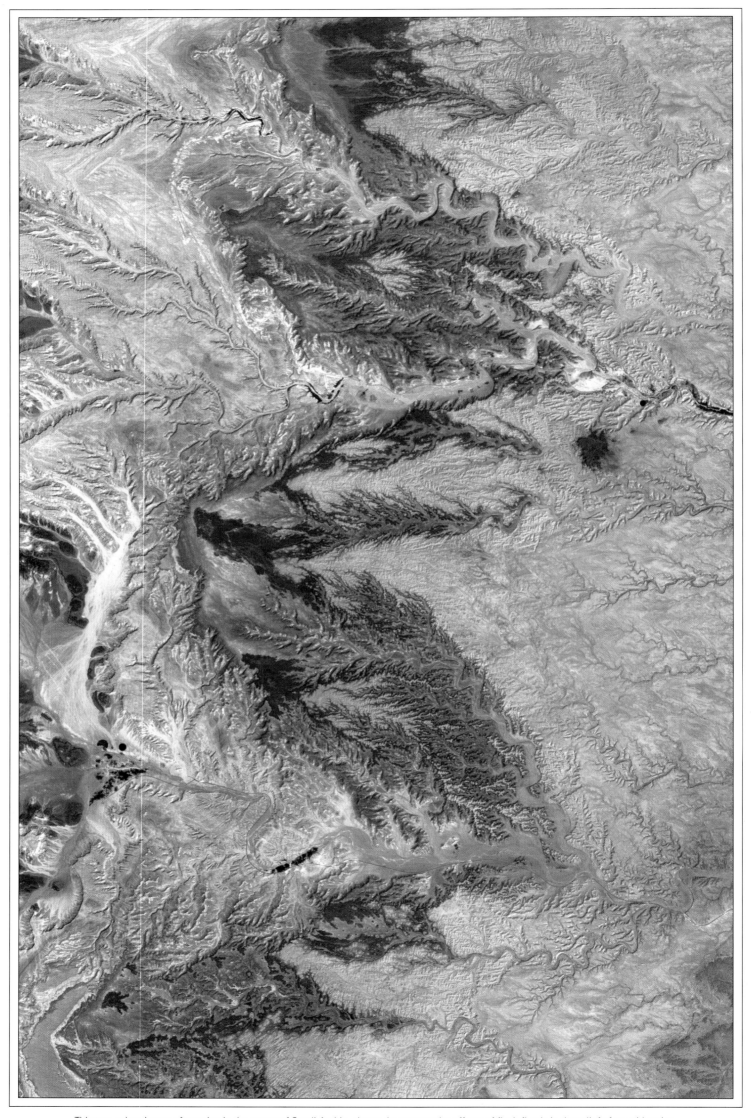

This true colour image of a region in the centre of Saudi Arabia, shows the spectacular effects of flash floods in the relief of an arid region.

Satellite
Maps
OF THE
World

Eighty-nine full colour satellite
maps covering the entire world
from Pole to Pole, each map
interpreted and enhanced with
elevation data and overlaid
with cartographic detail.
These comprehensive maps
provide a unique perspective
of our world - seen for the
very first time as it truly is.

Europe

60° N A   1   30° W   B   20°   C   70° 10°   D   0°   E   10°   F   20°

Reykjavik

ICELAND

NORWEGIAN
SEA

N
O
R
W
A
Y

S
W
E
D
E
N

FAEROES
(Den.)

SHETLAND

Gulf of Bothnia

ORKNEY

Oslo

SCOTLAND

Stockholm

Ta

NORTH
SEA

DENMARK
København
(Copenhagen)

BALTIC SEA

Baile Átha Cliath
(Dublin)
IRELAND

N.
IRELAND

UNITED

KINGDOM

LITHUA

ATLANTIC

WALES   ENGLAND

Amsterdam

BERLIN

RUSSIA

WARSZAWA
(WARSAW)

OCEAN

LONDON   NETHER-
LANDS

GERMANY

POLAND

English Channel   BRUXELLES
(BRUSSELS) BELGIUM

CHANNEL
ISLANDS

Luxembourg
LUXEMBOURG

PRAHA
(PRAGUE)
CZECH REPUBLIC

Bay
of
Biscay

PARIS

WIEN
(VIENNA)

SLOVAKIA

Bratislava

FRANCE

Bern LIECHTENSTEIN AUSTRIA

Budapest

MASSIF

SWITZERLAND

SLOVENIA Zagreb

HUNGARY

CENTRAL

Mt. Blanc
4808

A L P S

CROATIA

R O

PORTUGAL

ANDORRA

MONACO SAN MARINO

ADRIATIC SEA

BOSNIA-
HERZEGOVINA BEOGRAD
Sarajevo   (BELGRADE)

LISBOA
(LISBON)

MADRID

SPAIN

CORSE
(CORSICA)
(Fr.)

I
T
A
L
Y

YUGOSLAVIA

ISLAS BALEARES
(BALEARIC ISLANDS)
MENORCA

VATICAN
CITY

Tirana
(Tirane)

Skopje
(S

MACEDONIA

Strait of Gibraltar

GIBRALTAR (U.K.)
CEUTA (Sp.)

IBIZA   MALLORCA

SARDEGNA
(SARDINIA)
(Italy)

ROMA
(ROME)

ALBANIA

Rabat

MELILLA (Sp.)

ALGER
(ALGIERS)

M E D I T E R R A N E A N

TYRRHENIAN
SEA

IONIAN
SEA

GREECE

MOROCCO

Tunis

SICILIA
(SICILY)

ATH
(ATH

HAUTS PLATEAUX

MALTA

S
E
A

HAUT ATLAS

GRAND ERG OCCIDENTAL

ALGERIA

TUNISIA

Tarábulus
(Tripoli)

KH
(CR

GRAND ERG ORIENTAL

L I B Y A

D   0°   E   10°   F   20°

© Copyright

Scale 1 : 17 500 000

0   250   500   750   1000 km

24

Belgium and the Netherlands

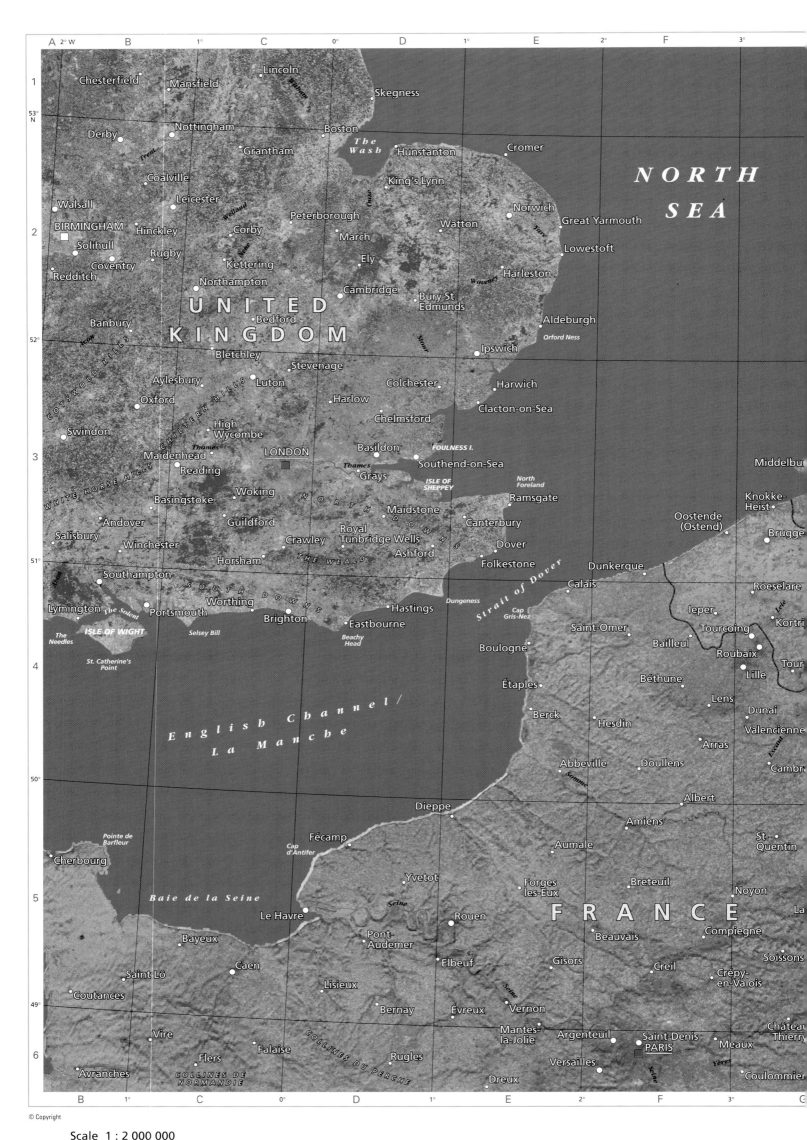

© Copyright

Scale 1 : 2 000 000

0   50   100 km

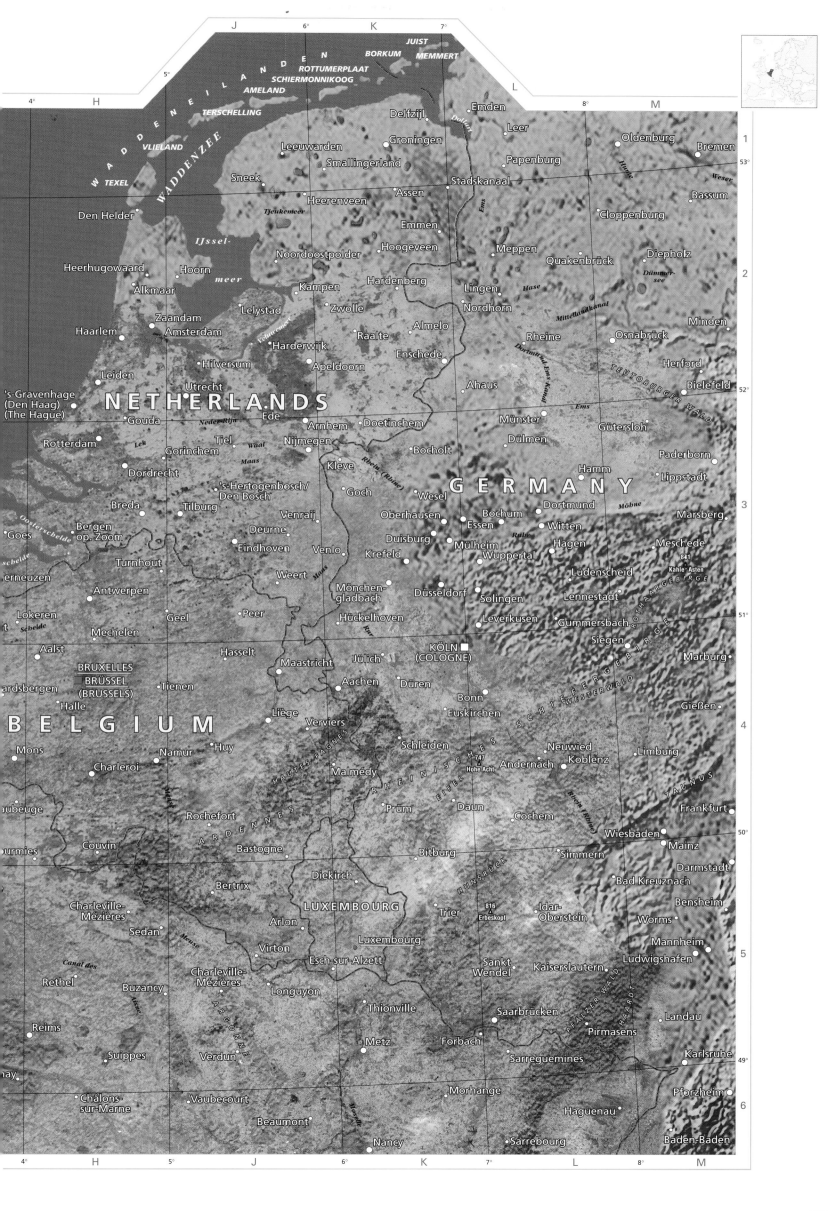

© Copyright

Scale 1 : 5 000 000

0   100   200   300 km

29

European Russia

Scale 1 : 9 000 000

0   200   400   600 km

© Copyright

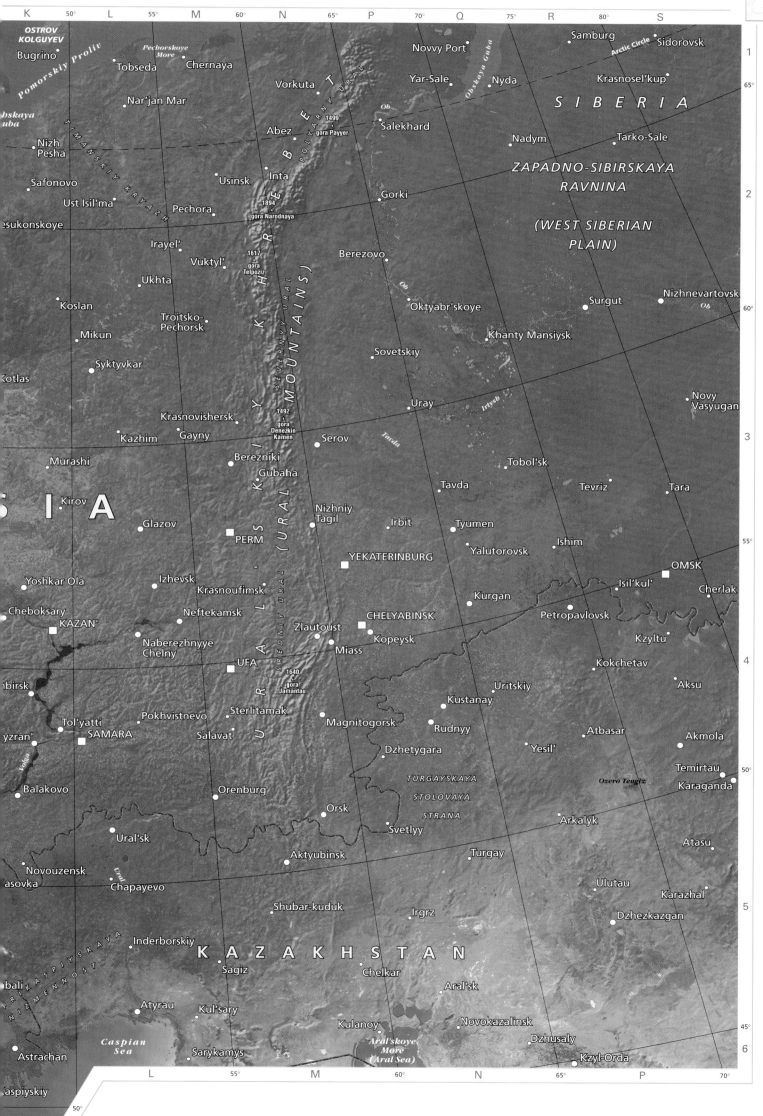

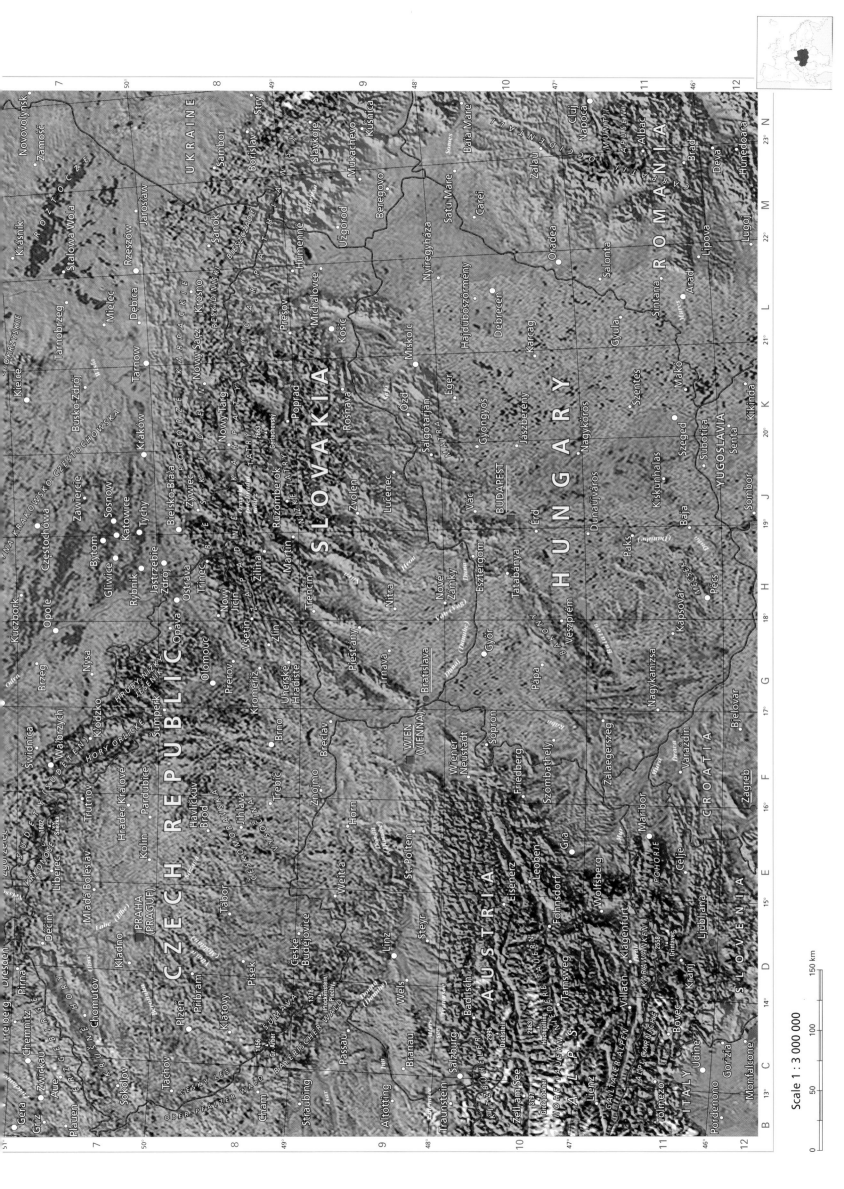

Scale 1 : 3 000 000

Germany

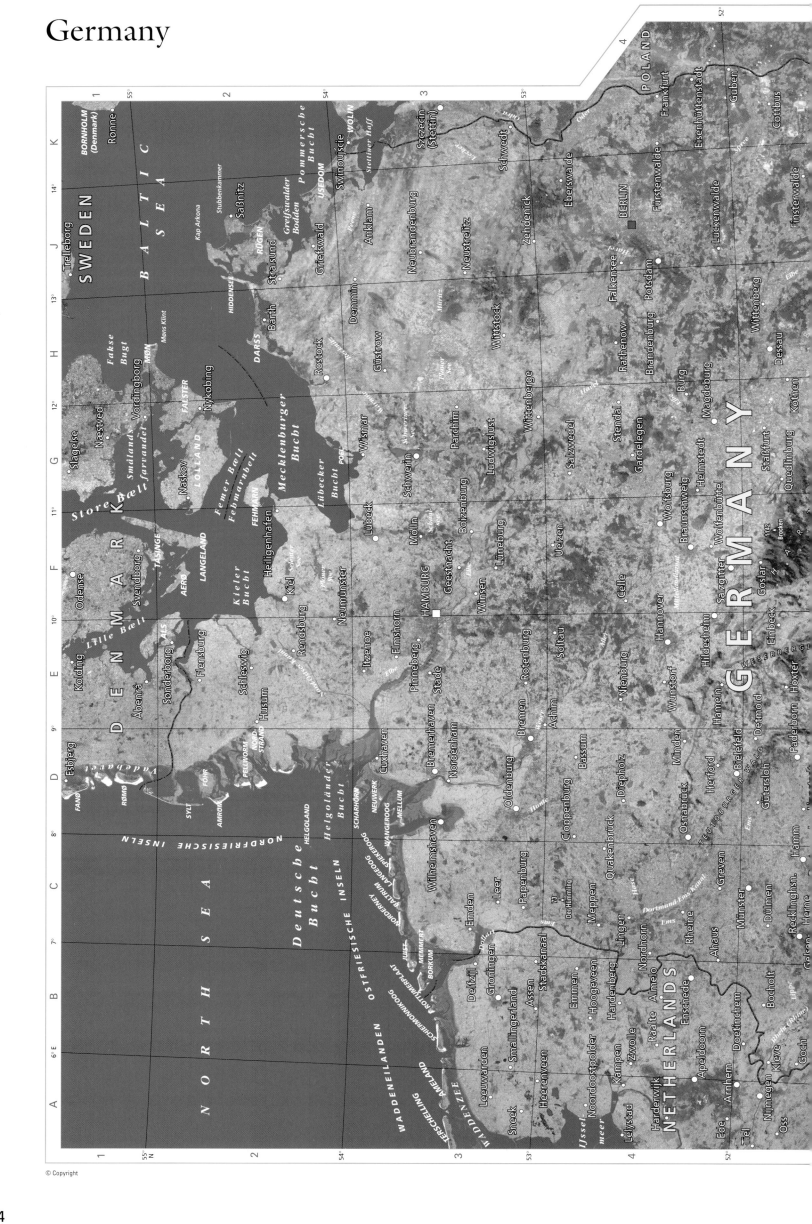

Scale 1 : 2 250 000

0   50   100   150 km

35

United Kingdom and Ireland

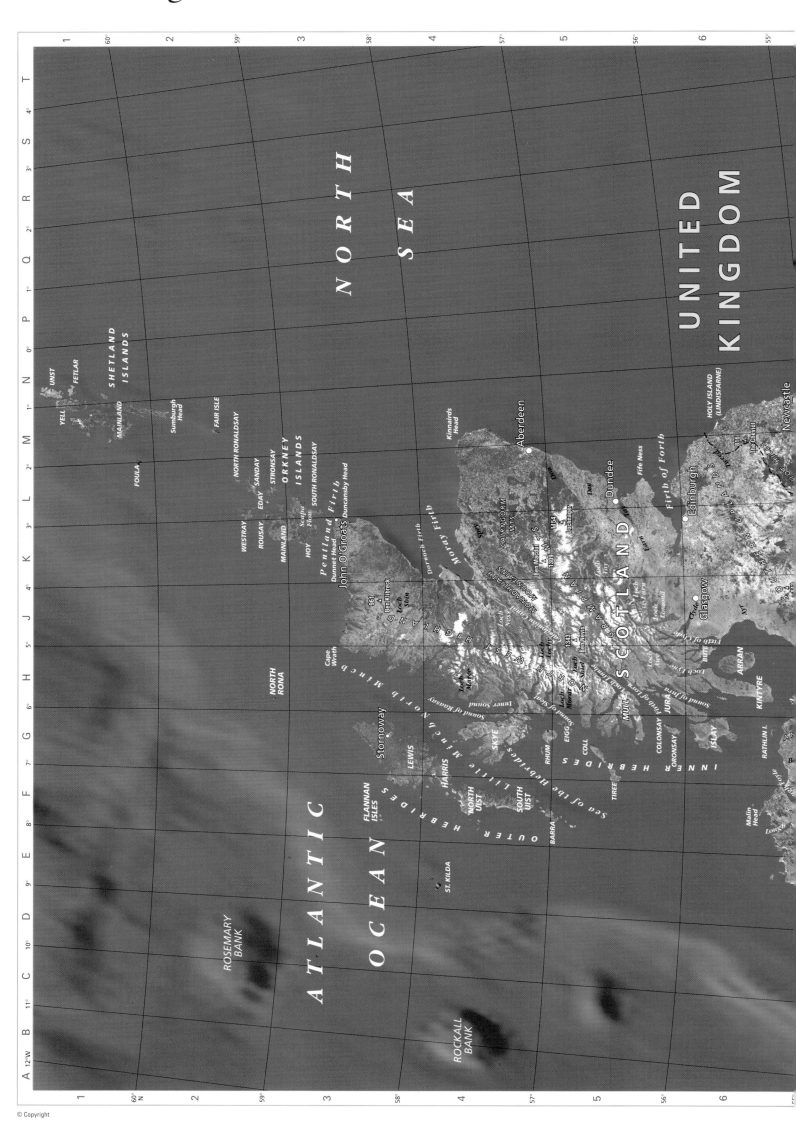

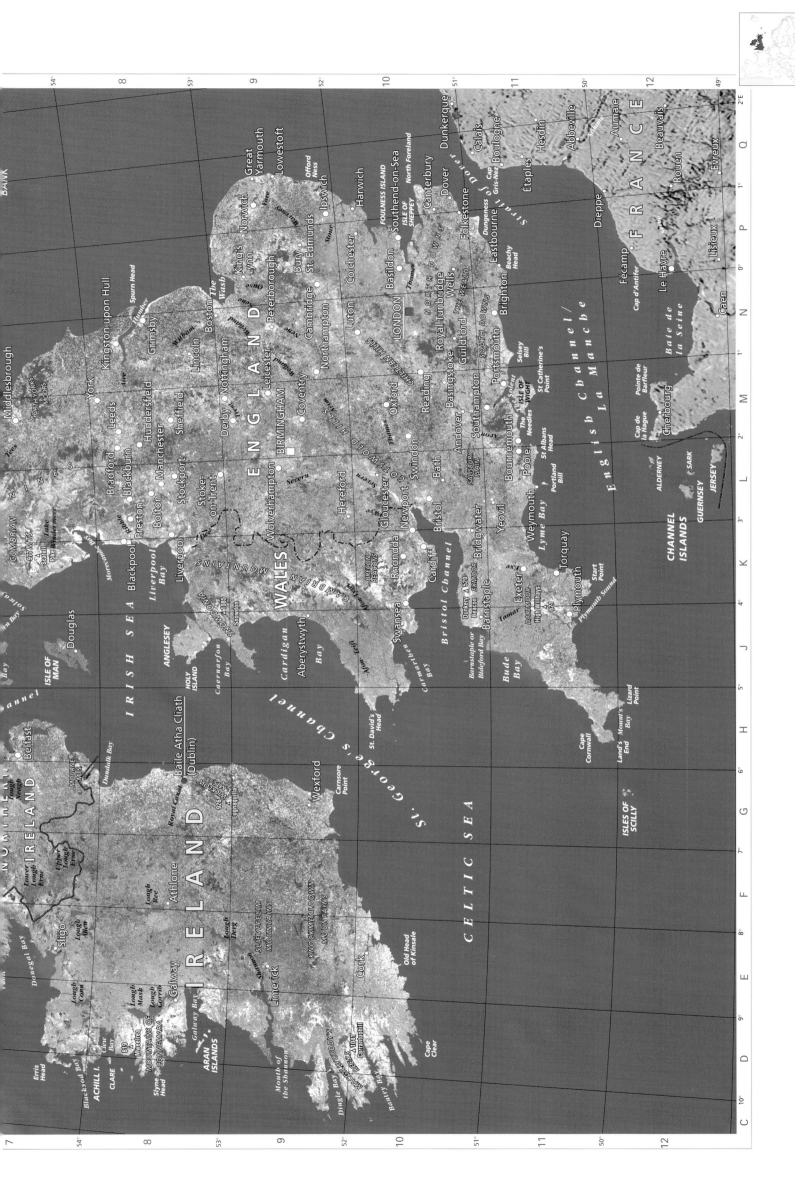

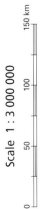

Scale 1 : 3 000 000

0   50   100   150 km

37

France

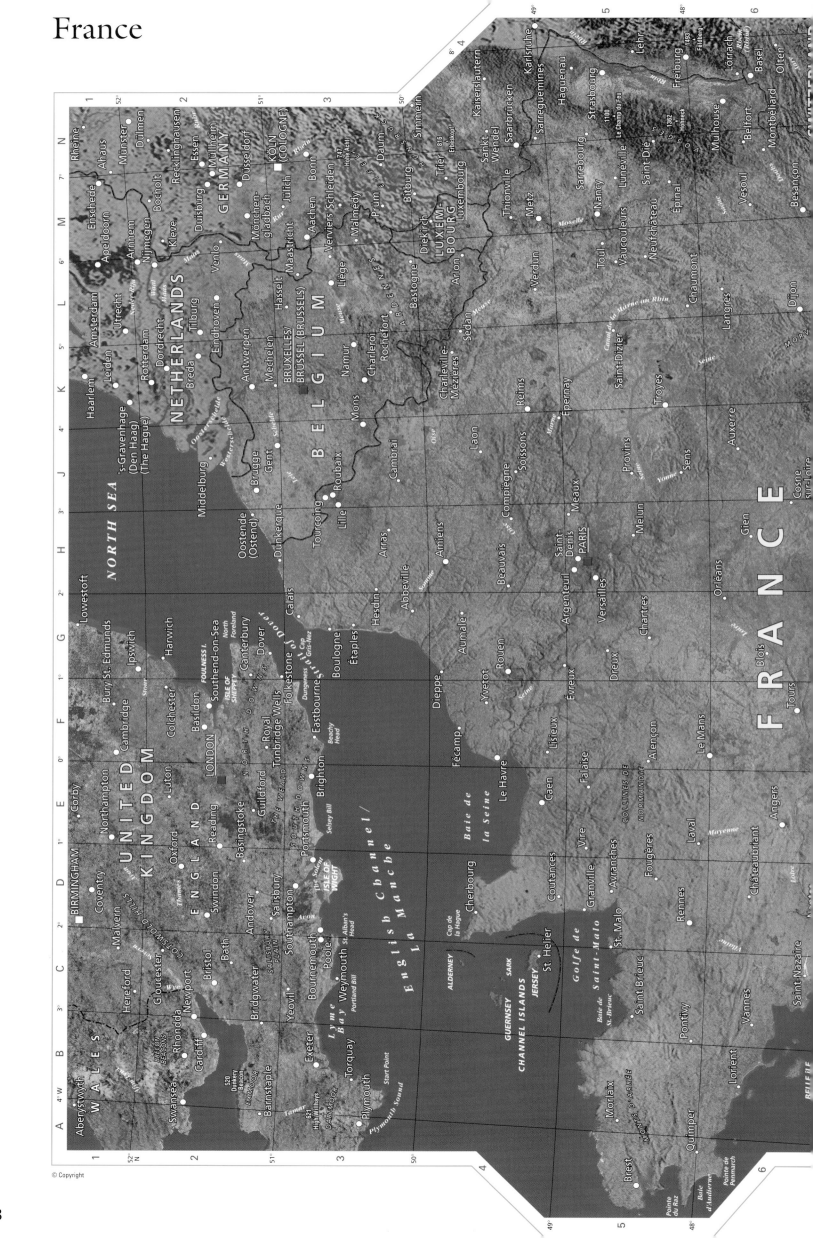

© Copyright

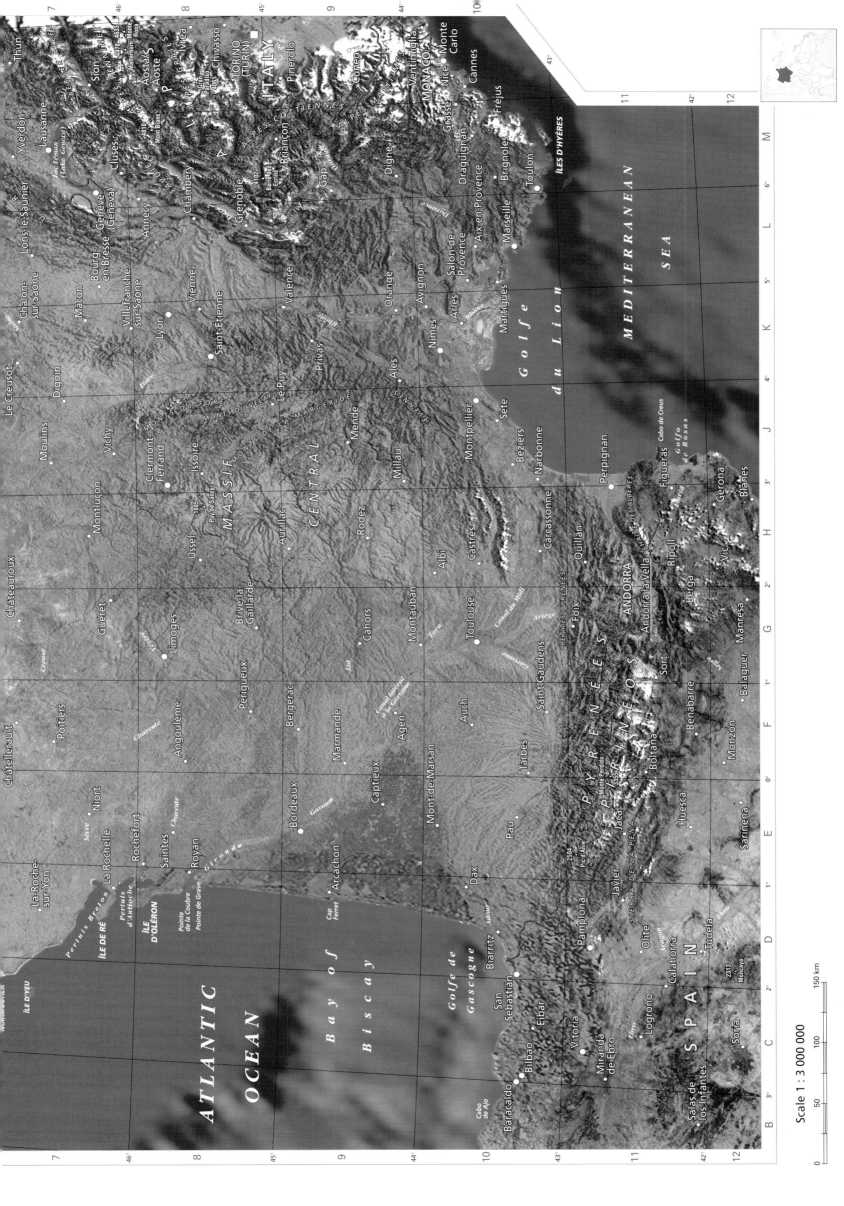

Scale 1 : 3 000 000

Spain and Portugal

© Copyright

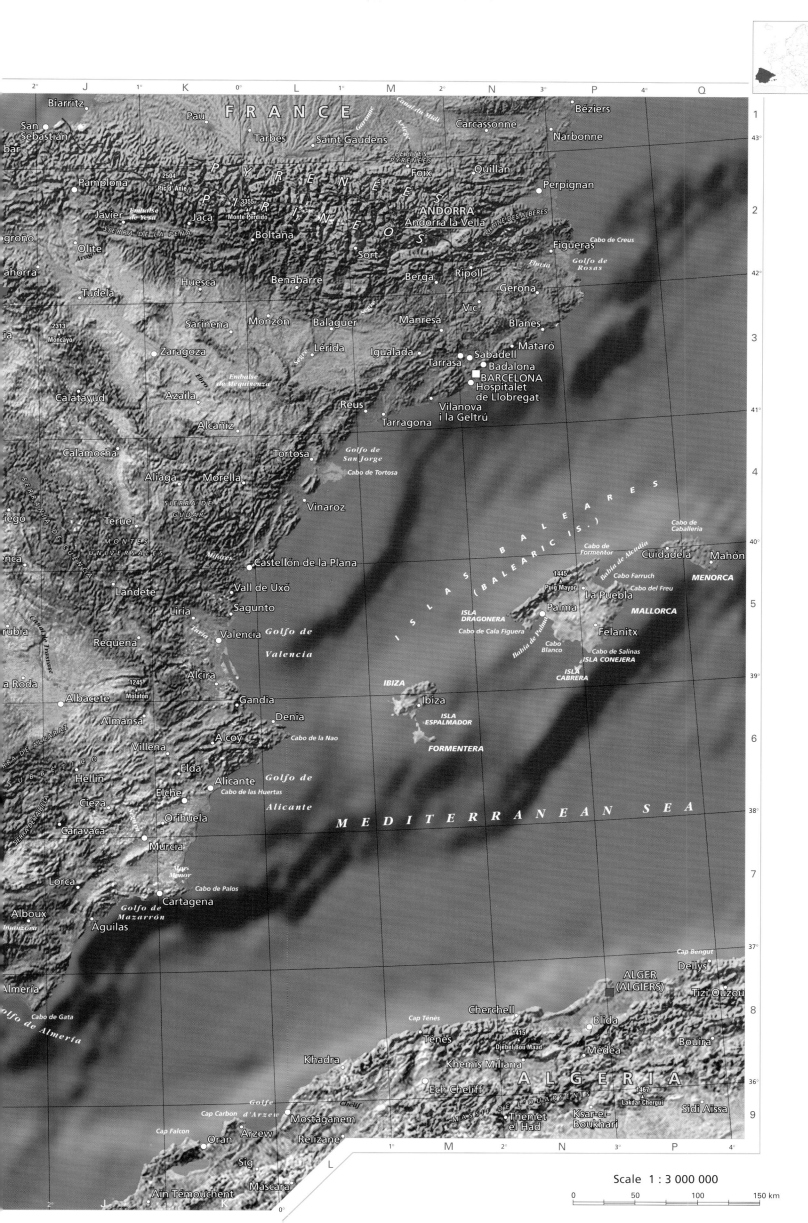

Biarritz
San Sebastián
bar
Pamplona
Javier
Embalse de Yesa
Jaca
Pau
Tarbes
Saint Gaudens
FRANCE
Carcassonne
Béziers
Narbonne
groño
Olite
ahorra
Tudela
Huesca
Boltaña
Benabarre
Berga
Ripoll
PYRÉNÉES
2504
Pic d'Anie
3355
Monte Perdido
SIERRA DE LA PEÑA
Aragón
ANDORRA
Andorra la Vella
Foix
Quillan
Perpignan
CHAÎNE DES ALBÈRES
PETITES PYRÉNÉES
Garonne
Canal du Midi
Ariège
Sort
Vic
Figueras
Cabo de Creus
Golfo de Rosas
Fluvia
Gerona
Blanes

2313
Moncayo
ia
Zaragoza
Calatayud
Azaila
Alcañiz
Sariñena
Monzón
Balaguer
Lérida
Igualada
Manresa
Segre
Segre
Tarrasa
Sabadell
Mataró
Badalona
BARCELONA
Hospitalet
de Llobregat
Reus
Vilanova
i la Geltrú
Tarragona
Embalse
de Mequinenza
Ebro

Calamocha
Aliaga
Morella
Tortosa
Golfo de
San Jorge
Cabo de Tortosa
SIERRA DE
GÚDAR
Vinaroz
SERRANÍA DE CUENCA
iego
Teruel
MONTES
UNIVERSALES
Mijares
Castellón de la Plana
Vall de Uxó
Sagunto
Landete
Liria
Turia
B A L E A R E S
(B A L E A R I C   I S .)
I S L A S
Cabo de
Caballería
Cabo de
Formentor
Bahía de Alcudia
Cabo Farruch
Cuidadela
Mahón
MENORCA
1445
Puig Mayor
La Puebla
Cabo del Freu
Palma
MALLORCA
ISLA
DRAGONERA
Felanitx
Cabo de Cala Figuera
Bahía de Palma
Cabo
Blanco
Cabo de Salinas
ISLA CONEJERA
ISLA
CABRERA

nca
rubia
Requena
Valencia
Golfo de
Valencia
Alcira
IBIZA
Ibiza
ISLA
ESPALMADOR
FORMENTERA

a Roda
Albacete
1245
Molatón
Almansa
Villena
Gandia
Denia
Alcoy
Cabo de la Nao

Hellín
Cieza
Caravaca
Elda
Elche
Alicante
Orihuela
SIERRA DE ALCARAZ
SUBBÉTICO
SIERRA DE TABILLA
Segura
Cabo de las Huertas
Golfo de
Alicante
M E D I T E R R A N E A N   S E A

Murcia
Lorca
Mar
Menor
Cabo de Palos

Alboux
Inganora
Águilas
Cartagena
Golfo de
Mazarrón

Almería
Golfo de Almería
Cabo de Gata
Cap Bengut
ALGER
(ALGIERS)
Dellys
Tizi Ouzou

Cherchell
Cap Ténès
Blida
Bouira

Ténès
Djebel Bou Maad
1415
Médéa

Khadra
Khemis Miliana
A L G E R I A
1467
Lakdar Chergui
Sidi Aïssa

Golfe
d'Arzew
Cap Carbon
Chélif
Ech Cheliff
MASSIF DE L'OUARSENIS
Theniet
el Had
Ksar-el-
Boukhari

Cap Falcon
Oran
Arzew
Mostaganem
Relizane

Sig
Mascara
Aïn Témouchent

Scale 1 : 3 000 000

0   50   100   150 km

The Alpine States

Scale 1 : 2 250 000

0   50   100   150 km

© Copyright

Italy

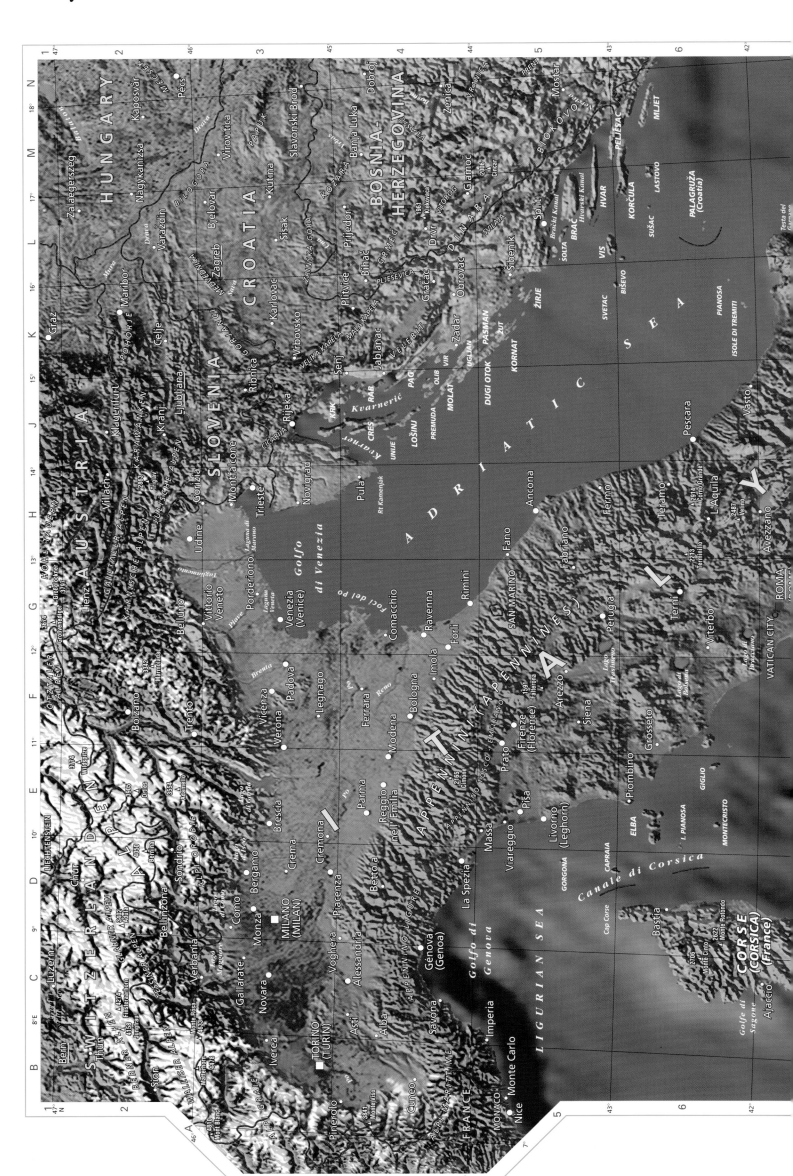

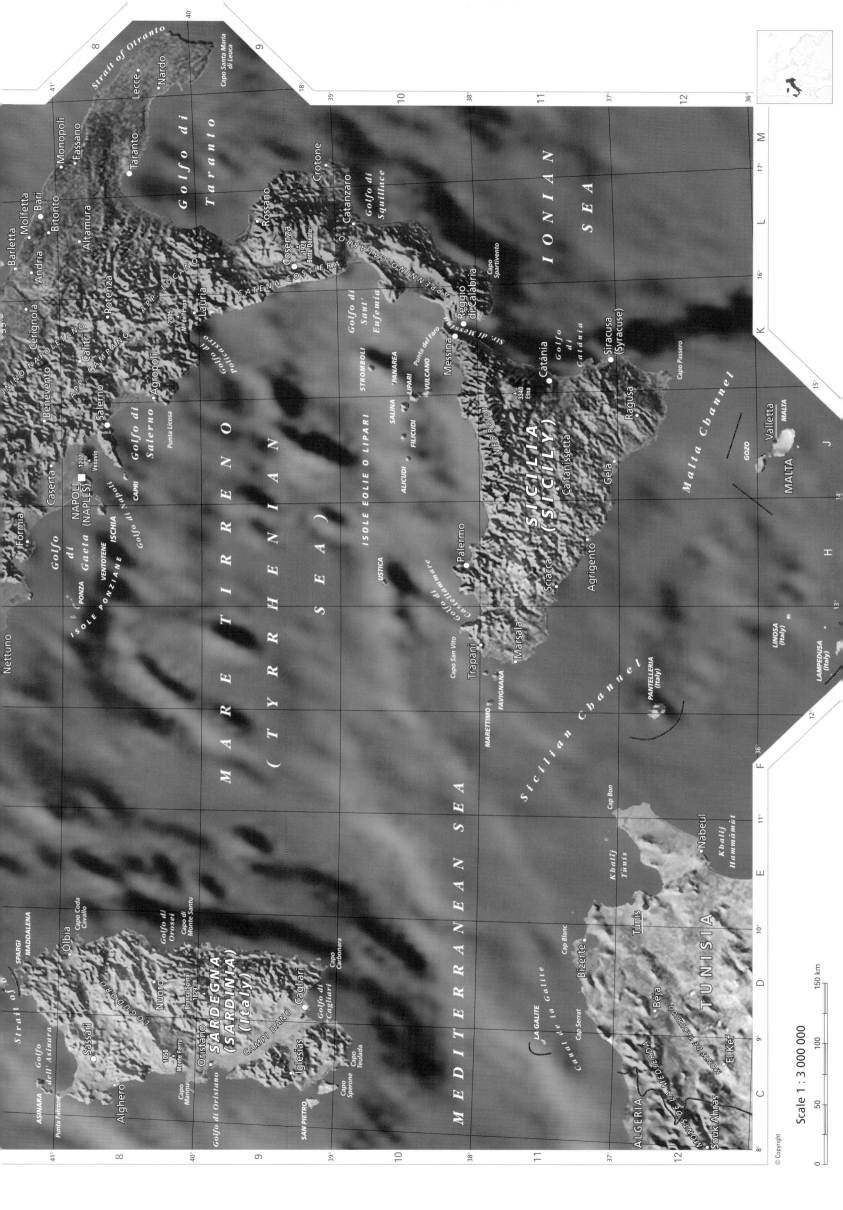

The Balkans

Košice

A 14° E   B   15°   C   16°   D   17°   E   18°   F   19°   G   20°

SLOVAKIA

Wels
Donau (Danube)
Steyr
Sankt Pölten
WIEN (VIENNA)
Trnava
Nitra
Lučenec
Kazincbarcika
 Özd
Miskolc
Nyíregy

Scheibbs
Bratislava
Nové Zámky
Komárno
Neusiedler See
Sopron
Győr
Vác
Eger
Gyöngyös
Hajdúböszörmen

Liezen
Wiener Neustadt
Tatabánya
BUDAPEST
Jászberény
Debrecen

AUSTRIA
Kapfenberg
Leoben
Hartberg
Szombathely
Pápa
Veszprem
Székesfehérvár
Cegléd
Érd
Kecskemét
Karcag
Orad

Fohrsdorf
Graz

Wolfsberg
Klagenfurt
Maribor
Zalaegerszeg
HUNGARY
Szentes
Békéscsaba
Gyula

Villach
Triglav 2863
Kranj
Celje
Nagykanizsa
Kaposvár
Szekszárd
Szeged
Makó
Arad

SLOVENIA
Ljubljana
Varaždin
Pécs
Baja
Subotica
Orosháza

Trieste
Ribnica
Zagreb
Bjelovar
Virovitica
Drava
Sombor
Senta
Kikinda
Timişoara

Rijeka
Karlovac
Sisak
Kutina
CROATIA
Osijek
Bečej
Zrenjanin
Rsita

Pula
Senj
Vrbovsko
Nova Gradiska
Vukovar
Vinkovci
Novi Sad
Fruška Gora
Vršac

Bihać
Prijedor
Slavonski Brod
Sremska Mitrovica
BEOGRAD (BELGRADE)

Jablanac
Zadar
Banja Luka
Dobroj
Bijeljina
Šabac
Smederevo
Požarevac

Obrovac
Gračac
Drvar
Tuzla
Valjevo

Glamoč
Cincar 2006
BOSNIA-
Zenica
Sarajevo
Čačak
Svetozarevo

Šibenik
Sinj
HERZEGOVINA
Titovo Užice
Kraljevo
Kruševac

Split
Arzano
Mostar
Pljevlja
YUGOSLAVIA

Hvar
Korčula
Novi Pazar
Kosovska/ Mitrovica
Lesko

Lastovo
Mljet
Nikšić
Peć
Priština
Vranj

Dubrovnik
Podgorica
Deravica 2656
Dragobia
Dakovica
Prizren

Jezerce 2692
Shkodër
Kumar

ADRIATIC SEA
Bicaj
Titov vrh 2747
Tetovo
Skopje

San Severo
Manfredonia
Peshkopia
Korab 2764
MACED

Foggia
Golfo di Manfredonia
ALBANIA
Tirane (Tirana)
Prilep

Cerignola
Barletta
Durrës
Elbasani
Bitola

ITALY
Bari
Bitonto
Monopoli
Kënet'e Karavastas
Ohrid

Calitri
Altamura
Fasano

C   16°   D   17°   E   18°   F   19°   G   20°   21°   J

© Copyright

Scale 1 : 3 000 000
0   50   100   150 km

46

Greece and West Turkey

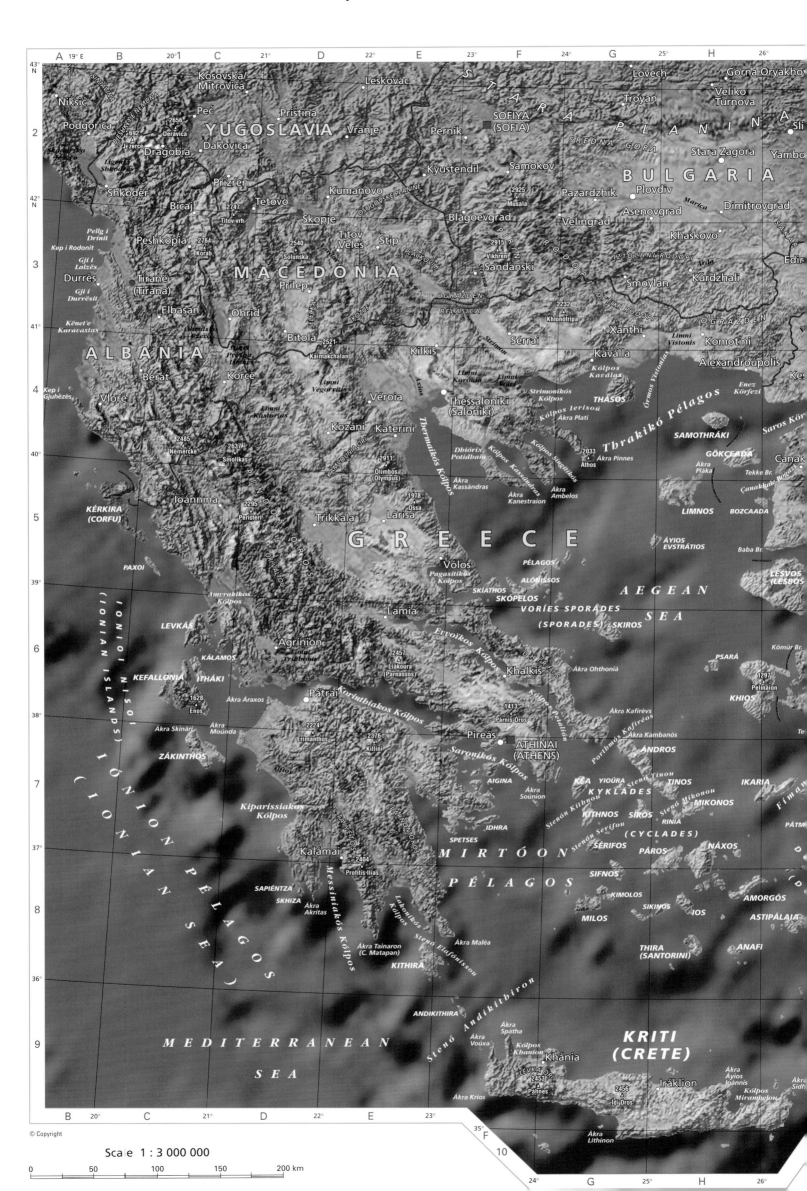

© Copyright

Scale 1 : 3 000 000

0   50   100   150   200 km

Turkey

Scale 1 : 5 000 000

0   100   200   300 km

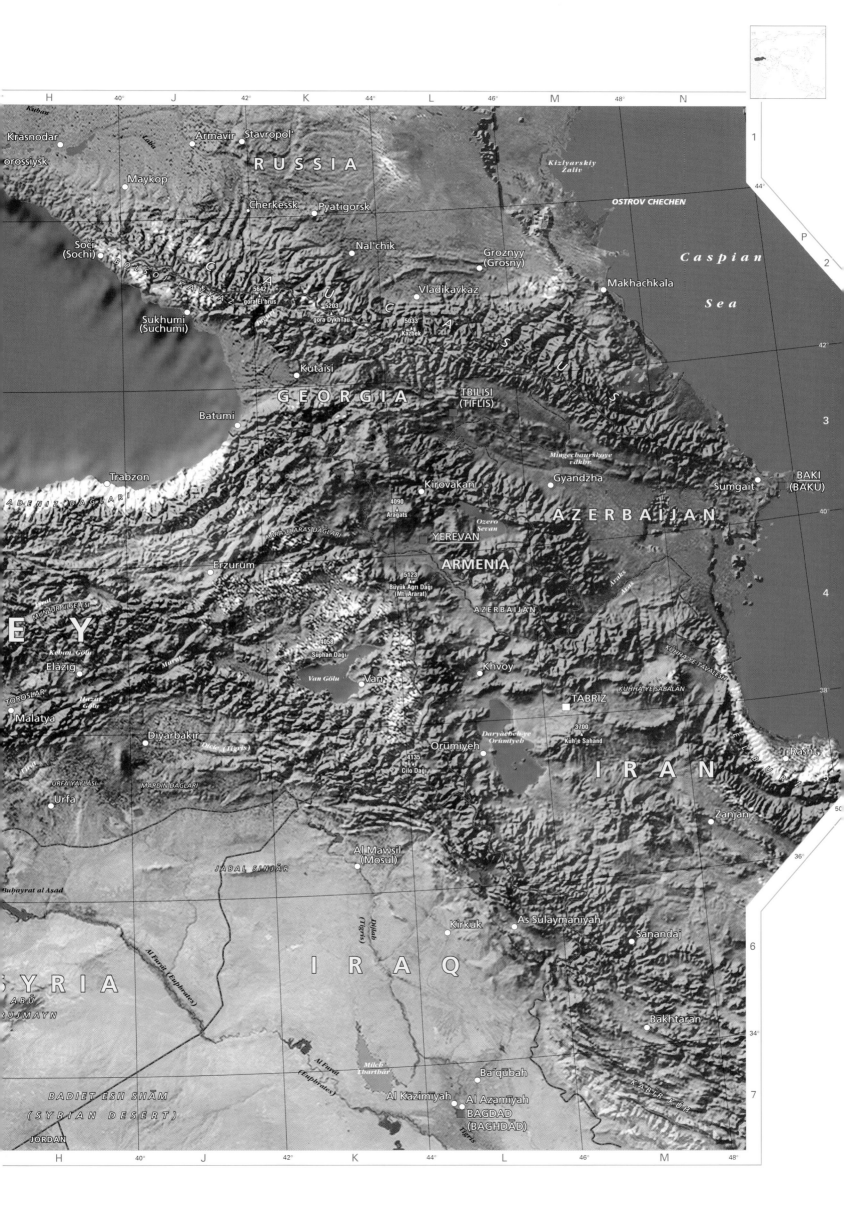

Kuban

Krasnodar

orossiysk

Armavir   Stavropol'

RUSSIA

1

Maykop

Laba

Cherkessk   Pyatigorsk

44°

Nal'chik

OSTROV CHECHEN

Kizlyarskiy
Zaliv

Caspian

P

Soči
(Sochi)

B O L S O J

Groznyy
(Grosny)

2

K A V K A Z

C   A

Vladikavkaz

Makhachkala

gora El'brus
5642

5203

Sea

Sukhumi
(Suchumi)

gora Dykh Tau

U   C

5033
Kazbek

42°

C   A

Kutaisi

S   U

Batumi

GEORGIA

S

TBILISI
(TIFLIS)

3

Mingechaurskoye
vdkhr.

Trabzon

Kirovakan

Gyandzha

Sumgait

BAKI
(BAKU)

ADENIZ DAĞLARI

4090
Aragats

Ozero
Sevan

AZERBAIJAN

40°

KARASU ARAS DAĞLARI

YEREVAN

Erzurum

ARMENIA

4

E Y

5123
Büyük Ağrı Dağı
(Mt. Ararat)

AZERBAIJAN

Araks

MUNZUR SILSELESI

4058
Süphan Dağı

Khvoy

KÜHHA-YE TAVALESH

Keban Gölü

Aras

Elâziğ

Murat

Van Gölü

Van

KÜHHA-YE SABALAN

TOROSLAR

*Hazar
Gölü*

TABRIZ

Malatya

Daryächeh-ye
Orümiyeh

3700
Küh-e Sahand

Diyarbakır

Dicle (Tigris)

Orümiyeh

Rasht

5

Firat

URFA YAYLASI

MARDIN DAĞLARI

4135
Cilo Dağı

E L B U R Z

Urfa

50°

Buḥayrat al Asad

36°

Al Mawsil
(Mosul)

JABAL SINJÂR

KABIR KÜH

*Dijlah
(Tigris)*

Kirkūk

As Sulaymaniyah

Sanandaj

6

I R A Q

S Y R I A

Al Furât (Euphrates)

Bakhtaran

34°

*ABŪ
RUJMAYN*

*Al Furât
(Euphrates)*

Milch
Tharthär

Ba'qubah

7

*BADIET ESH SHÂM
(SYRIAN DESERT)*

Al Kāzimīyah

Al Azamiyah

BAGDAD
(BAGHDAD)

JORDAN

Tigris

Middle East

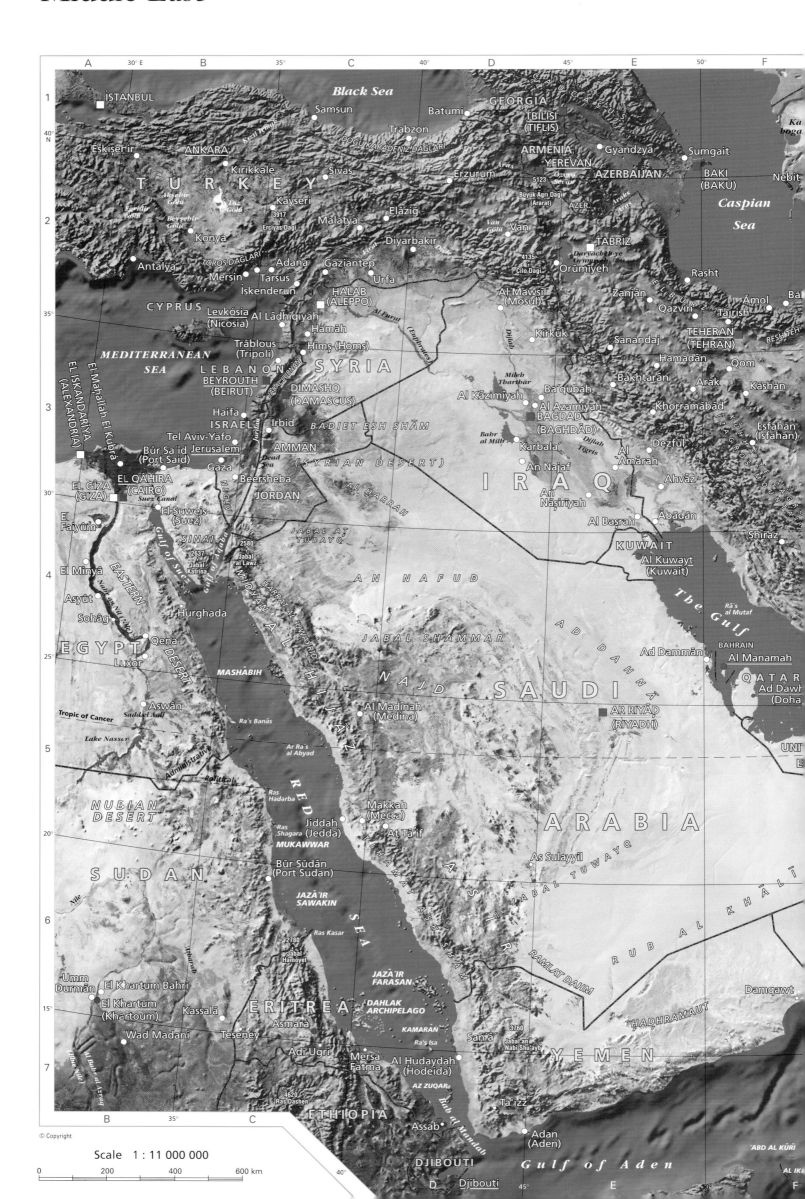

Scale 1 : 11 000 000

0   200   400   600 km

© Copyright

Israel, Jordan and Lebanon

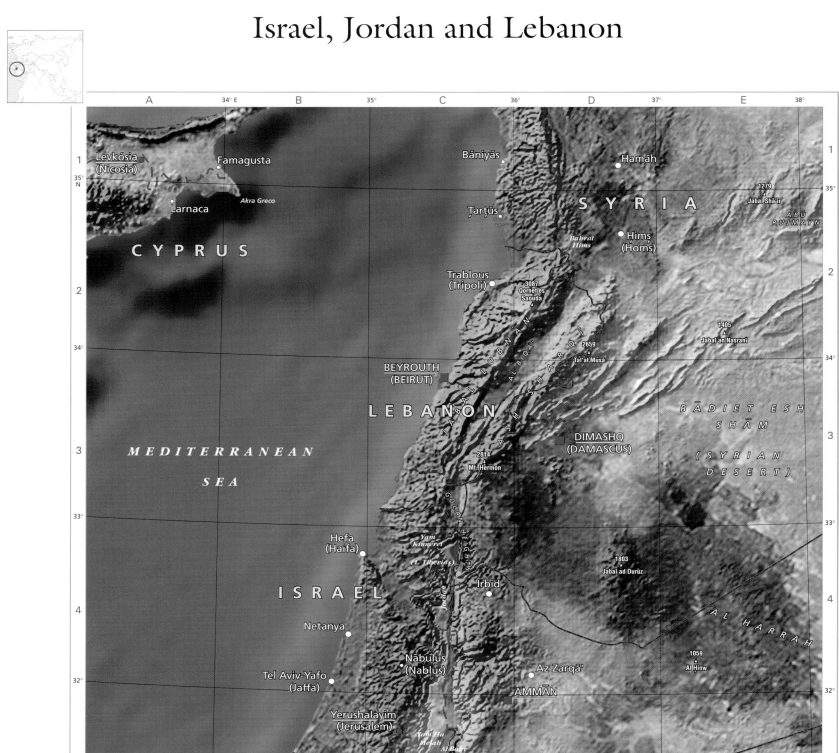

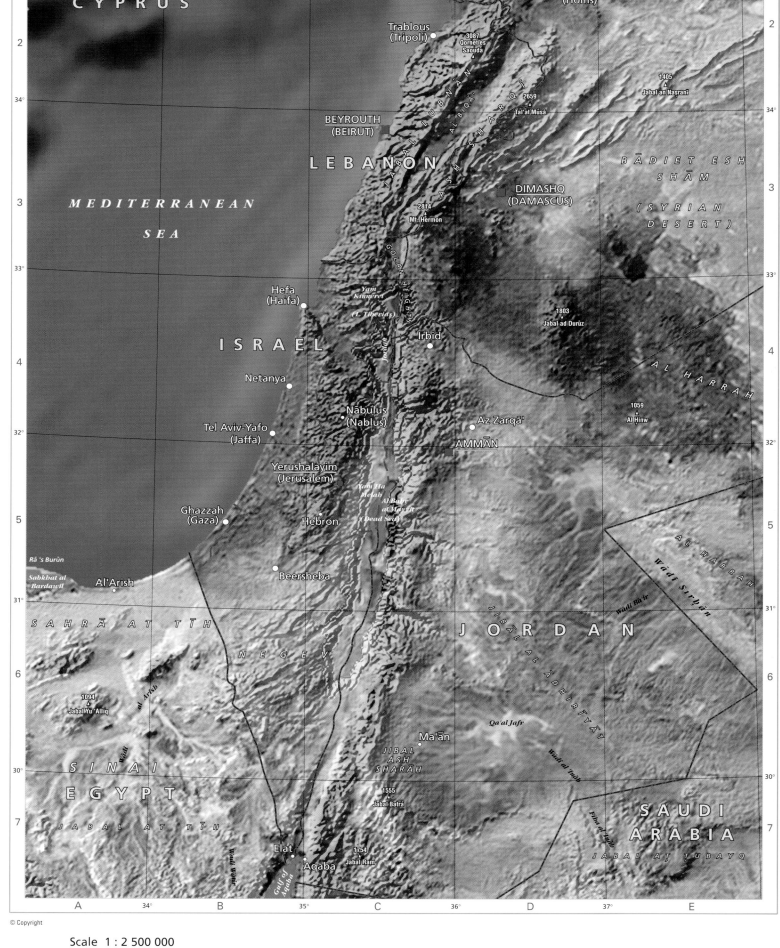

Scale 1 : 2 500 000

| 0 | 50 | 100 | 150 km |

The Gulf States

Scale 1 : 5 000 000

0   100   200   300 km

55

Africa

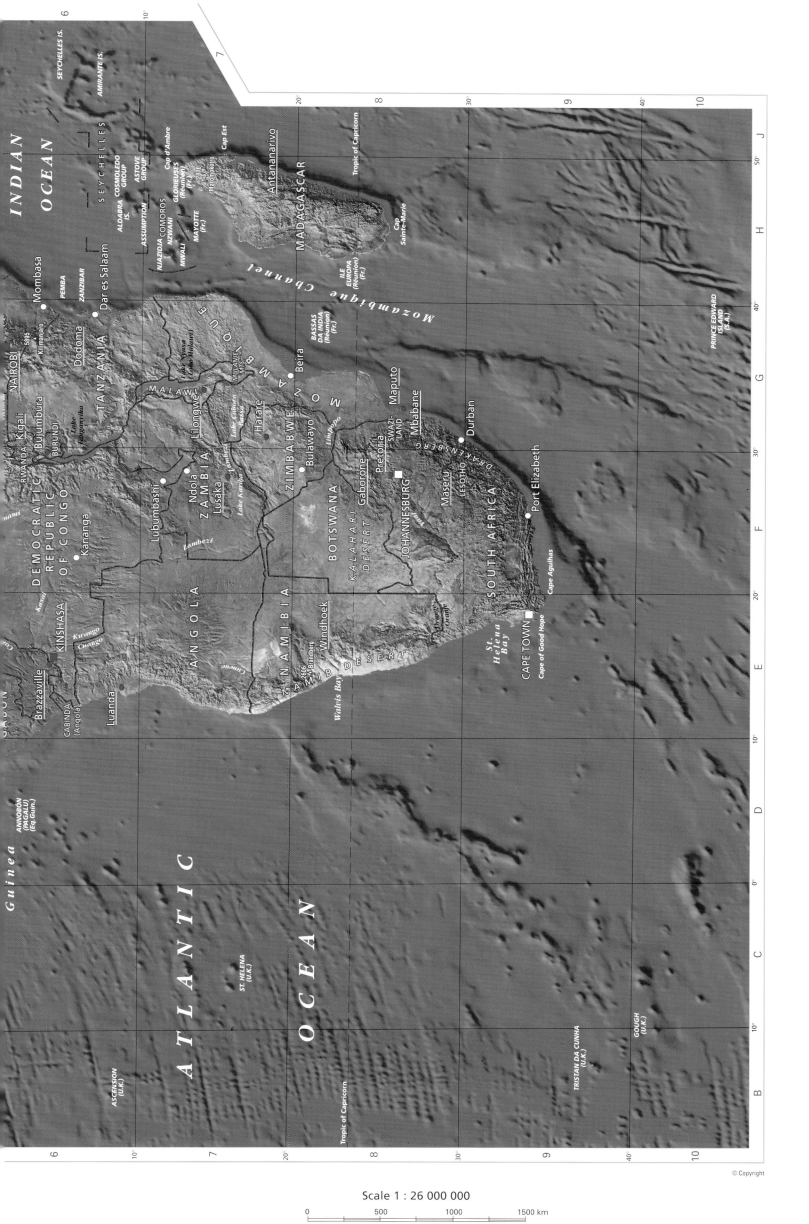

Scale 1 : 26 000 000

0   500   1000   1500 km

© Copyright

57

Northwest Africa

① AÇÔRES (AZORES) (Port.)
CORVO
FLORES
GRACIOSA
SÃO JORGE
FAIAL
TERCEIRA
PICO
SÃO MIGUEL
FORMIGAS
SANTA MARIA

Funchal
MADEIRA (Port.)
PORTO SANTO

ILHAS SELVAGENS (Madeira)

LA PALMA
GOMERA
TENERIFE
3710
HIERRO
Piço de Teide
GRAN CANARIA
Santa Cruz
Las Palmas
ISLAS CANARIAS (CANARY ISLANDS) (Spain)
LANZAROTE
FUERTEVENTURA
Cap Juby

Cádiz
Málag
Gibra
Strait of Gibraltar
Tanger (Tangier)
Ceuta
Tétou
Kénitra
Salé
Rabat
DÂR-EL-BEIDÂ (CASABLANCA)
Fès
Ta
Meknès
Jbel Bou
Naceur
Ras Beddouza
Safi
MOROCC
ATLAS
Er Rac
Marrakech
Beni Mellal
Cap Sim
4165
H 1 G H
4071
Cap Rhir
Jebel Toubkal
Irhil M'Goun
3340
Agadir
Taroudannt
Ouarzazate
Guelmine
ANTI ATLAS
Tan-Tan
JEBEL OUARKZIZ
Laâyoune
Saguia el-Hamra
Es Semara
Sebkha de Tindouf
Tindouf
Cabo Bojador

ATLANTIC
Tropic of Cancer
Bir Mogreïn
Aïn Ben Tili
ERG IGUIDI
M'CHERRAH
EL EGLAB
Chouatinet
Ad Dakhla
Punta Sarga
WESTERN SAHARA (MOROCCO)
Sebkhet Oumm ed Droûs Telli
OCEAN
Bahía de Rio de Oro
Sebkhet Oumm ed Droûs Guebli
Oued el Ma
M DENNAH
ERG CHEC

Nouâdhibou
Râs Nouâdhibou
Zouérat
S
A
Dakhlet Nouâdhibou
ILE TIDRA
Atâr
EL DJOUF
Taoudenni
Cap Timiris
Chinguetti
Akjoujt
Sebkra du Ndaghamcha
MAURITANIA
Nouakchott
Tidjikja
EL MREYYÉ
HODH
St Louis
Dagana
AOUKAR
MA
Kaédi
Kiffa
'Ayoûn el Atroûs
Cap Vert
Thiès
DAKAR
Kaolack
SENEGAL
Lac Faguibine
Tombouctou
Niger
Banjul
GAMBIA
Tambacounda
Kayes
Lac Niangay
GOURMA
Gao
Cap Roxo
GUINEA-BISSAU
Medina Gounas
MONTS MANDINGUES
KAARTA
Lac Débo
MACINA
S
A
H
SAHEL
Bissau
MASSIF DU TAMGUE
FOUTA DJALLON
Labé
Bamako
Ségou
Mopti
Djibo
Dori
ORANGO
GUINEA
Tougan
BURKINA
Cap Verga
Kindia
LOMA MOUNTAINS
Kankan
Bobo Dioulasso
Ouagadougou
Conakry
Black Volta
FASO

© Copyright

Scale 1 : 10 000 000
0   200   400   600 km

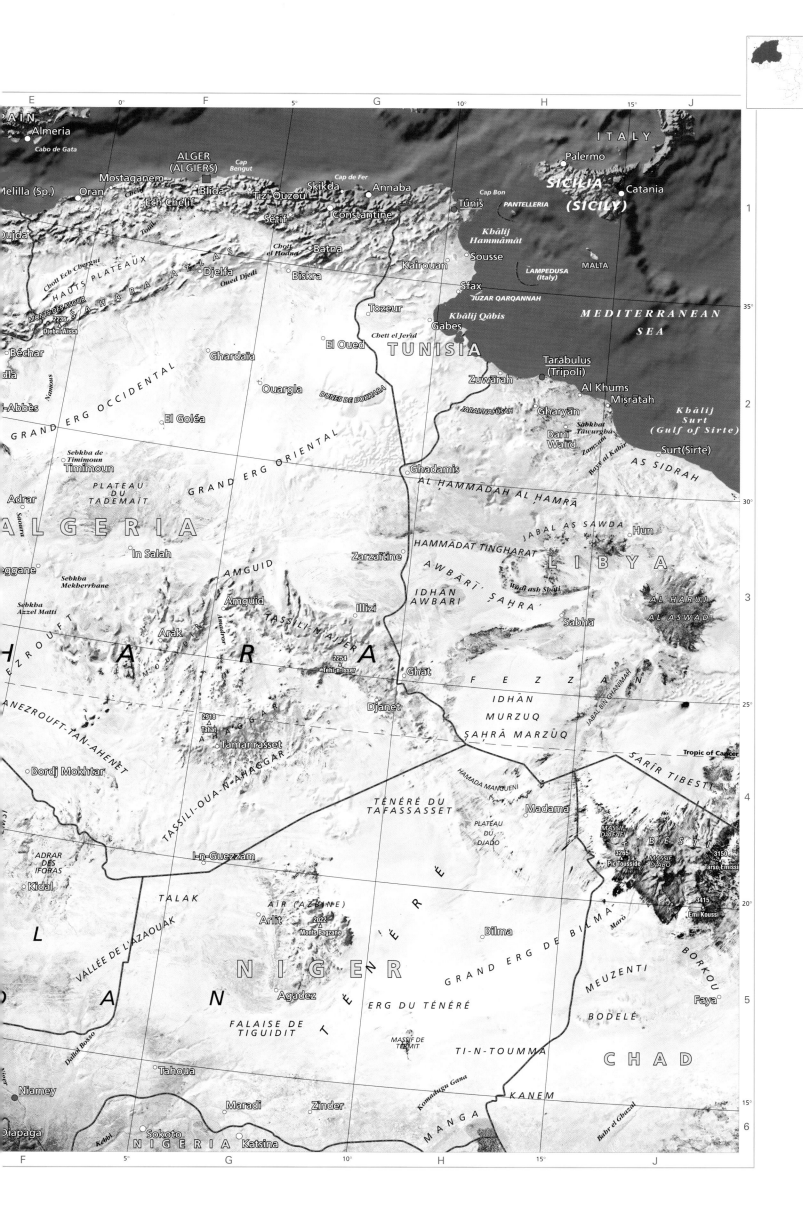

Northeast Africa

MEDITERRANEAN

TUNISIA
Zuwārah
Tarābulus (Tripoli)
Al Khums
Misrātah
Banghāzī (Benghazi)
AL JABAL AL AKHDAR
Tubruq
Ra's al Milḥ

BARQAH AL BAHRĪYA

Gharyān
JABAL NAFŪSAH
Banī Walīd
Sabkhat Tāwurghā
Khalij Surt (Gulf of Sirte)

KATTA
SENH

Ghadāmis
Surt (Sirte)
AS SIDRAH
Ajdābiyā
Sabkhat Ghuzayyil
Sabkhat Shunayn

AL HAMMĀDAH AL ḤAMRĀ
JABAL AS SAWDA
Hun

AS ṢAḤRĀ AL LĪBĪYAH (LIBYAN DESERT)

Zarzaïtine
HAMMĀDAT TINGHARAT
AWBĀRĪ ṢAḤRĀ

WĀḤĀT JĀLŪ

ALGERIA
IDHĀN AWBARI
Wādī ash Shāṭi
Sabhā
AL HARŪJ AL ASWAD

SARĪR KALANSHIYŪ

Illizi

LIBYA

2254
Tchi-n-Isser
TASSILI-N-AJJER
Ghāt
FEZZĀN
IDHĀN MURZUQ
JABAL BIN GHANĪMAH
ṢAḤRĀ RABYĀNAH
AL KHUFRAH
Al Khufrah

S A H A R A

Djanet
Tropic of Cancer
ṢAḤRĀ MARZŪQ

AS ṢAḤ

HAMADA MANGUENI
SARĪR TIBESTY

TÉNÉRÉ DU TAFASSASSET
Madama

PLATEAU DU DJADO

MASSIF D'AFAFI
T I B E S T I
3265 MASSIF D'ABO
Pic Toussidé
3150 Tarso Emissi

NIGER
3415 Emi Koussi
ERDI
ERDI MA
DÉPRESSION DE MOURDI

Bilma
GRAND ERG DE BILMA
MEUZENTI BORKOU
Faya

T É N É R É
ERG DU TÉNÉRÉ
BODELÉ
ENNEDI

MASSIF DE TERMIT
TI-N-TOUMMA

CHAD

MANGA
KANEM
Howa

Hadejia
Komadugu Gana
Bahr el Ghazal
MASSIF DU KAPKA

JABAL DARFŪR

S A H E L
SU

Ati
OUADDAÏ
Abéché
El Geneina
El Fasher

Maiduguri
Lac Tchad (Lake Chad)
N'Djamena
Mongo
3088 Jabal Marrah
Nyala

Gongola
Massenya
DARSILA

Maroua
MONTS MANDARA
Bongor
Chari
Bahr Salamat
Noukale

Benue
Laï
Bahr Aouk
Birao
DAR ROUNGA
Lol
AS ṢA

NIGERIA
Sarh
Moundou
CENTRAL AFRICAN REPUBLIC

CAMEROON
MASSIF DES BONGOS

© Copyright

Scale 1 : 10 000 000
0   200   400   600 km

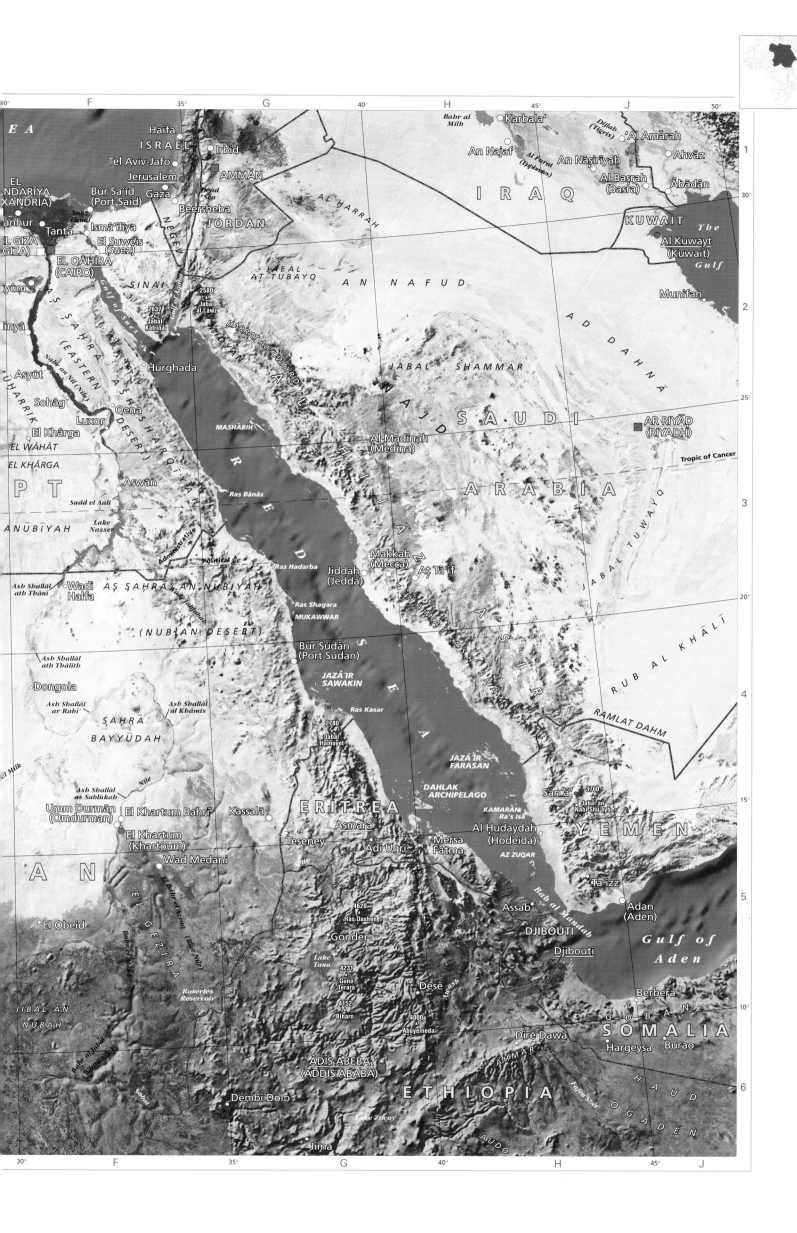

F · 35° · G · 40° · H · 45° · J · 50°

EA

E Haifa
ISRAEL Irbid
Tel Aviv-Jafo
Jerusalem AMMĀN
EL Bûr Sa'îd Gaza Dead Sea
NDARÏYA (Port Said) Beersheba JORDAN
XANDRIA) JORDAN
anhur Tanta Ismâ'îliya NEGEV
EL GIZA El Suweis
(GIZA) (Suez) 2580
EL QÂHIRA JABAL al Lawz
(CAIRO) SINAI AT TUBAYQ AN NAFUD
iyûm 2637
Jabal Katrîna JABAL SHAMMAR

Bahr al Mill Karbala' 'Al Amārah
An Najaf Al Furat An Nāsirīyah Ahvāz
(Euphrates)
Djilab (Tigris)
IRAQ Al Başrah Ābādān
(Basra)
KUWAIT The
Al Kuwayt
(Kuwait) Gulf

Munifah

AD DAHNĀ

AS SAHRA
(EASTERN
AS SHARQÏYA
inyâ Nab. au Nil (Nile)
Asyût
DESERT)
Sohâg Hurghada
UHARRIK Qena
Luxor
El Khârga
EL WÂHÂT

MASHÂBIH

Al-Madinah
(Medina)

SAUDI AR RIYĀD
(RIYADH)

Tropic of Cancer

EL KHÂRGA Aswân
PT Sadd el Aali
ANÜBÏYAH Lake Nasser
Ras Bânâs
N

A R A B I A

JABAL TUWAYQ

Asb Shallâl Wadi
ath Thâni Halfa
AŞ ŞAHRA AN NUBIYAH
Ras Hadarba Jiddah Makkah
(Jedda) (Mecca) At Ta'if
(NUBIAN DESERT)
Ras Shagara
MUKAWWAR
Asb Shallâl
ath Thâlith
Bûr Sūdān
Dongola (Port Sudan)
JAZĀ'IR
Asb Shallâl SAWAKIN
ar Rabi' Ras Kasar
ŞAHRA 2780
BAYYUDAH Jabal
Hamoyet
El Milk JAZĀ'IR
Nile FARASAN
Asb Shallâl DAHLAK
as Sablûkah ARCHIPELAGO
Umm Durmân KAMARĀN San'ā' 3760
(Omdurman) El Khartum Bahrî Kassalā Ra's Isā Jabal an
El Khartum ERITREA Al Hudaydah Nabi Shu'ayb
(Khartoum) Asmara (Hodeida) YEMEN
Teseney Adi Ugri Mersa
Wad Medani Fatma
AZ ZUQAR

RUB AL KHĀLĪ

RAMLAT DAHM

Ta'izz

AN
EL GEZIRA
El Obeid 4620
Ras Dashen Assab Adan
El Bahr er Azraq (Blue Nile) Gonder (Aden)
DJIBOUTI
Lake Djibouti
Tana Berbera
Roseries 4231
Reservoir Gûna Terara Dese SOMALIA
JIBÂL AN 4152 4000 Dirê Dawa Hargeysa Burao
NÜBAH Biharn Abuyemeda AHMAR
ÄDÏS ÂBEBA
(ADDIS ABABA)
Dembî Dolo **ETHIOPIA**
Lake Zilway
Jima

Bab al Mandab
Gulf of
Aden

GUBAN
HAUD
OGADEN
AUDO

30° · F · 35° · G · 40° · H · 45° · J

61

West Africa

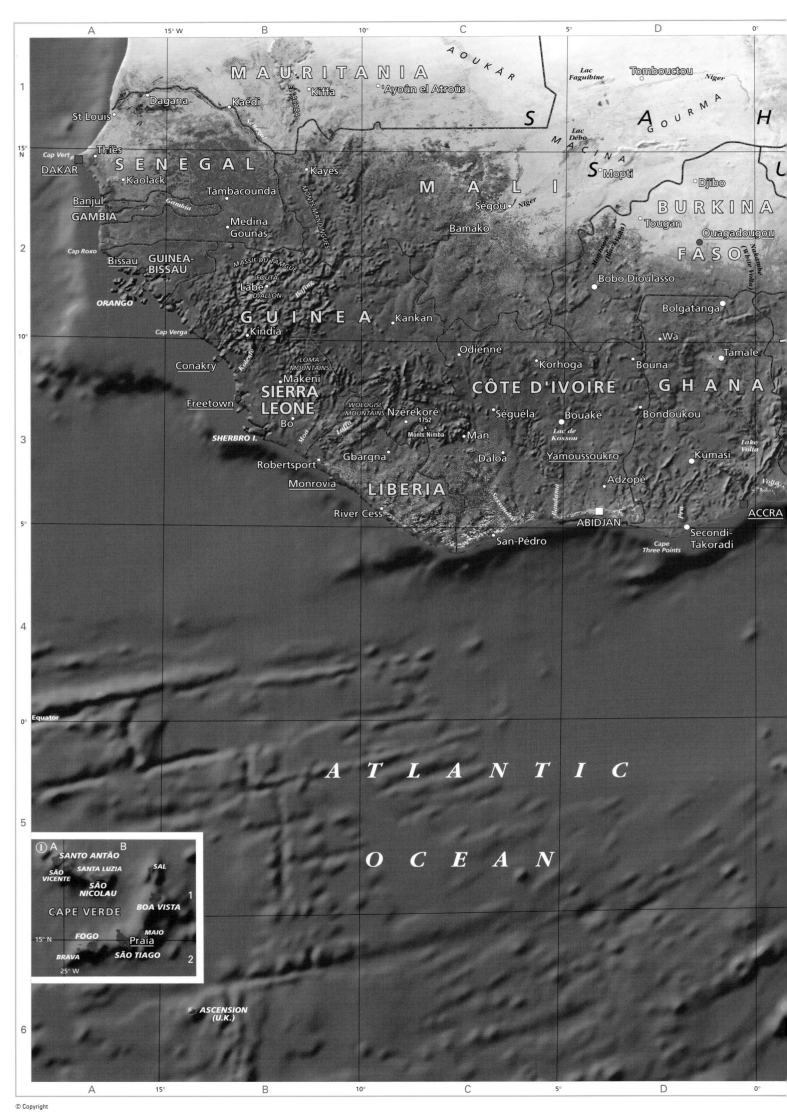

Scale 1 : 10 000 000

0   200   400   600 km

© Copyright

ERG DU TÉNÉRÉ

BODELÉ

ERG DU
DJOURAB

Agadez

FALAISE DE
TIGUIDIT

MASSIF DE
TERMIT

TI-N-TOUMMA

E

L

D

Dilia Bosso

N I G E R

MANGA

KANEM

C H A D

N

Tahoua

Niamey

Zinder

Lac Tchad
(Lake Chad)

Ati

Abéché

Maradi

Hadejia

N'Djamena

Lac Fitri

Sokoto

Katsina

Maiduguri

1613

Mongo

Birnin-Kebb

Gusau

Kano

Mont du Guéra

Kandi

Ka

Zaria

Massenya

ngou

Kaduna

Maroua

Bongor

Chari

Bahr Salamat

NIN

Niger

Kumo

MONTS
MANDARA

Laï

Sarh

Parakou

Kainji
Reservoir

Minna

Jos

JOS PLATEAU

Yola

Garoua

Moundou

Bahr Aouk

Bida

Abuja

N I G E R I A

Lac de
Lagdo

Saki

Ilorin

2049
Hoséré Vokré

Ngaoundéré

Oshogbo

Makurdi

Benue

GOTEL
MOUNTAINS

MASSIF DU YADE

C E N T R A L

Ogbomosho

IBADAN

Akure

Bozoum

Bossangoa

eokuta

Ikeja

Benin-City

Enugu

Bamenda

2740
Monts Bambouto

A F R I C A N

to-

Niger

Sanaga

Bouar

R E P U B L I C

Sibut

Cotonou

LAGOS

Uyo

Calabar

Nkongsamba

Bertoua

Berbérati

Bangui

ight of Benin

Port Harcourt

Mouths of the Niger

4095
Mont Cameroun

C A M E R O O N

Mbaïki

Ubangi

Malabo

Douala

Yaoundé

BIOKO
(FERNANDO
PÓO)

Gulf of

Ouésso

Ubangi

Impfondo

Zaïre

Guinea

PRÍNCIPE

EQUATORIAL
GUINEA

Cabo San Juan

Lulonga

SÃO TOMÉ AND PRÍNCIPE

Libréville

C O N G O

SÃO TOMÉ

São Tomé

Baie du Cap Lopez

Owando

Mbandaka

Equator

Cap
Lopez

G A B O N

DEMOCRATIC
REPUBLIC OF
CONGO

Port Gentil

ANNOBÓN
(PAGALU)
(Eq. Guinea)

MASSIF DU CHAILLU

Congo

Lac
Mai-Ndombe

Kuto

Kwa

Lukenie

PLATEAUX BATÉKÉ

Bandunda

Kasai

Zaïre

Brazzaville

KINSHASA

Kikwit

Pointe Noire

CABINDA
(Angola)

Matadi

Chutes de
Livingstone

Ponta da Narca

M'banza
Congo

Kwango

Kwilu

Uíge

Baía do Bengo

A N G O L A

Luanda

Malanje

Central Africa

© Copyright

Scale 1 : 10 000 000

0   200   400   600 km

Southern Africa

Scale 1 : 10 000 000

0   200   400   600 km

© Copyright

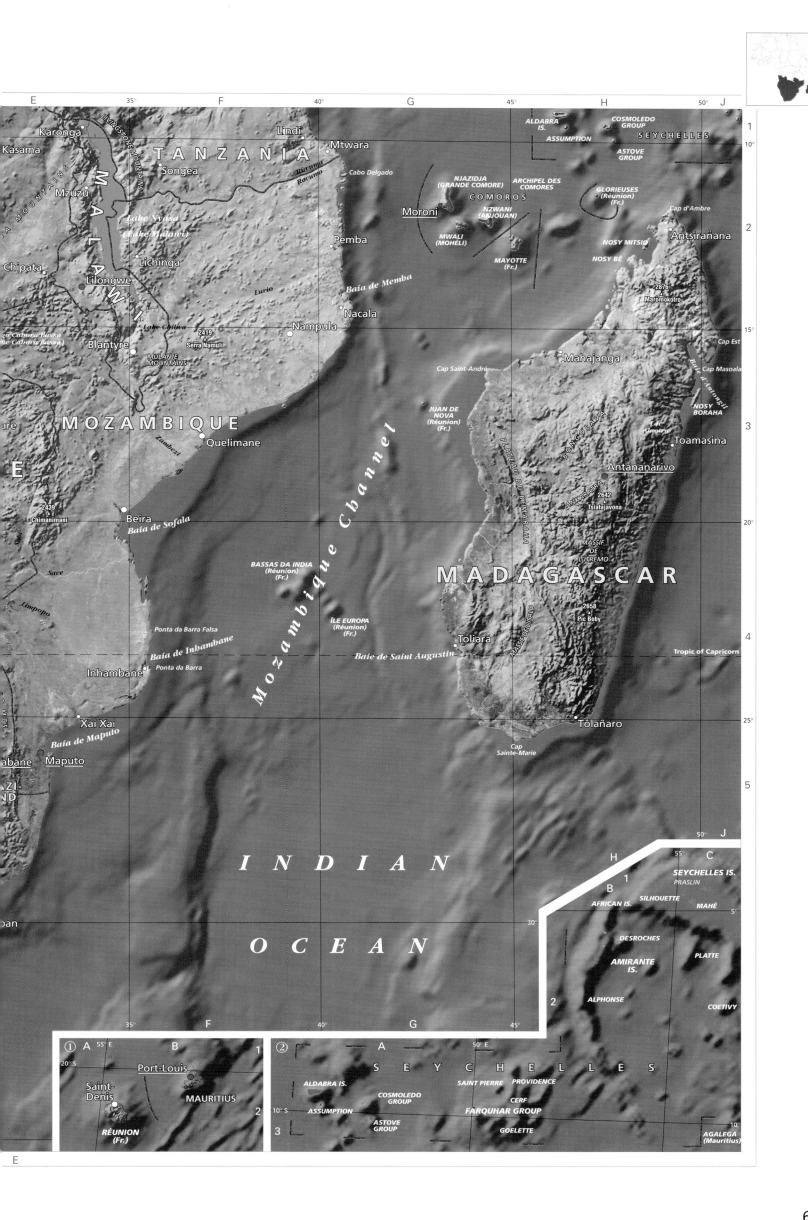

E   35°   F   40°   G   45°   H   50°   J

1

E
Kasama   Karonga   ALDABRA   COSMOLEDO   1
                                                                                          IS.   GROUP   SEYCHELLES
                        Songea   Lindi   ASSUMPTION   ASTOVE   10°
        Mzuzu   Mtwara   GROUP
                                    Cabo Delgado   NJAZIDJA   ARCHIPEL DES
Chipata   (GRANDE COMORE)   COMORES   GLORIEUSES
        Lichinga   Lake Nyasa   COMOROS   (Réunion)   2
               (Lake Malawi)   Pemba   Moroni   NZWANI   (Fr.)   Cap d'Ambre
        Lilongwe   (ANJOUAN)   NOSY MITSIO
                                                                  MWALI   Antsiranana
                              Lurio   Baía de Memba   (MOHÉLI)   NOSY BÉ
                                                                        MAYOTTE   2876
ga Cahora Bassa   Nacala   (Fr.)   Maromokotro
de Cahora Bassa)
Blantyre   2419   Nampula   Cap Est   15°
           Serra Namuli   Baie d'Antongil Cap Masoala
        MULANJE   Cap Saint-André   Mahajanga
        MOUNTAINS

MOZAMBIQUE   JUAN DE   NOSY
                                                                NOVA   BORAHA
        Zambezi   Quelimane   (Réunion)   BONGOLAVA
E   (Fr.)   PLATEAU DU BEMARAHA   Lac   Toamasina
                                                                                                                          Alaotra   3
                                                                                                     Antananarivo
                                                                                          ANKARATRA   2642
2439   Tsiafajavona
Chimanimani   Beira   20°
        Baía de Sofala   MASSIF
Save   DE
        BASSAS DA INDIA   L'ITREMO
        (Réunion)   MADAGASCAR
Limpopo   (Fr.)

        Ponta da Barra Falsa   ÎLE EUROPA   2658
                              (Réunion)   Pic Boby
Inhambane   Ponta da Barra   (Fr.)   Baie de Saint Augustin   Toliara   Tropic of Capricorn   4

Xai Xai   25°
                                                                        Tôlañaro
abane   Baía de Maputo   Cap
Maputo   Sainte-Marie
ZI-
ND   5

                                                                                                    50°   J

                    I   N   D   I   A   N   H   55°   C
                                                                                            SEYCHELLES IS.
                                                                          1   PRASLIN
                                                                          B
                                                                   AFRICAN IS.   SILHOUETTE   MAHÉ
                                                                                                                   5°
                                                                                            30°
                    O   C   E   A   N   DESROCHES
                                                                                            PLATTE
                                                          AMIRANTE
                                                          IS.
                                                                   ALPHONSE
                                                                                            COETIVY
                    35°   F   40°   G   45°

① A   55° E   B   1   ② A   50° E
20° S   Port-Louis   S E Y C H E L L E S
Saint-   ALDABRA IS.   SAINT PIERRE   PROVIDENCE
Denis   MAURITIUS   2   COSMOLEDO   CERF
        RÉUNION   2   GROUP   FARQUHAR GROUP   AGALEGA
        (Fr.)   10° S ASSUMPTION   (Mauritius)
                                  3   ASTOVE   GOELETTE
E   GROUP   10°

67

Asia

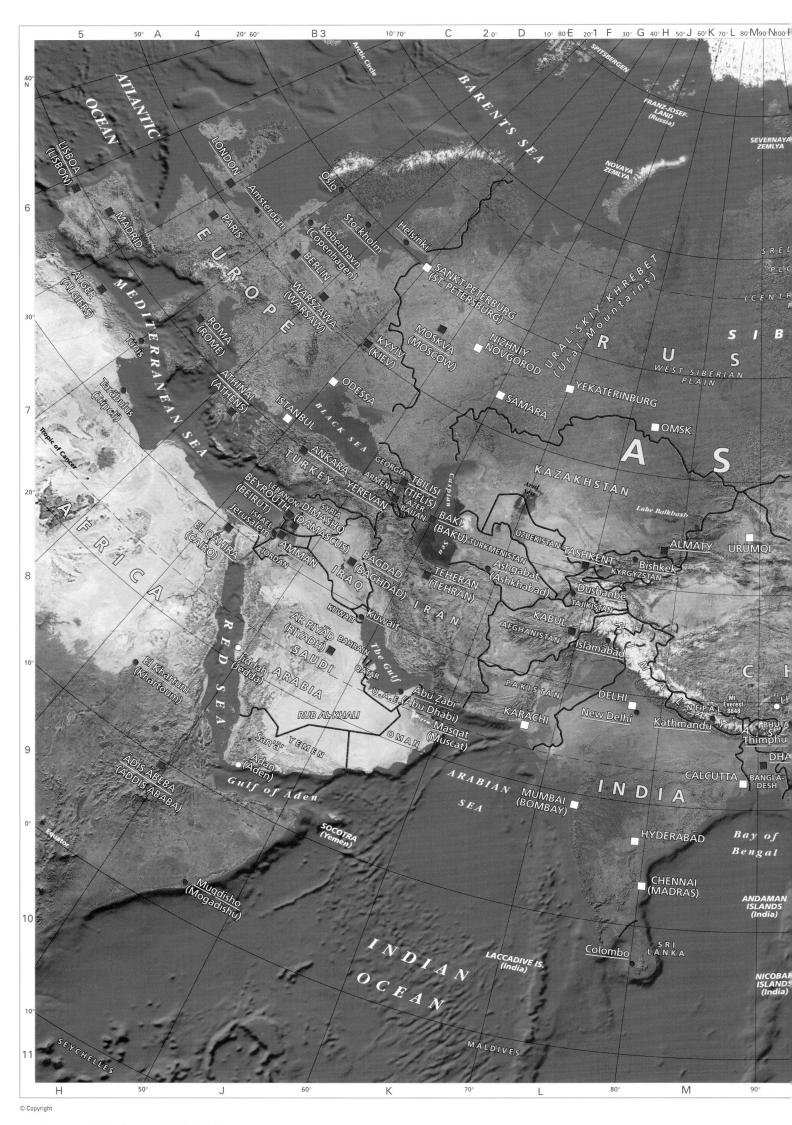

ATLANTIC OCEAN

LISBOA (LISBON)

MADRID

ALGER (ALGIERS)

Tunis

Tarābulus (Tripoli)

MEDITERRANEAN SEA

EUROPE

LONDON

Amsterdam

PARIS

BERLIN

WARSZAWA (WARSAW)

ROMA (ROME)

ATHINAI (ATHENS)

ISTANBUL

Oslo

Stockholm

København (Copenhagen)

Helsinki

SANKT-PETERBURG (ST. PETERSBURG)

MOSKVA (MOSCOW)

KYYIV (KIEV)

ODESSA

BLACK SEA

ANKARA

TURKEY

BEYROUTH (BEIRUT)

LEBANON DIMASHQ (DAMASCUS)

SYRIA

ISRAEL Jerusalem

JORDAN AMMAN

EL QÂHIRA (CAIRO)

AFRICA

GEORGIA TBILISI (TIFLIS)

ARMENIA YEREVAN

AZER. BAKI BAJAN (BAKU)

Caspian Sea

NIZHNIY NOVGOROD

SAMARA

URAL'SKIY KHREBET (Ural Mountains)

RUSSIA

YEKATERINBURG

OMSK

WEST SIBERIAN PLAIN

KAZAKHSTAN

Aral Sea

Lake Balkhash

BARENTS SEA

SPITSBERGEN

FRANZ-JOSEF-LAND (Russia)

NOVAYA ZEMLYA

SEVERNAYA ZEMLYA

SIB

RUS

AS

Arctic Circle

Tropic of Cancer

IRAQ BAGDAD (BAGHDAD)

IRAN TEHERAN (TEHRAN)

TURKMENISTAN

Ashgabat (Ashkhabad)

UZBEKISTAN TASHKENT

ALMATY

ÜRÜMQI

Bishkek KYRGYZSTAN

Dushanbe TAJIKISTAN

KUWAIT Kuwait

AR RIYĀD (RIYADH)

SAUDI ARABIA

BAHRAIN QATAR

The Gulf

U.A.E. Abu Zabi (Abu Dhabi)

OMAN Masqat (Muscat)

KABUL AFGHANISTAN

Islāmābād

PAKISTAN

KARACHI

DELHI

New Delhi

MT. Everest 8848

Kathmandu

NEPAL

BHUTAN Thimphu

INDIA

Jiddah (Jedda)

El Khartum (Khartoum)

RED SEA

RUB AL KHALI

San'ā' YEMEN

Adan (Aden)

ĀDIS ĀBEBA (ADDIS ABABA)

Gulf of Aden

Muqdisho (Mogadishu)

SOCOTRA (Yemen)

ARABIAN SEA

MUMBAI (BOMBAY)

HYDERABAD

CHENNAI (MADRAS)

CALCUTTA

BANGLA-DESH

DHA

Bay of Bengal

ANDAMAN ISLANDS (India)

Equator

INDIAN OCEAN

LACCADIVE IS. (India)

Colombo

SRI LANKA

MALDIVES

NICOBAR ISLANDS (India)

SEYCHELLES

© Copyright

Equatorial Scale   1 : 28 500 000

0   400   800   1200   1600 km

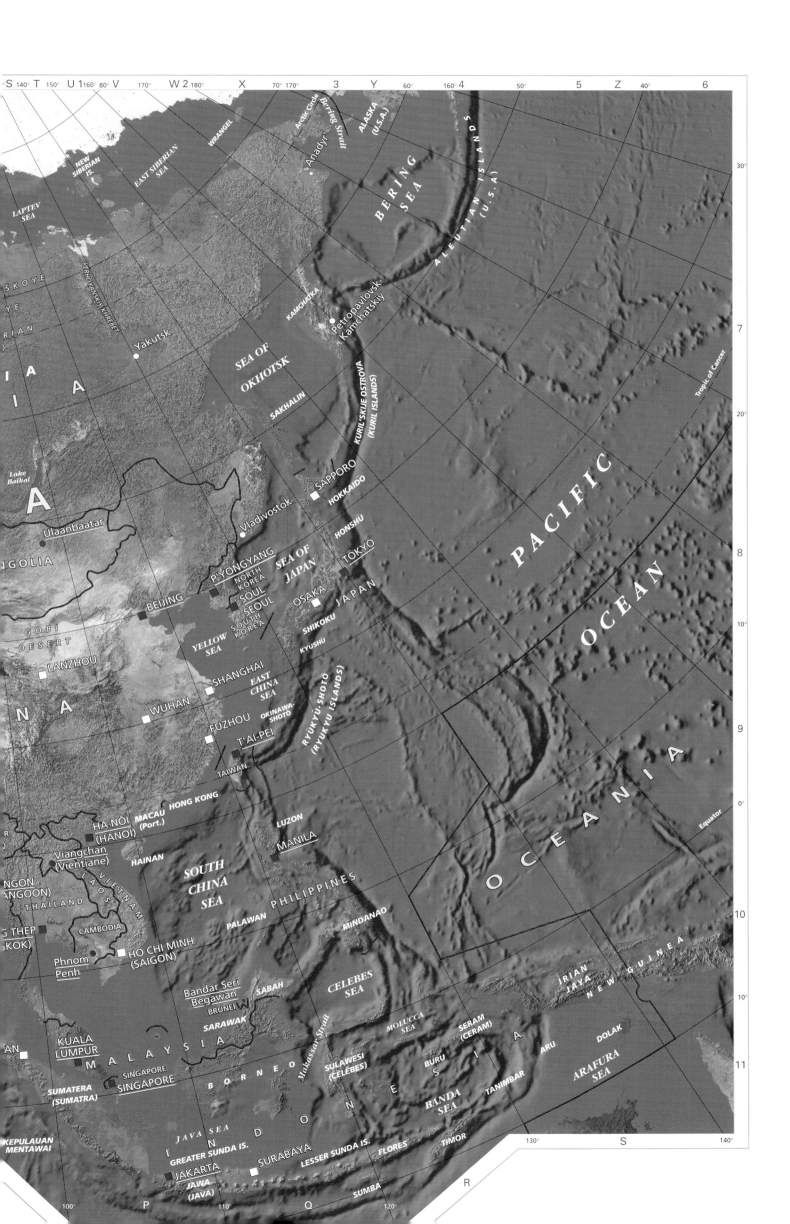

© Copyright

Scale 1 : 12 000 000

0   200   400   600 km

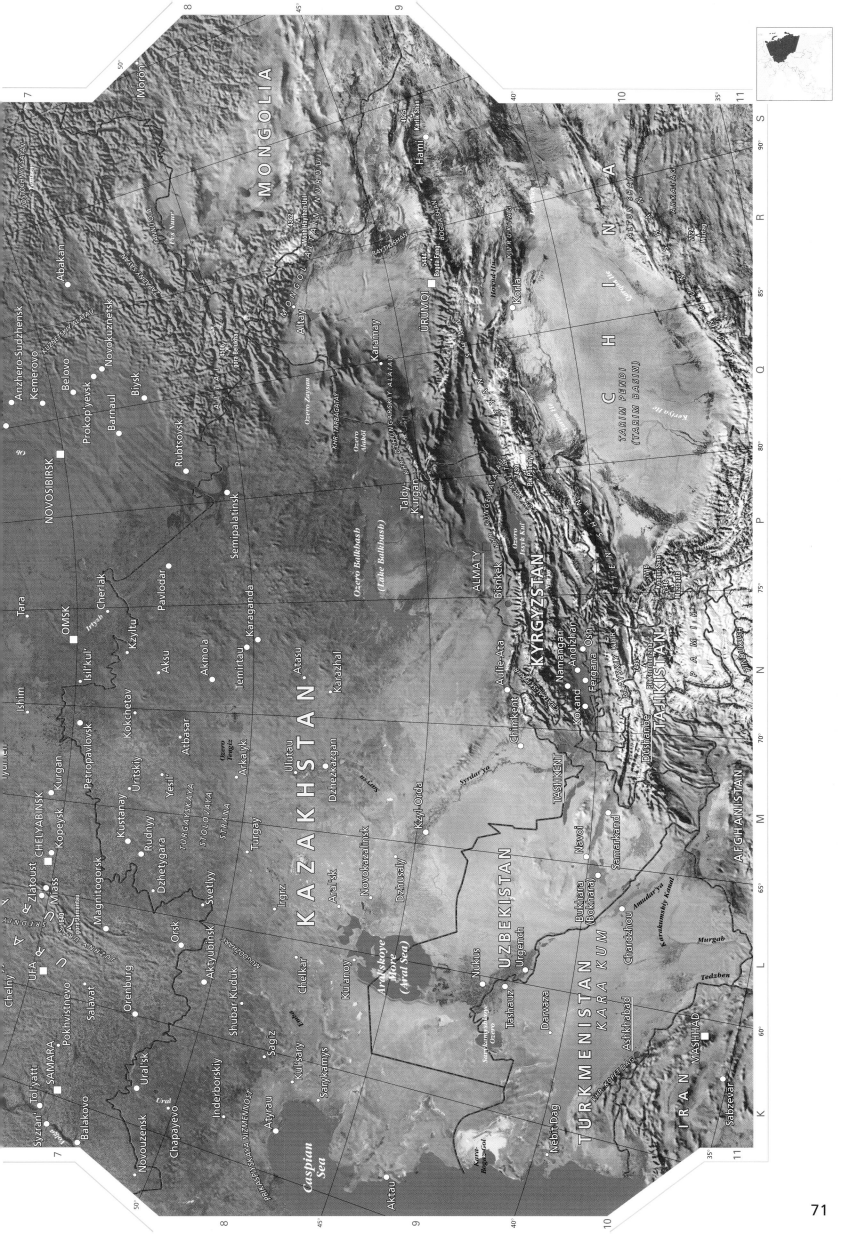

A 75° E   65° N B   80°   C 3   85°   D   70° 90°   E   95°   2 F   100°   G   105°

110° J 115° K 120° L 125° M 130°
H
1
75°

MORE LAPTEVYKH
OSTROV BOL'SHOY BEGICHEV
(LAPTEV SEA)
OSTF STOLB

Tarko-Sale
Sidorovsk
Krasnosel'kup
Igarka
Noril'sk
Kheta
Khatanga
Novorybnoye
Anabar
Olenëkskiy Zaliv

4

60° N

Surgutikha
GORY PUTORANA
Chirinda
ANABARSKOYE PLOSKOGORYE
Kotuy
Tiksi
Guba Buorkhaya

Komsa
SREDNESIBIRSKOYE PLOSKOGORYE
Tura
Udachnyy
Muna
Olenëk
Zhigansk

Bajkit
(CENTRAL SIBERIAN PLATEAU)
Nizh. Tunguska

5

Lesosibirsk
R U S S I A
Vilyuy

60°
N

Nizh. Tunguska

55°

Krasnoyarsk
Yenisey
Angara
Vilyuyskoye Vdkhr.
Yerbogachen
Aldan

Ust-Ilimsk
Lensk
Lena
Yakutsk

6

Bratsk
PATOMSKOYE NAGORYE
Lena
Amga

Bratskoye Vdkhr.
Nizhneudinsk
LENO-ANGARSKOYE PLATO
Nizhneangarsk
STANOVOYE NAGORYE
Aldan
ALDANSKOYE NAGORYE

BAIKALSKIY KHREBET
2467
Gora Golets-Skalistyy

50°

3492
Gora Munku Sardyk
VOSTOCHNYY SAYAN
Angarsk
Irkutsk
BARGUZINSKIY KHREBET
Ozero Baykal (Lake Baikal)

Hövsgöl Nuur
Ulan-Ude
Zeyskoye Vdkhr.
Zeya
KHREBET DZAGDY

Mörön
STANOVOY KHREBET

7

Chita
Shilka
Argun
Ergun He

Khilok
YABLONOVYY KHREBET

Orhon
2519
Gora Burun-Sabartuj
Ergun Zuoqi

Tuul Gol
Onon
Amur (Heilong Jiang)
Zeya
KHREBET TUKURINGRA
Blagoveshchensk
BUREINSK

Ulaanbaatar
CHENTIJN NURUU
Kerulen
Choybalsan
Hulun Nur
Nen Jiang

45°

Bulgan
M O N G O L I A
Buyr Nuur
Khabarov

8

Saynshand
Qiqihar
Amur (Heilong Jiang)
Anui

G O B I   D E S E R T
C H I N A
Hegang

Baicheng
Jiamusi
Songhua Jiang

Erenhot
HARBIN
Jixi
Ozero Khanka

40°

Mudanjiang
(L. Khanka)

BAOTOU
Bairin Zuoqi
CHANGCHUN
JILIN
Ussuriysk

Hohhot
Mudan Jiang

9

ZHANGJIAKOU
Vladivostok

Datong
DA HINGGAN LING
Songhua Jiang
Nakhod

H   110°   J   115°   K   120°   L   125°

M
NORTH KOREA
N
130°

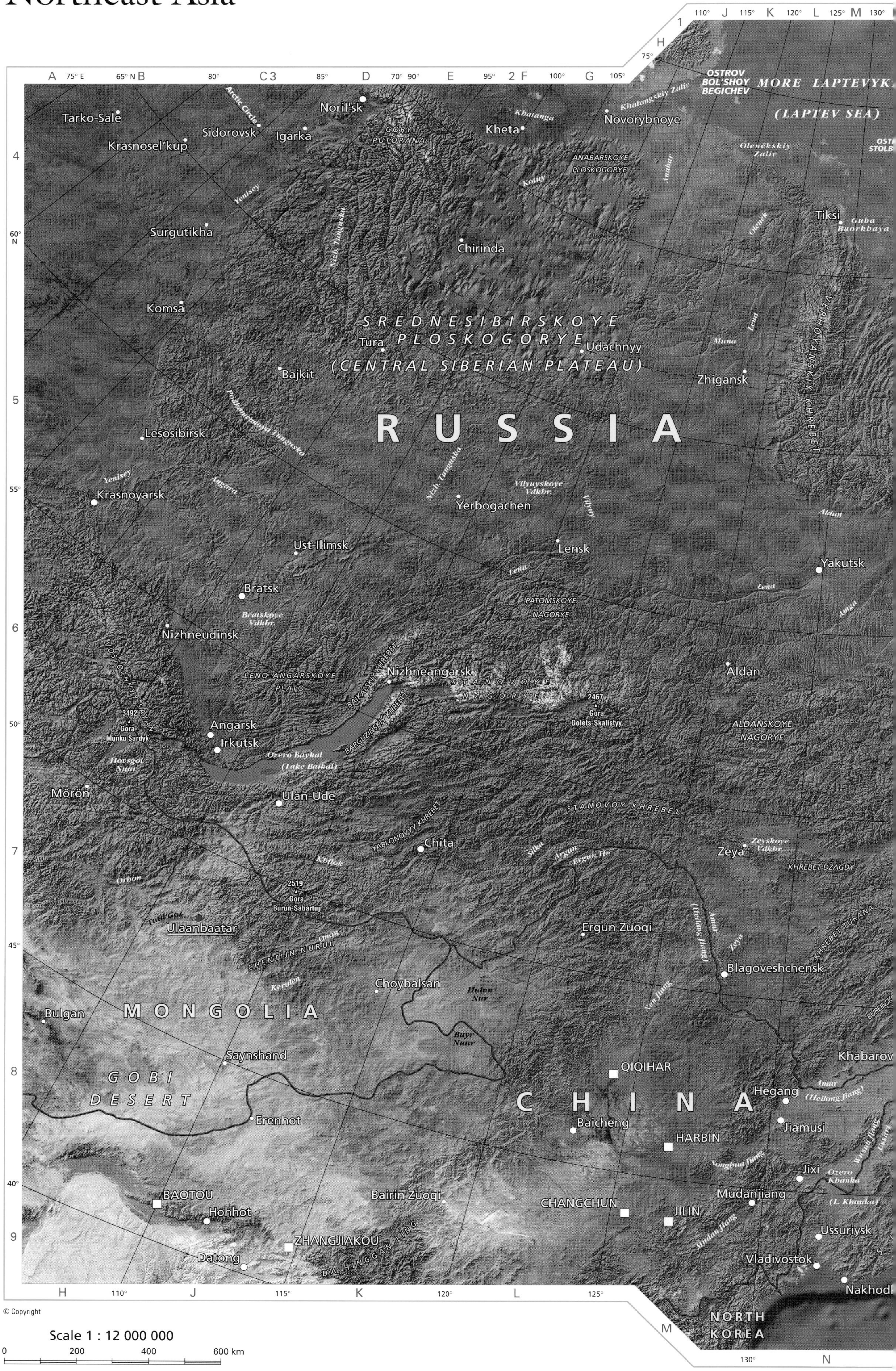

© Copyright

Scale 1 : 12 000 000
0   200   400   600 km

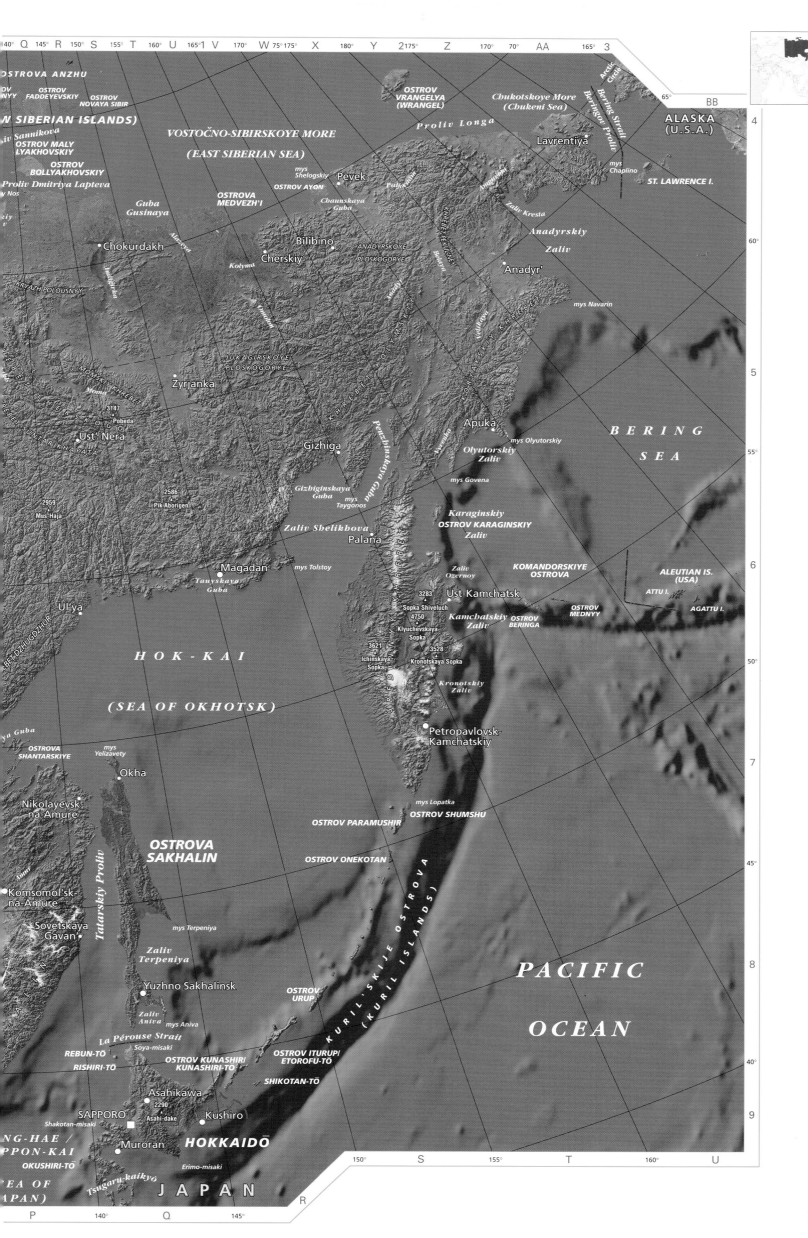

OSTROVA ANZHU

W SIBERIAN ISLANDS)

Sannikova
OSTROV MALY
LYAKHOVSKIY

OSTROV
BOLLYAKHOVSKIY
Proliv Dmitriya Lapteva

OSTROV
FADDEYEVSKIY
OSTROV
NOVAYA SIBIR

OSTROV
VRANGELYA
(WRANGEL)

*Chukotskoye More
(Chukeni Sea)*

Proliv Longa

Lavrentiya

ALASKA
(U.S.A.)

*mys
Chaplino*

ST. LAWRENCE I.

Arctic
Circle

Bering Strait
Beringou Proliv

65°

BB

VOSTOČNO-SIBIRSKOYE MORE

(EAST SIBERIAN SEA)

mys Shelogskiy

OSTROV AYON

*Chaunskaya
Guba*

Pevek

Anadyrskiy
Zaliv

mys Navarin

Guba
Gusinaya

• Chokurdakh

OSTROVA
MEDVEZH'I

Bilibino

Cherskiy

ANADYRSKOYE
PLOSKOGORYE

• Anadyr'

Zaliv Kresta

60°

Kolyma

Alazeya

Indigirka

KRYAZH POLOUSNYY

JUKAGIRSKOYE
PLOSKOGORYE

KHREBET PEKULNEY

Zyrjanka

Kolyma

Omolon

5

MONSKIY KHREBET

Moma

3147
▲ Pobeda

BERING

SEA

Ust'-Nera

Anyuy

Veliktoya

Apuka

mys Olyutorskiy

55°

Mus-Haja
2959
▲

2586
Pik Aborigen

Gizhiga

*Gizbiginskaya
Guba*

*mys
Taygonos*

Olyutorskiy
Zaliv

mys Govena

Karaginskiy
OSTROV KARAGINSKIY
Zaliv

ZEBET CHERSKOGO

Zaliv Shelikhova

Palana

KOMANDORSKIYE
OSTROVA

ALEUTIAN IS.
(USA)

Magadan

mys Tolstoy

*Zaliv
Ozernoy*

3283
▲

Ust-Kamchatsk

ATTU I.

AGATTU I.

60°

*Tauyskaya
Guba*

Sopka Shiveluch

Kamchatskiy
Zaliv

OSTROV
BERINGA

OSTROV
MEDNYY

Ul'ya

HOK-KAI

4750
▲ Klyuchevskaya
Sopka

3621
Ichinskaya
Sopka ▲

3528
▲
Kronotskaya Sopka

50°

(SEA OF OKHOTSK)

Kronotskiy
Zaliv

*Petropavlovsk-
Kamchatskiy*

OSTROVA
SHANTARSKIYE

*mys
Yelizavety*

Okha

70°

Nikolayevsk-
na-Amure

mys Lopatka

OSTROV SHUMSHU

OSTROV PARAMUSHIR

Komsomol'sk-
na-Amure

OSTROVA
SAKHALIN

OSTROV ONEKOTAN

45°

Sovetskaya
Gavan

mys Terpeniya

Zaliv
Terpeniya

PACIFIC

80°

Yuzhno Sakhalinsk

OSTROV
URUP

OCEAN

*Zaliv
Aniva*
mys Aniva

La Pérouse Strait

REBUN-TŌ
RISHIRI-TŌ

Soya-misaki

OSTROV KUNASHIRI
KUNASHIRI-TŌ

OSTROV ITURUP/
ETOROFU-TŌ

SHIKOTAN-TŌ

40°

Asahikawa

2290
Asahi-dake ▲

SAPPORO

Kushiro

9

Shakotan-misaki

Erimo-misaki

HOKKAIDŌ

NG-HAE /
PPON-KAI

OKUSHIRI-TŌ

Muroran

Tsugaru-kaikyō

JAPAN

EA OF
APAN)

R

© Copyright

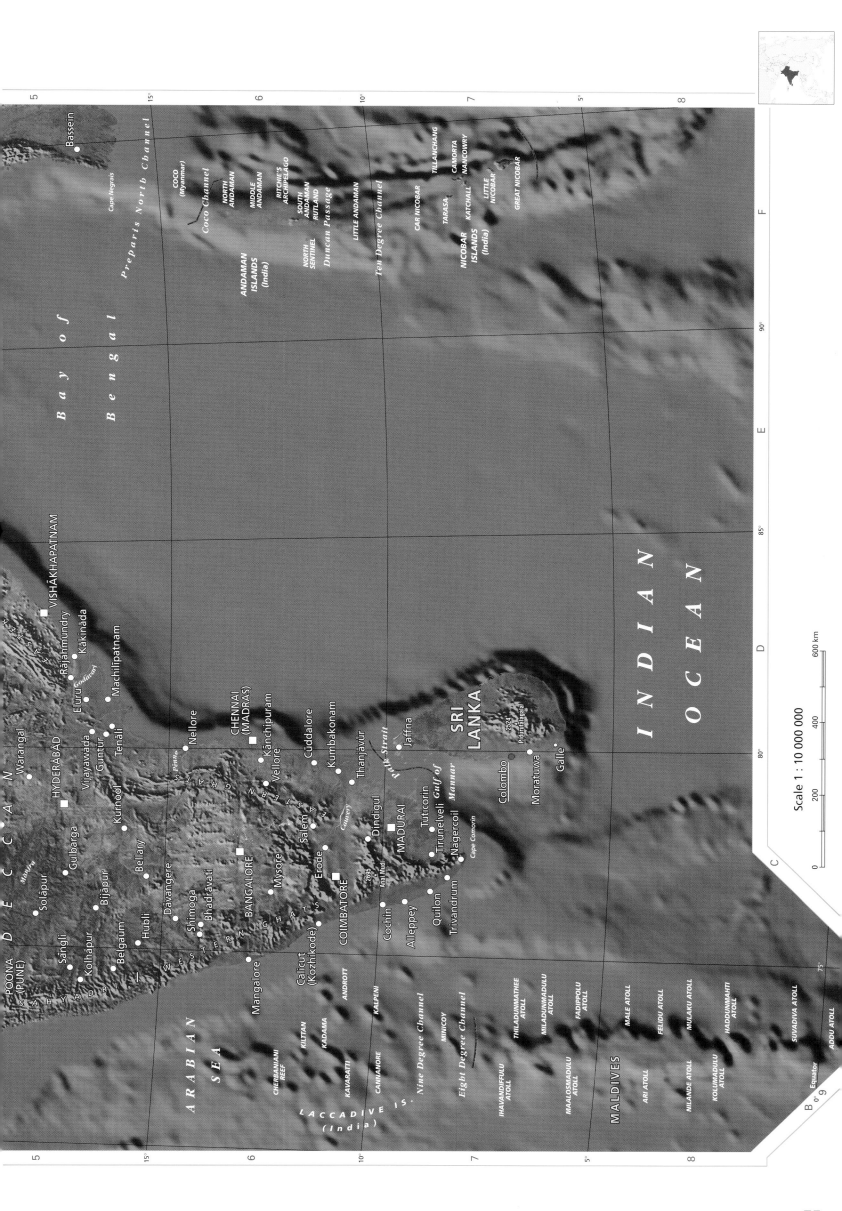

Scale 1 : 10 000 000

0   200   400   600 km

Southeast Asia

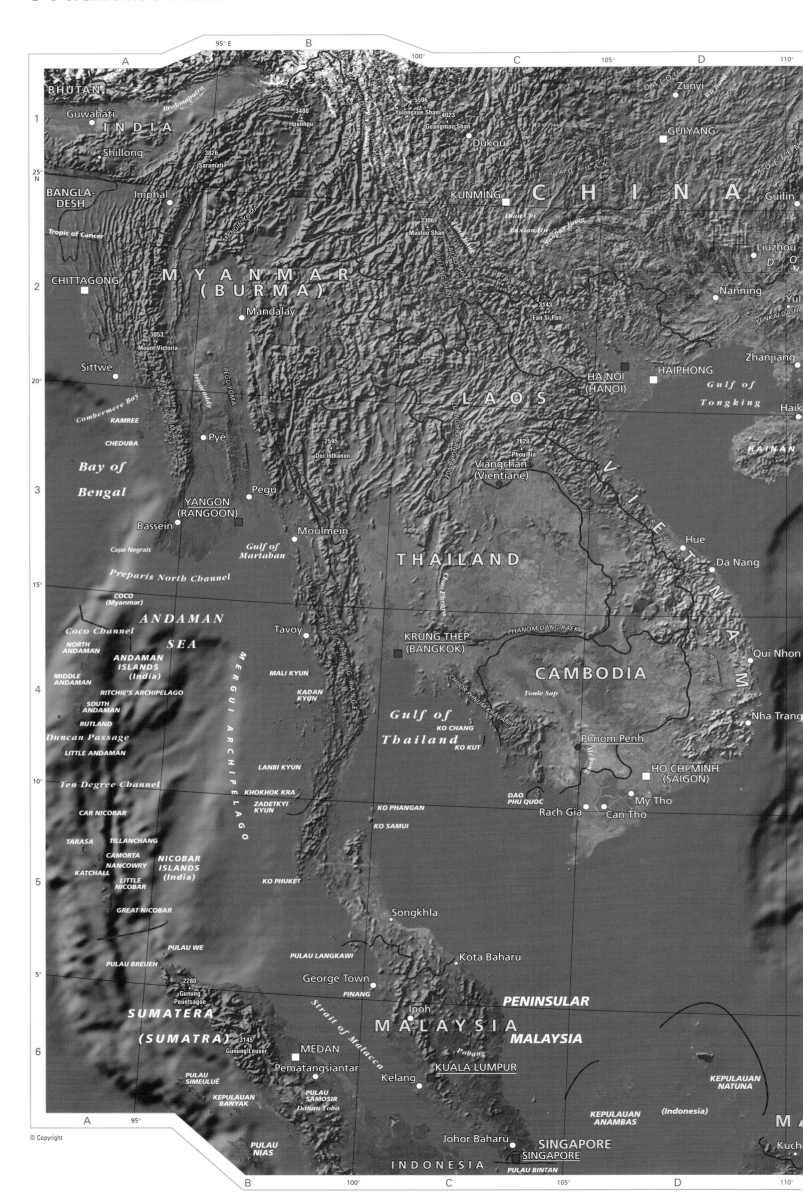

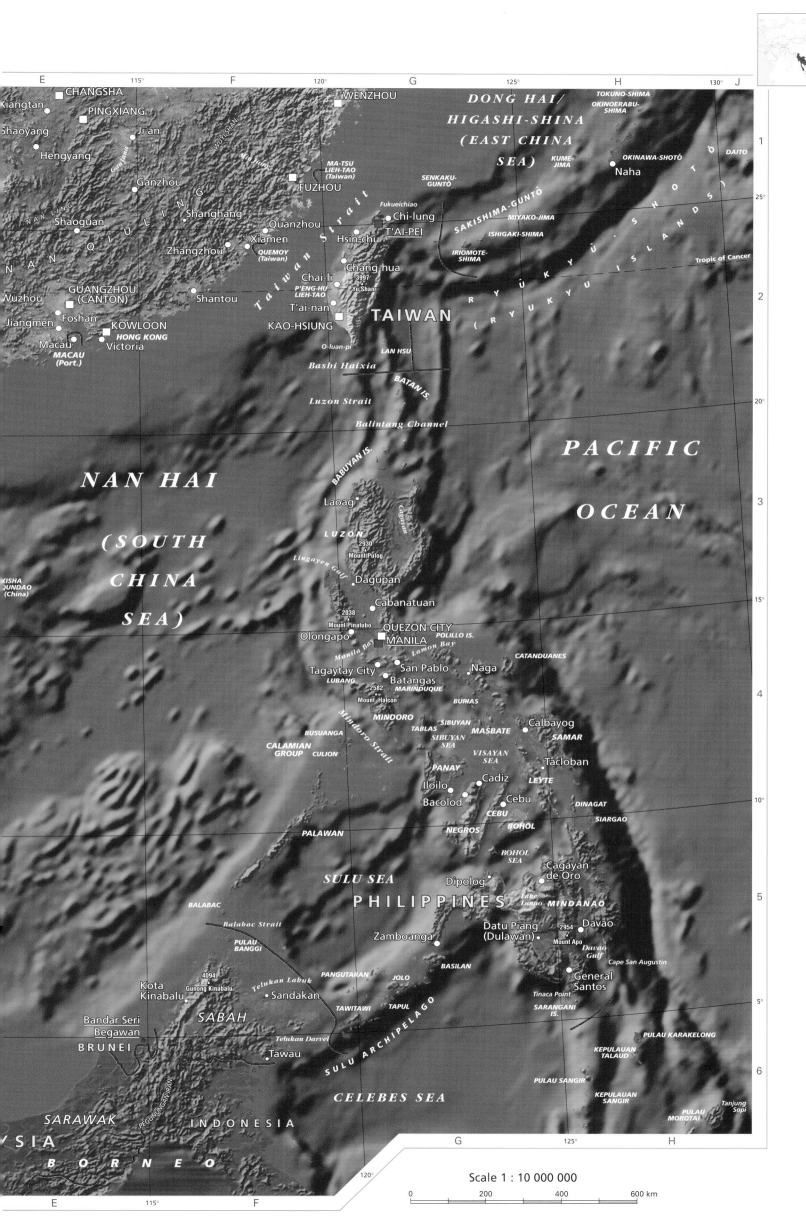

CHANGSHA
PINGXIANG
Xiangtan
Shaoyang
Hengyang
Ji'an
Ganzhou
Shaoguan
Shanghang
Zhangzhou
Xiamen
QUEMOY
(Taiwan)
Quanzhou
FUZHOU
MA-TSU
LIEH-TAO
(Taiwan)
WENZHOU

DONG HAI/
HIGASHI-SHINA
(EAST CHINA
SEA)

TOKUNO-SHIMA
OKINOERABU-
SHIMA

KUME-
JIMA
Naha

OKINAWA-SHOTŌ

DAITO

SENKAKU-
GUNTŌ

SAKISHIMA-GUNTŌ

MIYAKO-JIMA

ISHIGAKI-SHIMA

Tropic of Cancer

25°

Chi-lung
T'AI-PEI
Hsin-chu
Chang-hua
3997
Yu Shan
Chai-li
P'ENG-HU
LIEH-TAO
T'ai-nan
KAO-HSIUNG
TAIWAN
O-luan-pi
LAN HSU
Bashi Haixia
BATAN IS.

Fukueichiao

IRIOMOTE-
SHIMA

RYŪKYŪ ISLANDS
(RYŪKYŪ SHOTŌ)

Taiwan Strait

Wuzhou
GUANGZHOU
(CANTON)
Shantou
Jiangmen
Foshan
KOWLOON
HONG KONG
Victoria
Macau
MACAU
(Port.)

NAN QIULING

NAN LING

VUYISHAN

Min Jiang

Gan Jiang

Luzon Strait
Balintang Channel

PACIFIC

OCEAN

NAN HAI

(SOUTH

CHINA

SEA)

XISHA
QUNDAO
(China)

BABUYAN IS.
Laoag
LUZON
2930
Mount Pulog
Lingayen Gulf
Dagupan
Cabanatuan
2038
Mount Pinatubo
Olongapo
QUEZON CITY
MANILA
Manila Bay
Tagaytay City
LUBANG
San Pablo
Batangas
2582
Mount Halcon
MARINDUQUE
MINDORO
Mindoro Strait
BUSUANGA
CALAMIAN
GROUP
CULION
POLILLO IS.
Lamon Bay
Naga
CATANDUANES

Cagayan

TABLAS
SIBUYAN
SEA
PANAY
Iloilo
Bacolod
NEGROS
PALAWAN
BURIAS
MASBATE
VISAYAN
SEA
Cadiz
Cebu
CEBU
BOHOL
Calbayog
SAMAR
Tacloban
LEYTE
DINAGAT
SIARGAO

BOHOL
SEA
SULU SEA
Dipolog
PHILIPPINES
Cagayan
de Oro
Lake
Lanao
MINDANAO
BALABAC
Balabac Strait
PULAU
BANGGI
4094
Gunong Kinabalu
Kota
Kinabalu
Telukan Labuk
Sandakan
SABAH
Bandar Seri
Begawan
BRUNEI
Tawau
Telukan Darvel
SULU ARCHIPELAGO
TAWITAWI
TAPUL
JOLO
PANGUTARAN
BASILAN
Zamboanga
Datu Piang
(Dulawan)
2954
Mount Apo
Davao
Davao
Gulf
Cape San Augustin
General
Santos
Tinaca Point
SARANGANI
IS.
PULAU KARAKELONG
KEPULAUAN
TALAUD
PULAU SANGIR
KEPULAUAN
SANGIR
PULAU
MOROTAI
Tanjung
Sopi
CELEBES SEA
SARAWAK
INDONESIA
BORNEO
PEGUNUNGAN IRAN

SIA

Scale 1 : 10 000 000

0   200   400   600 km

China

© Copyright

Scale 1 : 10 000 000

0   200   400   600 km

MONGOLIA

GOBI DESERT

BADAIN JARAN SHAMO

C H I N A

LAOS   VIETNAM

NAN HAI
(SOUTH CHINA S

Gulf of
Tongking

MONGOL ALTAIN NURUU

Bon-Cagan-
Nur

3802
Ih-Oba-Ula

3957
Barun
Bagdo-Ula

4925
Karlik Shan

Shule He

GOV'ALTAIN NURUU

Bulgan

Saynshand

Erenhot

Ruo Shui

Huang Ho

BAOTOU   HOHHOT   ZHANGJIAKOU

Datong   BEIJING

DA HING-GAN LING

Buyr
Nuur

Keruten

QILIAN SHAN

Har Hu

Yinchuan

Huang He

Wutai Shan
3058

Baoding   TIANJI

Qinghai Hu
(Koko Nor)

3266
Haixin Shan

4070
Maomao Shan

Xining

LANZHOU

TAIYUAN   SHIJIAZHUANG

Cangzhou

5730
Har Sai Shan

Gyaring Hu   Ngoring Hu

A-NYEMAQEN SHAN

BAYAN HAR SHAN

SHALUI SHAN

MIN SHAN

Wei He

HANDAN

Huang He

JINAN

Z

Baoji   XI'AN   LUOYANG   ZHENGZHOU

3767
Taibai Shan

QIN LING   Han Shui

Kaifeng   Xuzhou

DABA SHAN

Nanyang   Bengbu

Xiangfan   Xinyang   HUAINAN

NANJIN

DABIESHAN

DAXUE SHAN

7556
Gongga Shan

CHENGDU

Wanxian

Yichang   HEFEI   Wu

Shashi   WUHAN   Anqing

Chang Jiang

ZIGONG   CHONGQING

Jinsha Jiang

DALOU SHAN

Wu Jiang

Changde

Dongting Hu

Jiujiang   Jingdezh

WULING SHAN

5596
Yulongxue Shan

4023
Guangmao Shan

Dukou

Zunyi

GUIYANG

YUN-GUI GAOYUAN

Xiangtan   CHANGSHA   NANCHANG

Payang Hu

PINGXIANG   Ji'an

WUYI SHAN

Shaoyang   Hengyang   Guijiang   Shanghang

Ganzhou   Quan

KUNMING

Deng Chi

Dian Chi

Fuxian Hu

Nampan Jiang

3306
Maotou Shan

WULIANG SHAN

AILAO SHAN

XUEFENG SHAN

Guilin

NAN LING

Shaoguan   Q

Shanghang

Zhangzhou

Tropic of Cancer

3143
Fan Si Pan

Liuzhou   DONG NAN   Wuzhou

Nanning   Xijiang

GUANGZHOU
(CANTON)   Xiamen

QUE
(Tai

Yulin   Foshan   Jiangmen   KOWLOON

HONG KONG

Macau   Victoria

MACAU
(Port.)   Zhanjiang

Shantou

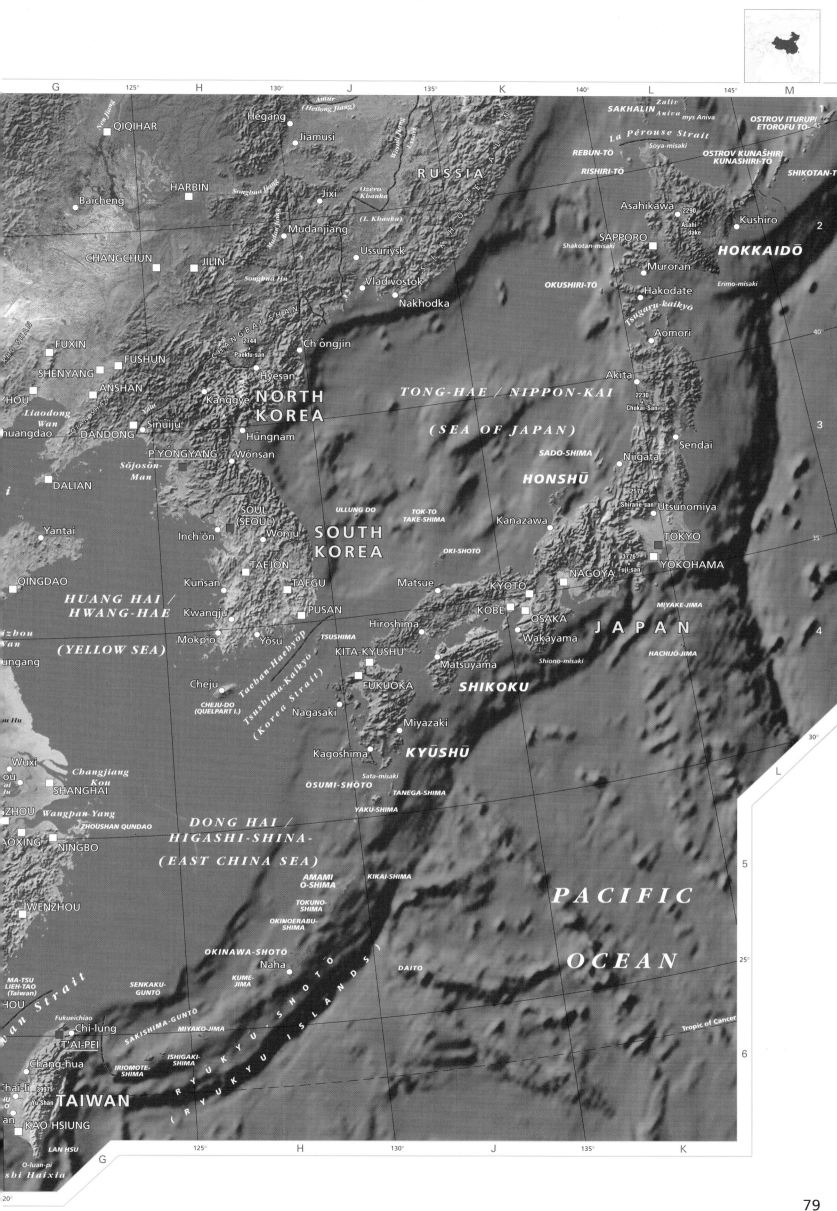

Japan and Korea

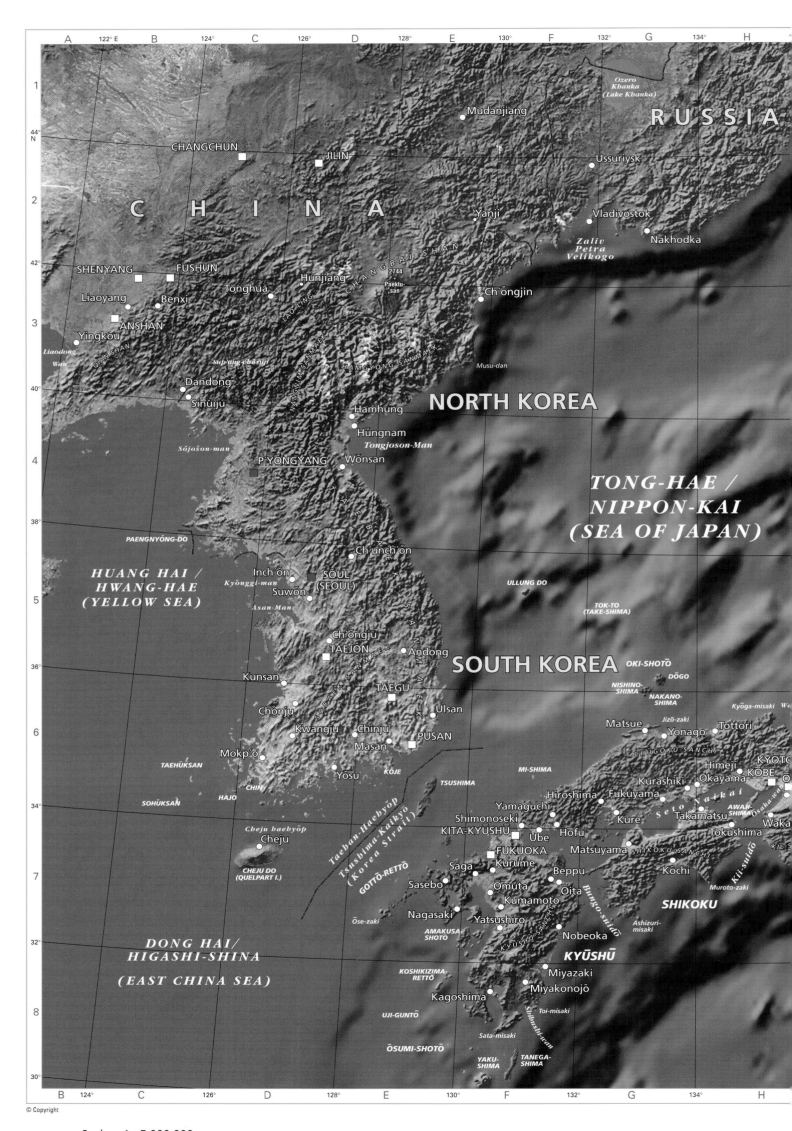

Scale   1 : 5 000 000

0   100   200   300 km

© Copyright

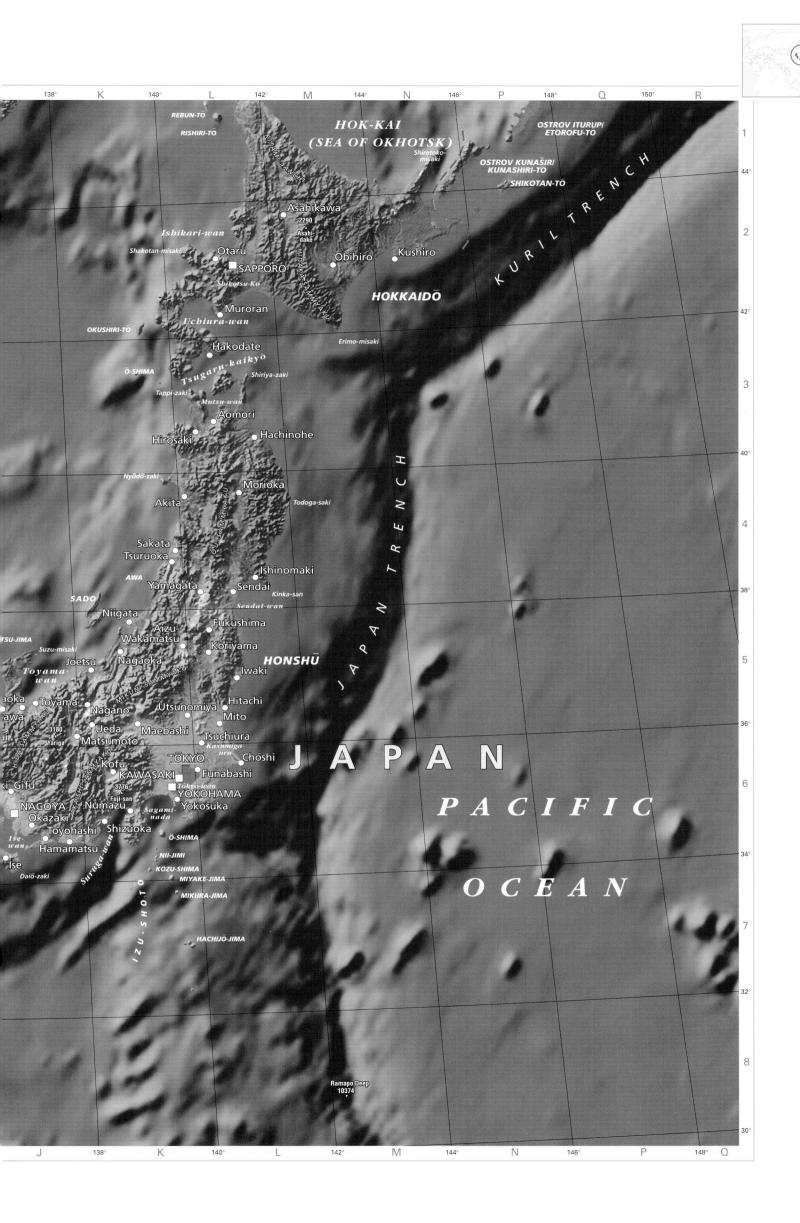

138° K 140° L 142° M 144° N 146° P 148° Q 150° R

44°

REBUN-TO
RISHIRI-TO

HOK-KAI
(SEA OF OKHOTSK)

OSTROV ITURUP/
ETOROFU-TO

1

Shiretoko-
misaki

OSTROV KUNAŠIRI/
KUNASHIRI-TO

SHIKOTAN-TO

KURIL TRENCH

44°

Asahikawa
2290
Asahi-
dake

Ishikari-wan

Otaru
SAPPORO

KITAMI-SANCHI

Obihiro
Kushiro

2

42°

Shakotan-misaki

Shikotsu-Ko

HOKKAIDŌ

Muroran

HIDAKA-SAMMYAKU

OKUSHIRI-TO
Uchiura-wan

42°

O-SHIMA

Hakodate

Erimo-misaki

Tsugaru-kaikyō

Shiriya-zaki

3

40°

Tappi-zaki
Mutsu-wan

Aomori

Hachinohe

Hirosaki

Nyūdō-zaki

Morioka

JAPAN TRENCH

40°

Akita

OU-SAMMYAKU

Todoga-saki

4

38°

Sakata
Tsuruoka

AWA

Yamagata

Ishinomaki

Sendai

Kinka-san

SADO

Sendai-wan

38°

Niigata

Fukushima

Aizu-
Wakamatsu

Kōriyama

ATSU-JIMA

Suzu-misaki

HONSHŪ

5

36°

Jōetsu
Nagaoka

MIKUNI-SAMMYAKU

Iwaki

Toyama-
wan

Toyama
Nagano
Utsunomiya
Hitachi

awa

Ueda
Maebashi
Mito

ki
3180
Yariga

Matsumoto
Tsuchiura

Kasumiga-
ura

TŌKYŌ
Chōshi

J A P A N

36°

Kofū
KAWASAKI

HIDA-SAMMYAKU

Gifu

Funabashi

Tokyo-wan
3776

YOKOHAMA

P A C I F I C

6

34°

NAGOYA
Okazaki
Numazu
Yokosuka

AKAISHI-SAMMYAKU

Fuji-san
Sagami-
nada

Toyohashi
Shizuoka

Ise-
wan

O-SHIMA

Hamamatsu

NII-JIMI

Ise

Daiō-zaki

KOZU-SHIMA
MIYAKE-JIMA

O C E A N

34°

IZU-SHOTO

MIKURA-JIMA

SURUGA-WAN

7

32°

HACHIJO-JIMA

32°

8

Ramapo Deep
10374

30°

J 138° K 140° L 142° M 144° N 146° P 148° Q

30°

Malaysia

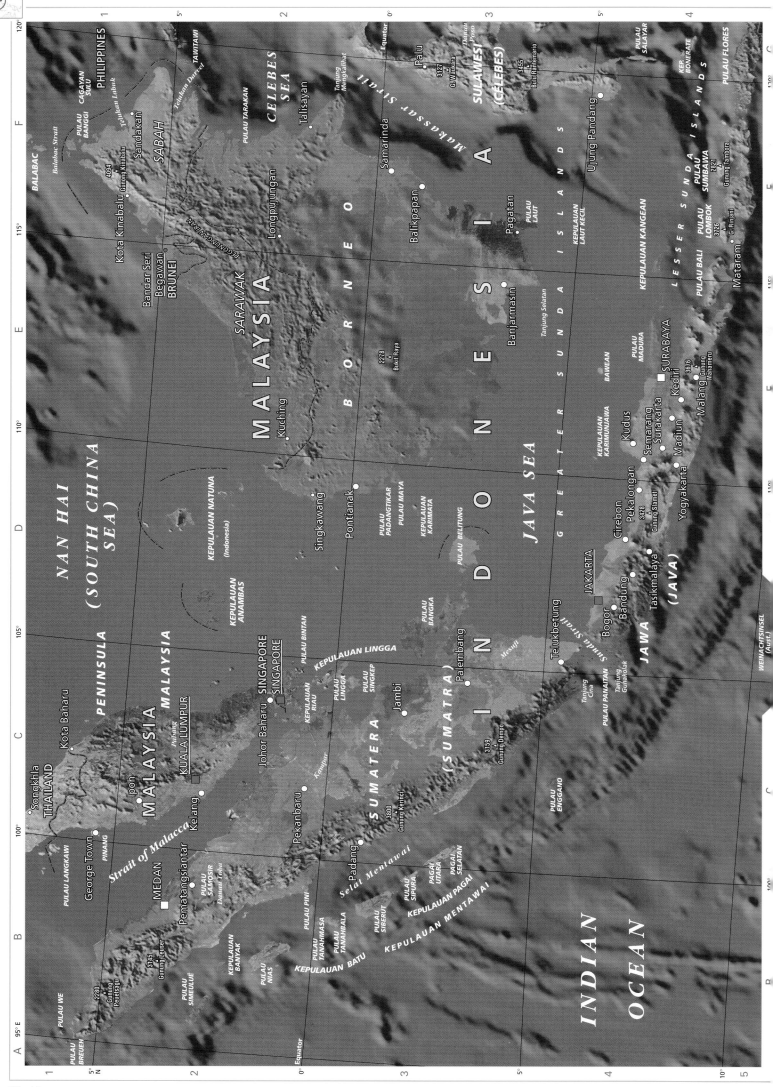

PHILIPPINES

BALABAC
Balabac Strait
PULAU
BANGGI
CAGAYAN
SULU
Teluken Labuk
Sandakan
Teluken Darvel
TAWITAWI

CELEBES
SEA

SABAH
Kota Kinabalu
Gunong Kinabalu 4094

PULAU TARAKAN

Tanjung Mengkalihat

Talisayan

Pahu
Poso
Palu
3127
G. Watukara
SULAWESI
(CELEBES)

PULAU
SALAYAR

KEP.
BONERATE

PULAU FLORES

3455
Bulu Rantemario

MALAYSIA

SARAWAK

Bandar Seri
Begawan
BRUNEI

PEGUNUNGAN IRAN

Longpujungan

Samarinda

B O R N E O

MALAYSIA

Balikpapan

Pagatan
PULAU
LAUT
KEPULAUAN
LAUT KECIL

KEPULAUAN KANGEAN

LESSER SUNDA ISLANDS

Ujung Pandang

PULAU
SUMBAWA
2821
Gunung Tambora

Kuching

2278
Bukit Raya

Banjarmasin

Tanjung Selatan

I N D O N E S I A

G R E A T E R   S U N D A   I S L A N D S

PULAU BALI
PULAU
LOMBOK
3726
G. Rinjani
Mataram

SURABAYA
Kediri
3676
Gunung
Mahameru
Malang
Gunung
Mahameru

NAN HAI
(SOUTH CHINA
SEA)

KEPULAUAN NATUNA
(Indonesia)

Singkawang

Pontianak

PULAU
PADANGTIKAR
PULAU MAYA

KEPULAUAN
KARIMATA

PULAU BELITUNG

BAWEAN
PULAU
MADURA

KEPULAUAN
KARIMUNJAWA
Kudus
Semarang
Surakarta
Madiun
3428
Gunung Slamet
Yogyakarta

JAVA SEA

PENINSULA

MALAYSIA

KEPULAUAN
ANAMBAS

SINGAPORE
PULAU BINTAN

KEPULAUAN LINGGA

PULAU
BANGKA

JAKARTA
Cirebon
Pekalongan

Bogor
Bandung
Tasikmalaya

Songkhla
THAILAND
Kota Baharu

MALAYSIA
Pahang
KUALA LUMPUR

Ipoh

Johor Baharu
SINGAPORE
SINGAPORE

KEPULAUAN
RIAU
PULAU
LINGGA
PULAU
SINGKEP

Jambi

Palembang
Musi

Telukbetung

Sunda Strait

Tanjung
Cina
PULAU PANAITAN

JAWA
(JAVA)

WEINACHTSINSEL
(Aust.)

George Town
PINANG
Kelang

PULAU LANGKAWI

Strait of Malacca

MEDAN
Pematangsiantar
PULAU
SAMOSIR
Danau Toba

Pekanbaru
Kampar

3800
Gunung Kerinci

Padang
Selat Mentawai

3159
Gunung Dempo

SUMATERA

(SUMATRA)

Tanjung
Guhakolak

PULAU
ENGGANO

PULAU WE
PULAU
BREUEH
2280
Gunung
Peuetsagu

3145
Gunung Leuser

KEPULAUAN
BANYAK
PULAU
NIAS

KEPULAUAN BATU
PULAU
TANAHMASA
PULAU
TANAHBALA

PULAU PINI

PULAU
SIBERUT
PAGAI
UTARA
PAGAI
SELATAN

KEPULAUAN PAGAI

PULAU
SIPURA

KEPULAUAN MENTAWAI

PULAU
SIMEULUE

INDIAN

OCEAN

Equator

Equator

Massау Strait

© Copyright

Scale 1 : 10 000 000

0   200   400   600 km

82

Indonesia

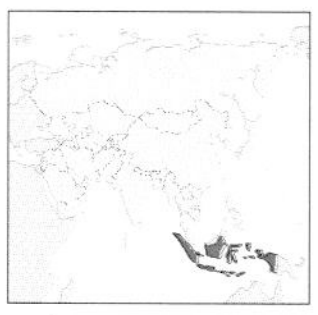

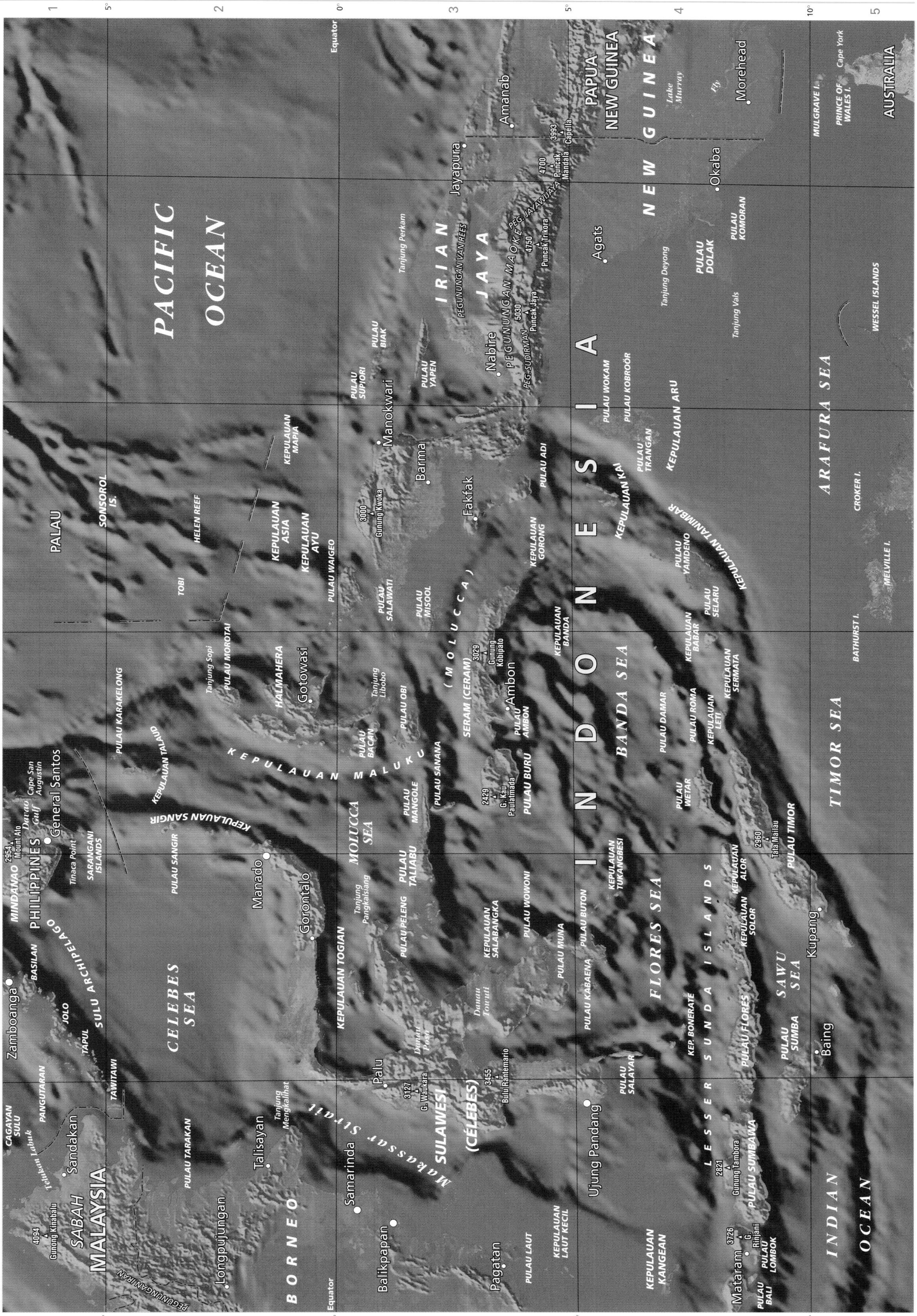

PACIFIC OCEAN
PALAU
SONSOROL IS.
HELEN REEF
TOBI
KEPULAUAN ASIA
KEPULAUAN AYU
KEPULAUAN MAPIA
PULAU WAIGEO
PULAU SUPIORI
PULAU BIAK
PULAU YAPEN
Manokwari
PULAU SALAWATI
PULAU MISOOL
Gunung Kwoka
3000
Barma
Fakfak
Jayapura
Amanab
PAPUA NEW GUINEA
NEW GUINEA
IRIAN JAYA
Tanjung Perkam
PEGUNUNGAN VAN REES
PEGUNUNGAN MAOKE
PEG. JAYAWIJAYA
PEG. SUDIRMAN
Puncak Jaya
5030
Puncak Trikora
4750
Puncak Mandala
4700
Capella
3993
Nabire
Agats
Okaba
Morehead
Lake Murray
Fly
Cape York
PRINCE OF WALES I.
MULGRAVE I.
AUSTRALIA
Tanjung Deyong
PULAU DOLAK
PULAU KOMORAN
Tanjung Vals
WESSEL ISLANDS
ARAFURA SEA
CROKER I.
MELVILLE I.
BATHURST I.
KEPULAUAN ARU
PULAU WOKAM
PULAU KOBROOR
PULAU TRANGAN
PULAU ADI
KEPULAUAN KAI
KEPULAUAN TANIMBAR
PULAU YAMDENO
PULAU SELARU
KEPULAUAN GORONG
INDONESIA
BANDA SEA
KEPULAUAN BANDA
KEPULAUAN BABAR
KEPULAUAN SERMATA
KEPULAUAN LETI
PULAU ROMA
PULAU DAMAR
PULAU WETAR
TIMOR SEA
PULAU TIMOR
Tata Mailau
2960
Kupang
SAWU SEA
KEPULAUAN ALOR
KEPULAUAN SOLOR
LESSER SUNDA ISLANDS
PULAU FLORES
PULAU SUMBA
Baing
KEP. BONERATE
FLORES SEA
PULAU KABAENA
PULAU SALAYAR
Ujung Pandang
PULAU SUMBAWA
Gunung Tambora
2821
G. Rinjani
3726
Mataram
PULAU LOMBOK
PULAU BALI
KEPULAUAN KANGEAN
INDIAN OCEAN
KEPULAUAN LAUT KECIL
PULAU LAUT
Pagatan
Balikpapan
Samarinda
BORNEO
Longpujungan
PEGUNUNGAN IRAN
SABAH
MALAYSIA
Gunung Kinabalu
4094
Sandakan
Teluk Labuk
CAGAYAN SULU
PANGUTARAN
TAWITAWI
TAPUL
JOLO
SULU ARCHIPELAGO
BASILAN
Zamboanga
PULAU TARAKAN
Talisayan
Tanjung Mengkalihat
Makassar Strait
SULAWESI (CELEBES)
Palu
G. Waukara
3127
Bulu Rantemario
3455
Danau Poso
Danau Towuti
CELEBES SEA
KEPULAUAN TOGIAN
Gorontalo
Manado
Tanjung Pangkalsiang
PULAU PELENG
KEPULAUAN SALABANGKA
PULAU WOWONI
PULAU MUNA
PULAU BUTON
KEPULAUAN TUKANGBESI
PULAU TALIABU
PULAU MANGOLE
MOLUCCA SEA
PULAU SANANA
PULAU BURU
G. Kau Paulamada
2429
PULAU AMBON
Ambon
SERAM (CERAM)
Gunung Kobipato
3029
(MOLUCCA)
PULAU BACAN
PULAU OBI
Tanjung Libobo
KEPULAUAN MALUKU
HALMAHERA
Gotowasi
PULAU MOROTAI
Tanjung Sopi
PULAU KARAKELONG
KEPULAUAN TALAUD
KEPULAUAN SANGIR
PULAU SANGIR
SARANGANI ISLANDS
Tinaca Point
MINDANAO
PHILIPPINES
Mount Apo
2954
Davao Gulf
Cape San Augustin
General Santos
Equator

© Copyright

Scale 1 : 10 000 000

0 200 400 600 km

Oceania

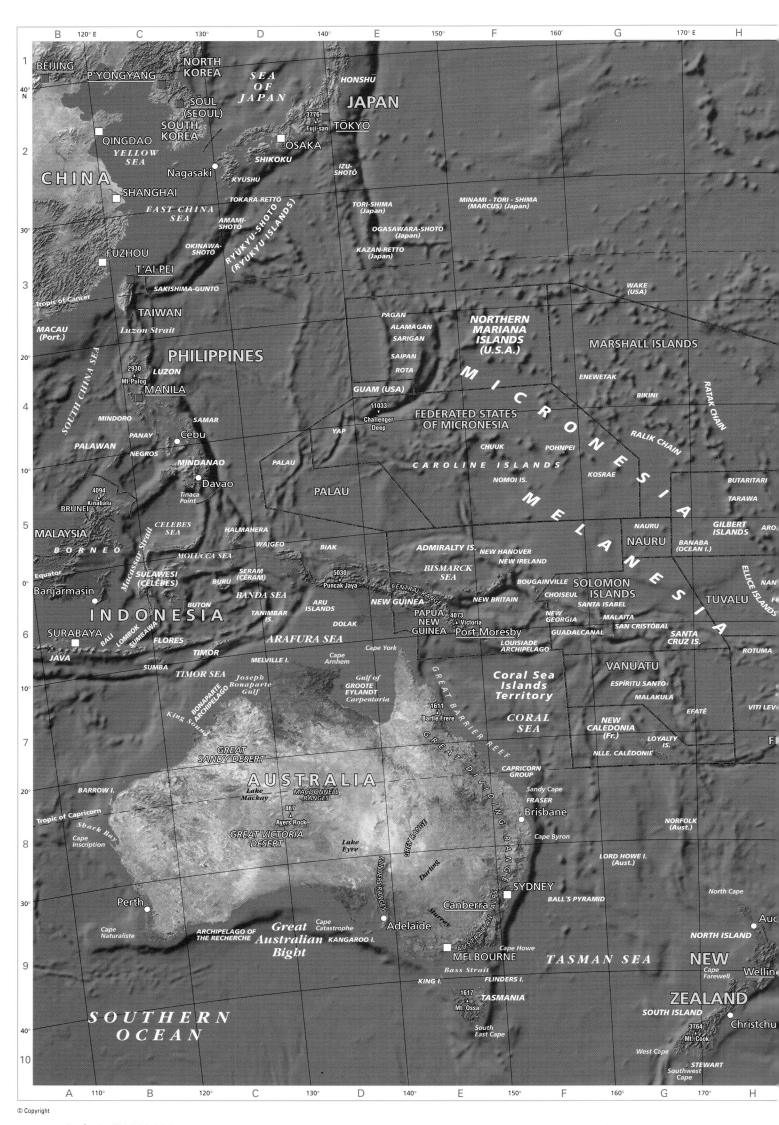

© Copyright

Scale 1 : 35 000 000

0   500   1000   1500   2000 km

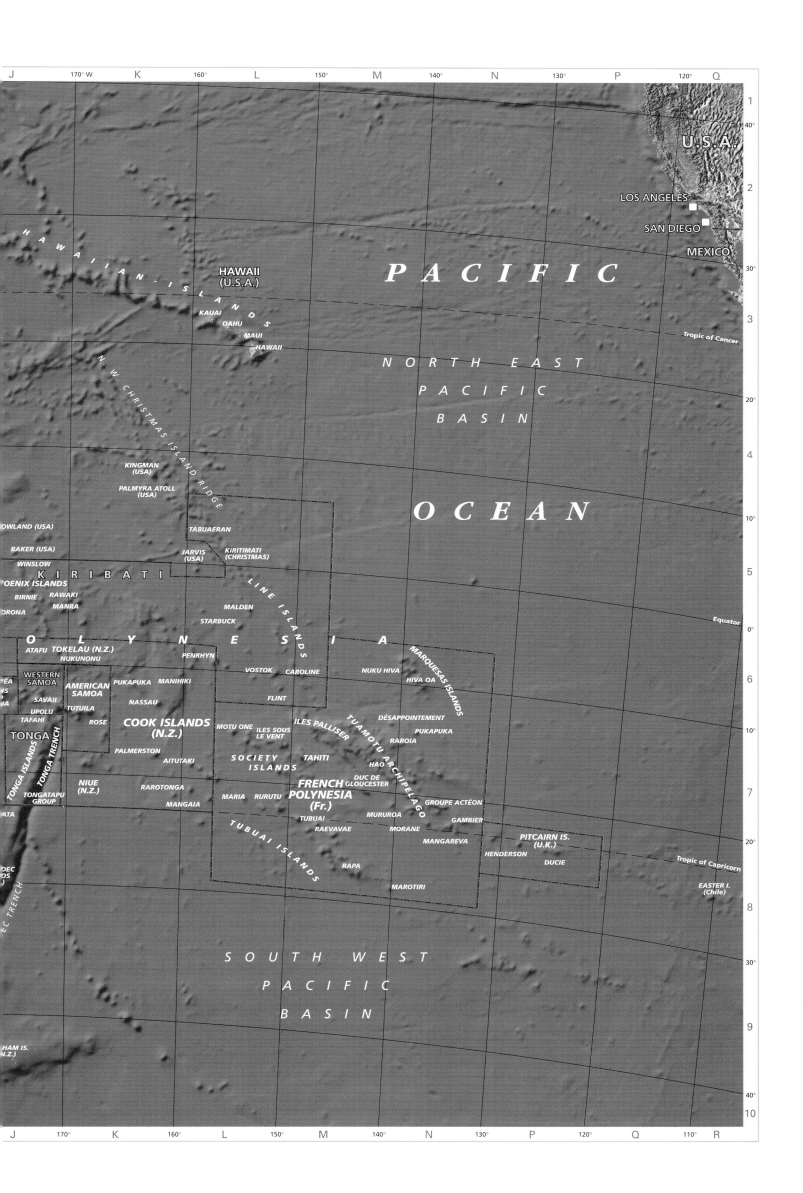

J   170° W   K   160°   L   150°   M   140°   N   130°   P   120°   Q

U.S.A.

LOS ANGELES
SAN DIEGO
MEXICO

P A C I F I C

HAWAII
(U.S.A.)
KAUAI
OAHU
MAUI
HAWAII

N O R T H   E A S T

P A C I F I C

B A S I N

Tropic of Cancer

O C E A N

KINGMAN
(USA)

PALMYRA ATOLL
(USA)

TABUAERAN

OWLAND (USA)

BAKER (USA)

WINSLOW

JARVIS
(USA)

KIRITIMATI
(CHRISTMAS)

K I R I B A T I

Equator

OENIX ISLANDS

BIRNIE   RAWAKI
ORONA   MANRA

MALDEN

STARBUCK

L I N E   I S L A N D S

O   L   Y   N   E   S   I   A

ATAFU   TOKELAU (N.Z.)
NUKUNONU

PENRHYN

VOSTOK   CAROLINE

NUKU HIVA

M A R Q U E S A S   I S L A N D S

HIVA OA

WESTERN
SAMOA

PUKAPUKA   MANIHIKI

ÉA
IS
IA

AMERICAN
SAMOA

NASSAU

FLINT

SAVAII

UPOLU   TUTUILA

TAFAHI   ROSE

COOK ISLANDS
(N.Z.)

MOTU ONE
ILES SOUS
LE VENT

ILES PALLISER

DÉSAPPOINTEMENT

PUKAPUKA

RAROIA

T U A M O T U   A R C H I P E L A G O

TONGA

PALMERSTON

AITUTAKI

*S O C I E T Y
I S L A N D S*

TAHITI

HAO

DUC DE
GLOUCESTER

NIUE
(N.Z.)

RAROTONGA

FRENCH
POLYNESIA
(Fr.)

T O N G A   I S L A N D S

T o n g a   T R E N C H

TONGATAPU
GROUP

MANGAIA

MARIA   RURUTU

MARIA

GROUPE ACTÉON

MURUROA

MORANE

GAMBIER

TUBUAI

RAEVAVAE

MANGAREVA

PITCAIRN IS.
(U.K.)

HENDERSON

DUCIE

Tropic of Capricorn

ATA

T U B U A I   I S L A N D S

RAPA

MAROTIRI

EASTER I.
(Chile)

EC TRENCH

DEC
DS

S O U T H   W E S T

P A C I F I C

B A S I N

HAM IS.
N.Z.)

J   170°   K   160°   L   150°   M   140°   N   130°   P   120°   Q   110°   R

Australia

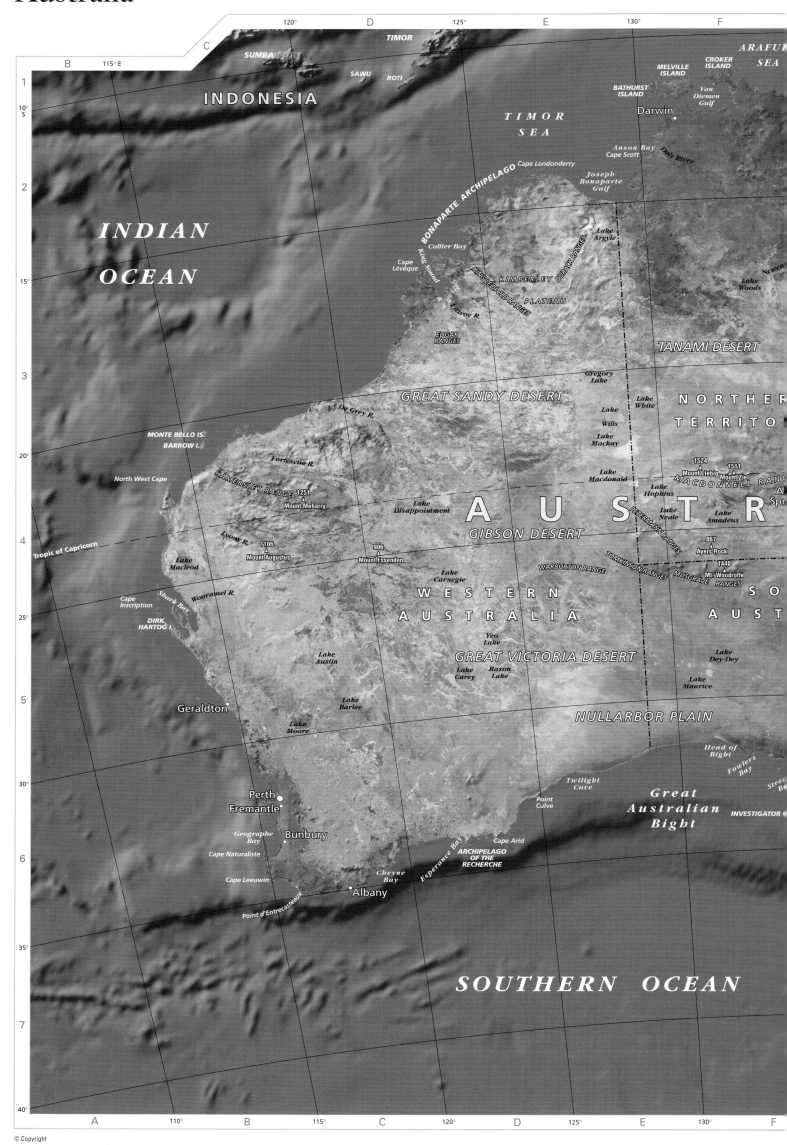

Scale 1 : 12 000 000

0   200   400   600 km

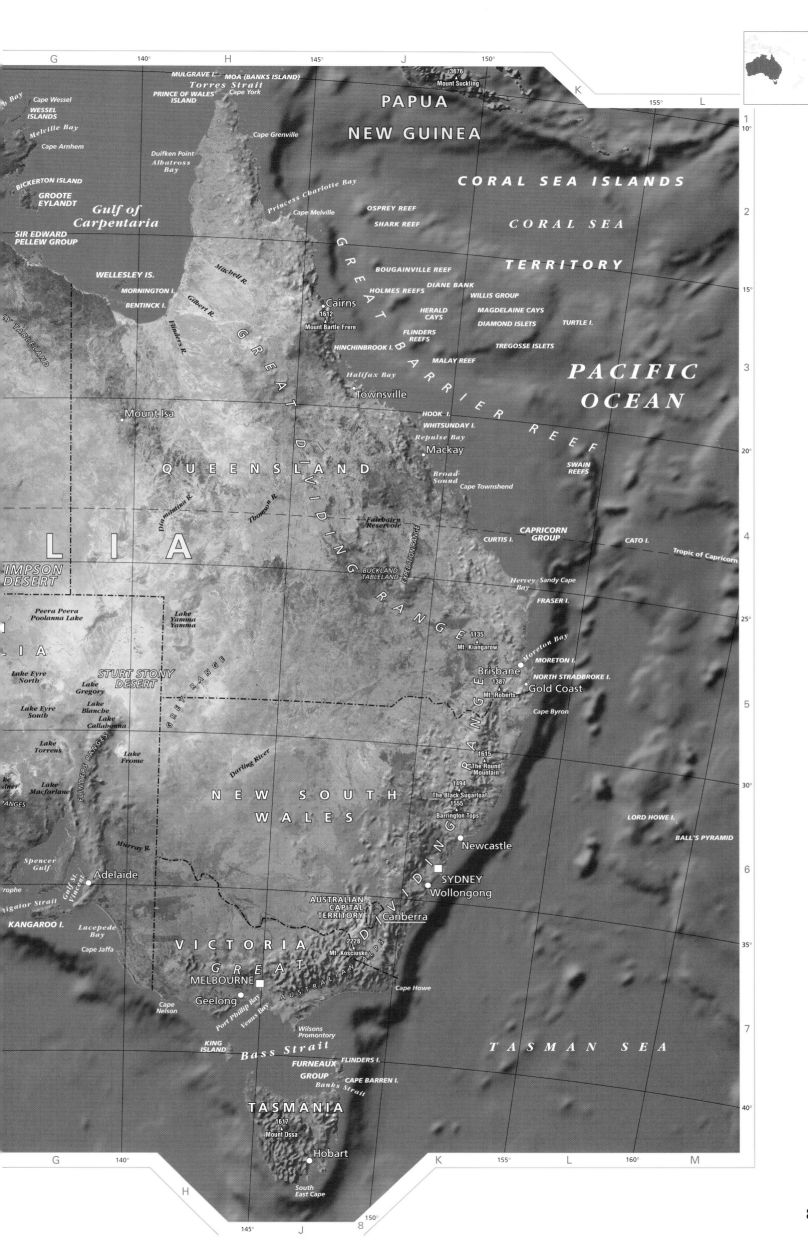

PAPUA

NEW GUINEA

3676
Mount Suckling

MULGRAVE I.   MOA (BANKS ISLAND)
Torres Strait
PRINCE OF WALES   Cape York
ISLAND

Cape Wessel
WESSEL
ISLANDS

Melville Bay

Cape Arnhem

Cape Grenville

CORAL SEA ISLANDS

CORAL   SEA

BICKERTON ISLAND

GROOTE
EYLANDT

*Gulf of
Carpentaria*

Duifken Point
Albatross
Bay

Princess Charlotte Bay

Cape Melville

OSPREY REEF

SHARK REEF

TERRITORY

SIR EDWARD
PELLEW GROUP

WELLESLEY IS.

Mitchell R.

BOUGAINVILLE REEF

HOLMES REEFS   DIANE BANK

WILLIS GROUP

MORNINGTON I.

Gilbert R.

Cairns

HERALD
CAYS

MAGDELAINE CAYS

BENTINCK I.

1612
Mount Bartle Frere

Flinders R.

FLINDERS
REEFS

DIAMOND ISLETS

TURTLE I.

HINCHINBROOK I.

TREGOSSE ISLETS

MALAY REEF

**PACIFIC
OCEAN**

Halifax Bay

Townsville

HOOK I.

WHITSUNDAY I.

Repulse Bay

Mount Isa

QUEENSLAND

Mackay

GREAT   DIVIDING   RANGE

Broad-
Sound

Cape Townshend

SWAIN
REEFS

Diamantina R.

Thomson R.

Fairbairn
Reservoir

CAPRICORN
GROUP

LIA

*IMPSON
DESERT*

CURTIS I.

CATO I.

Tropic of Capricorn

BUCKLAND
TABLELAND

EXPEDITION RANGE

Hervey
Bay

Sandy Cape

Peera Peera
Poolanna Lake

Lake
Yamma
Yamma

FRASER I.

*STURT STONY
DESERT*

1135
Mt. Kiangarow

Moreton Bay

MORETON I.

Lake Eyre
North

Brisbane

NORTH STRADBROKE I.

1387

LIA

Lake
Gregory

Lake
Blanche

GREY RANGE

Mt. Roberts

Gold Coast

Lake Eyre
South

Lake
Callabonna

Cape Byron

Lake
Torrens

Lake
Frome

1615
The Round
Mountain

LORD HOWE I.

Darling River

1494
The Black Sugarloaf

BALL'S PYRAMID

FLINDERS RANGES

Lake
Macfarlane

**NEW   SOUTH
WALES**

1555
Barrington Tops

ANGES

Murray R.

Newcastle

Spencer
Gulf

Adelaide

DIVIDING   RANGE

SYDNEY

Gulf St.
Vincent

Wollongong

rophe

AUSTRALIAN
CAPITAL
TERRITORY

igator Strait

Canberra

KANGAROO I.

Lacepede
Bay

VICTORIA

2228
Mt. Kosciusko

Cape Jaffa

GREAT

MELBOURNE

AUSTRALIAN ALPS

Cape Howe

Geelong

Cape
Nelson

Port Phillip Bay

Venus Bay

Wilsons
Promontory

TASMAN   SEA

KING
ISLAND

Bass   Strait

FURNEAUX
GROUP

FLINDERS I.

CAPE BARREN I.

Banks Strait

TASMANIA

1617
Mount Ossa

Hobart

South
East Cape

10°

2

15°

3

20°

4

25°

Tropic of Capricorn

5

30°

6

35°

7

40°

New Zealand

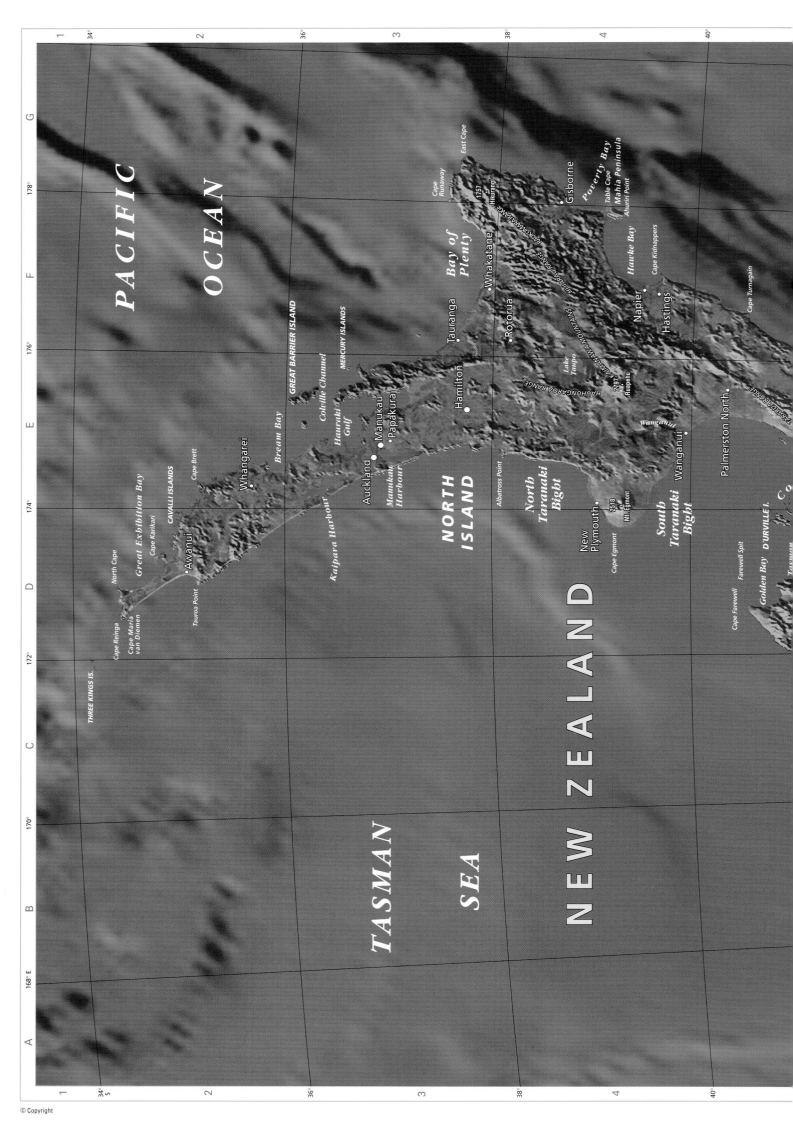

Scale   1 : 4 000 000

0   100   200 km

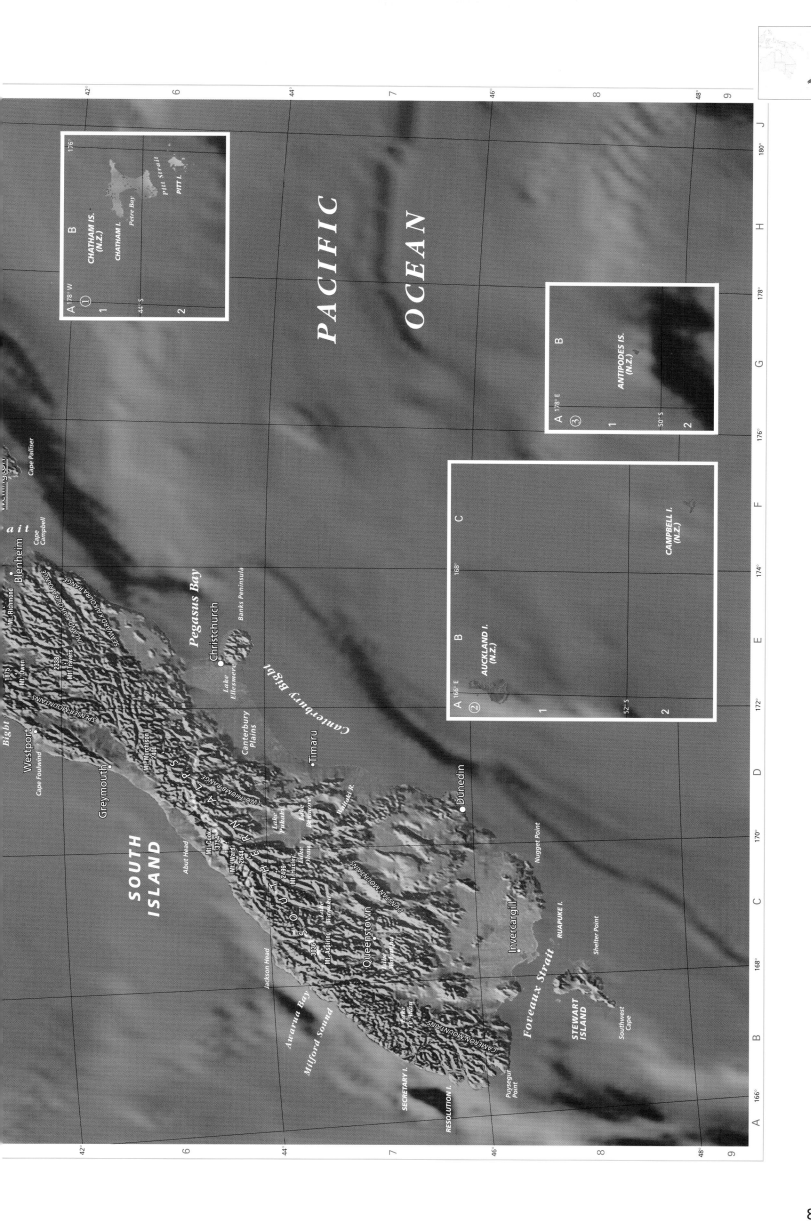

PACIFIC

OCEAN

SOUTH
ISLAND

CHATHAM IS.
(N.Z.)

CHATHAM I.

Petre Bay

Pitt Strait

PITT I.

ANTIPODES IS.
(N.Z.)

CAMPBELL I.
(N.Z.)

AUCKLAND I.
(N.Z.)

Cape Palliser

Cape Campbell

Mt. Richmond

Blenheim

Mt. Owen

Mt. Travers

SPENSER MOUNTAINS

Westport

Cape Foulwind

Greymouth

Mt. Murchison

Pegasus Bay

Christchurch

Banks Peninsula

Lake Ellesmere

Canterbury Plains

Canterbury Bight

Timaru

Abut Head

Mt. Cook

Mt. Ward

Mt. Huxley

Lake Pukaki

Lake Tekapo

Waitaki R.

Dunedin

Jackson Head

Mt. Aspiring

Queenstown

Lake Wakatipu

Lake Wanaka

Lake Hawea

DUNSTAN MOUNTAINS

Nugget Point

Invercargill

RUAPUKE I.

Shelter Point

Foveaux Strait

STEWART
ISLAND

Southwest Cape

Awarua Bay

Milford Sound

Lake Te Anau

CAMERON MOUNTAINS

SECRETARY I.

RESOLUTION I.

Puysegur Point

North America

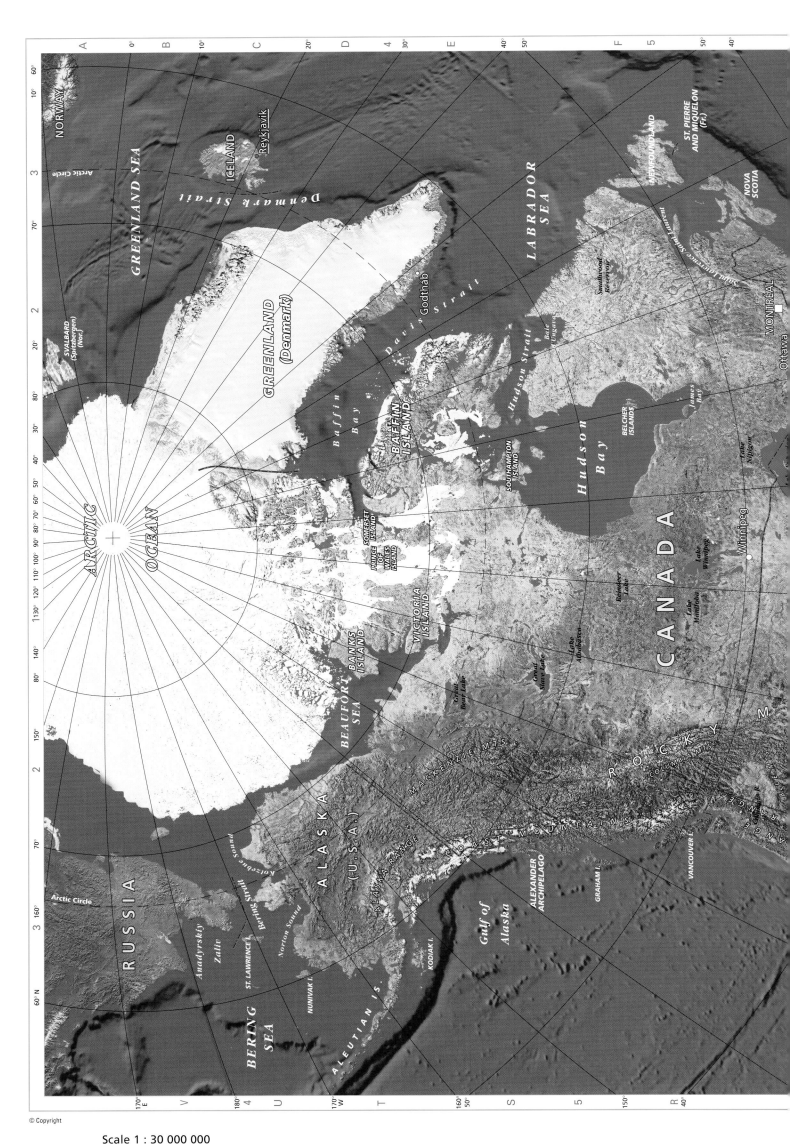

Scale 1 : 30 000 000

0   500   1000   1500   2000 km

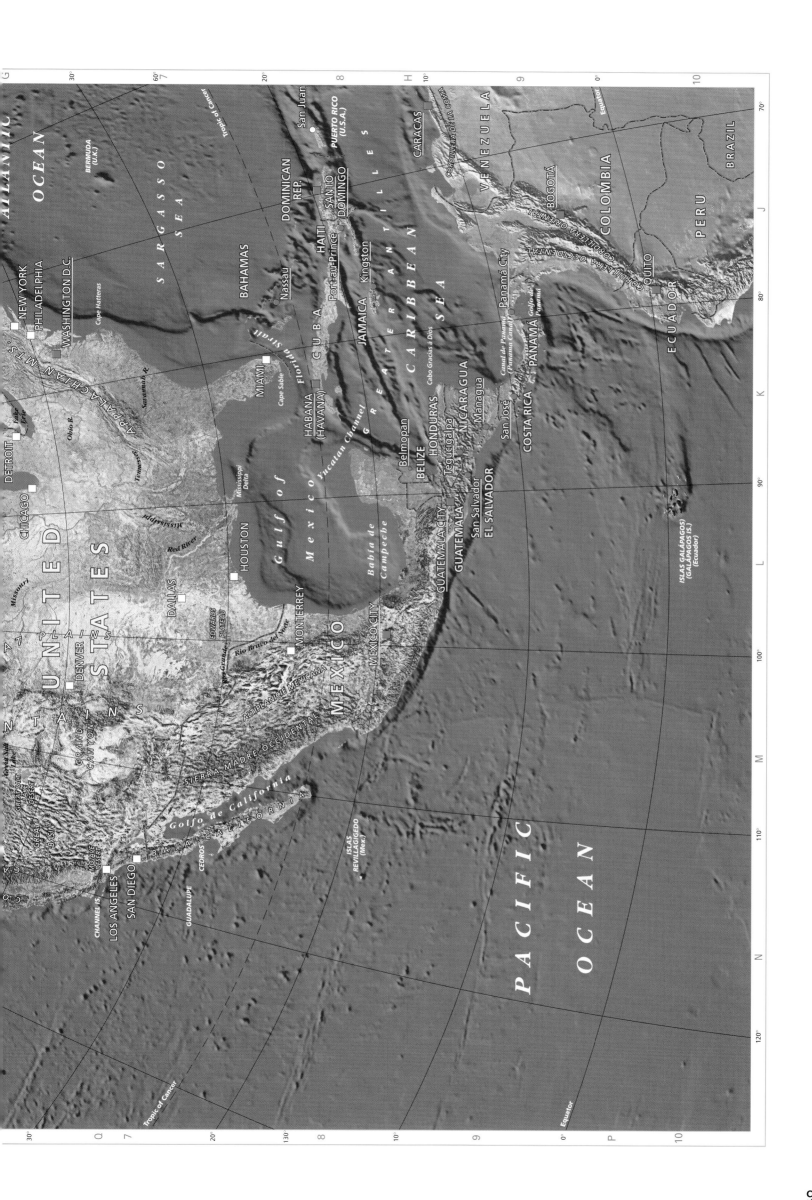

ATLANTIC

OCEAN

SARGASSO SEA

BERMUDA (U.K.)

NEW YORK
PHILADELPHIA
WASHINGTON D.C.
DETROIT
CHICAGO
Cape Hatteras
Lake Erie
Ohio R.
Tennessee R.
Savannah R.

APPALACHIAN MTS.

UNITED STATES

GREAT PLAINS
Missouri
Mississippi
Red River
Mississippi Delta

DENVER
DALLAS
EDWARDS PLATEAU

ROCKY MOUNTAINS
GRAND CANYON
GREAT BASIN
GREAT SALT LAKE
MOJAVE DESERT
Great Salt Lake

LOS ANGELES
CHANNEL IS.
SAN DIEGO

GUADALUPE
CEDROS
BAJA CALIFORNIA

Golfo de California

SIERRA MADRE OCCIDENTAL

ISLAS REVILLAGIGEDO (Mex.)

Rio Bravo del Norte

MONTERREY

ALTIPLANICIE MEXICANA

MEXICO

MEXICO CITY

Tropic of Cancer

MIAMI
Cape Sable
Florida Strait

HOUSTON

Gulf of Mexico

Bahía de Campeche

BAHAMAS

Nassau

HABANA (HAVANA)

CUBA

Yucatán Channel

DOMINICAN REP.
HAITI
Port-au-Prince
SANTO DOMINGO

San Juan
PUERTO RICO (U.S.A.)

JAMAICA
Kingston

GREATER ANTILLES

LESSER ANTILLES

CARIBBEAN SEA

Cabo Gracías a Diós

GUATEMALA
GUATEMALA CITY
San Salvador
EL SALVADOR
BELIZE
Belmopan
HONDURAS
Tegucigalpa
NICARAGUA
Managua
San José
COSTA RICA

Panamá City
Canal de Panamá (Panama Canal)
PANAMA
Golfo de Panamá

CARACAS

CORDILLERA DE LA COSTA

VENEZUELA

BOGOTÁ

COLOMBIA

CORDILLERA OCCIDENTAL
CORDILLERA ORIENTAL

QUITO
ECUADOR

PERU

BRAZIL

Equator

ISLAS GALÁPAGOS (GALÁPAGOS IS.) (Ecuador)

PACIFIC

OCEAN

Tropic of Cancer

Equator

G
30°
60°
20°
H
10°
9
0°
10

30°
20°
130°
10°
9
0°
10

70°
J
80°
K
90°
L
100°
110°
M
120°

91

Canada

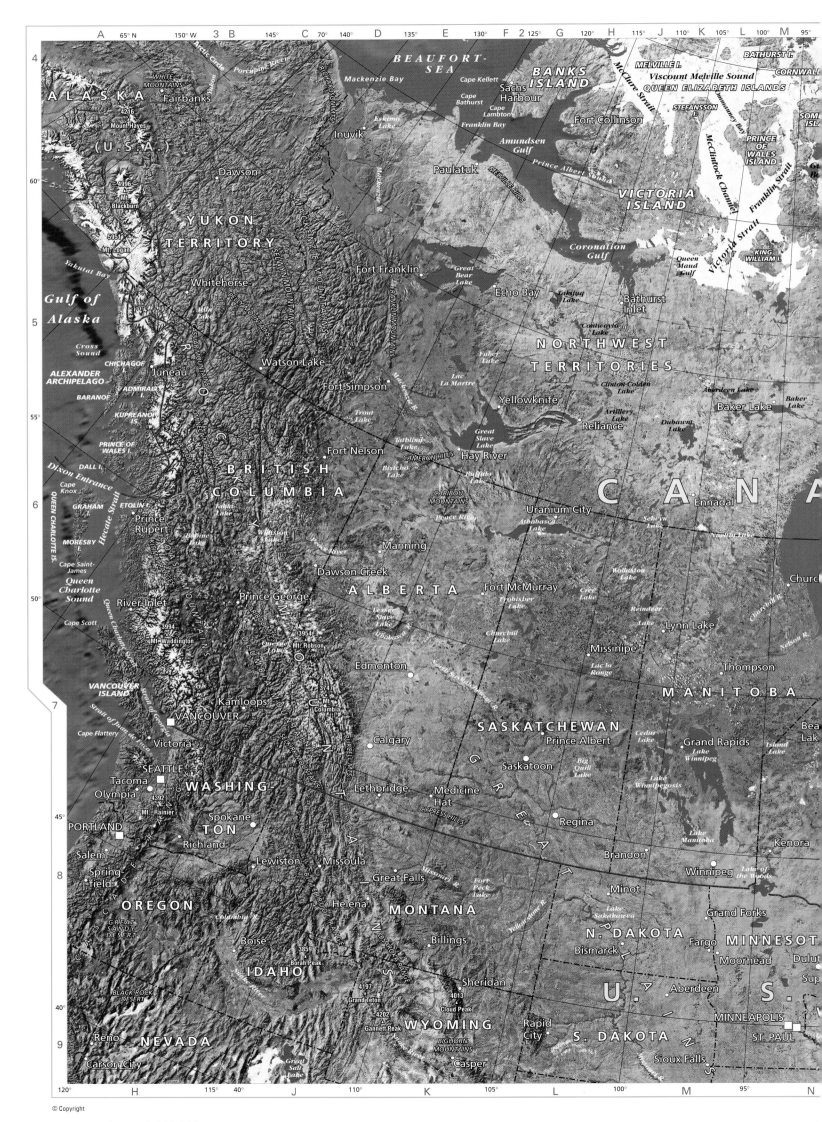

© Copyright

Scale 1 : 12 000 000

0   200   400   600 km

United States of America

Scale 1 : 13 400 000

0   200   400   600   800 km

95°   H   90°   J   85°   K   80°   L   75°   M   70°   N

Kenora
Ogoki
Lake Mistassini

ONTARIO

QUÉBEC

Albany R.

Timmins

Thunder Bay

Lake Nipigon

Lac Saint-Jean

Lake Superior

Lake of the Woods

Duluth

Sault Sainte Marie

North Bay

MONTRÉAL

MAINE

MINNESOTA
rhead
Superior

Québec

Saint Lawrence River

Ottawa River

ST. PAUL

Ottawa

MINNEAPOLIS

WISCONSIN

MICHIGAN

Lake Huron

ADIRONDACK MOUNTAINS

VER- MONT

Augusta

1917 Washington

Appleton

Lake Michigan

Burlington

Montpelier

NEW HAMP- SHIRE

Concord

Mason City

Madison

MILWAUKEE

Grand Rapids

Flint

TORONTO

Lake Ontario

Hamilton

Rochester

Syracuse

Albany

MASSA- CHUSETS

BOSTON

Cape Cod

IOWA

Rockford

Lansing

Niagara Falls

BUFFALO

NEW YORK

Hartford

CONNECT- ICUT

PROVIDENCE

RHODE I.

es Moines

aha

Davenport

CHICAGO

South Bend

DETROIT

Toledo

Erie

Lake Erie

CLEVELAND

Akron

PENNSYLVANIA

PITTSBURGH

Jersey City

NEW YORK

Long Island Sound

Burlington

Peoria

ILLINOIS

INDIANA

OHIO

Columbus

Allentown

NEWARK

Trenton

PHILADELPHIA

NEW JERSEY

SAS ITY

Springfield

INDIANAPOLIS

Dayton

Clarksburg

Ohio R.

Harrisburg

MARY- LAND

BALTIMORE

DELAWARE

ka

Jefferson City

CINCINNATI

WEST VIRGINIA

Frankfort

Charleston

WASHINGTON D.C.

O

ST. LOUIS

MISSOURI

Evansville

Louisville

KENTUCKY

VIRGINIA

Richmond

Cape Charles

Norfolk

Chesapeake Bay

Springfield

Paducah

APPALACHIAN MOUNTAINS

Winston-Salem

Greensboro

Raleigh

Pamlico Sound

sa

OZARK PLATEAU

Nashville

Knoxville

BLUE RIDGE

Arkansas R.

Tennessee R.

N. CAROLINA

Cape Hatteras

ARKANSAS

Memphis

Chattanooga

Charlotte

S

Little Rock

Columbia

Wilmington

Cape Fear

MISSISS- IPPI

Birmingham

ATLANTA

S. CAROLINA

LAS

Shreveport

ALABAMA

Macon

Charleston

Jackson

Montgomery

GEORGIA

Savannah R.

Red River

Columbus

Savannah

ATLANTIC

Baton Rouge

Mobile

Alabama R.

Tallahassee

Jacksonville

OCEAN

mont

LOUISIANA

Gulfport

HOUSTON

NEW ORLEANS

Cape San Blas

FLORIDA

ORDA

Gulf of Mexico

Orlando

Cape Canaveral

TAMPA

St. Petersburg

Lake Okeechobee

Fort Lauderdale

GRAND BAHAMA

GREAT ABACO

MIAMI

BAHAMAS

Cape Sable

NASSAU

ELEUTHERA

Straits of Florida

ANDROS

Nassau

CAT

FLORIDA KEYS

SAN SALVADOR

GREAT EXUMA

LONG ISLAND

Tropic of Cancer

Marianao

HABANA (HAVANA)

Santa Clara

ACKLINS

MAYAGUANA

Pinar del Rio

CUBA

TURKS AND CAICOS ISLANDS (U.K.)

GREAT INAGUA

Cancún

Camagüey

United States, Northwest

© Copyright

Scale 1 : 6 250 000

0   100   200   300 km

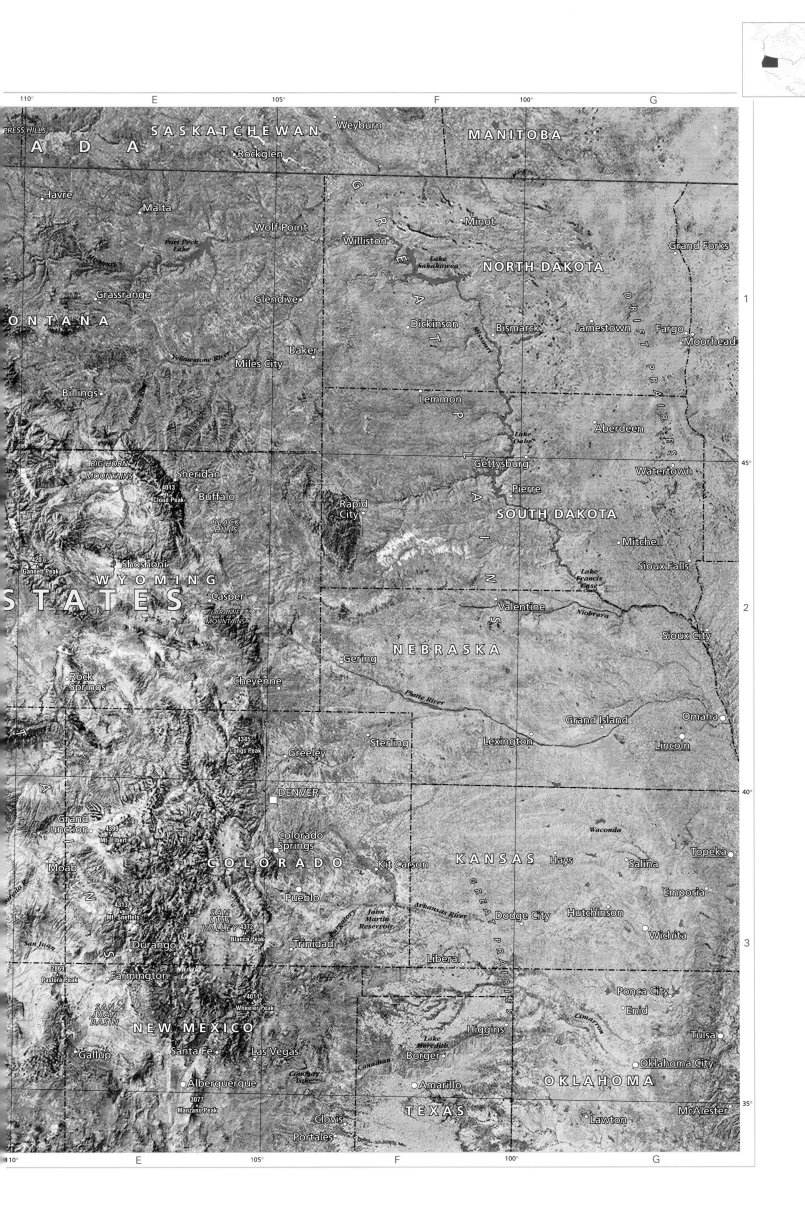

PRESS HILLS

SASKATCHEWAN   Weyburn   MANITOBA

A D A

Rockglen

Havre

Malta

Wolf Point   Williston   Minot   NORTH DAKOTA   Grand Forks

Fort Peck
Lake

Lake
Sakakawea

Grassrange   Glendive   Dickinson   Bismarck   Jamestown   Fargo

O N T A N A   Moorhead

Missouri

Baker

Miles City

Billings   Yellowstone River   Lemmon   Aberdeen

Lake
Oahe

BIG HORN
MOUNTAINS   Sheridan   Gettysburg   Watertown

4013   Buffalo
Cloud Peak   Pierre

Rapid
City   SOUTH DAKOTA

BLACK
HILLS   Mitchell

4207   Shoshoni   Lake
Gannett Peak   Francis
Case   Sioux Falls

W Y O M I N G

S T A T E S   Casper   Valentine   Niobrara   Sioux City

LARAMIE
MOUNTAINS   N E B R A S K A

Rock   Gering
Springs   Cheyenne   Platte River   Grand Island   Omaha

4345   Sterling   Lexington   Lincoln
Longs Peak   Greeley

DENVER

Grand   4399   Colorado   Waconda
Junction   Mt. Elbert   Springs   K A N S A S   Topeka

Moab   C O L O R A D O   Kit Carson   Hays   Salina

4313   Pueblo   Emporia
Mt. Sneffels   GREAT
SAN   John   Arkansas River
LUIS   Martin   Dodge City   Hutchinson   Wichita
VALLEY   4372   Reservoir
San Juan   Blanca Peak   Trinidad   PRAIRIES
Durango   Liberal

2869   Farmington
Pastora Peak

4011   Ponca City
SAN   Wheeler Peak   Enid
JUAN
BASIN   N E W   M E X I C O   Higgins   Tulsa

Lake
Meredith   Oklahoma City
Gallup   Santa Fe   Las Vegas   Borger   O K L A H O M A

Conchas   Canadian
Alberquerque   Lake   Amarillo   Lawton   McAlester

3077   T E X A S
Manzano Peak
Clovis

Portales

G
R
E
A
T

P
L
A
I
N
S

DRIFT PRAIRIES

United States, Northeast

MANITOBA

Gull Bay

Lake Nipigon

Geraldton

Kapusk

ONTARIO

Marathon

Lake of the Woods

Fort Frances

Thunder Bay

Grand Forks

Red Lakes

N. DAK.

Bemidji

Leech Lake

ISLE ROYALE

MICHIPICOTEN

Chapleau

Fargo

Moorhead

Duluth

Superior

Ashland

GOGEBIC RANGE

Lake Superior

Sault Sainte Marie

LA

Brainerd

Mille Lacs

MINNESOTA

SUPERIOR UPLAND

Marquette

Watertown

MINNEAPOLIS

ST. PAUL

Eau Claire

Wausau

Alpena

S. DAK.

Minnesota

WISCONSIN

Green Bay

Appleton

Lake Michigan

Traverse City

Lake Huron

Mankato

Winona

Pentenwell Lake

Lake Winnebago

MICHIGAN

Flint

Sioux Falls

Mason City

Rock

Fond du Lac

Bay City

Niobrara

Sioux City

Fort Dodge

Dubuque

Madison

MILWAUKEE

Racine

Grand Rapids

Lansing

DETROIT

Rockford

IOWA

Cedar Rapids

Davenport

CHICAGO

South Bend

Fort Wayne

Toledo

NEBR.

Missouri R.

Des Moines

Illinois R.

INDIANA

OHIO

Omaha

Des Moines

Burlington

Peoria

ILLINOIS

Columb

Lincoln

Chillicothe

Quincy

Springfield

INDIANAPOLIS

Dayton

KANSAS CITY

UNITED STATES

CINCINNATI

Topeka

ST. LOUIS

Effingham

Ohio R.

Emporia

Jefferson City

Missouri R.

Rolla

Louisville

Frankfort

KANSAS

Lake of the Ozarks

MISSOURI

Evansville

Lexington

Joplin

Springfield

PLATEAU

Cape Girardeau

KENTUCKY

Ponca City

OZARK

Paducah

CUMBERLAND PL

Tulsa

BOSTON MTS.

Jonesboro

Nashville

Knoxville

AP

OKLAHOMA

Arkansas R.

Fort Smith

ARKANSAS

Memphis

TENNESSEE

McAlester

OACHITA MTS.

Little Rock

Chattanooga

Hartwell Reservoir

Huntsville

Tennessee R.

MISSISSIPPI

GEORGIA

SO

Mississippi

ALABAMA

© Copyright

Scale 1 : 6 250 000

0   100   200   300 km

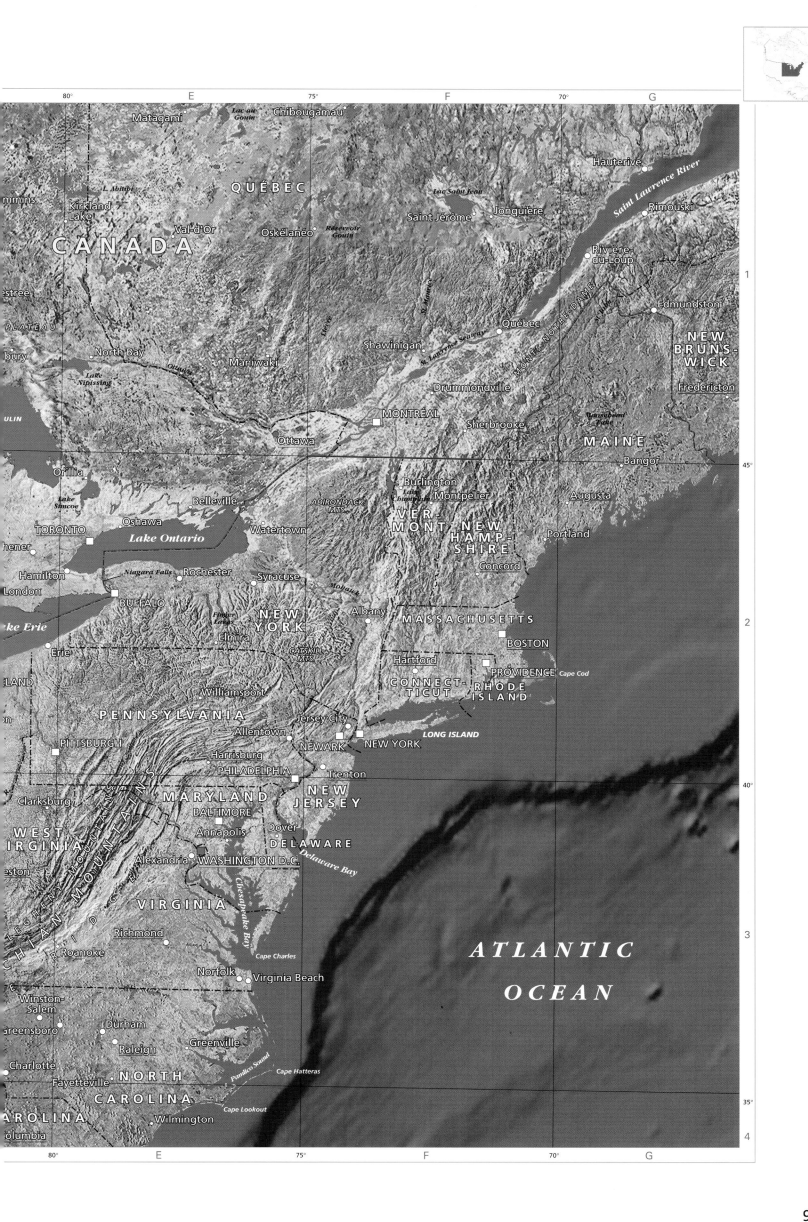

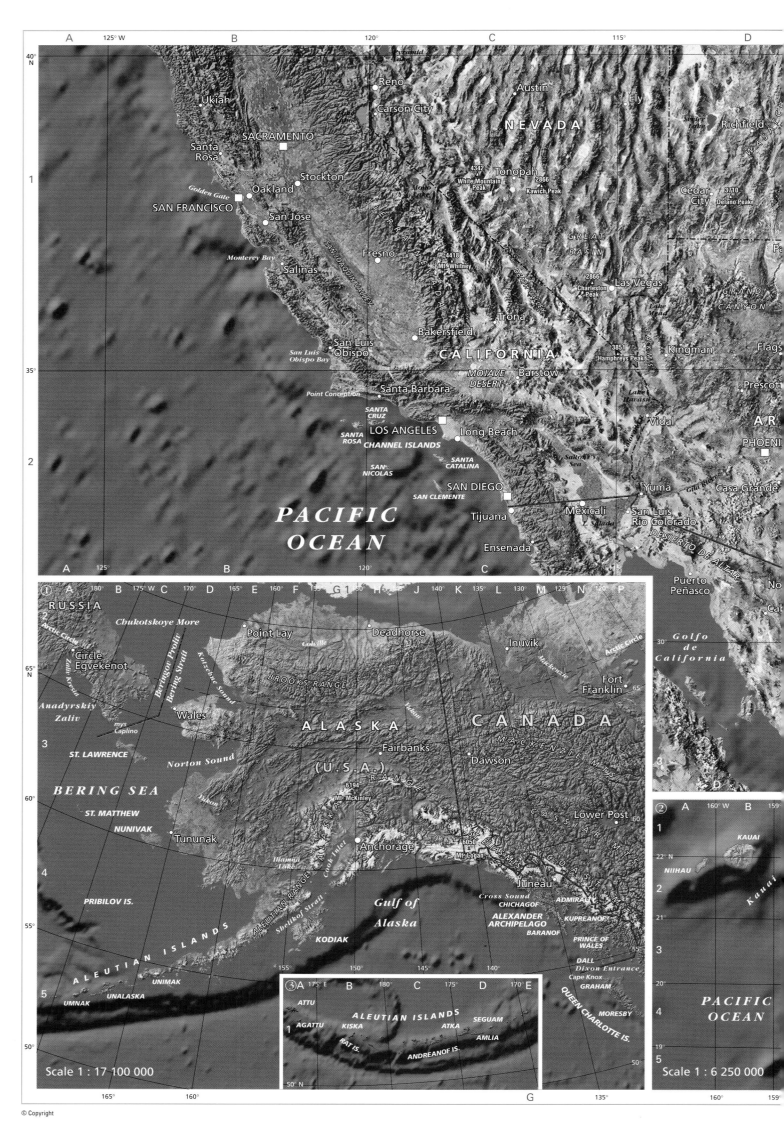

Scale 1 : 17 100 000

Scale 1 : 6 250 000

© Copyright

Scale 1 : 6 250 000

0   100   200   300 km

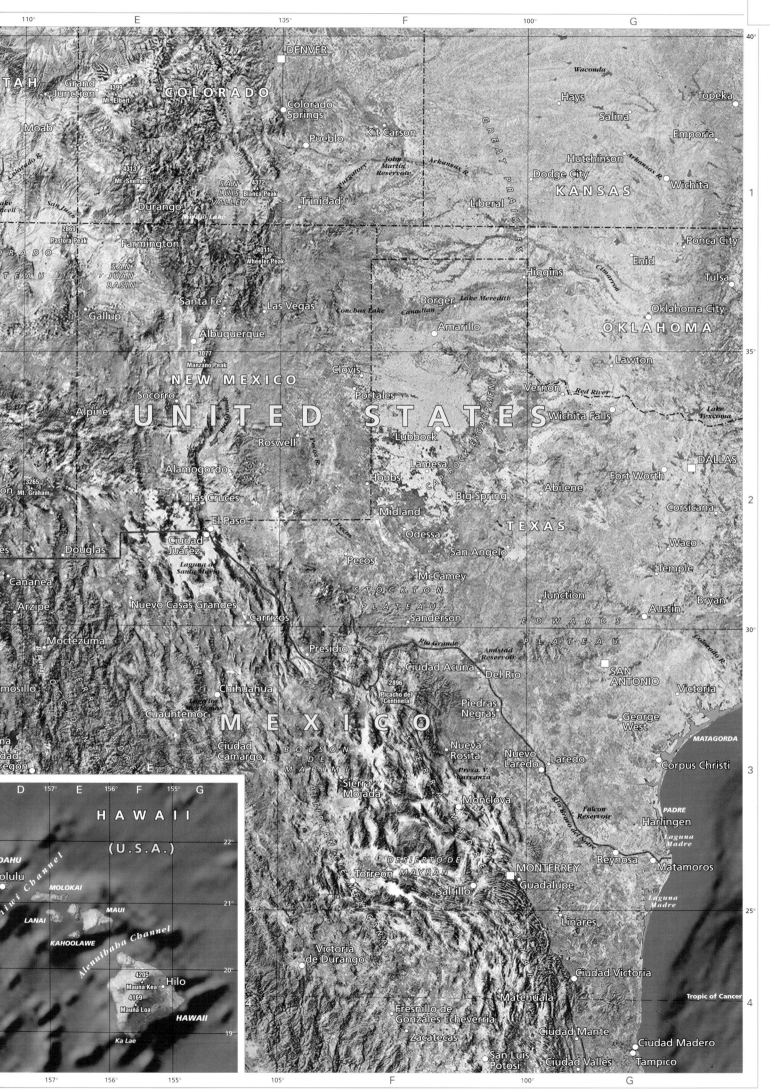

UTAH

Grand
Junction
4399
Mt. Elbert
COLORADO
DENVER
Moab
Colorado
Springs
Colorado R.
Kit Carson
4313
Mt. Sneffels
SAN
LUIS
VALLEY
Durango
4372
Blanca Peak
Trinidad
Pueblo
John
Martin
Reservoir
Purgatory
Arkansas R.

Waconda
Hays
Salina
Topeka
Emporia

GREAT PRAIRIES

Hutchinson
Arkansas R.
Dodge City
Liberal
KANSAS
Wichita

2869
Pastora Peak
Farmington
SAN
JUAN
BASIN
4011
Wheeler Peak
Higgins
Cimarron
Enid
Ponca City
Tulsa

Gallup
Santa Fe
Las Vegas
Conchas Lake
Borger
Canadian
Lake Meredith
Oklahoma City
OKLAHOMA

Albuquerque
Amarillo

3077
Manzano Peak
NEW MEXICO
Clovis
Lawton

Socorro
UNITED STATES
Portales
Vernon
Red River
Lake
Texcoma

Alpine
Wichita Falls

Roswell
Pecos R.
Lubbock

3265
Mt. Graham
Alamogordo
Lamesa
CAP ROCK ESCARPMENT
Fort Worth
DALLAS

Hobbs
Abilene
Corsicana

Las Cruces
Midland
Big Spring
TEXAS
Waco

Douglas
El Paso
Odessa
San Angelo
Temple

Ciudad
Juárez
Pecos R.
Pecos
McCamey
Junction
Bryan
Austin

Cananea
Laguna de
Santa María
STOCKTON
PLATEAU
Sanderson
EDWARDS

Arzipe
Nuevo Casas Grandes
Carrizos
PLATEAU
Colorado R.

Moctezuma
SIERRA OCCIDENTAL
Presidio
Rio Grande
Amistad
Reservoir
PLATEAU

mosillo
Chihuahua
Ciudad Acuna
Del Rio
SAN
ANTONIO
Victoria

Cuauhtemoc
2896
Picacho del
Centinela
Piedras
Negras
George
West
MATAGORDA

na
dad
regón
MEXICO
Ciudad
Camargo
BOLSÓN
DE
MAPIMI
SIERRA MADRE
Nueva
Rosita
Nuevo
Laredo
Laredo
Corpus Christi

Sierra
Mojada
Presa V.
Guavanza
Monclova
Falcon
Reservoir
PADRE
Harlingen
Laguna
Madre

ALTIPLANICIE MEXICANA
DESIERTO DE
MAYRAN
Torreón
Rio Bravo del Norte
MONTERREY
Reynosa
Matamoros

Saltillo
Guadalupe
Laguna
Madre

Linares

Victoria
de Durango
Ciudad Victoria

Matehuala
Tropic of Cancer

Fresnillo de
Gonzáles Echeverria
Ciudad Mante
Ciudad Madero

Zacatecas
Ciudad Valles
Tampico

San Luis
Potosí

HAWAII

(U.S.A.)

OAHU
olulu
MOLOKAI
Kaiwi Channel
LANAI
MAUI
KAHOOLAWE
Alenuihaha Channel
4205
Mauna Kea
Hilo
4169
Mauna Loa
HAWAII
Ka Lae

United States, Southeast

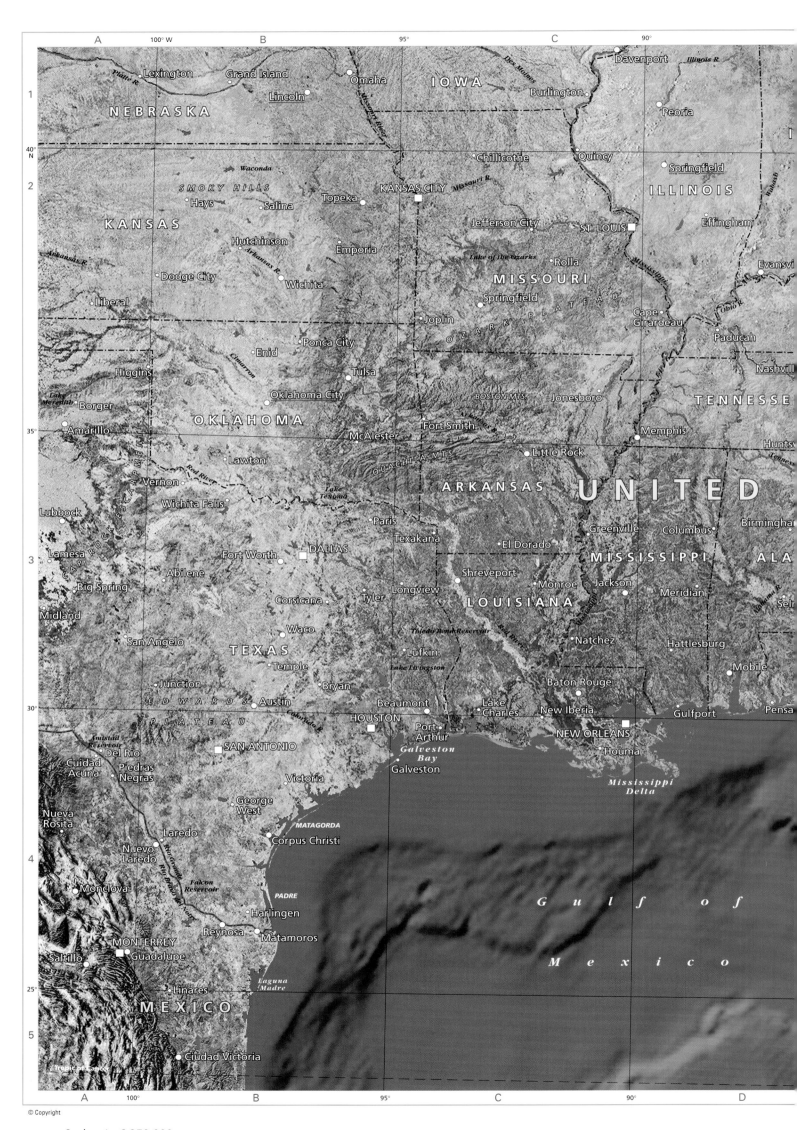

Scale   1 : 6 250 000

0   100   200   300 km

© Copyright

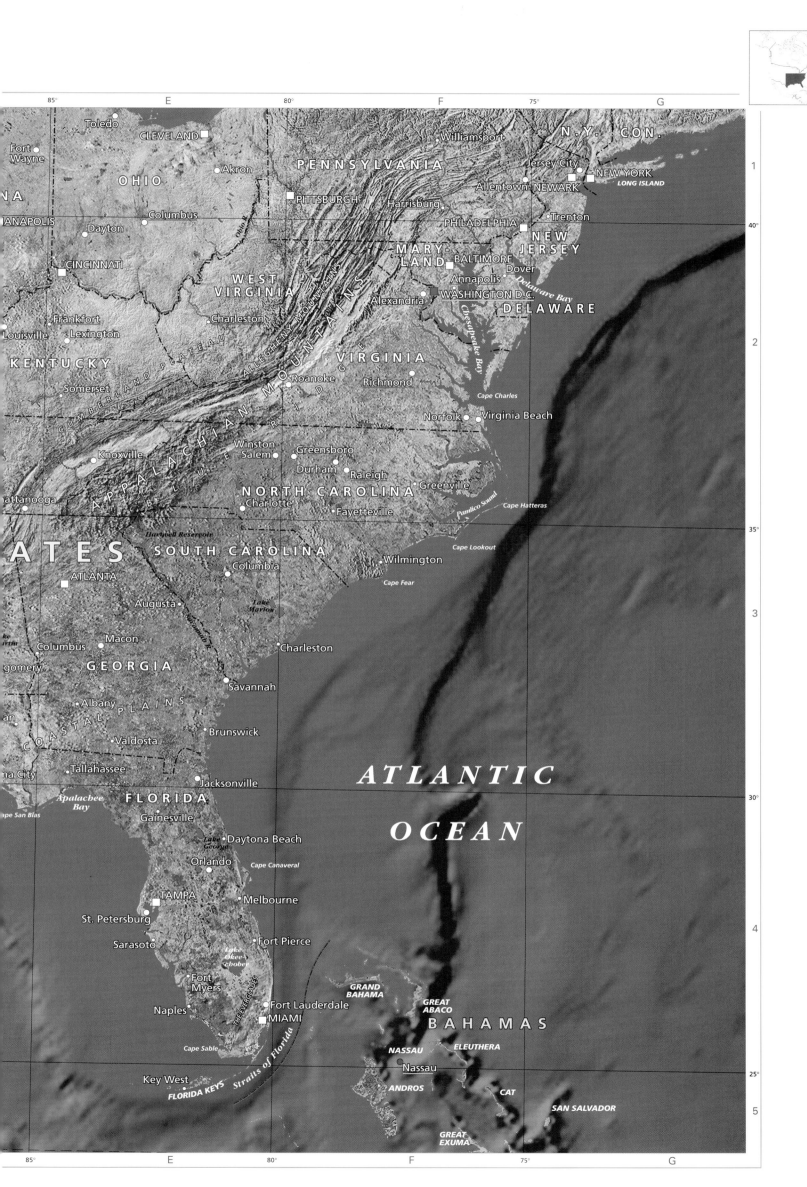

Central America and the Caribbean

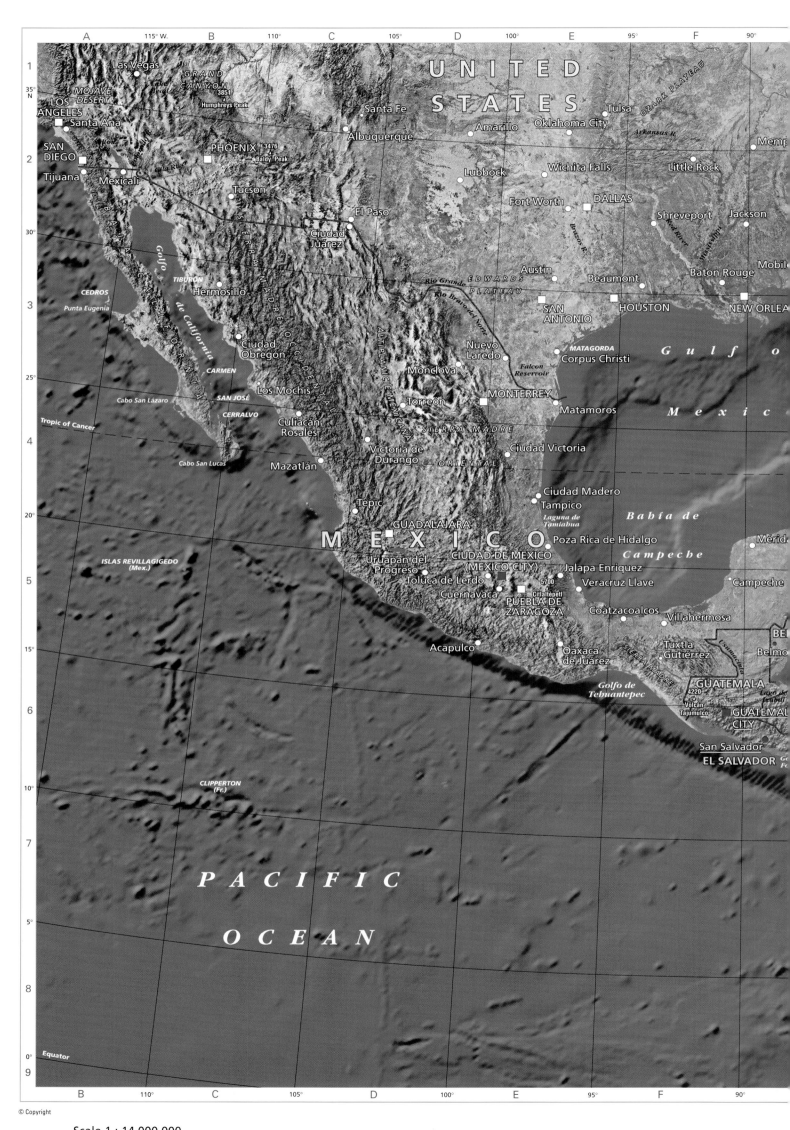

Scale 1 : 14 000 000

0   200   400   600   800 km

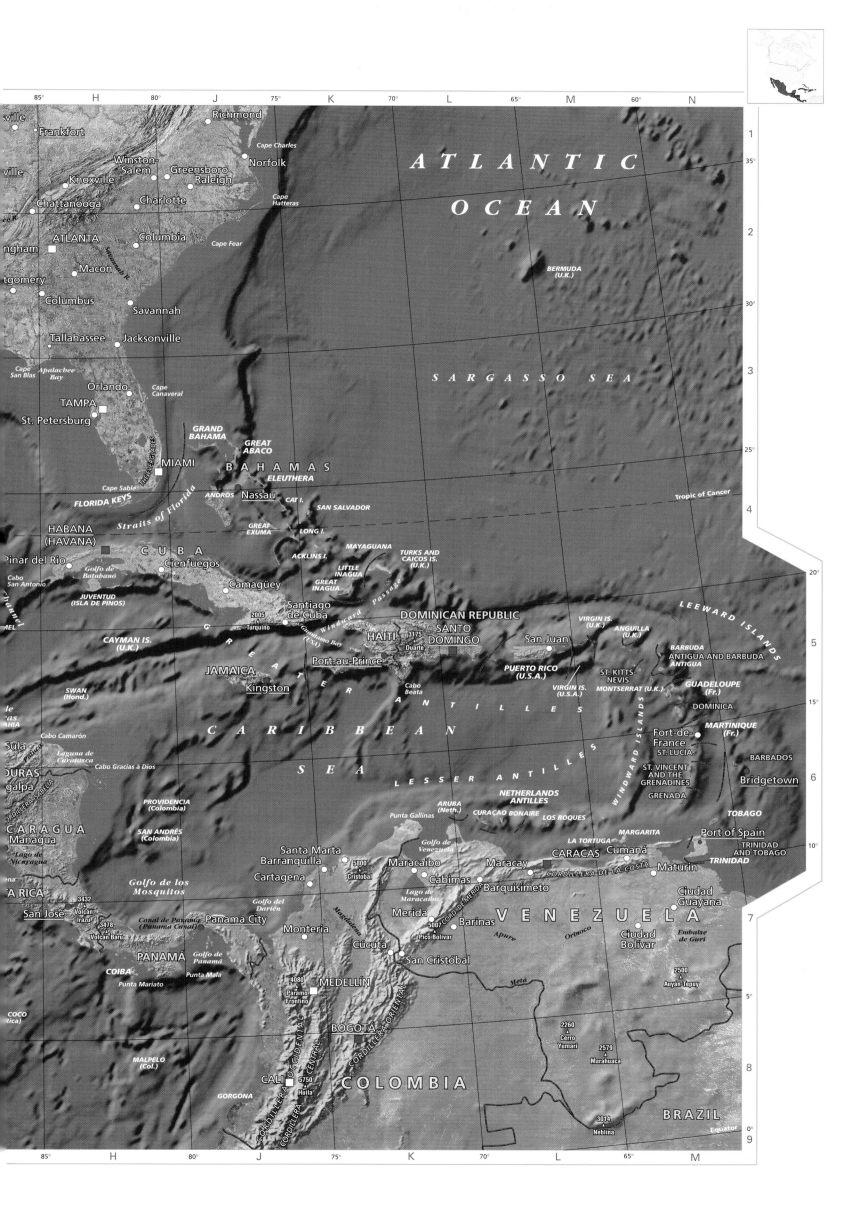

ATLANTIC

OCEAN

1

35°

—ville • Frankfort • Richmond

—ville Cape Charles

—ville Winston- • Greensboro • Norfolk
Knoxville Salem Raleigh
Chattanooga • Charlotte Cape Hatteras

2

tgomery ATLANTA • Columbia
□ Cape Fear

• Macon

• Columbus Savannah

30°

Tallahassee Jacksonville

Cape Apalachee
San Blas Bay

3

Orlando Cape
Canaveral

TAMPA
St. Petersburg □

SARGASSO SEA

BERMUDA
(U.K.)

GRAND
BAHAMA

MIAMI GREAT
ABACO

Cape Sable BAHAMAS
FLORIDA KEYS ELEUTHERA

25°

Nassau CAT I.
ANDROS SAN SALVADOR

Tropic of Cancer

4

HABANA Straits of Florida GREAT
(HAVANA) EXUMA LONG I.
Pinar del Rio □ CUBA
Cabo Golfo de Cienfuegos ACKLINS I. MAYAGUANA
San Antonio Batabanó LITTLE TURKS AND
JUVENTUD Camagüey INAGUA CAICOS IS.
(ISLA DE PINOS) GREAT (U.K.)
20° INAGUA

2005 Santiago LEEWARD
Turquino de Cuba DOMINICAN REPUBLIC ISLANDS
CAYMAN IS. HAITI 3175 SANTO VIRGIN IS.
(U.K.) Duarte DOMINGO (U.K.) ANGUILLA
San Juan (U.K.)
5 JAMAICA Port-au-Prince BARBUDA
PUERTO RICO ANTIGUA AND BARBUDA
Kingston Cabo (U.S.A.) ST. KITTS- ANTIGUA
SWAN Beata VIRGIN IS. NEVIS
(Hond.) (U.S.A.) MONTSERRAT (U.K.) GUADELOUPE
CARIBBEAN (Fr.)
DOMINICA 15°
SEA Fort-de- MARTINIQUE
Cabo Camarón France (Fr.)
URAS Laguna de ST. LUCIA
galpa Caratasca Cabo Gracias á Dios BARBADOS
6 LESSER ANTILLES ST. VINCENT
AND THE Bridgetown
PROVIDENCIA GRENADINES
(Colombia) NETHERLANDS GRENADA
ANTILLES TOBAGO
CARAGUA SAN ANDRES ARUBA
Managua (Colombia) Punta Gallinas (Neth.) CURAÇAO BONAIRE Port of Spain
Lago de LOS ROQUES MARGARITA TRINIDAD
10° Nicaragua Golfo de LA TORTUGA AND TOBAGO
Santa Marta Venezuela Cumaná TRINIDAD
A RICA Barranquilla 5800 Maracaibo CARACAS Maturín
Cristobal Maracay CORDILLERA DE LA COSTA
Cartagena Cabimas Barquisimeto
3432 Golfo de los Lago de Ciudad
San José Volcán Mosquitos Golfo del Maracaibo Guayana
Irazú Darién Mérida VENEZUELA
3478 Canal de Panamá 5007 Barinas
Volcán Barú (Panama Canal) Panama City Pico Bolívar Apure Orinoco Ciudad 7
Monteria Bolívar 2500
PANAMÁ Cúcuta Metá Embalse Auyán-Tepuy
COIBA Golfo de San Cristóbal de Guri
Panamá 5°
Punta Mala 4080 MEDELLÍN
Punta Mariato Páramo
MALPELO Frontino
(Col.) 2260
Cerro 2579
Yumari Marahuaca
BOGOTÁ 8
CALI 5750
GORGONA Huila COLOMBIA 3014
Neblina BRAZIL
Equator 0°
9

South America

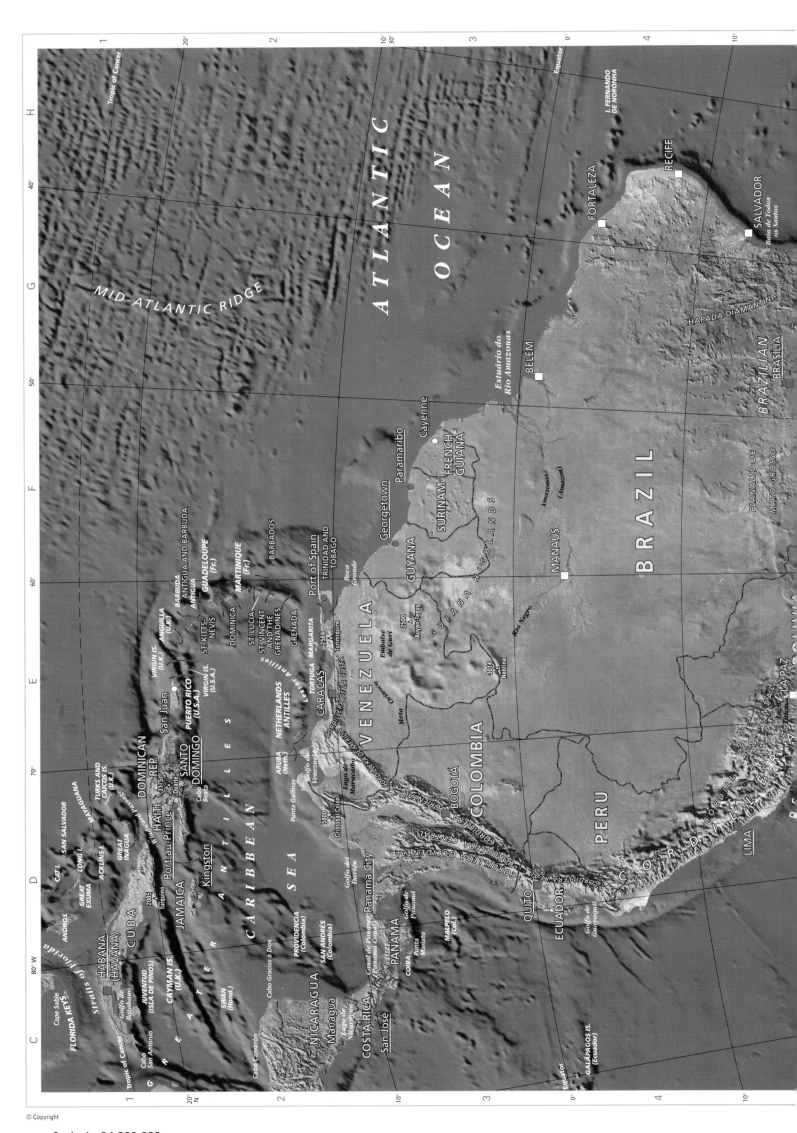

ATLANTIC OCEAN

MID-ATLANTIC RIDGE

BRAZIL

BRAZILIAN

PERU

COLOMBIA

VENEZUELA

GUYANA

SURINAM

FRENCH GUIANA

ECUADOR

Cayenne

Paramaribo

Georgetown

CARACAS

BOGOTÁ

QUITO

LIMA

LA PAZ

BELÉM

MANAUS

FORTALEZA

RECIFE

SALVADOR

I. FERNANDO DE NORONHA

CHAPADA DIAMANTINA

GUIANA HIGHLANDS

PLANALTO DE MATO GROSSO

BRASÍLIA

Estuário do Rio Amazonas

Amazonas (Amazon)

Rio Negro

Orinoco

Meta

CARIBBEAN SEA

GREATER ANTILLES

Lesser Antilles

CUBA

HAITI

DOMINICAN REP.

JAMAICA

PUERTO RICO (U.S.A.)

VIRGIN IS. (U.K.)

VIRGIN IS. (U.S.A.)

ANGUILLA (U.K.)

ANTIGUA AND BARBUDA

BARBUDA

ANTIGUA

GUADELOUPE (Fr.)

DOMINICA

MARTINIQUE (Fr.)

ST. LUCIA

ST. VINCENT AND THE GRENADINES

BARBADOS

GRENADA

TRINIDAD AND TOBAGO

NETHERLANDS ANTILLES

ARUBA (Neth.)

CAYMAN IS. (U.K.)

TURKS AND CAICOS IS. (U.K.)

ACKLINS I.

LONG I.

CAT I.

SAN SALVADOR

MAYAGUANA

GREAT INAGUA

GREAT EXUMA

ANDROS

NICARAGUA

COSTA RICA

PANAMA

HABANA (HAVANA)

SANTO DOMINGO

Port-au-Prince

Kingston

San Juan

Managua

San José

PANAMÁ

Panama City

CARACAS

St. Kitts-Nevis

Port of Spain

MARGARITA

TORTUGA

San Antonio

Cabo San Antonio

Cabo Gracias a Dios

PROVIDENCIA (Colombia)

SAN ANDRÉS (Colombia)

COIBA

SWAN (Hond.)

MALPELO (Col.)

GALÁPAGOS IS. (Ecuador)

JUVENTUD (ISLA DE PINOS)

Golfo de Batabanó

Golfo de Venezuela

Lago de Maracaibo

Golfo del Darién

Golfo de Panamá

Golfo de Guayaquil

Punta Gallinas

Cabo Beata

Punta Mariato

Cabo Camarón

Canal de Panamá (Panama Canal)

Cristóbal Colón

Tiuna

Embalse de Guri

Auyán-Tepuy

Neblina

Turimiquire

Roca Grande

Boca Grande

FLORIDA KEYS

Straits of Florida

Cape Sable

Tropic of Cancer

Equator

CORDILLERA DE LA COSTA

CORDILLERA DE MÉRIDA

CORDILLERA OCCIDENTAL

CORDILLERA CENTRAL

CORDILLERA ORIENTAL

CORDILLERA REAL

CORDILLERA ORIENTAL

2369

2500

3014

3775

2005

5800

Turquino

Duarte

© Copyright

Scale 1 : 24 300 000

0   200   400   600   800   1000 km

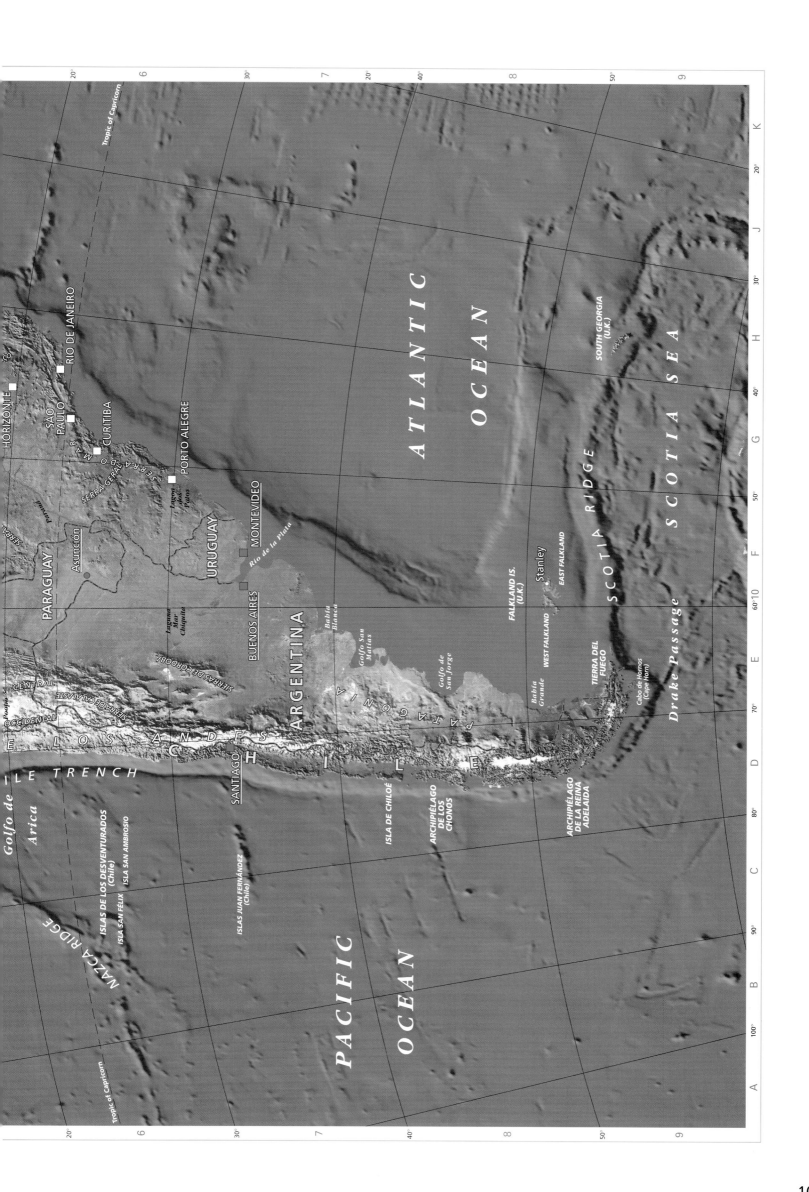

107

South America, North

CARIBBEAN SEA

LESSER ANTILLES

ST. VINCENT AND THE GRENADINES

GRENADA

TOBA

Punta Gallinas

ARUBA (Neth.)

NETHERLANDS ANTILLES
CURAÇAO BONAIRE

LOS ROQUES

LA TORTUGA

MARGARITA

Port of Spain

TRIN

NICARAGUA

SAN ANDRÉS (Colombia)

Lago de Nicaragua

Santa Marta

Barranquilla

Cartagena

5800
Cristobal Colón

Golfo de Venezuela

Maracaibo

Cabimas

Lago de Maraca

CARACAS

Maracay

Barcelona

Cumaná

TURIN

Barquisimeto

CORDILLERA DE LA COSTA

Turimiquire
2569

Maturin

Delta del Orinoco

San José

Golfo de los Mosquitos

Colón

Panama City

Golfo del Darién

Monteria

Magdalena

Cúcuta

Merida
5007

Pico Bolívar

Barinas

CORD. DE MERIDA

Calabozo

VENEZUELA

Ciudad Guayana

Embalse de Guri

COSTA RICA

3478
Volcán Barú

PANAMA

Canal de Panamá (Panama Canal)

Golfo de Panamá

Punta Mala

San Cristóbal

Apure

Orinoco

2100
Cerro

Cerro Guaiquinima
2500

Canaima

Auyán Tepuy

281

COIBA

Punta Mariato

4080
Páramo Frontino

MEDELLÍN

Bucaramanga

Meta

2441
Cerro Yavi

LA GRAN SABANA

Rora

Cabo Corrientes

Sogamoso

CORDILLERA ORIENTAL

2260
Cerro Yumari

GUIANA

MALPELO (Col.)

Buenaventura

BOGOTÁ

Orocué

Obando

La Esmeralda

Boa Vista

Marahuaca
2579

CALI

5750
Huila

Palmira

COLOMBIA

Rio

3014
Neblina

GORGONA

Neiva

MESA DE YAMBI

Tumaco

Pasto

Mitú

QUITO

Equator

Esmeraldas

5897
Volcán Cotopaxi

Macujer

Uaupés

Japurá

Rio Negro

Boiaçu

Bahía de Manta

ECUADOR

Pantoja

La Pedrera

Içá

Fonte Boa

MANA

GUAYAQUIL

Chimborazo
6310

Golfo de Guayaquil

Cuenca

Iquitos

Solimões

Amazonas (Amazon)

Coari

Sullana

Borja

Juruá

Carauari

Piura

Yurimaguas

Bahía de Sechura

Punta Negra

PERU

Eirunepé

BRAZ

Pôrto Velho

Chiclayo

Cajamarca

Pucallpa

Aripuanã

Trujillo

6746
Huascarán

Rio Branco

SERRA DOS PARECI

Chimbote

Huánuco

Guajará Mirim

90° W

CULPEPPER

ISLAS GALÁPAGOS (GALAPAGOS ISLANDS) (Ecuador)

WENMAN

PINTA

GENOVESA

0° Equator

MARCHENA

FERNANDINA

SAN SALVADOR

SANTA CRUZ

SAN CRISTÓBAL

ISABELA

SANTA MARIA

ESPAÑOLA

Bolognesi

Iñapari

Lago Rogaguado

Vilhen

Huancayo

LIMA

Cusco

Ixiamas

Trinidad

Punta Carreta

Ica

Nazca

Nevado Palomani
5999

BOLIVIA

Nevado de Ampato
6310

Puno

Lago Titicaca

6485
Nevado de Illampu

Cochabamba

Arequipa

LA PAZ

Santa Cruz

PACIFIC

Tanca

6542
Nevado de Sajama

Oruro

Lago de Poopó

Sucre

Arica

Potosí

OCEAN

Golfo de Arica

Iquique

CORDILLERA OCCIDENTAL

PAMPA DEL TAMARUGAL

Salar de Uyuni

CH

BO

Tarija

Calama

6020
Cerro Nuevo Mundo

Tartagal

PAR

CHILE

ARGENTINA

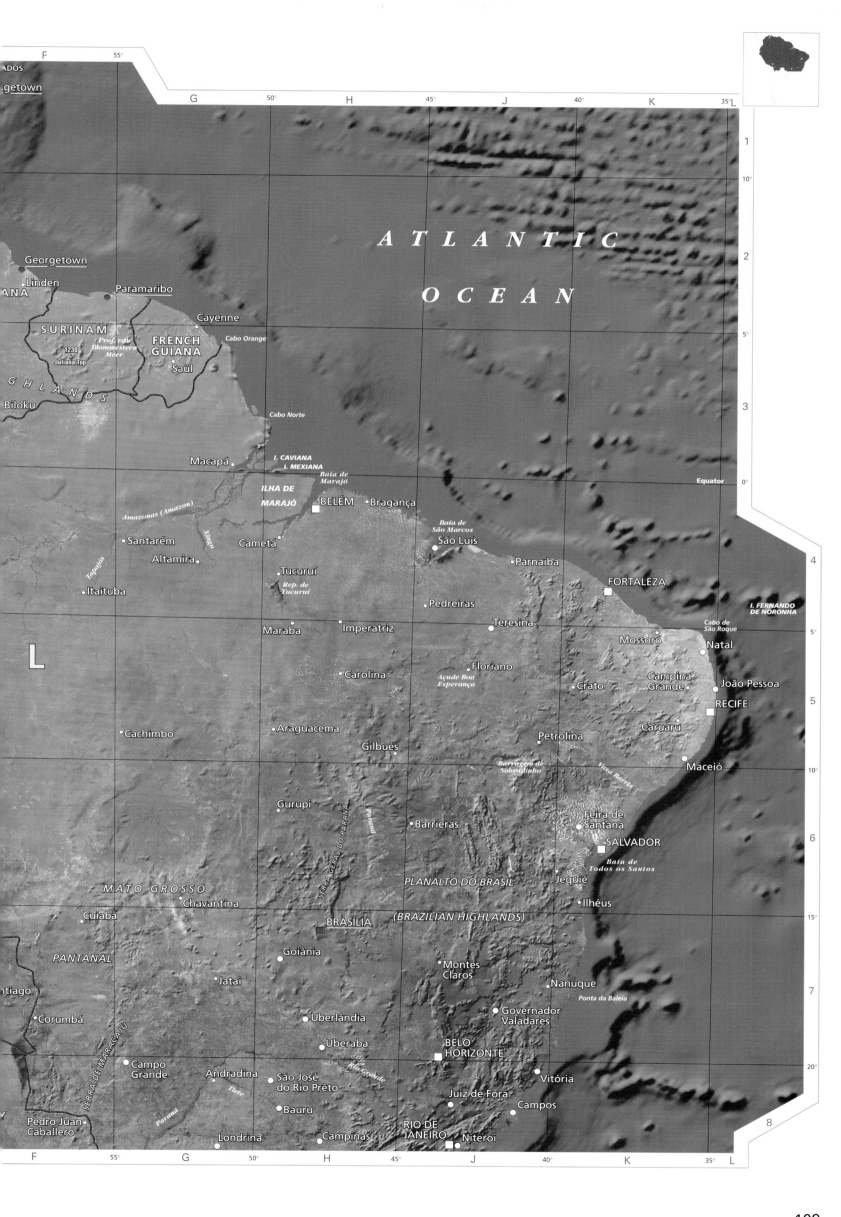

South America, South

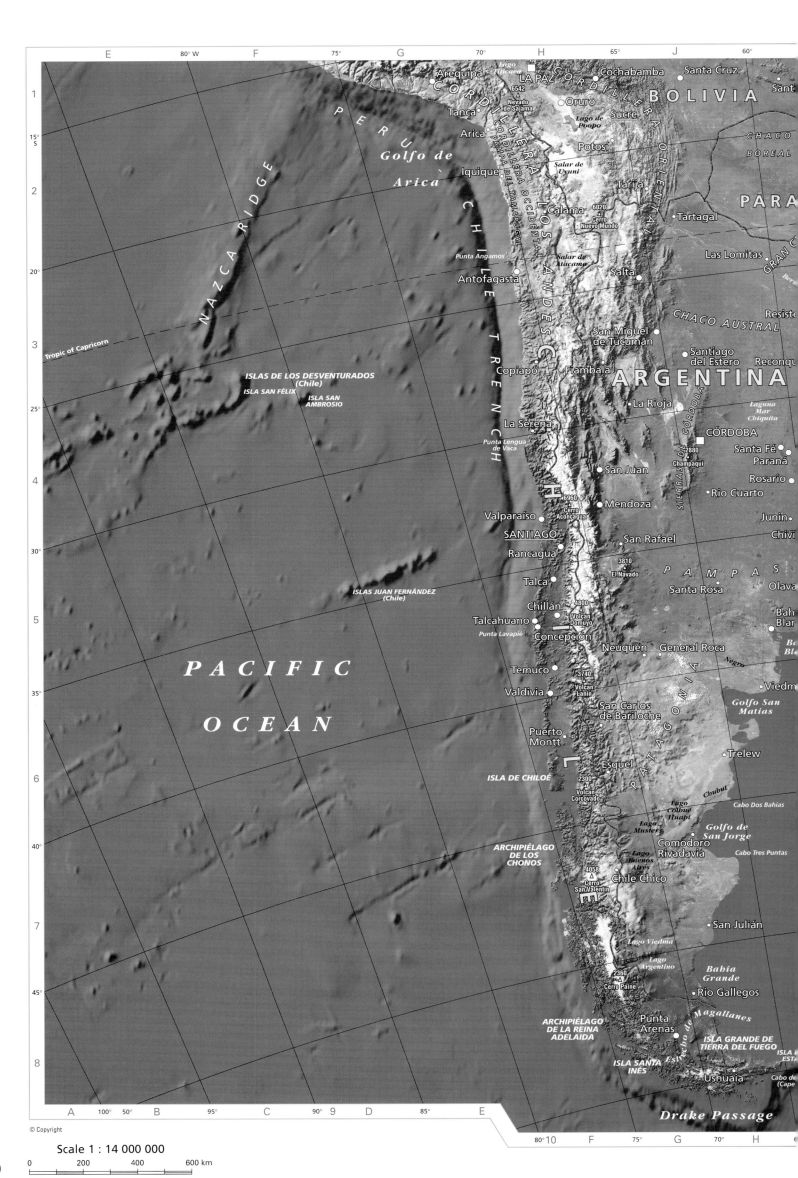

Golfo de Arica

PERU BASIN

NAZCA RIDGE

Tropic of Capricorn

ISLAS DE LOS DESVENTURADOS
(Chile)
ISLA SAN FÉLIX
ISLA SAN
AMBROSIO

PACIFIC

OCEAN

ISLAS JUAN FERNÁNDEZ
(Chile)

PERU-CHILE TRENCH

Arequipa
Lago
Titicaca
LA PAZ
6542
Nevado
de Sajama
Tanca
Arica
Iquique
Punta Angamos
Antofagasta
6020
Cerro
Nuevo Mundo

Cochabamba
Santa Cruz
Sant
BOLIVIA
Oruro
Lago de
Poopó
Sucre
Potosí
Salar de
Uyuni
Tarija
CHACO
BOREAL
PARA

Calama
Salar de
Atacama
Salta
Tartagal
Las Lomitas
GRAN C

CHACO AUSTRAL
Resiste

Copiapó
San Miguel
de Tucumán
Flambala
Santiago
del Estero
Reconq
ARGENTINA

La Rioja
Laguna
Mar
Chiquita

La Serena
Punta Lengua
de Vaca
CÓRDOBA
2880
Champaquí
Santa Fé
Paraná

San Juan
Río Cuarto
Rosario

6960
Cerro
Aconcagua
Mendoza
Junin
Chivi

Valparaíso
SANTIAGO
Rancagua
San Rafael
P A M P A S
3810
El Navado
Santa Rosa
Olava

Talca
Santa Rosa

Chillán
Talcahuano
4800
Volcán
Domuyo
Bah
Blan

Punta Lavapié
Concepción
Neuquén
General Roca
Bo
Ble

Temuco
3740
Volcán
Lanin
Río Negro
Viedm

Valdivia
San Carlos
de Bariloche
Golfo San
Matías

Puerto
Montt

ISLA DE CHILOÉ
2300
Volcán
Corcovado

Esquel
Trelew
Chubut
Cabo Dos Bahias

Lago
Colhué
Huapi
Golfo de
San Jorge

Lago
Musters
Comodoro
Rivadavia
Cabo Tres Puntas

ARCHIPIÉLAGO
DE LOS
CHONOS
Lago
Buenos
Aires

4058
Cerro
San Valentín
Chile Chico

San Julián

Lago Viedma

Lago
Argentino
Bahía
Grande

2360
Cerro Paine
Río Gallegos

ARCHIPIÉLAGO
DE LA REINA
ADELAIDA
Punta
Arenas
Estrecho de Magallanes

ISLA GRANDE DE
TIERRA DEL FUEGO
ISLA
ESTA

ISLA SANTA
INÉS
Ushuaia
Cabo
(Cape

Drake Passage

© Copyright

Scale 1 : 14 000 000
0   200   400   600 km

110

VTANAL

Uberlândia

Governador
Valadares

Ponta de Baleia

nbá

Campo
Grande

Uberaba

BELO
HORIZONTE

São José
do Rio Prêto

Vitória

2

Andradina

Bauru

Juiz de Fora

20°

BRAZIL

Campos

Y

Campinas

Niterói

Pedro Juan
Caballero

Londrina

SÃO PAULO

RIO DE
JANEIRO

3

oncepción

Santos

Represa
de
Itaipu

Cascavel

CURITIBA

Tropic of Capricorn

Caaguazú

sunción

25°

osa

Encarnación

Erechim

Florianópolis

entes

Posadas

4

Uruguaiana

Santa
Maria

PÔRTO ALEGRE

30°

Rivera

Pelotas

Lagoa dos
Patos

URUGUAY

Lagoa
Mirim

Rio Grande

Negro

Embalse
del Rio
Negro

ercedes

5

MONTEVIDEO

Rio de la Plata

OS
S

35°

Mar del Plata

6

ATLANTIC

OCEAN

40°

7

45°

8

FALKLAND IS.
(U.K.)

Stanley

ID

50°

EAST FALKLAND

SOUTH GEORGIA
(U.K.)

9

SCOTIA RIDGE

SCOTIA   SEA

10

Polar Regions

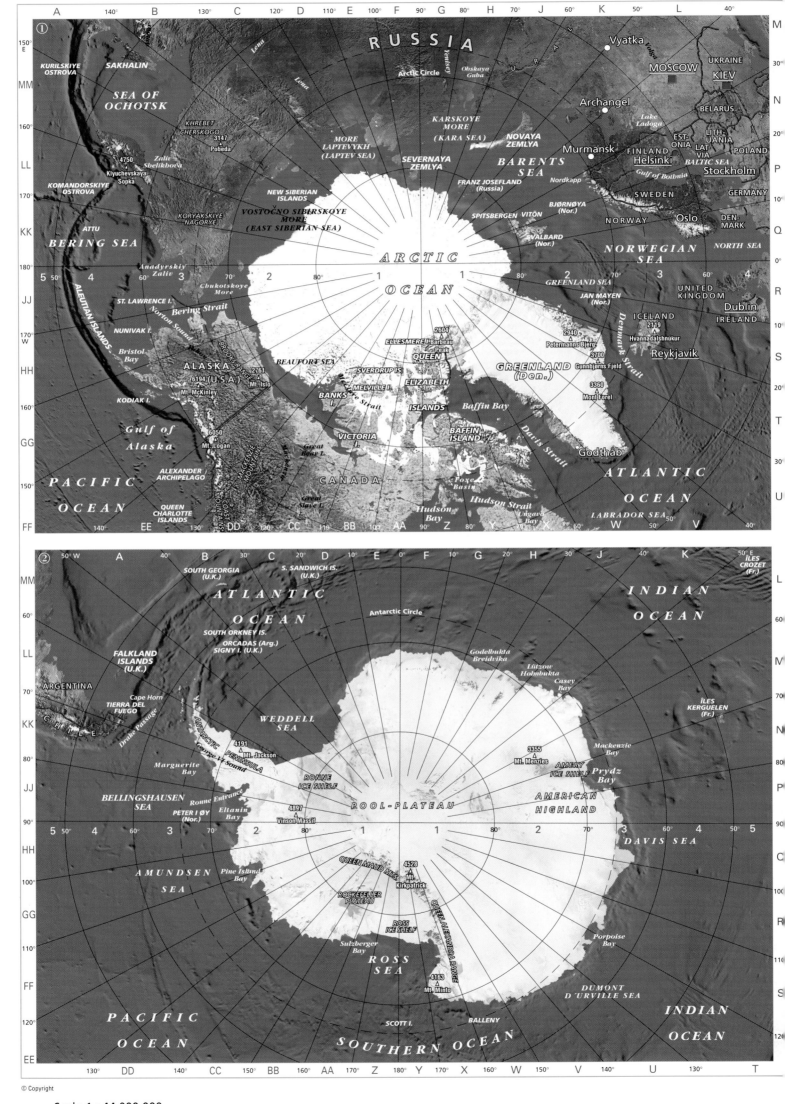

Scale 1 : 44 000 000

0   500   1000   1500   2000 km

Satellite Atlas
OF THE
WORLD

Using the Index

All the placenames and features appearing in this atlas are included in this index. The same feature name may appear on several different pages. In order to avoid duplication, the name will generally be referred to the largest scale map on which the feature appears.

Placename or feature name ——— **Echo Bay**	*Canada*	•	92	H3
Ecija	*Spain*	•	40	E7
Ecuador	*South America*	A	108	B4
Eday	*United Kingdom*	°	36	L2
Ede	*Netherlands*	•	27	J2
Edgar Ranges	*Australia*	▲▲	86	D3
Country or group of countries within ——— Edgell Island	**Canada**	°	93	U4
which the name appears Edinburgh	*United Kingdom*	■	36	K6
Edirne	*Turkey*	°	48	J3
Edmonton	*Canada*	°	92	H6
Edmundston	*Canada*	•	99	G1
Symbols to indicate the type of ——— Edremit	*Turkey*	•	49	K5
feature (see box below) Edremit Körfezi	*Turkey*	►	49	J5
Edwards Plateau	*United States*	▲▲	101	G2
Efate	*Vanuatu*	°	84	G7
Effingham	*United States*	•	98	C3
Eger	*Hungary*	•	46	H2
Page number ——— Egersund	*Norway*	•	**29**	C7
Eğridir Gölü	*Turkey*	♪	50	D4
Egypt	*North Africa*	A	60	E3
Eibar	*Spain*	•	41	H1
Eifel	*Germany*	▲▲	35	B6
Grid reference ——— Eigg	*United Kingdom*	°	36	**G5**
Eight Degree Channel	*Arabian Sea*	►	75	B7
Einbeck	*Germany*	•	34	E5
Eindhoven	*Netherlands*	•	27	J3
Eirunepe	*Brazil*	•	108	D5
Eisenach	*Germany*	•	35	F6
Eisenhüttenstadt	*Germany*	•	34	K4
Eisleben	*Germany*	•	34	G5

Explanation of symbols used

⊘	Physical region, feature	■	Capital City
⬡	Island or Island group, Rocky reef, Coral reef	○	State capital
▲	Mountain, volcano, peak	A	Country names
▲▲	Mountain range	a	State or province name
⌐	Cape, point	♪	Lake or salt lake
✔	River, canal	⌣	Sea, ocean
•	Place name	►	Gulf, strait, bay
		✳	Point/Place of interest

Facts and Figures

Dimensions of the Earth

Circumference of the Equator	40,076 km
Total surface area of the Earth	510,100,933 km²
Area of dry land (29.2%)	149,408,563 km²
Area of sea (70.8%)	360,692,370 km²

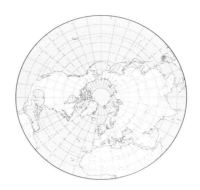

Continental Land Surface

1. Asia 43,608,000 km²

2. Africa 30,335,000 km²

3. North America 25,349,000 km²

4. South America 17,611,000 km²

5. Antarctica 13,340,000 km²

6. Europe 10,498,000 km²

7. Australia and Oceania 8,923,000 km²

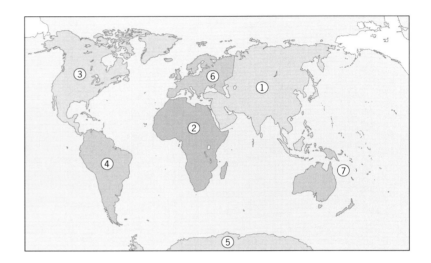

Largest Countries according to area

1. Russia 17,100,000 km²

2. Canada 9,976,139 km²

3. China 9,572,980 km²

4. United States 9,363,166 km²

5. Brazil 8,511,996 km²

6. Australia 7,682,300 km²

7. India 3,166,829 km²

8. Argentina 2,780,092 km²

9. Sudan 2,505,813 km²

10. Algeria 2,381,740 km²

Oceans and largest inland waters

1. Caspian Sea (Salt) (Asia) 371,000 km²

2. Lake Superior (N. America) 83,270 km²

3. Lake Victoria (Africa) 68,800 km²

4. Lake Huron (N. America) 60,700 km²

5. Lake Michigan (N. America) 58,020 km²

6. Aral Sea (Salt) (Asia) 36,000 km²

7. Lake Tanganyika (Africa) 32,900 km²

8. Great Bear Lake (N. America) 31,790 km²

9. Lake Baikal (Asia) 30,500 km²

10. Great Slave Lake (N. America) 28,440 km²

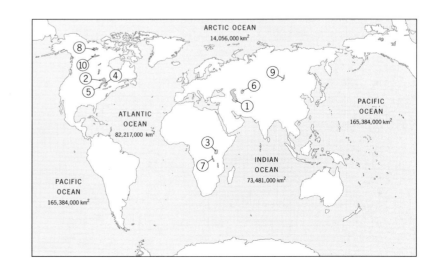

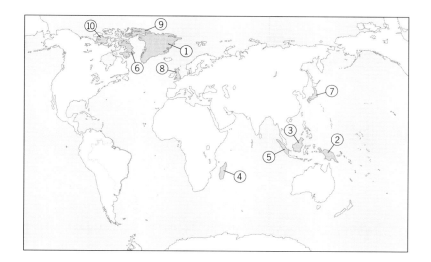

Largest islands of the world

1.	Greenland	2,175,600 km²
2.	New Guinea	808,510 km²
3.	Borneo	757,050 km²
4.	Madagascar	594,180 km²
5.	Sumatra	524,100 km²
6.	Baffin Island	476,070 km²
7.	Honshu	230,455 km²
8.	Great Britain	229,870 km²
9.	Ellesmere Island	212,690 km²
10.	Victoria Island	212,200 km²

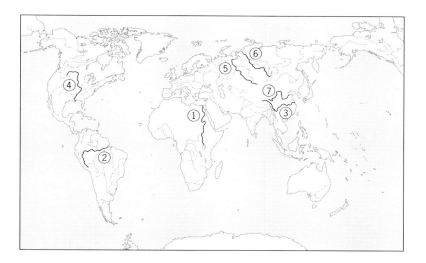

Longest rivers of the world

1.	Nile (Africa)	6,695 km
2.	Amazon (S. America)	6,515 km
3.	Chang-Jiang/Yangtze (Asia)	6,380 km
4.	Mississippi-Missouri (N. America)	6,019 ‹m
5.	Ob-Irtysh (Asia)	5,570 km
6.	Jenisey-Angara (Asia)	5,550 km
7.	Huang He-Yellow River (Asia)	5,464 km

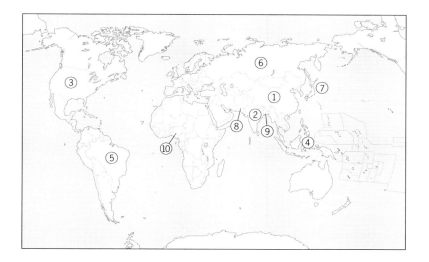

Largest countries according to population

1.	China	1,185,000,000
2.	India	903,000,000
3.	United States	257,000,000
4.	Indonesia	188,000,000
5.	Brazil	159,000,000
6.	Russia	150,000,000
7.	Japan	124,900,000
8.	Pakistan	122,400,000
9.	Bangladesh	122,280,000
10.	Nigeria	92,800,000

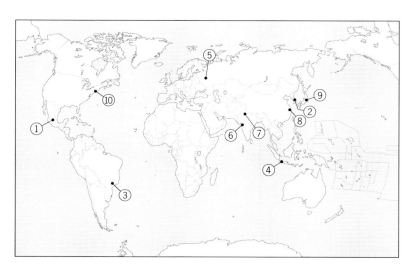

Largest cities of the world

1.	Mexico City	15,047,000
2.	Seoul	10,628,000
3.	Sao Paulo	9,480,427
4.	Jakarta	9,000,000
5.	Moscow	8,967,000
6.	Bombay	8,400,000
7.	Delhi	8,380,000
8.	Shanghai	8,214,436
9.	Tokyo	7,976,000
10.	New York	7,322,564

Index

Name	Location		Page	Grid
Avrillac	France	•	39	H9
Awa	Japan		81	K4
Awaji-Shima	Japan		80	H6
Awanui	New Zealand	•	88	D2
Awarua Bay	New Zealand	►	89	B7
Awash	Ethiopia	✓	65	G1
Awbari' Sahra'	Libya	⊙	60	B2
Axios	Greece	✓	48	E4
Ayamonte	Spain	•	40	C7
Aydin	Turkey	○	49	K7
Aydin Daglari	Turkey	▲	49	K6
Ayers Rock	Australia	*	86	F5
Aylesbury	United Kingdom	•	26	B3
'Ayoûn el Atroûs	Mauritania	•	58	D5
Ayr	United Kingdom	✓	36	J6
Az Zahirah	Oman	⊙	55	G5
Az Zarqa'	Jordan	•	54	D4
Az Zuqar	Yemen		61	H5
Azaila	Spain	•	41	K3
Azaouâd	Mali	⊙	58	E5
Azare	Switzerland	✓	42	C3
Azbine (Aïr)	Niger	▲	59	G5
Azerbaijan	Asia	A	51	M3
Azuaga	Spain	•	40	E6

B

Name	Location		Page	Grid
Ba'qubah	Iraq	•	52	D3
Baai van Benin	Atlantic Ocean	►	63	E3
Bab al Mandab	Indian Ocean	►	61	H5
Baba Burun	Turkey		48	H5
Baba Burun	Turkey		49	P3
Babine Lake	Canada	✓	92	F6
Babol	Iran	•	52	F2
Babuyan Islands	Philippines		77	G3
Bacau	Romania	•	47	P3
Backnang	Germany	•	35	E8
Bacolod	Philippines	•	77	G4
Bad Hersfeld	Germany	•	35	E6
Bad Ischl	Austria	•	32	C10
Bad Kissingen	Germany	•	35	F6
Bad Kreuznach	Germany	•	27	L5
Bad Salzungen	Germany	•	35	F6
Badain Jaran Shamo	China	⊙	78	C2
Badajoz	Spain	○	40	D6
Badalona	Spain	•	41	N3
Baden-Baden	Germany	•	35	D8
Badiet esh Sham (Syrian Desert)	Syria	⊙	54	E3
Baffin Bay	North America	►	93	T2
Baffin Island	Canada		93	Q2
Bafing	West-Africa	✓	62	B2
Bafra Burun	Turkey		50	F3
Bagdad (Baghdad)	Iraq	■	52	D3
Baghdad (Bagdad)	Iraq	■	52	D3
Bahamas	Atlantic Ocean	A	105	J3
Bahawalpur	Pakistan	•	53	K4
Bahia	Honduras		105	G5
Bahía Blanca	Argentina	►	110	J6
Bahía Blanca	Argentina	•	110	J6
Bahía de Alcudia	Spain	►	41	P5
Bahía de Algeciras	Spain	►	40	E8
Bahía de Campeche	Mexico	►	104	F4
Bahía de Manta	Ecuador	►	108	A4
Bahía de Palma	Spain	►	41	N5
Bahía de Rio de Oro	Western Sahara	►	58	B4
Bahía de Santander	Spain	►	40	G1
Bahía de Sechura	Peru	►	108	A5
Bahía Grande	Argentina	►	110	H9
Bahr al Jabal (White Nile)	Central Africa	✓	64	E2
Bahr al Mill	Iraq	✓	52	D3
Bahr Aouk	Central Africa	✓	64	B2
Bahr el Abiad	Africa	✓	61	F5
Bahr el Ghazal	Central Africa	✓	60	C5
Bahr Salamat	Chad	✓	63	H3
Bahrain	Middle East	A	55	D3
Bahrat Hims	Syria	✓	54	D2
Baía de Inhambane	Mozambique	►	67	F4
Baía de Maputo	Mozambique	►	67	E5
Baía de Marajó	Brazil	►	109	H4
Baía de Memba	Mozambique	►	67	G2
Baía de São Marcos	Brazil	►	109	J4
Baía de Setúbal	Spain	►	40	A6
Baía de Sofala	Mozambique	►	67	F4
Baía de Todos os Santos	Brazil	►	109	K6
Baía do Bengo	Angola	►	63	G6
Baia Mare	Romania	•	47	L2
Baicheng	China	•	79	G1
Baie d'Antongil	Madagascar	►	67	H3
Baie d'Audierne	France	►	38	A6
Baie de Bourgneuf	France	►	38	C6
Baie de la Seine	France	►	38	E4
Baie de Saint Augustin	Madagascar	►	67	G4
Baie de St.-Brieuc	France	►	38	C5
Baie des Chaleurs	Canada	►	93	T7
Baie du Cap Lopez	Gabon	►	63	F5
Baikalskiy Khrebet	Russia	▲	72	H5
Baile Átha Cliath	Ireland	■	37	G8
Baile Átha Cliath (Dublin)	Ireland	■	37	H8
Bailleul	France	•	26	F4
Baing	Indonesia	•	83	B5
Bairin Zuoqi	China	•	72	K8
Baja	Hungary	•	46	F3
Baja California	Mexico	⊙	104	B3
Bakadzicite	Bulgaria	▲	49	J2
Baker	United States	•	97	F1
Baker	United States		85	J5
Baker Lake	Canada	•	92	M4
Baker Lake	Canada	✓	92	N4
Bakersfield	United States	•	100	C1
Bakhtaran	Iran	○	51	M6
Baki (Baku)	Azerbaijan	■	51	P3
Bakir	Turkey	✓	49	J5
Bakony	Hungary	▲	46	F2
Balabac	Philippines	■	82	F1
Balabac Strait	Malaysia	►	82	F1
Balaguer	Spain	•	41	L3
Balakovo	Russia	•	31	K4
Balashov	Russia	•	30	J4
Balaton	Hungary	✓	43	N4
Baldy Peak	United States	▲	104	C2
Balearic Isles (Islas Baleares)	Spain		41	M5
Bali	Indonesia		82	E4
Balikpapan	Indonesia	•	82	F3
Balikesir	Turkey	○	50	B4
Balintang Channel	South East Asia	►	77	G2
Ball's Pyramid	Australia		87	L6
Balleny	Antarctica		112	(2)X3
Balta	Ukraine	•	47	S2
Baltic Sea	Europe		29	J9
Baltijssk	Russia	•	33	J3
Baltimore	United States	•	99	E3
Baltrum	Germany		34	C3
Bam	Iran	•	55	H2
Bamako	Mali	■	62	C2
Bamberg	Germany	•	35	F7
Bamenda	Cameroon	•	63	G3
Bampur	Iran	✓	53	G4
Banaadir	Somalia		65	G3
Banaba (Ocean Island)	Kiribati (Pacific Ocean)		84	G6
Banbury	United Kingdom	•	26	B2
Banda Sea	Indonesia		83	C4
Bandama	West Africa	✓	62	C3
Bandar Seri Begawan	Brunei	■	82	E2
Bandar-e' 'Abbas	Iran	○	55	G3
Bandar-e Lengeh	Iran	•	55	F3
Bandirma	Turkey	•	49	L4
Bandirma Körfezi	Turkey	►	49	L4
Bandudu	Democratic Republic of Congo	•	64	B4
Bandung	Indonesia	•	82	D4
Bangalore	India	○	75	C6
Bangang Co	China	✓	74	C2
Bangassou	Central African Republic	•	64	C3
Banghazi (Benghazi)	Libya	○	60	C1
Bangkok (Krung Thep)	Thailand	■	76	C4
Bangladesh	Southern Asia	A	74	E4
Bangor	United States	•	99	G2
Bangui	Central African Republic	■	64	B3
Bani Walid	Libya	•	60	B1
Baniyas	Syria	•	54	C1
Banja Luka	Bosnia-Herzegovina	•	43	N6
Banjarmasin	Indonesia	•	82	E3
Banjul	Gambia	■	58	B6
Banks Island	Canada	•	92	G2
Banks Island (Moa)	Australia		87	H2
Banks Peninsula	New Zealand	►	89	D6
Banks Strait	Australia	►	87	J8
Bann	United Kingdom	✓	37	G6
Bantry Bay	Ireland	►	37	D10
Baoding	China	•	78	F3
Baoji	China	•	78	D4
Baotou	China	•	78	E2
Baracaldo	Spain	•	39	B10
Baranof Island	United States		100	(1)K4
Baranovichi	Belarus	•	29	P10
Barbados	Caribbean	A	105	N6
Barbeau Peak	Canada	▲	112	(1)Y1
Barbuda	Caribbean	•	105	M5
Barcelona	Spain	○	41	N3
Barcelona	Venezuela	○	108	E1
Barcotta	Spain	•	40	D6
Bareilly	India	•	74	C3
Barents Sea	Northern Asia	•	70	D3
Barguzinskiy Khrebet	Russia	▲	72	H6
Bari	Italy	•	45	L7
Barinas	Venezuela	○	108	C2
Barisal	Bangladesh	•	74	F4
Barkly Tableland	Australia	▲	87	G3
Barletta	Italy	•	46	D8
Barma	Indonesia	•	83	D3
Barnaul	Russia	○	71	Q7
Barnstaple	United Kingdom	•	38	B2
Barnstaple or Bideford Bay	United Kingdom	►	37	J10
Barqah al Bahriyah	Egypt	⊙	60	E1
Barquisimeto	Venezuela	○	108	D1
Barra	United Kingdom		36	F4
Barracaldo	Spain	•	40	G8
Barragem de Sobradinho	Brazil	✓	109	J6
Barranquilla	Colombia	○	108	C1
Barre des Ecrins	France	▲	39	M8
Barreiro	Portugal	•	40	A6
Barrieras	Brazil	•	109	J6
Barrington Tops	Australia	▲	87	K6
Barrow Island	Australia	•	86	B4
Barstow	United States	•	100	C2
Barth	Germany	•	34	H2
Bartle Frere	Australia	▲	84	E7
Bartoszyce	Poland	•	32	K4
Barun Bagdo-Ula	Mongolia	▲	78	C1
Basel	Switzerland	○	42	C3
Bashi Haixia	Taiwan / Philippines	►	79	F6
Basilan	Philippines		83	B1
Basildon	United Kingdom	•	37	P10
Basingstoke	United Kingdom	•	26	B3
Basra (Al Basrah)	Iraq	•	52	E3
Bass Strait	Australia	►	87	H8
Bassano d.Grappa	Italy	•	43	G5
Bassas da India (Réunion)	Southern Africa		67	F4
Bassein	Myanmar (Burma)	•	76	A3
Bassum	Germany	•	34	D4
Bastia	France	•	44	D6
Bastogne	Belgium	•	27	J4
Bataklik Gölü	Turkey	✓	49	R7
Batan Islands	Philippines		77	G2
Batangos	Philippines		77	G4
Bath	United Kingdom	•	38	C2
Bathurst Inlet	Canada	•	92	K2
Bathurst Island	Australia		86	E2
Bathurst Island	Canada		92	L1
Batna	Algeria	•	59	G1
Baton Rouge	United States	○	102	C3
Batumi	Georgia	○	51	J3
Bauru	Brazil	•	109	H8
Bautzen	Germany	•	35	K5
Bawean	Indonesia		82	E4
Bay City	United States	•	99	D2
Bay of Bengal	India	►	75	E5
Bay of Biscay	France / Spain	►	40	F1
Bay of Fundy	Canada	►	93	T8
Bay of Islands	Canada	►	93	V7
Bay of Plenty	New Zealand	►	88	F3
Bayan Har Shan	China	▲	78	B4
Baydaratskaya Guba	Russia	►	70	L4
Baydhabo	Somalia	⊙	65	G3
Bayerische Alpen	Germany	▲	43	G3
Bayerischer Wald	Germany	⊙	35	H7
Bayeux	France	•	26	C5
Baykit	Russia	•	72	F4
Baynunah	United Arab Emirates	⊙	55	E5
Bayr Nuur	Mongolia	✓	72	K7
Bayreuth	Germany	•	35	G7
Baytik Shan	China	▲	71	R8
Bayy al Kabir	Libya	✓	60	B1
Baza	Spain	•	40	H7
Beachy Head	United Kingdom		38	F3
Bear Lake	United States	✓	96	D2
Bearskin Lake	Canada	•	92	N6
Beas de Segura	Spain	•	40	H6
Beaufort Sea	North Pole		92	E2
Beaumont	France	•	27	J6
Beaumont	United States	•	102	C3
Beauvais	France	•	26	F5
Becej	Yugoslavia	•	46	H4
Béchar	Algeria	•	59	E2
Úbeda	Spain	•	40	G6
Bedford	United Kingdom	•	26	C2
Beersheba	Israel	○	54	B5
Beijing	China	•	78	F2
Beira	Mozambique	○	67	F3
Beirut	Lebanon	•	54	C3
Beirut (Beyrouth)	Lebanon	■	54	C3
Beius	Romania	•	47	K3
Béja	Tunisia	•	45	C12
Beja	Portugal	•	40	C6
Béjar	Spain	•	40	E3
Békéscsaba	Hungary	•	46	J3
Bel'tsy	Moldova	•	47	R2
Belarus	Europe	A	30	H4
Belaya	Russia	✓	73	W3
Belcher Islands	Canada		93	Q5
Belém	Brazil	○	109	H4
Belfast	United Kingdom	○	37	H7
Belfort	France	•	38	M6
Belgaum	India	•	75	B5
Belgium	Europe	A	27	H4
Belize	Central America	A	104	G5
Bellary	India	•	75	C5
Belle Isle	Canada		93	W6
Belle Île	France	•	38	B6
Belleville	Canada	•	99	E2
Bellingham	United States	•	96	B1
Bellingshausen Sea	Antarctica	►	112	(2)JJ5
Bellinzona	Switzerland	•	42	E4
Belluno	Italy	•	43	H4
Belmopan	Belize	■	104	G5
Belo Horizonte	Brazil	○	109	J7
Belovo	Russia	•	71	R7
Beloye More (White Sea)	Russia	►	30	H1
Belozersk	Russia	•	30	H2
Bemidji	United States	•	98	B1
Ben Klibreck	United Kingdom	▲	36	J3
Ben Macdhui	United Kingdom	▲	36	K4
Ben Nevis	United Kingdom	▲	36	H5
Benabarre	Spain	•	41	L2
Benavente	Spain	•	40	E3
Bend	United States	•	96	B2
Benevento	Italy	•	45	J7
Bengbu	China	•	78	F4
Benghazi (Banghazi)	Libya	○	60	C1
Benguela	Angola	•	66	A2
Benguela	Angola	•	64	A6
Beni Mellal	Morocco	•	58	D2
Beni-Abbès	Algeria	•	59	E2
Benin	West Africa	A	63	E2
Benin-City	Nigeria	○	63	F3
Benoni	South Africa	•	66	D5
Bensheim	Germany	•	35	D7
Bentinck Island	Australia		87	G3
Benue	West Africa	✓	63	F3
Benwee Head	Ireland	►	37	D7
Benxi	China	•	80	C3
Beograd (Belgrade)	Yugoslavia	○	46	H5
Beppu	Japan	•	80	F7
Berat	Albania	•	48	C4

Name	Region	Page	Grid
Berbera	Somalia	65	H1
Berbérati	Central African Republic	63	H4
Berck	France	26	E4
Berdyansk	Ukraine	30	H5
Beregovo	Ukraine	47	K1
Berezniki	Russia	70	K6
Berezovo	Russia	31	N2
Berga	Spain	41	M2
Bergama	Turkey	49	K5
Bergamo	Italy	44	D3
Bergen	Norway	29	C6
Bergen op.Zoom	Netherlands	27	H3
Bergerac	France	39	F9
Bering Sea	Pacific Ocean	100	(2)C3
Beringov Proliv / Bering Strait	Russia/United States	100	(1)D2
Berlevåg	Norway	28	Q1
Berlin	Germany	34	J4
Bermejo	Argentina	110	K4
Bermuda	Atlantic Ocean	105	M2
Bern	Switzerland	42	C4
Bernay	France	26	D5
Berner Alpen	Switzerland	42	C4
Bernina	Switzerland / Italy	42	E4
Berounka	Czech Republic	33	C8
Bertix	Belgium	27	J5
Bertoua	Cameroon	63	G3
Besançon	France	38	M6
Beskid Niski	Poland	33	L8
Beskiden	Poland	33	H8
Béthume	France	26	F4
Bettola	Italy	42	E6
Bey Daglari	Turkey	50	C5
Beykoz	Turkey	49	M3
Beyrouth (Beirut)	Lebanon	54	C3
Beysehir Gölü	Turkey	50	D5
Béziers	France	39	J10
Bhadravati	India	75	C6
Bhagalpur	India	74	E3
Bharuch	India	74	B4
Bhatpara	India	74	E4
Bhavnagar	India	74	B4
Bhopal	India	74	C4
Bhubaneshwar	India	74	E4
Bhutan	Southern Asia	74	F3
Biak	Indonesia	84	D6
Bialystok	Poland	32	N4
Biarritz	France	39	D10
Biata Podlaska	Poland	33	N7
Biatystock	Poland	29	M10
Biberach	Germany	35	E8
Bicaj	Albania	46	H8
Bickerton Island	Australia	87	G2
Bida	Nigeria	63	F3
Biebrza	Poland	32	M4
Biel	Switzerland	42	C3
Bielefeld	Germany	34	D4
Bieler See	Switzerland	42	C3
Biella	Italy	42	D5
Bielsko-Biala	Poland	33	J8
Bieszczady	Poland	33	M8
Big Horn Mountains	United States	97	E2
Big Quill Lake	Canada	92	L6
Big Spring	United States	101	F2
Big Trout Lake	Canada	93	N6
Bighorn River	United States	97	E1
Bight of Benin	Atlantic Ocean	63	E3
Bihac	Bosnia Herzegovina	46	C5
Bihar	India	74	E3
Bijapur	India	75	C5
Bijeljina	Bosnia Herzegovina	46	G5
Bikaner	India	74	B3
Bikini	Marshall Islands	84	G4
Bilaspur	India	74	D4
Bilauktaung Range	Myanmar (Burma) / Thailand	76	B4
Bilbao	Spain	40	H1
Bilibino	Russia	73	V3
Billings	United States	94	E2
Bilma	Niger	59	H5
Bilogora	Croatia	46	D3
Biloku	Guyana	109	F3
Bioko (Fernando Póo)	Equatorial Guinea	63	F4
Biokovo	Bosnia-Herzegovina / Croatia	46	E6
Bîr Mogreïn	Mauritania	58	C3
Birao	Central African Republic	60	D5
Bîrlad	Romania	47	Q3
Birmingham	United Kingdom	37	M9
Birmingham	United States	102	D3
Birnie	Kiribati (Pacific Ocean)	85	J6
Birnin-Kebb	Nigeria	63	E2
Birzai	Lithuania	29	N8
Bisevo	Croatia	46	C7
Bishkek	Kyrgyzstan	71	P9
Biskra	Algeria	59	G2
Bismarck	United States	97	F1
Bismarck Sea	Papua New Guinea	84	E6
Bissau	Guinea-Bissau	62	A2
Bistcho Lake	Canada	92	H4
Bistrita	Romania	47	M2
Bitburg	Germany	35	B7
Bitola	Macedonia	48	D3
Bitonto	Italy	46	D8
BItteroot Range	United States	96	C1
Biwa-Ko	Japan	81	J6
Biysk	Russia	71	R7
Bizerte	Tunisia	45	D11
Bjelovar	Croatia	46	D4
Bjeshkët e Nemuna	Yugoslavia / Albania	46	G7
Bjørnevatn	Norway	28	Q2
Bjørnøya	Norway	112	(1)N2
Black Forest	Germany	42	D3
Black Hills	United States	97	E2
Black Mountains	United States	100	D1
Black Rock Desert	United States	96	C2
Black Sea	Europe	50	N2
Black Volta (Mouhoun)	West Africa	62	E3
Blackburn	United Kingdom	37	L8
Blackpool	United Kingdom	37	K8
Blacksod Bay	Ireland	37	C8
Blagoevgrad	Bulgaria	48	F2
Blagoveshchensk	Russia	72	M6
Blanca Peak	United States	97	E3
Blanes	Spain	41	N3
Blantyre	Malawi	67	E3
Blåvands Huk	Denmark	29	D9
Blenheim	New Zealand	89	E5
Bletchley	United Kingdom	26	C3
Blida	Algeria	59	F1
Blida	Algeria	41	P8
Bloemfontein	South Africa	66	D5
Blois	France	38	G6
Blönduós	Iceland	28	(1)D2
Blue Mountains	United States	96	C2
Blue Nile (El Bahr el Azraq)	Africa	61	F5
Blue Ridge	United States	99	D3
Blyot Island	Canada	93	R2
Bo	Sierra Leone	62	B3
Bo Hai	China	79	F3
Boa Vista	Cape Verde	62	(1)B1
Boa Vista	Brazil	108	E3
Bobo Dioulasso	Burkina Faso	58	E6
Bóbr	Poland	32	E6
Bobruysk	Belarus	30	F4
Bocholt	Germany	34	B5
Bochum	Germany	34	C5
Bodelé	Chad	59	J5
Boden	Sweden	28	L4
Bodensee	Germany / Switzerland	35	E5
Bodo	Norway	28	H3
Boende	Democratic Republic of Congo	64	C4
Bogda Feng	China	71	R9
Bogda Shan	China	71	R9
Bogor	Indonesia	82	D4
Bogotá	Colombia	108	C3
Bohol	Philippines	77	G5
Bohol Sea	Philippines	77	G5
Boise	United States	96	C2
Boizenburg	Germany	34	F3
Boknafjorden	Norway	29	C7
Bolaçu	Brazil	108	E4
Boleslawiec	Poland	33	E6
Bolgatanga	Ghana	62	D2
Bolivia	South America	108	D7
Bollnäs	Sweden	29	J6
Bolmen	Sweden	29	G8
Bologna	Italy	44	F4
Bolognesi	Peru	108	C5
Bolsoj Kavkaz	Russia / Georgia	51	H2
Bolsón de Mapimi	Mexico	101	E3
Boltaña	Spain	41	L2
Bolton	United Kingdom	37	L8
Bolu	Turkey	49	P4
Bolu Daglari	Turkey	50	E3
Bolzano	Italy	42	G4
Bømlo	Norway	29	C7
Bomu	Central Africa	64	D3
Bon-Cagan-Nur	Mongolia	78	B1
Bonaire	Central America	105	L6
Bonaparte Archipelago	Australia	86	D3
Bondo	Democratic Republic of Congo	64	C3
Bondoukov	Côte D'Ivoire	62	D3
Bongolava	Madagascar	67	H3
Bongor	Chad	60	C5
Bonn	Germany	35	C6
Bor	Yugoslavia	47	K5
Bor Dagi	Turkey	50	C5
Borah Peak	United States	96	D2
Borazjan	Iran	55	D2
Bordeaux	France	39	E9
Bordj Mokhtar	Algeria	59	F4
Borgames	Iceland	28	C2
Børgefjellet	Norway	28	G4
Borger	United States	101	F1
Borislav	Ukraine	33	N8
Borja	Peru	108	B4
Borkou	Chad	60	C4
Borkum	Germany	34	B3
Borlänge	Sweden	29	H6
Borneo	South East Asia	82	E2
Bornes	Indonesia	83	A2
Bornholm	Denmark	29	H9
Bornholmsgattet	Europe	29	H9
Borovichi	Russia	30	G3
Bosna	Croatia	44	M4
Bosnia-Herzegovina	Europe	46	E5
Bosporus (Karadeniz Bogazi)	Turkey	50	C3
Bossangoa	Central African Republic	63	H3
Boston	United Kingdom	26	C2
Boston	United States	99	F2
Boston Mountains	United States	102	C2
Botosani	Romania	47	P2
Botswana	Southern Africa	66	C4
Botte Donato	italy	45	L9
Bottrop	Germany	35	B5
Bouaké	Ivory Coast	62	D3
Bouar	Central African Republic	64	B2
Bougainville	Papua New-Guinea	84	F6
Bougainville Reef	Australia	87	J3
Bouira	Algeria	41	P8
Boulogne	France	38	G3
Bouna	Côte D'Ivoire	62	D3
Bourg-en-Bresse	France	39	L7
Bourges	France	39	H6
Bournemouth	United Kingdom	37	L11
Bovec	Slovenia	33	C11
Boxmeer	Netherlands	27	J3
Boyoma Falls	Democratic Republic of Congo	64	D3
Boz Burun	Turkey	50	C3
Boz Daglari	Turkey	49	K6
Bozburun Dagi	Turkey	49	N7
Bozca Ada	Turkey	48	H5
Bozeman	United States	96	D1
Bozoum	Central African Republic	63	H3
Brac	Croatia	46	D6
Bracki Kanal	Croatia	46	D6
Brad	Romania	33	M12
Bradford	United Kingdom	37	L8
Bragança	Portugal	40	D3
Brahmapur	India	75	D5
Brahmaputra	Southern Asia	74	E3
Braila	Romania	47	Q4
Brainerd	United States	98	B2
Brandberg	Namibia	66	A4
Branden	Canada	92	L7
Brandenburg	Germany	34	H4
Brandon	Canada	94	F2
Brasília	Brazil	109	H7
Brasov	Romania	47	N4
Bratislava	Slovakia	33	G9
Bratsk	Russia	72	G5
Bratskoye Vdkhr.	Russia	72	G5
Braunau	Austria	43	J2
Braunschweig	Germany	34	F4
Brava	Cape Verde	62	(1)A2
Bravo	Europe	46	H4
Bray Island	Canada	93	R3
Brayança	Brazil	108	H4
Brazil	South America	108	D5
Brazilian Highlands (Planalto do Brasil)	Brazil	109	J7
Brazos River	United States	104	E2
Brazzaville	Congo	63	G5
Bream Bay	New Zealand	88	E2
Breaza	Romania	47	N2
Breclav	Czech Republic	33	F9
Breclav	Slovakia	43	M2
Brecon Beacons	United Kingdom	37	K10
Breda	Netherlands	27	H3
Breida Fjördur	Iceland	28	(1)B2
Breivikbotn	Norway	28	M1
Brekken	Norway	28	F5
Bremen	Germany	34	D3
Bremerhaven	Germany	34	D3
Brenta	Italy	44	F3
Brescia	Italy	44	E3
Breslau (Wroclaw)	Poland	33	G6
Brest	France	38	A5
Brest	Belarus	30	E4
Breteuil	France	26	F5
Bria	Central African Republic	64	C5
Briançon	France	39	M9
Bridgetown	Barbados	105	N6
Bridgwater	United Kingdom	38	B2
Brienzer See	Switzerland	42	C4
Brighton	United Kingdom	37	N11
Brignoles	France	42	B7
Brisbane	Australia	87	K5
Bristol	United Kingdom	37	L10
Bristol Bay	United States	112	(1)HH4
Bristol Channel	United Kingdom	37	J10
British Columbia	Canada	92	F5
Brive-la-Gaillarde	France	39	G8
Brno	Czech Republic	33	F8
Broad Sound	Australia	87	J4
Brocken	Germany	34	F5
Brooks Range	Alaska	112	GG3
Brooks Range	United States	100	(1)F2
Bruchsal	Germany	35	D7
Brugge	Belgium	26	G3
Bruncu Spina	Sardinia (Italy)	45	D9
Brunei	Asia	82	E2
Brunswick	United States	103	E3
Bruxelles / Brüssel (Brussels)	Belgium	27	H4
Bryan	United States	101	G2
Bryansk	Russia	30	G4
Brzeg	Poland	32	G6
Bubiyan	Kuwait	55	C2
Bucaramanga	Colombia	108	C2
Bucharest (Bucuresti)	Romania	47	P5
Buckland Tableland	Australia	87	J4
Bucuresti (Bucharest)	Romania	47	P5
Budapest	Hungary	46	G2
Bude Bay	United Kingdom	37	J11
Budennovsk	Russia	30	J6
Büdingen	Germany	35	E6
Buenaventura	Colombia	108	B3
Buenos Aires	Argentina	111	K5
Buffalo (Wyo.)	United States	97	E2
Buffalo (N.Y.)	United States	99	E2
Buffalo Lake	Canada	92	J5
Bug	Ukraine / Poland	30	E4
Bugrino	Russia	31	K1
Buhayrat al Asad	Syria	51	H5

Caribbean Sea	*Central America*	105	J5
Cariboo Mountains	*Canada*	92	G6
Carlisle	*United Kingdom*	37	L7
Carmarthen Bay	*United Kingdom*	37	J10
Carmen	*Mexico*	104	B3
Carmona	*Spain*	40	E7
Carnsore Point	*Ireland*	37	G9
Carolina	*Brazil*	109	H5
Caroline	*Kiribati (Pacific Ocean)*	85	L6
Caroline Islands	*Micronesia*	84	E5
Carpathian Mountains	*Ukraine / Romania*	47	M1
Carpathians (Západné Karpaty)	*Poland / Slovakia*	33	H9
Carpatii Occidentali	*Romania*	33	M11
Carpi	*Italy*	42	F6
Carrantuohill	*Ireland*	37	D10
Carrizos	*Mexico*	101	E2
Çarsamba	*Turkey*	50	E5
Carson City	*United States*	96	C3
Cartagena	*Spain*	41	K7
Cartagena	*Colombia*	108	B1
Caruaru	*Brazil*	109	K5
Casa Grande	*United States*	100	D2
Casablanca (Dar-el-Beida)	*Morocco*	58	D2
Casale Monferrato	*Italy*	42	D5
Cascade	*United States*	96	C2
Cascade Range	*United States*	96	B2
Cascavel	*Brazil*	111	L3
Cascina	*Italy*	42	F7
Caserta	*Italy*	45	J7
Casey Bay	*Antarctica*	112	(2)K3
Casper	*United States*	97	E2
Caspian Sea	*Europe*	51	N2
Cassai	*Central Africa*	64	C5
Cassiar Mountains	*Canada*	100	(1)L3
Castelfranco Veneto	*Italy*	43	H5
Castellón de la Plana	*Spain*	41	K4
Castelo Branco	*Portugal*	40	C5
Castlereagh Bay	*Australia*	87	G2
Cat Island	*Bahamas*	105	J4
Catanduanes	*Philippines*	77	G4
Catánia	*Sicily*	45	K11
Catanzaro	*Italy*	45	L10
Catena Costiera	*Italy*	45	L9
Cato Island	*Australia*	87	L4
Catskill Mountains	*United States*	99	F2
Caucasus	*Asia*	51	J2
Cauvery	*India*	75	C6
Cavado	*Portugal*	40	B3
Cavalli Islands	*New Zealand*	88	D2
Çavus Burun	*Turkey*	49	N8
Cayenne	*French Guiana*	109	G3
Cayman Islands	*Caribbean*	105	H5
Cebu	*Philippines*	77	G4
Cebu	*Philippines*	77	G4
Cedar City	*United States*	96	D3
Cedar Lake	*Canada*	92	L6
Cedar Rapids	*United States*	98	B2
Cedros	*Mexico*	104	A3
Cegléd	*Hungary*	46	G2
Celebes Sea	*Indonesia*	83	B2
Célebes (Sulawesi)	*Indonesia*	83	A3
Celje	*Slovenia*	43	L4
Celle	*Germany*	34	F4
Celtic Sea	*United Kingdom*	37	E10
Cento	*Italy*	42	G6
Central African Republic	*Central Africa*	64	D4
Central Alps	*Switzerland*	42	D4
Central Makran Range	*Pakistan*	53	H4
Central Range	*Papua New-Guinea*	84	E6
Central Siberian Plain (Srednesibirskoye Ploskogorye)	*Russia*	72	F4
Cerf	*Seychelles*	67	(2)B2
Cerignola	*Italy*	46	C8
Cernjahovsk	*Russia*	30	D4
Cerralvo	*Mexico*	104	B4
Cerro Aconcagua	*Argentina*	110	H5
Cerro Guaiquinima	*Venezuela*	108	E2
Cerro Nuevo Mundo	*Bolivia*	108	D8
Cerro Paine	*Chile*	110	G9
Cerro San Valentin	*Chile*	110	G8
Cerro Yavi	*Venezuela*	108	D2
Cerro Yumari	*Venezuela*	108	D3
Cervonograd	*Ukraine*	33	P7
Cesena	*Italy*	43	H6
Ceské Budejovice	*Czech Republic*	33	D9
Ceskomoravská Vysocina	*Czech Republic*	33	E8
Cesky Les	*Czech Republic*	33	B8
Ceuta	*Spain*	40	E9
Cévennes	*France*	39	J10
Ch'ongjin	*North Korea*	80	E3
Ch'ongju	*South Korea*	80	D5
Ch'unch'on	*South Korea*	80	D5
Chablais	*France*	42	B4
Chaco Austral	*Argentina*	110	J4
Chaco Boreal	*Paraguay*	110	J3
Chad	*West Africa*	60	C4
Chagai Hills	*Pakistan*	53	H4
Chai-li	*Taiwan*	79	F6
Chaîne des Albéres	*France*	41	N2
Chalbi Desert	*Kenya*	65	F3
Challenger Deep	*Oceania*	84	E4
Chalon-sur-Saône	*France*	39	K7
Châlons-sur-Marne	*France*	27	H6
Cham	*Germany*	35	H7
Chambal	*India*	74	C3
Chambery	*France*	39	L8
Champaqui	*Argentina*	110	J5
Chandigarh	*India*	74	C2
Chang Jiang	*China*	78	F4
Chang-hua	*Taiwan*	77	G2
Changbai Shan	*East Asia*	80	D3
Changchun	*China*	79	G2
Changde	*China*	78	E5
Changjiang Kou	*China*	79	G4
Changsha	*China*	78	E5
Channel Islands	*United Kingdom*	37	K12
Chao Phraya	*South East Asia*	76	C3
Chapada Damantina	*Brazil*	106	G4
Chapayevo	*Kazakhstan*	31	L4
Chapleau	*Canada*	98	D1
Chardzhou	*Turkmenistan*	71	L10
Charente	*France*	39	F8
Chari	*Africa*	60	C5
Charleroi	*Belgium*	27	H4
Charles Island	*Canada*	93	S4
Charleston (W.Va)	*United States*	103	E2
Charleston (S.C.)	*United States*	103	E3
Charleston Peak	*United States*	100	C1
Charleville-Mézières	*France*	27	H5
Charlotte	*United States*	103	E2
Charlottetown	*Canada*	93	U7
Chartres	*France*	38	G5
Châteauroux	*France*	39	G7
Châteauxbriant	*France*	38	D6
Châtellerault	*France*	39	F7
Château-Thierry	*France*	26	G5
Chatham Islands	*New Zealand*	89	(1)B1
Chatkal'skiy Khrebet	*Kyrgyzstan*	71	N9
Chattanooga	*United States*	103	D2
Chaumont	*France*	38	L5
Chaunskaya Guba	*Russia*	73	V3
Chavantina	*Brazil*	109	G6
Chaves	*Portugal*	40	C3
Cheb	*Czech Republic*	35	H6
Cheboksary	*Russia*	31	K3
Cheduba	*Myanmar (Burma)*	76	A3
Cheju	*South Korea*	80	D7
Cheju Do (Quelpart I.)	*South Korea*	80	D7
Cheju-Haehyop	*East Asia*	80	D7
Chelif	*Algeria*	59	F1
Chelkar	*Kazakhstan*	31	M5
Chelm	*Poland*	33	N6
Chelmsford	*United Kingdom*	26	D3
Chelyabinsk	*Russia*	31	N3
Chemnitz	*Germany*	35	J6
Chenachane	*Algeria*	58	E3
Chengdu	*China*	78	C4
Chennai (Madras)	*India*	75	D6
Chentijn Nuruu	*Mongolia*	72	H7
Cherbaniani Reef	*India*	75	B6
Cherbourg	*France*	38	D4
Cherepovets	*Russia*	30	H3
Cherkassy	*Ukraine*	30	G5
Cherkessk	*Russia*	51	K1
Cherlak	*Russia*	31	Q4
Chernaya	*Russia*	31	M1
Chernigov	*Ukraine*	30	G4
Chernovtsy	*Ukraine*	30	F5
Cherski	*Russia*	73	U3
Cherzhell	*Algeria*	41	N8
Chesapeake Bay	*United States*	99	E3
Chëshskaya Guba	*Russia*	70	H4
Chesterfield	*United Kingdom*	26	B1
Chesterfield Inlet	*Canada*	93	N4
Chett el Jerid	*Tunisia*	59	G2
Cheviot	*United Kingdom*	37	K6
Chew Bahir	*Ethiopia*	65	F3
Cheyenne	*United States*	97	F2
Cheyne Bay	*Australia*	86	C6
Chi-lung	*Taiwan*	77	G1
Chia-li	*Taiwan*	77	G2
Chiavari	*Italy*	42	E6
Chibougamou	*Canada*	99	F1
Chicago	*United States*	98	C2
Chichagof	*United States*	100	(1)K4
Chiclana de la Frontera	*Spain*	40	D8
Chiclayo	*Peru*	108	B5
Chiemsee	*Germany*	35	H9
Chier	*Italy*	42	C5
Chigu Co	*China*	74	F3
Chihuahua	*Mexico*	101	E3
Chile	*South America*	110	H4
Chile Chico	*Chile*	110	G8
Chillán	*Chile*	110	G6
Chillicothe	*United States*	98	B3
Chiltern Hills	*United Kingdom*	37	M10
Chimanimari	*Zimbabwe*	67	E3
Chimbote	*Peru*	108	B5
Chimkent	*Kazakhstan*	71	M9
Chin	*North Korea*	80	D6
China	*East Asia*	78	B4
Chingola	*Zambia*	64	D6
Chingola	*Zambia*	66	D2
Chinguetti	*Mauritania*	58	C4
Chinju	*South Korea*	80	E6
Chioggia	*Italy*	45	H5
Chipata	*Zambia*	65	E6
Chirinda	*Russia*	72	G3
Chisinau	*Moldova*	30	F5
Chita	*Russia*	72	J6
Chitato	*Angola*	64	C5
Chittagong	*Bangladesh*	74	F4
Chivasso	*Italy*	42	C5
Chivilcoy	*Argentina*	110	K6
Chobe	*South Africa*	66	C3
Choiseul	*Solomon Islands*	84	F6
Chojnice	*Poland*	32	G3
Chokai-San	*Japan*	79	K3
Choke	*Ethiopia*	65	F1
Chokurdah	*Russia*	73	R2
Cholet	*France*	39	E6
Chomutov	*Czech Republic*	33	C7
Chongqing	*China*	78	D5
Chonju	*South Korea*	80	D6
Choshi	*Japan*	81	L6
Chott Ech Chergui	*Algeria*	59	E2
Chott el Hodna	*Algeria*	59	G1
Choybalsan	*Mongolia*	72	J7
Christchurch	*New Zealand*	89	E6
Christmas Island	*Australia*	82	D5
Chubut	*Argentina*	110	H7
Chugoku-Sanchi	*Japan*	80	G6
Chukeni Sea (Chukotskoye More)	*Russia*	73	Z3
Chukotskoye More (Chukeni Sea)	*Russia*	73	Z3
Chuor Phnum Krâvanh	*South East Asia*	76	C4
Chur	*Switzerland*	42	E4
Churchill	*Canada*	92	N5
Churchill Lake	*Canada*	92	J5
Churchill River	*Canada*	92	M5
Churchill River	*Canada*	93	U6
Chutes de Livingstone	*Democratic Republic of Congo*	63	G6
Chuuk	*Micronesia*	84	F5
Cicarija	*Croatia*	46	B4
Ciechanów	*Poland*	32	K5
Ciechanowiec	*Poland*	32	M5
Cienfuegos	*Cuba*	105	H4
Ciezq	*Spain*	41	J6
Cihanbeyli Platosu	*Turkey*	49	Q6
Cilo Dagı	*Turkey*	51	K5
Cimarron	*United States*	102	B1
Cimone	*Italy*	44	E4
Cîmpina	*Romania*	47	N4
Cîmpulung	*Romania*	47	N4
Cincar	*Bosnia Hersogovina*	46	E6
Cincinnati	*United States*	98	D3
Circle Egvekenot	*Russia*	100	B2
Cirebon	*Indonesia*	82	D4
Citlaltépetl	*Mexico*	104	E5
Città di Castello	*Italy*	43	H7
Ciudad Acuna	*Mexico*	101	E3
Ciudad Bolívar	*Venezuela*	108	E2
Ciudad Camargo	*Mexico*	101	E3
Ciudad de Mexico (Mexico City)	*Mexico*	104	D5
Ciudad Guayana	*Venezuela*	108	E2
Ciudad Juárez	*Mexico*	104	C2
Ciudad Madero	*Mexico*	104	G4
Ciudad Mante	*Mexico*	101	G4
Ciudad Obregón	*Mexico*	104	C3
Ciudad Real	*Spain*	40	G6
Ciudad Valles	*Mexico*	101	G4
Ciudad Victoria	*Mexico*	104	E4
Ciudadela	*Spain*	41	P5
Clacton-on-Sea	*United Kingdom*	26	E3
Clare	*Ireland*	37	C8
Clarksburg	*United States*	99	D3
Clermont-Ferrand	*France*	39	J8
Cleveland	*United States*	99	D2
Clew Bay	*Ireland*	37	D8
Clinton-Golden Lake	*Canada*	92	K4
Clipperton	*France*	104	C6
Cloppenburg	*Germany*	34	D4
Cloud Peak	*United States*	97	E2
Clovis	*United States*	101	F2
Cluj Napoca	*Romania*	47	L3
Cluses	*France*	39	M7
Clyde	*Canada*	93	T2
Clyde	*United Kingdom*	36	K6
Coalville	*United Kingdom*	26	B2
Coari	*Brazil*	108	E4
Coast Mountains	*Canada*	92	F6
Coast Range	*United States*	96	B2
Coastal Plains	*United States*	103	D3
Coats Island	*Canada*	93	Q4
Coatzacoalcos	*Mexico*	104	F5
Coburg	*Germany*	35	F6
Cochabamba	*Bolivia*	108	D7
Cochem	*Germany*	35	C6
Cochin	*India*	75	C7
Coco Channel	*Andaman Islands*	75	F6
Coco Islands	*Myanmar*	75	F6
Coetivy	*Seychelles*	67	(2)C2
Coiba	*Panama*	108	A2
Coimbatore	*India*	75	C6
Coimbra	*Portugal*	40	B4
Colchester	*United Kingdom*	26	D3
Coll	*United Kingdom*	36	G5
Collier Bay	*Australia*	86	D3
Collines de Normandie	*France*	38	E5
Collines du Perche	*France*	26	D6
Colmar	*France*	42	C2
Cologne (Köln)	*Germany*	35	B6
Colombia	*South America*	108	C3
Colombo	*Sri Lanka*	75	C7
Colón	*Panama*	108	B2
Colonsay	*United Kingdom*	36	G5
Colorado	*United States*	97	E3
Colorado Plateau	*United States*	96	D3
Colorado River	*United States*	97	D3
Colorado Springs	*United States*	97	F3
Columbia	*United States*	103	E3
Columbia Mountains	*Canada*	92	G6
Columbia Plateau	*United States*	96	C2
Columbia River	*United States*	96	B1
Columbus (GA.)	*United States*	103	E3

Columbus (Ohio)	United States	103	D3
Columbus	United States	102	D3
Colville	United States	100	(1)F2
Colville Channel	New Zealand	88	E3
Comacchio	Italy	43	H6
Combermere Bay	Myanmar	76	A3
Como	Italy	42	E5
Comodoro Rivodaavia	Argentina	110	H8
Comoros	Indian Ocean	67	G2
Compiègne	France	26	F5
Comrat	Moldova	47	R3
Conakry	Guinea	62	B3
Concepción	Chile	110	G6
Concepción	Paraguay	109	F8
Conchas Lake	United States	101	F1
Concord	United States	99	F2
Conegliano	Italy	43	H5
Congo	Congo	64	B4
Congo	West Africa	63	H5
Congo	West Africa	63	H4
Connecticut	United States	99	F2
Constanta	Romania	47	R5
Constantina	Spain	40	E7
Constantine	Algeria	59	G1
Contwoyto Lake	Canada	92	J3
Cook Inlet	United States	100	(1)G3
Cook Islands	New Zealand	85	K7
Cook Strait	New Zealand	88	E5
Coos Bay	United States	96	B2
Copenhagen (København)	Denmark	29	F9
Copiapó	Chile	110	G4
Coral Sea	Australia	87	K2
Coral Sea Islands Territory	Micronesia	84	E7
Corby	United Kingdom	26	C2
Corcaigh (Cork)	Ireland	37	E10
Cordillera Cantábrica	Spain	40	D2
Cordillera Central	Colombia	108	B3
Cordillera de la Costa	Venezuela	108	D2
Cordillera de Merida	Venezuela	108	C2
Cordillera Isabella	Nicaragua	105	G6
Cordillera los Andes	South America	108	B5
Cordillera Occidental	Colombia	108	B3
Cordillera Occidental	Chile	110	H2
Cordillera Oriental	Colombia	108	C3
Cordillera Oriental	South America	108	D7
Córdoba	Spain	40	F7
Córdoba	Argentina	110	J5
Corfu (Kérkira)	Greece	48	B5
Coria	Spain	40	D5
Cork (Corcaigh)	Ireland	37	E10
Corlu	Turkey	49	K3
Corno Grande	Italy	44	H6
Cornwallis Island	Canada	92	M2
Coronation Gulf	Canada	92	J3
Corpus Christi	United States	102	B4
Corrientes	Argentina	111	K4
Corsica	Corsica	45	C6
Corsicana	United States	101	G2
Corumbá	Brazil	109	F7
Corvallis	United States	96	B2
Corvo (Azores)	Portugal	58	(1)A2
Cosenza	Italy	45	L9
Cosmoledo Group	Seychelles	67	(2) A2
Cosne-sur-Loire	France	38	H6
Costa Rica	Central America	105	G6
Côte d'Ivoire	West Africa	62	C3
Cotonou	Benin	63	E3
Cotswold Hills	United Kingdom	37	L10
Cottbus	Germany	35	K5
Coulommiers	France	26	G6
Coutances	France	26	B5
Couvin	Belgium	27	H4
Coventry	United Kingdom	37	M9
Covilha	Portugal	40	C4
Cozumel	Mexico	105	G4
Crailsheim	Germany	35	F7
Craiova	Romania	47	L5
Crato	Brazil	109	K5
Cree Lake	Canada	92	K5
Creil	France	26	F5
Crema	Italy	42	E5
Cremona	Italy	42	F5
Crépy-en-Valois	France	26	F5
Cres	Croatia	46	B5
Crete (Kriti)	Greece	48	G9
Creuse	France	39	G7
Cristobal Colón	Panama / Costa Rica	108	C1
Croatia	Europe	46	D4
Croker Island	Australia	86	F2
Cromer	United Kingdom	26	E2
Cross Sound	United States	100	(1)K4
Crotone	Italy	45	M9
Crown Prince Frederik Island	Canada	93	P2
Cserhát	Hungary	46	G2
Cuando	South Africa	66	C3
Cuango	Central Africa	64	B5
Cuanza	Angola	66	B2
Cuanza	Central Africa	64	B5
Cuauhtemoc	Mexico	101	C3
Cuba	Caribbean	105	H4
Cubango	South Africa	66	B3
Cúcuta	Colombia	108	C2
Cuddalore	India	75	D6
Cudskoje ozero / Peipsi järv	Estonia / Russia	29	P7
Cuenca	Spain	41	H4
Cuenca	Ecuador	108	B4
Cuernavaca	Mexico	104	E5
Cui-ling	Taiwan	78	G5
Cuiabá	Brazil	109	F7
Cuidad-Rodrigo	Spain	40	D4
Cuíto	South Africa	66	B3
Culiacán Rosales	Mexico	104	C4
Culion	Philippines	77	F4
Culpepper	Ecuador	108	(1)A1
Cumaná	Venezuela	108	E1
Cumberland Plateau	United States	98	D3
Cumberland Sound	Canada	93	T3
Cumbrian Mountains	United Kingdom	37	K7
Cunene	Angola / Namibia	66	A3
Cuneo	Italy	42	C6
Cüo Dagi	Turkey	52	D2
Curaçao	Central America	105	L6
Curitiba	Brazil	111	M4
Curtis Island	Australia	87	K4
Cusco	Peru	108	C6
Cuttack	India	74	E4
Cuxhaven	Germany	34	D3
Cyclades (Kyklades)	Greece	48	G7
Cypress Hills	Canada	97	D1
Cyprus	Europe	49	Q9
Czech Republic	Europe	33	D8
Czestochówa	Poland	33	J7

D

D'Urville Island	New Zealand	88	D5
Da Hinggan Ling	China	78	F2
Da Nang	Vietnam	76	D3
Da Yunhe	China	78	F3
Daba Shan	China	78	D4
Dabie Shan	China	78	E4
Dachstein	Austria	33	C10
Dagana	Senegal	58	B5
Dagupan	Philippines	77	G3
Dahlak-Archipelago	Eritrea	52	D6
Daio-Zaki	Japan	81	J6
Daito	Japan	79	J5
Dakar	Senegal	58	B6
Dakhlet Nouâdhibou	Mauritania	58	B5
Dakovica	Yugoslavia	48	C2
Dalälven	Sweden	29	J6
Dalian	China	79	G3
Dall Island	United States	100	(1)L4
Dallas	United States	102	B3
Dallol Bosso	Niger	59	F6
Dalma'	United Arab Emirates	55	E4
Daloa	Côte D'Ivoire	62	C3
Dalou	China	76	D1
Dalou Shan	China	78	D5
Daly River	Australia	86	F2
Damascus (Dimashq)	Syria	54	D3
Damqawt	Yemen	52	F6
Danau Poso	Indonesia	83	B3
Danau Toba	Indonesia	82	B2
Danau Towuti	Indonesia	83	B3
Dandong	China	79	G2
Danube (Donau)	Europe	42	E2
Danzig (Gdansk)	Poland	32	H3
Dao Phu Quoc	Vietnam	76	C4
Dar es Salaam	Tanzania	65	F5
Dar Rounga	Central Africa	64	C2
Dar Sila	Chad	64	C1
Dar-el-Beida (Casablanca)	Morocco	58	D2
Darbhanga	India	74	E3
Dardanelles	Turkey	49	J4
Darling River	Australia	87	H6
Darmstadt	Germany	35	D7
Darss	Germany	34	H2
Dartmoor	United Kingdom	38	A3
Darvaza	Turkmenistan	53	G1
Darwin	Australia	86	F2
Daryacheh-ye Bakhtegan	Iran	55	E2
Daryacheh-ye Hamun-e-Hırmand	Iran	53	H3
Daryacheh-ye Maharlu	Iran	55	E2
Daryacheh-ye Orumıyeh	Iran	51	L5
Daryacheh-ye Tashk	Iran	53	F4
Dasht-e-Lut	Iran	55	H1
Datong	China	78	E2
Datu Piang (Dulawan)	Philippines	77	G5
Daugava	Latvia	29	P8
Daugavpils	Latvia	29	P9
Daum	Germany	35	B6
Davangere	India	75	C6
Davao	Philippines	77	H5
Davao Gulf	Philippines	77	H5
Davenport	United States	98	B2
Davis Strait	North America	93	V3
Dawson	Canada	100	(1)K3
Dawson Creek	Canada	92	G5
Dax	France	39	D10
Daxue Shan	China	78	C4
Dayton	United States	98	D3
Daytona Beach	United States	103	E4
Dayyinah	United Arab Emirates	55	E4
De Grey River	Australia	86	C4
Dead Sea	Middle East	52	C3
Dead Sea (Al Bahr al Mayyi)	Jordan	54	C5
Dead Sea (Yam Ha Melah)	Israel	54	C5
Deadhorse	Alaska	100	(1)H1
Death Valley	United States	100	C1
Debica	Poland	33	L7
Debrecen	Hungary	46	J2
Deccan	India	75	C5
Dedegöl Dagı	Turkey	50	D5
Dee	United Kingdom	36	L4
Dee	United Kingdom	37	K8
Deer Lake	Canada	93	V7
Dehra Dun	India	74	C2
Dej	Romania	47	L2
Del Rio	United States	101	F3
Delaware	United States	99	E3
Delaware Bay	United States	99	E3
Delfzijl	Netherlands	27	KI
Delhi	India	74	C3
Delitzsch	Germany	34	H5
Dellys	Algeria	41	P8
Delta del Orinoco	Venezuela	108	E2
Dembi Dolo	Ethiopia	65	E2
Demmin	Germany	34	J3
Democratic Republic of Congo	Central Africa	64	C4
Den Haag	Netherlands	27	G2
Den Helder	Netherlands	27	H2
Denia	Spain	41	L6
Denizli	Turkey	50	C5
Denmark	Europe	29	D9
Denmark Strait	Greenland	93	AA4
Denver	United States	97	F3
Dépression de Mourdi	Chad	60	D4
Der Hümmling	Germany	34	C4
Deravica	Yugoslavia / Albania	46	H7
Derby	United Kingdom	37	M9
Des Moines	United States	98	B2
Des Moines	United States	98	B2
Désappointement	French Polynesia	85	M7
Dese	Ethiopia	61	G5
Desierto de Altar	Mexico	100	D2
Desierto de Mayran	Mexico	101	F3
Desroches	Seychelles	67	(2) B2
Dessau	Germany	34	H5
Detmold	Germany	34	D5
Detroit	United States	98	D2
Détroit d'Honguedo	Canada	93	U7
Détroit de Jacques-Cartier	Canada	93	U6
Deurne	Netherlands	27	J3
Deva	Romania	47	K4
Devil River Peak	New Zealand	88	D5
Devoluy	France	42	A6
Devon Island	Canada	93	P1
Deyyer	Iran	55	E3
Dezful	Iran	52	E3
Dhaka	Bangladesh	74	F4
Dhaulagiri	Nepal	74	D3
Dhiórix Potidhaia	Greece	48	F4
Dhirfis	Greece	48	F6
Dhule	India	74	B4
Ídi Óros	Greece	48	G9
Diamantina River	Australia	87	H4
Diamond Islets	Australia	87	K3
Dian Chi	China	76	C2
Diane Bank	Australia	87	J3
Diapaga	Burkina Faso	59	F6
Dickinson	United States	97	F1
Dicle (Tigris)	Middle East	55	B1
Diekirch	Luxembourg	27	K5
Diepholz	Germany	34	D4
Dieppe	France	38	G4
Digne	France	39	M9
Digoin	France	39	J7
Dijlah (Tigris)	Middle East	52	E3
Dijon	France	38	L6
Dimashq (Damascus)	Syria	54	D3
Dimitrovgrad	Bulgaria	47	N7
Dinagat	Philippines	77	H4
Dinara	Bosnia-Herzegovina / Croatia	46	D5
Dindigul	India	75	C6
Dingle Bay	Ireland	37	C9
Dipolog	Philippines	77	G5
Dire Dawa	Ethiopa	61	H6
Dirk Hartog Island	Australia	86	B5
Disko	Greenland	93	V2
District of Columbia (D.C.)	United States	99	E3
Dixon Entrance	United States	100	(1)L5
Diyarbakır	Turkey	51	J5
Djanet	Algeria	60	A3
Djebel Aïssa	Algeria	59	E2
Djebel Bou Maad	Algeria	41	N8
Djelfa	Algeria	59	F2
Djibo	Burkina Faso	58	E6
Djibouti	North East Africa	61	H5
Djibouti	Djibouti	61	H5
Dnepr	Ukraine	30	G5
Dnepropetrovsk	Ukraine	30	H5
Dnezhskaya Guba	Russia	30	H2
Dobbacio	Italy	43	H4
Doboj	Bosnia Hersogovina	44	N4
Dobreta Turnu Severin	Romania	47	K5
Dobrich	Bulgaria	47	Q6
Dobrich	Bulgaria	50	B2
Dobrudzansko Plato	Bulgaria	47	Q6
Dodecanes (Dodekanissa)	Greece	48	J7
Dodekanissa (Dodecanes)	Greece	48	J7
Dodge City	United States	97	G3
Dodoma	Tanzania	65	F5
Doetinchem	Netherlands	27	K3
Dogen Co	China	74	F2
Dogo	Japan	80	G5
Dogu Karadeniz Daglari	Turkey	52	C1
Doha (Ad Dawhah)	Qatar	52	F4
Doi Inthanon	Thailand	76	B3
Dolak	Indonesia	84	D6
Dôle	France	38	L6
Dollart	Germany / Netherlands	27	L1
Dominica	Caribbean	105	M5
Dominican Republic	Caribbean	105	K5
Don	United Kingdom	36	L4

Name	Location	Page	Grid
Don	Russia	30	H4
Don Benito	Spain	40	E6
Donau (Danube)	Europe	42	E2
Donauwörth	Germany	35	F8
Donegal Bay	Ireland	37	E7
Donegal Mountains	Ireland	37	E7
Donetsk	Ukraine	30	H5
Dong Hai / Higashi-Shina-Kai (East China Sea)	South East Asia	79	H5
Dongnan Qiuling	China	78	E6
Dongola	Sudan	61	F4
Dongting Hu	China	78	E5
Dønna	Norway	28	F3
Dordrecht	Netherlands	27	H3
Dori	Burkina Faso	58	E6
Dornbirn	Austria	42	E3
Dornoch Firth	United Kingdom	36	K4
Dorotea	Sweden	28	J4
Dortmund	Germany	34	C5
Dortmund-Ems-Kanal	Germany	34	C4
Dothan	United States	103	D3
Douala	Cameroon	63	G4
Doubs	France	38	M6
Douglas	United Kingdom	37	J7
Douglas	United States	101	E2
Doullens	France	26	F4
Douro	Spain	40	G3
Dover	United Kingdom	37	Q10
Dover	United States	99	E3
Dovrefjell Snøhetta	Norway	29	D5
Dragan	Sweden	28	H4
Draguignan	France	42	B7
Drake Passage	South America	110	G10
Drakensberg	South Africa / Lesotho	66	D6
Dráma	Greece	47	M8
Drammen	Norway	29	F7
Drau	Europe	46	C3
Dráva	Europe	44	L2
Dresden	Germany	35	J5
Dreux	France	26	E6
Drift Prairies	United States	97	G1
Drina	Europe	46	G5
Drogobia	Albania	46	H7
Drummondville	Canada	99	F1
Drvar	Bosnia Hersogovina	46	D5
Drweca	Poland	32	J4
Duarte	Dominican Republic	105	K5
Dubai (Dubayy)	United Arab Emirates	55	F4
Dubawnt Lake	Canada	92	L4
Dubayy (Dubai)	United Arab Emirates	55	F4
Dublin (Baile Átha Cliath)	Ireland	37	H8
Dubrovnik	Croatia	46	F7
Dubuque	United States	98	B2
Duc de Gloucester	French Polynesia	85	M7
Ducie	Pitcairn Islands	85	P8
Duero	Spain	40	G3
Dugi	Croatia	46	B5
Dugi Otok	Croatia	44	J5
Duifken Point	Australia	87	H2
Duisburg	Germany	35	B5
Duitse Bocht	North Sea	34	C2
Dukou	China	78	C5
Dulawan (Datu Piang)	Philippines	77	G5
Dülmen	Germany	34	C5
Duluth	United States	98	B1
Dümmersee	Germany	27	M2
Dumont d´Urville Sea	Antarctica	112	(2)U3
Duna	Europe	46	F3
Dunai	France	26	G4
Dunaj (Danube)	Europe	33	G10
Dunaújuáros	Hungary	33	H11
Dunav	Europe	30	F6
Duncan Passage	Andaman Islands	75	F6
Duncansby Head	United Kingdom	36	L3
Dundalk Bay	Ireland	37	G8
Dundee	United Kingdom	36	L5
Dunedin	New Zealand	89	D7
Dunes de Dokhara	Algeria	59	G2
Dungeness	United Kingdom	37	P11
Dungu	Democratic Republic of Congo	64	D3
Dunkerque	France	26	F3
Dunkery Beacon	United Kingdom	37	K10
Dunnet Head	United Kingdom	37	K3
Dunstan Mountains	New Zealand	89	C7
Duqm	Oman	53	G6
Durack Ranges	Australia	86	E3
Durance	France	39	M9
Durango	United States	97	E3
Durban	South Africa	67	E5
Düren	Germany	35	B6
Durgapur	India	74	E4
Durham	United States	99	E3
Durmitor	Yugoslavia	46	G6
Durrës	Albania	48	B3
Durresi	Albania	46	G8
Dushanbe	Tajikistan	53	J2
Düsseldorf	Germany	35	B5
Düzce	Turkey	49	P4
Dvinskaya Guba	Russia	30	H1
Dytiki Rodópi	Greece	48	G3
Dzhambul	Kazakhstan	71	N9
Dzhetygara	Kazakhstan	31	N4
Dzhezkazgan	Kazakhstan	71	M8
Dzhizak	Uzbekistan	53	J1
Dzhusaly	Kazakhstan	31	N6

E

Name	Location	Page	Grid
Earn	United Kingdom	36	K5
East Cape	New Zealand	88	G3
East China Sea (Dong Hai / Higashi-Shina-Kai)	South East Asia	79	H5
East Falkland	South Atlantic Ocean	111	K9
East London	South Africa	66	D6
East Siberian Sea (Vostocno-Sibirskoye More)	Russia	73	T2
Eastbourne	United Kingdom	26	D4
Easter Island	Chile	85	Q8
Eastern Desert (As Sahra´ ash Sharqiyah)	Egypt	61	F3
Eastern Ghats	India	75	D5
Eau Claire	United States	98	B2
Eber Gölü	Turkey	49	P6
Eberswalde	Germany	34	J4
Ebro	Spain	41	K3
Ech Cheliff	Algeria	41	M8
Echo Bay	Canada	92	H3
Écija	Spain	40	E7
Ecuador	South America	108	B4
Eday	United Kingdom	36	L2
Ede	Netherlands	27	J2
Edgar Ranges	Australia	86	D3
Edgell Island	Canada	93	U4
Edinburgh	United Kingdom	36	K6
Edirne	Turkey	48	J3
Edmonton	Canada	92	H6
Edmundston	Canada	99	G1
Edremit	Turkey	49	K5
Edremit Körfezi	Turkey	49	J5
Edwards Plateau	United States	101	G2
Efaté	Vanuatu	84	G7
Effingham	United States	98	C3
Eger	Hungary	46	H2
Egersund	Norway	29	C7
Egridir Gölü	Turkey	50	D4
Egypt	North Africa	60	E3
Eibar	Spain	41	H1
Eifel	Germany	35	B6
Eigg	United Kingdom	36	G5
Eight Degree Channel	Arabian Sea	75	B7
Einbeck	Germany	34	E5
Eindhoven	Netherlands	27	J3
Eirunepé	Brazil	108	D5
Eisenach	Germany	35	F6
Eisenhüttenstadt	Germany	34	K4
Eisleben	Germany	34	G5
El ´Acaba	Mauritania	62	B1
El Bahr el Azraq (Blue Nile)	Africa	61	F5
El Djouf	Mauritania / Mali	58	D4
El Dorado	United States	101	C2
El Eglab	Algeria	58	D3
El Faiyûm	Egypt	61	E2
El Fasher	Sudan	60	E5
El Ferrol	Spain	40	B1
El Geneira	Sudan	60	D5
El Geziza	Sudan	61	F5
El Gîza (Giza)	Egypt	61	E1
El Goléa	Algeria	59	F2
El Iskandarîyah (Alexandria)	Egypt	61	E1
El Kef	Tunisia	45	C12
El Khârga	Egypt	61	F2
El Khartum Bahri	Sudan	61	F4
El Khartum (Khartoum)	Sudan	61	F4
El Mahallah El Kubrá	Egypt	52	B3
El Milk	Sudan	61	E4
El Minyâ	Egypt	61	E2
El Mreyyé	Mauritania / Mali	58	D5
El Navado	Argentina	110	H6
El Obeid	Sudan	61	F5
El Oued	Algeria	59	G2
El Paso	United States	101	E2
El Qâhira (Cairo)	Egypt	61	F2
El Salvador	Central America	104	F6
El Suweis	Egypt	52	B3
El Wâhât el Khârga	Egypt	61	F2
Elat	Israel	54	B7
Elâzig	Turkey	51	H4
Elba	Italy	44	E6
Elbasan	Albania	48	C3
Elbe	Germany / Czech Republic	35	J5
Elbe (Labe)	Germany / Czech Republic	35	K6
Elbeuf	France	26	E5
Elblag	Poland	30	D4
Elburz	Iran	52	E2
Elche	Spain	41	K6
Elda	Spain	41	K6
Eleuthera	Bahamas	103	F4
Elgon	Uganda / Kenya	65	E3
Elista	Russia	30	J5
Elk	Poland	32	M4
Ellesmere Island	Canada	11	(1)CC1
Ellice Inseln	Micronesia	84	H6
Elmira	United States	99	E2
Elsen Nur	China	74	F1
Elsenerz	Austria	33	D9
Eltanin Bay	Antarctica	112	(2)JJ2
Eluru	India	75	D5
Ely	United Kingdom	26	D2
Ely	United States	96	D3
Emån	Sweden	29	J8
Emba	Kazakhstan	71	K8
Embalse de Alcántara	Spain	40	D5
Embalse de Almendra	Spain	40	D3
Embalse de Cijara	Spain	40	F5
Embalse de Guri	Venezuela	108	E2
Embalse de Mequinenza	Spain	41	K3
Embalse de Ricabayo	Spain	40	E3
Embalse de Valdecañas	Spain	40	E5
Embalse de Yesa	Spain	41	J2
Embalse del Ebro	Spain	40	G1
Embalse del Río Negro	Uruguay	111	K5
Embalse del Zújar	Spain	40	E6
Emden	Germany	34	C3
Emissi	Chad	60	C4
Emmen	Netherlands	27	K2
Empoli	Italy	42	G7
Emporia	United States	98	A3
Ems	Germany	34	C4
Encantada	Mexico	94	C5
Encarnación	Paraguay	111	K4
Enentokiö	Finland	28	M2
Enewetak	Marshall Islands	84	G4
Enez Körfezi	Greece	48	H4
Engels´	Russia	30	K4
England	United Kingdom	37	L9
English Channel / La Manche	United Kingdom	37	L11
Enid	United States	97	G3
Ennadal	Canada	92	L4
Ennedi	Chad	60	D4
Enos	Greece	48	C6
Enschede	Netherlands	27	K2
Ensenada	Mexico	94	C5
Enugu	Nigeria	63	F3
Épernay	France	27	G5
Épinal	France	38	M5
Epupa Falls	Angola / Namibia	66	A3
Equatorial Guinea	West Africa	63	F4
Er Rachidia	Morocco	58	E2
Erbeskopf	Germany	35	C7
Erciyas Dagı	Turkey	50	F4
Erd	Hungary	46	F2
Erdek Körfezi	Turkey	50	B3
Erdi	Chad	60	D4
Erdi Ma	Chad	60	D4
Erechim	Brazil	111	L3
Erenhot	China	72	L6
Erfurt	Germany	35	G6
Erg Chech	Mali / Algeria	58	E4
Erg du Djourab	Chad	63	H1
Erg du Ténéré	Niger	59	H5
Erg Iguidi	Mauritania / Alger a	58	D3
Ergene	Turkey	48	J3
Ergun He	China	72	L6
Ergun Zuoqi	China	72	L6
Erie	United States	93	Q8
Erimanthos	Greece	48	D7
Erimo-Misaki	Japan	81	M3
Eritrea	Africa	61	G4
Erlangen	Germany	35	G7
Ermeraldas	Ecuador	108	B3
Erode	India	75	C6
Erzgebirge	Germany	35	J6
Erzurum	Turkey	51	J4
Es Semara	Western Sahara	58	C3
Esbjerg	Denmark	29	E9
Escaut	France	26	G4
Esch-sur-Alzett	Luxembourg	27	J5
Esfahan (Isfahan)	Iran	52	F3
Eshwege	Germany	35	F5
Eskilstuna	Sweden	29	J7
Eskimo Lake	Canada	92	E3
Eskisehir	Turkey	50	C4
Esler Dagı	Turkey	49	M7
Española	Ecuador	108	(1)B2
Esperance Bay	Australia	86	D6
Espíritu Santo	Vanuatu	84	G7
Espoo / Esbo	Finland	29	M6
Esquel	Argentina	110	G7
Essen	Germany	35	C5
Estonia	Europe	29	N7
Estrecho de Magallanes	South America	110	G9
Esztergom	Hungary	33	H10
Étaples	France	26	E4
Eternity Range	Antarctica	112	(2)LL3
Ethiopia	Central Africa	65	F2
Etna	Sicily	45	J11
Etolin Island	Canada	92	E6
Etosha Pan	Namibia	66	B3
Eugene	United States	96	B2
Euphrates (Al Furat)	Middle East	52	C2
Eureka	United States	96	B2
Euskirchen	Germany	35	B6
Evans Strait	Canada	93	Q4
Evansville	United States	98	C3
Evaz	Iran	55	F3
Évora	Portugal	40	C6
Évreux	France	26	E5
Évros	Greece / Turkey	50	B3
Evvoïkos Kólpos	Greece	48	F6
Exe	United Kingdom	37	K11
Exeter	United Kingdom	37	K11
Exmoor	United Kingdom	38	B2
Expedition Range	Australia	87	J5

F

Name	Location	Page	Grid
Faber Lake	Canada	92	H4
Fabriano	Italy	44	G5
Fadippolu Atoll	Maldives	75	B7
Faeroes	Denmark	24	D1
Fafen Shet'	Ethiopia	61	H6
Fagaras	Romania	47	M4
Faial (Azores)	Portugal	58	(1)B2

G

Ginzo de Limra	*Spain*	40	C2
Gironde	*France*	39	E8
Gisborne	*New Zealand*	88	G4
Gisors	*France*	26	E5
Giurgiu	*Romania*	47	N6
Giza (El Gîza)	*Egypt*	61	E1
Gizhiga	*Russia*	73	U4
Gizhiginskaya Guba	*Russia*	73	T4
Gji i Durrësit	*Albania*	48	B3
Gji i Lalzës	*Albania*	48	B3
Gjøvik	*Norway*	29	F6
Glåma	*Norway*	29	F6
Glamoc	*Bosnia Hersogovina*	46	D5
Glarner Alpen	*Switzerland*	44	C2
Glasgow	*United Kingdom*	36	J6
Glazov	*Russia*	31	L3
Glendive	*United States*	97	F1
Glittertind	*Norway*	29	E6
Gliwice	*Poland*	33	H7
Glogów	*Poland*	32	F6
Glommersträst	*Sweden*	28	K4
Glorieuses (Réunion)	*South Africa*	67	H2
Gloucester	*United Kingdom*	38	C2
Gmunden	*Austria*	43	J3
Gniezno	*Poland*	32	G3
Goba	*Ethiopia*	65	G2
Gobi Desert	*China / Mongolia*	78	D2
Goch	*Germany*	34	B5
Godavari	*India*	74	C5
Godelbukta Breidvika	*Antarctica*	112	(2)H3
Godhaun	*Greenland*	93	W3
Godthåb	*Greenland*	93	W4
Goelette	*Seychelles*	67	(2) B3
Goes	*Netherlands*	27	G3
Gogebic Range	*United States*	98	B1
Goiânia	*Brazil*	109	H7
Gökırmak	*Turkey*	50	E3
Gök Tepe	*Turkey*	49	M8
Gökçeada	*Turkey*	48	H4
Gökora Körfezi	*Turkey*	49	K8
Golan Heights	*Israel*	54	C3
Gold Coast	*Australia*	87	K5
Goldap	*Poland*	32	M3
Golden Bay	*New Zealand*	88	D5
Golden Gate	*United States*	96	B3
Golfe d'Arzew	*Algeria*	41	K9
Golfe de Gascogne	*France*	38	C10
Golfe de Saint-Malo	*France*	38	C5
Golfe de Valinco	*Corsica*	44	C7
Golfe di Sagone	*Corsica*	44	C6
Golfe du Lion	*France / Spain*	39	K10
Golfo de Alicante	*Spain*	41	L6
Golfo de Almería	*Spain*	41	H8
Golfo de Arica	*South America*	110	G2
Golfo de Batabanó	*Cuba*	105	H4
Golfo de Cádiz	*Spain / Portugal*	40	C8
Golfo de Fonseca	*El Salvador*	104	G6
Golfo de Guayaquil	*Ecuador*	108	A4
Golfo de Honduras	*Honduras*	105	G5
Golfo de los Mosquitos	*Central America*	105	H6
Golfo de Mazarrón	*Spain*	41	J7
Golfo de Panamá	*Panama*	105	J7
Golfo de Rosas	*Spain*	41	P2
Golfo de San Jorge	*Spain*	41	L4
Golfo de San Jorge	*Argentina*	110	H8
Golfo de Tehuantepec	*Mexico*	104	F5
Golfo de Valencia	*Spain*	41	L5
Golfo de Venezuela	*Venezuela*	108	C1
Golfo del Darién	*Central America*	108	B2
Golfo dell' Asinara	*Sardinia (Italy)*	45	C7
Golfo di Cagliari	*Sardinia (Italy)*	45	D9
Golfo di Castellammare	*Sicily (Italy)*	45	G10
Golfo di Catánia	*Sicily (Italy)*	45	K11
Golfo di Gaeta	*Italy*	45	H7
Golfo di Genova	*Italy*	42	D6
Golfo di Manfredonia	*Italy*	45	L7
Golfo di Napoli	*Italy*	45	H8
Golfo di Oristano	*Sardinia (Italy)*	45	C9
Golfo di Orosei	*Sardinia (Italy)*	45	D8
Golfo di Policastro	*Italy*	45	K9
Golfo di Salerno	*Italy*	45	J8
Golfo di Sant' Eufemia	*Italy*	45	K10
Golfo di Squillace	*Italy*	45	L10
Golfo di Taranto	*Italy*	45	L8
Golfo di Trieste	*Italy*	43	J5
Golfo di Venezia	*Italy*	44	G3
Golfo San Matias	*Argentina*	110	J7
Gomel'	*Belarus*	30	G4
Gomera (Canary Islands)	*Spain*	58	B3
Gonder	*Ethiopia*	61	G5
Gongga Shan	*China*	78	C5
Gongola	*Central Africa*	60	B5
Goodland	*United States*	94	F4
Goose Lake	*United States*	96	B2
Göppingen	*Germany*	35	E8
Gor'kovskoye Vdkhr.	*Russia*	30	J3
Gora Belukha	*Russia*	71	R8
Gora Burun-Sabartuj	*Russia*	72	H7
Gora Denezkin Kamen	*Russia*	31	M2
Gora Dykh Tau	*Russia / Georgia*	51	K2
Gora El'brus	*Russia / Georgia*	51	J2
Gora Golets-Skalistyy	*Russia*	72	K5
Gora Jamantau	*Russia*	31	M4
Gora Munku Sardyk	*Russia*	72	G6
Gora Narodnaya	*Russia*	31	N1
Gora Payyer	*Russia*	31	N1
Gora Telpoziz	*Russia*	31	M2
Gorakhpur	*India*	74	D3
Gorgona	*Italy*	44	D5
Gorgona	*Colombia*	108	B3
Gorinchem	*Netherlands*	27	H3
Gorizia	*Italy*	43	J5
Gorjanci	*Slovakia/ Croatia*	46	C4
Gorki	*Russia*	31	P1
Görlitz	*Germany*	35	K5
Gorlovka	*Ukraine*	30	H5
Gorna Oryahovitsa	*Bulgaria*	47	N6
Gorontalo	*Indonesia*	83	B2
Gory Byrranga	*Russia*	70	S3
Gory Putorana	*Russia*	70	S4
Góry Swietokrzyskie	*Poland*	33	K6
Gorzów Wielkopolski	*Poland*	32	E5
Goslar	*Germany*	34	F5
Göta älv	*Sweden*	29	F8
Gotel Mountains	*Nigeria*	63	G3
Gotha	*Germany*	35	F6
Gotland	*Sweden*	29	K8
Gotowasi	*Indonesia*	83	C2
Gotska Sandön	*Sweden*	29	K7
Göttingen	*Germany*	34	F5
Gotto-Retto	*Japan*	80	E7
Gouda	*Netherlands*	27	H2
Gough Is.	*Atlantic Ocean*	57	B10
Gourma	*Mali*	62	D1
Gov'altain Nuruu	*Mongolia*	78	C2
Governador Valadares	*Brazil*	109	J7
Gozo	*Malta*	45	J12
Gracac	*Croatia*	46	C5
Graciosa (Azores)	*Portugal*	58	(1)B2
Graham Island	*Canada*	100	(1)L5
Grampian Mountains	*United Kingdom*	36	J5
Gran Canaria (Canary Islands)	*Spain*	58	B3
Gran Chaco	*Argentina / Paraguay*	110	J3
Gran Paradiso	*Italy*	42	C5
Gran Pilastro	*Austria / Italy*	43	G4
Granada	*Spain*	40	G7
Grand Bahama	*Bahamas*	105	J3
Grand Ballon d'Alsace	*France*	35	C9
Grand Canyon	*United States*	100	D1
Grand Erg de Bilma	*Niger*	60	B4
Grand Erg Occidental	*Algeria*	59	E3
Grand Erg Oriental	*Algeria*	59	F3
Grand Forks	*United States*	98	A1
Grand Junction	*United States*	97	E3
Grand Rapids	*United States*	98	C2
Grand Teton	*United States*	92	J8
Grande Casse	*France*	42	B5
Grande Comore (Njazidja)	*Comoros*	67	G2
Grândola	*Portugal*	40	B6
Granite Peak	*United States*	96	C2
Grantham	*United Kingdom*	26	C2
Granville	*France*	38	D5
Grasse	*France*	42	B7
Grassrange	*United States*	97	E1
Grays	*United Kingdom*	26	D3
Graz	*Austria*	43	L3
Great Abaco	*Bahamas*	105	J3
Great Australian Bight	*Australia*	86	E6
Great Barrier Island	*New Zealand*	88	E3
Great Barrier Reef	*Australia*	87	J3
Great Basin	*United States*	100	C1
Great Bear Lake	*Canada*	92	G3
Great Dividing Range	*Australia*	87	H3
Great Exhibition Bay	*New Zealand*	88	D2
Great Exuma	*Bahamas*	105	J4
Great Falls	*United States*	96	D1
Great Inagua	*Caribbean*	105	K4
Great Karoo	*South Africa*	66	C6
Great Nicobar	*India*	75	F7
Great Plains	*United States*	97	F1
Great Prairies	*United States*	101	F1
Great Salt Lake	*United States*	96	D2
Great Salt Lake Desert	*United States*	96	D6
Great Sandy Desert	*Australia*	86	D4
Great Sandy Desert	*United States*	96	B2
Great Slave Lake	*Canada*	92	H4
Great Victoria Desert	*Australia*	86	D5
Great Yarmouth	*United Kingdom*	26	E2
Greater Antilles	*Caribbean*	105	J4
Greater Sunda Islands	*Indonesia*	82	D4
Greece	*Europe*	48	D5
Greeley	*United States*	97	F2
Green Bay	*United States*	98	C2
Greenland (Denmark)	*North Atlantic Ocean*	93	X3
Greenland Sea	*Iceland*	28	B1
Greensboro	*United States*	103	F2
Greenville (Miss.)	*United States*	102	C3
Greenville (N.C.)	*United States*	103	F2
Gregory Lake	*Australia*	86	E4
Greifswalder Bodden	*Germany*	34	J2
Gremikha	*Russia*	30	H1
Grenada	*Caribbean*	105	M6
Grenen	*Denmark*	29	F8
Grenoble	*France*	39	L8
Greven	*Germany*	34	C4
Grey Islands	*Canada*	93	V6
Grey Range	*Australia*	87	H5
Greymouth	*New Zealand*	89	D6
Griefswald	*Germany*	34	J2
Grimsby	*United Kingdom*	37	N8
Grímsey	*Iceland*	28	(1)E1
Griz	*Germany*	35	G6
Grmec	*Bosnia-Herzegovina*	46	D5
Grodno	*Belarus*	29	N10
Groningen	*Netherlands*	27	K1
Groot Karas Berg	*Namibia*	66	B5
Groote Eylandt	*Australia*	87	G2
Großer Arber	*Germany*	35	J7
Großer Beerberg	*Germany*	35	F6
Großglockner	*Austria*	43	H3
Grosseto	*Italy*	44	F6
Großvenediger	*Austria*	44	G1
Grotli	*Norway*	29	D6
Groupe Acteón	*French Polynesia*	85	N8
Groznyy (Grosny)	*Russia*	51	L2
Grudziadz	*Poland*	32	H4
Guadalajara	*Spain*	40	G4
Guadalajara	*Mexico*	104	D4
Guadalcanal	*Solomon Islands*	84	F7
Guadalimar	*Spain*	40	G6
Guadalquivir	*Spain*	40	E7
Guadalupe	*Mexico*	101	E3
Guadeloupe	*Caribbean*	105	M5
Guadelupe	*Spain*	40	E5
Guadiana	*Spain / Portugal*	40	C7
Guadix	*Spain*	40	G7
Guajará Mirim	*Brazil*	108	D6
Guam	*United States (Pacific Ocean)*	84	E4
Guangmao Shan	*China*	76	C1
Guangzhou	*China*	78	E6
Guantamo Bay	*United States (Caribbean)*	105	K5
Guarda	*Portugal*	40	C4
Guardo	*Spain*	40	F2
Guatemala	*Central America*	104	F5
Guatemala City	*Guatemala*	104	F6
Guayaquil	*Ecuador*	108	A4
Guayma	*Mexico*	100	C3
Guba Buorkhaya	*Russia*	72	M2
Guba Gusinaya	*Russia*	73	S2
Gubakha	*Russia*	31	M3
Guban	*Somalia*	65	G1
Guben	*Germany*	34	K5
Águeda	*Spanje / Portugal*	40	D4
Guelmine	*Morocco*	58	C3
Guéret	*France*	39	G7
Guernsey	*United Kingdom*	37	L12
Gueru	*Zimbabwe*	66	D3
Guge	*Ethiopia*	65	F2
Guiana Highlands	*South America*	108	E3
Guildford	*United Kingdom*	26	C3
Guilin	*China*	78	E5
Guinea	*West Africa*	62	B2
Guinea-Bissau	*West Africa*	62	A2
Guise	*France*	27	G5
Guiyang	*China*	78	D5
Gujranwala	*Pakistan*	53	K3
Gujrat	*Pakistan*	74	B2
Gulbarga	*India*	75	C5
Gulbere	*Latvia*	29	P8
Gulf of Aden	*Middle East*	61	J5
Gulf of Alaska	*North Pacific Ocean*	92	D5
Gulf of Aqaba	*Saudi Arabia / Egypt*	61	F2
Gulf of Boothia	*Canada*	92	N2
Gulf of Bothnia	*Sweden / Finland*	28	K6
Gulf of California	*Mexico*	104	B3
Gulf of Carpentaria	*Australia*	87	G2
Gulf of Finland	*Finland / Estonia / Russia*	29	N7
Gulf of Gdansk	*Poland*	32	J3
Gulf of Guinea	*Atlantic Ocean*	63	E4
Gulf of Kachchh	*India*	74	A4
Gulf of Khambhat	*India*	74	B4
Gulf of Maine	*United States*	93	T8
Gulf of Mannar	*India / Sri Lanka*	75	C7
Gulf of Martaban	*South East Asia*	76	B3
Gulf of Mexico	*Central America*	104	F3
Gulf of Oman	*Middle East*	53	G4
Gulf of Riga	*Lithuania*	29	M8
Gulf of Sirte (Khalij Surt)	*Tunisia*	60	C1
Gulf of St. Lawrence	*Canada*	93	U7
Gulf of Suez	*Egypt*	52	B4
Gulf of Thailand	*South East Asia*	76	C4
Gulf of Tongking	*South East Asia*	76	D2
Gulf St. Vincent	*Australia*	87	G7
Gulfport	*United States*	102	D3
Gull Bay	*Canada*	98	C1
Gulu	*Uganda*	64	E3
Gummersbach	*Germany*	35	C5
Guna Terara	*Ethiopia*	61	G5
Güney Dogu Toroslar	*Turkey*	50	G4
Gunnbjørns Fjeld	*Greenland*	112	(1)U3
Gunong Kinabalu	*Malaysia*	82	F1
Guntur	*India*	75	C5
Gunung Dempo	*Indonesia*	82	C3
Gunung Kau Paulatmada	*Indonesia*	83	C3
Gunung Kerinci	*Indonesia*	82	C3
Gunung Kinabalu	*Malaysia*	83	A1
Gunung Kobipato	*Indonesia*	83	C3
Gunung Kwoka	*Indonesia*	83	D3
Gunung Leuser	*Indonesia*	82	B2
Gunung Mahameru	*Indonesia*	82	E4
Gunung Peuetsagoe	*Indonesia*	76	B6
Gunung Peuetsagu	*Indonesia*	82	B2
Gunung Rinjani	*Indonesia*	82	F4
Gunung Slamet	*Indonesia*	82	D4
Gunung Tambora	*Indonesia*	82	F4
Gunung Waukara	*Indonesia*	82	F3
Gunzenhausen	*Germany*	35	F7
Gurktaler Alpen	*Austria*	43	J4
Gurskøy	*Norway*	29	C5
Gurupi	*Brazil*	109	H6
Gusau	*Nigeria*	63	F2
Güstrow	*Germany*	34	H3
Gütersloh	*Germany*	34	D5
Guwahati	*India*	74	F3
Guyana	*South America*	109	F2
Güzelyurt Körfezi	*Cyprus*	49	Q9
Gwalior	*India*	74	C3

Iijoki	*Finland*	28	P4
IJssel-meer	*Netherlands*	27	J2
Ikaria	*Greece*	48	H7
Ikeja	*Nigeria*	63	E3
Île d'Anticosti	*Canada*	93	U7
Île d'Oléron	*France*	39	D8
Île d'Yeu	*France*	39	C7
Île de la Madeleine	*Canada*	93	U7
Île de Noirmoutier	*France*	39	C7
Île de Ré	*France*	39	D7
Île Europa (Réunion)	*South Africa*	67	G4
Îles Crozet	*South Atlantic Ocean*	112	(2)L5
Îles d'Hyères	*France*	39	M11
Îles Kerguelen	*South Atlantic Ocean*	112	(2)M4
Ile Tidra	*Mauritania*	58	B5
Iles Palliser	*French Polynesia*	85	M7
Iles Sous le Vent	*French Polynesia*	85	L7
Ilgaz Daglari	*Turkey*	50	E3
Ilha de Marajó	*Brazil*	109	H4
Ilhas Berlengas	*Portugal*	40	A5
Ilhas Farilhões	*Portugal*	40	A5
Ilhas Selvagens (Madeira)	*Portugal*	58	B2
Ilhéus	*Brazil*	109	K6
Iliamna Lake	*United States*	100	(1)F3
Illinois	*United States*	98	C2
Illinois River	*United States*	98	C2
Illizi	*Algeria*	60	A2
Iloilo	*Philippines*	77	G4
Ilorin	*Nigeria*	63	E3
Imatra	*Finland*	29	Q6
Imola	*Italy*	43	G6
Imperatriz	*Brazil*	109	H5
Imperia	*Italy*	42	D7
Impfondo	*Congo*	63	H4
Imphal	*India*	74	F4
In Salah	*Algeria*	59	F3
Inapari	*Peru*	108	D6
Inarijärvi	*Finland*	28	P2
Ince Burun	*Turkey*	49	K4
Incekum Burun	*Turkey*	50	E5
Inch'on	*South Korea*	80	D5
Indawgyi	*Myanmar*	74	G3
Inderborskiy	*Kazakhstan*	31	L5
India	*Southern Asia*	74	C4
Indian Ocean	*Indian Ocean*	68	J9
Indiana	*United States*	98	C2
Indianapolis	*United States*	98	C3
Indigirka	*Russia*	73	R3
Indonesia	*Asia*	82	C3
Indore	*India*	74	C4
Indus	*Southern Asia*	53	J4
Ingolstadt	*Germany*	35	G8
Inguri	*Georgia*	51	K2
Inhambane	*Mozambique*	67	F5
Inland Kaikoura Range	*New Zealand*	89	E6
Inn	*Europe*	42	F3
Inner Hebrides	*United Kingdom*	36	G5
Inner Sound	*United Kingdom*	36	H4
Innsbruck	*Austria*	42	G3
Inowroclaw	*Poland*	32	H4
Inta	*Russia*	31	N1
Inukjuak	*Canada*	93	Q5
Inuvik	*Canada*	100	L2
Invercargill	*New Zealand*	89	C8
Investigator Group	*Australia*	86	F6
Investigator Strait	*Australia*	87	G7
Ioánnina	*Greece*	48	C5
Ionian Islands (Ionioi Nisoi)	*Greece*	48	B5
Ionian Sea (Iónion Pélagos)	*Europe*	48	B7
Ionioi Nisoi (Ionian Islands)	*Greece*	48	B5
Iónion Pélagos (Ionian Sea)	*Europe*	48	B7
Ios	*Greece*	48	H8
Iowa	*United States*	98	B2
Ipoh	*Malaysia*	82	C2
Ipoly	*Europe*	46	G1
Ipswich	*United Kingdom*	37	Q9
Iqualuit	*Canada*	93	T4
Iquique	*Chile*	110	G3
Iquitos	*Peru*	108	C4
Iráklion	*Greece*	48	H9
Iran	*Middle East*	53	F3
Iraq	*Middle East*	52	D3
Irayel'	*Russia*	31	M2
Irbid	*Jordan*	54	C4
Ireland	*Europe*	37	D8
Irgiz	*Kazakhstan*	31	N5
Irhil M'Goun	*Morocco*	58	D2
Irian Jaya	*Indonesia*	83	E3
Irineos Enä	*France*	39	F11
Iringa	*Tanzania*	65	F5
Iriomote-Shima	*Japan*	79	G6
Irish Sea	*United Kingdom*	37	H8
Irkutsk	*Russia*	72	G6
'Irq Jaham	*Saudi Arabia*	55	B3
Irrawaddy	*South East Asia*	76	A2
Irtysh	*Russia*	71	N7
Isabela	*Ecuador*	108	(1)A2
Isafjordur	*Iceland*	28	B1
Isar	*Germany*	33	B9
Ischia	*Italy*	45	H8
Ise	*Japan*	81	J6
Ise-Wan	*Japan*	81	J6
Isère	*France*	42	A5
Isfahan (Esfahan)	*Iran*	52	F3
Isfendiyar Daglari	*Turkey*	50	E3
Ishigaki-Shima	*Japan*	79	G6
Ishikari-Wan	*Japan*	81	L2
Ishim	*Russia*	31	P3
Ishinomaki	*Japan*	81	L4

Isikli Gölü	*Turkey*	49	N6
Isil'kul	*Russia*	31	Q4
iskenderun	*Turkey*	50	G5
Iskenderun Körfezi	*Turkey*	50	F5
Iskur	*Bulgaria*	47	M6
Isla Cabrera	*Spain*	41	N5
Isla Caviana	*Brazil*	109	H3
Isla Conejera	*Spain*	41	P5
Isla de Alborán	*Spain*	40	G8
Isla de Chiloé	*Chile*	110	F7
Isla de los Estados	*Argentina*	110	J9
Isla del Coco	*Costa Rica*	105	G7
Isla Dragonera	*Spain*	41	M5
Isla Espalmador	*Spain*	41	M6
Isla Grande de Tierra del Fuego	*Chile / Argentina*	110	H9
Isla Mexiana	*Brazil*	109	H3
Isla San Ambrosio	*Chile*	110	F4
Isla San Félix	*Chile*	110	E4
Isla Santa Inés	*Chile*	110	G9
Islamabad	*Pakistan*	53	K3
Island Lake	*Canada*	92	N6
Islas Baleares (Balearic Isles)	*Spain*	41	M5
Islas Canarias (Canary Islands)	*Spain*	58	B3
Islas de los Desventurados	*Chile*	110	E4
Islas Galápagos			
(Galápagos-Islands)	*Ecuador*	108	(1)A1
Islas Juan Fernández	*Chile*	110	E5
Islas Revillagigedo	*Mexico*	104	B5
Islay	*United Kingdom*	36	G6
Isle of Man	*United Kingdom*	37	J7
Isle of Sheppey	*United Kingdom*	38	F2
Isle of Wight	*United Kingdom*	37	M11
Isle Royale	*United States*	98	C1
Isles of Scilly	*United Kingdom*	37	G12
Ismâ'ilîya	*Egypt*	61	F1
Isole di Tremiti	*Italy*	44	K6
Isole Eolie o Lipari	*Italy*	45	J10
Isole Ponziane	*Italy*	45	G8
Isparta	*Turkey*	49	N7
Israel	*Middle East*	54	B4
Issoire	*France*	39	J8
Istanbul	*Turkey*	50	C3
Itaituba	*Brazil*	109	F4
Italy	*Europe*	44	E3
Itbay	*Egypt*	61	F2
Itháki	*Greece*	48	C6
Itzehoe	*Germany*	34	E3
Ivano-Frankovsk	*Ukraine*	30	E5
Ivanovo	*Russia*	30	J3
Iverea	*Italy*	42	C5
Ivujivik	*Canada*	93	R4
Iwaki	*Japan*	81	L5
Ixiamas	*Bolivia*	108	D6
Izhevsk	*Russia*	31	L3
Izmail	*Ukraine*	47	R4
Izmir (Smyrna)	*Turkey*	50	B4
Izmit	*Turkey*	50	C3
Izmit Körfezi	*Turkey*	50	C3
Iznik Gölü	*Turkey*	50	C3
Iztochni Rodópi	*Bulgaria*	47	M8
Izu-Shoto	*Japan*	81	K7

J

J.A.D. Jensens Nunatakker	*Greenland*	93	X4
Jaaza'ir Sawakin	*Egypt*	52	C6
Jabal ad Duruz	*Syria*	54	D4
Jabal Akhdar	*Oman*	53	G5
Jabal al Lawz	*Saudi Arabia*	61	G2
Jabal an Nabi Shu'ayb	*Saudi Arabia*	61	H4
Jabal an Nasrani	*Syria*	54	E2
Jabal as Sawda	*Libya*	60	B2
Jabal ash Sham	*Oman*	55	G5
Jabal at Tih	*Egypt*	54	A7
Jabal at Tubayq	*Saudi Arabia*	52	C4
Jabal Batra	*Jordan*	54	C7
Jabal Bin Ghanimah	*Libya*	60	C3
Jabal Hamoyet	*Sudan / Eritrea*	61	G4
Jabal Katrina	*Egypt*	52	B4
Jabal Katrina	*Egypt*	61	F2
Jabal Lubnan	*Lebanon*	54	C3
Jabal Marrah	*Sudan*	60	D5
Jabal Nafusah	*Libya*	60	B1
Jabal Ram	*Jordan*	54	C7
Jabal Sha'ir	*Syria*	54	E2
Jabal Shammar	*Saudi Arabia*	52	C4
Jabal Sinjar	*Syria / Iraq*	51	J5
Jabal Tuwayq	*Saudi Arabia*	52	D6
Jabal Yu 'Alliq	*Egypt*	54	A6
Jabalpur	*India*	74	C4
Jabir	*Oman*	55	H5
Jablanac	*Croatia*	46	B5
Jaca	*Spain*	41	K2
Jackson	*United States*	102	C2
Jackson Head	*New Zealand*	89	C6
Jacksonville	*United States*	103	E3
Jaén	*Spain*	40	G7
Jaffa (Tel Aviv-Yafo)	*Israel*	54	B4
Jaffna	*Sri Lanka*	75	D7
Jahrom	*Iran*	55	E2
Jaipur	*India*	74	C3
Jakarta	*Indonesia*	82	D4
Jakobstad	*Finland*	28	M5
Jalapa Enriquez	*Mexico*	104	E5
Jamaica	*Caribbean*	105	J5
Jambi	*Indonesia*	82	C3
James Bay	*Canada*	93	Q6
Jamestown	*United States*	97	G1

Jammer Bugt	*Denmark*	29	E8
Jammu	*India*	74	C2
Jammu and Kashmir	*India*	74	C2
Jamnagar	*India*	74	A4
Jamsä	*Finland*	28	N6
Jamshedpur	*India*	74	E4
Jan Mayen	*Northern Europe*	112	(1)S2
Japan	*South East Asia*	80	H8
Japurá	*South America*	108	D4
Jaroslaw	*Poland*	33	M7
Jarvis	*United States*	85	K5
Jask	*Iran*	55	G4
Jastrzebie Zdrój	*Poland*	33	H8
Jászberény	*Hungary*	46	G2
Jatai	*Brazil*	109	G7
Java	*Indonesia*	82	D4
Java (Jawa)	*Indonesia*	82	F4
Java Sea	*Asia*	82	D3
Javier	*Spain*	41	J2
Javor Osat	*Bosnia-Herzegovina*	46	F5
Jawa (Java)	*Indonesia*	82	F4
Jayapura	*Indonesia*	83	F3
Jazireh-ye Khark	*Iran*	55	C2
Jaza'ir Farasan	*Saudi Arabia*	52	D6
Jaza'ir Sawakin	*Sudan*	61	G4
Jazirat Masirah	*Oman*	53	G5
Jazireh-ye Abu Musa	*Iran*	55	F3
Jazireh-ye Qeys	*Iran*	55	E3
Jbel Bou Naceur	*Morocco*	58	E2
Jbel Kelti	*Morocco*	40	E9
Jebel Ouarkziz	*Morocco / Algeria*	58	D3
Jebel Toubkal	*Morocco*	58	D2
Jedda (Jiddah)	*Saudi Arabia*	52	C5
Jefferson City	*United States*	98	B3
Jekabpils	*Latvia*	29	N8
Jelgava	*Latvia*	29	M8
Jena	*Germany*	35	G6
Jennersdorf	*Austria*	43	L4
Jequié	*Brazil*	109	K6
Jerez de la Frontera	*Spain*	40	E8
Jersey	*United Kingdom*	37	L12
Jersey City	*United States*	93	S8
Jerusalem (Yerushalayim)	*Israel*	52	B3
Jesi	*Italy*	43	J7
Jezercë	*Albania*	48	B2
Jezioro Mamry	*Poland*	32	L3
Jezioro Sniardwy	*Poland*	32	L4
Jhansi	*India*	74	C3
Ji'an	*China*	77	F1
Jiamusi	*China*	79	J1
Jiangmen	*China*	77	E2
Jibal al Adhiriyat	*Jordan*	54	D6
Jibal an Nubah	*Sudan*	61	F5
Jibal ash Sharah	*Jordan*	54	C6
Jiddah (Jedda)	*Saudi Arabia*	52	C5
Jihlava	*Czech Republic*	33	E8
Jilib	*Somalia*	65	G3
Jilin	*China*	79	H2
Jima	*Ethiopia*	65	F2
Jinan	*China*	78	F3
Jingdezhen	*China*	78	F5
Jinsha Jiang	*China*	78	C5
Jinzhou	*China*	79	G2
Jiujiang	*China*	78	F5
Jiuling Shan	*China*	78	E5
Jixi	*China*	79	J1
Jizo-Zaki	*Japan*	80	G6
João Pessoa	*Brazil*	109	K5
Jodhpur	*India*	74	B3
Joensuu	*Finland*	28	Q5
Joetsu	*Japan*	81	K5
Johannesburg	*South Africa*	66	D5
John Martin Reservoir	*United States*	97	F3
Johor Baharu	*Malaysia*	82	C2
Jokkamokk	*Sweden*	28	K3
Jökulsá á Brú	*Iceland*	28	(1)F2
Jökulsá-á Fjöllum	*Iceland*	28	(1)E2
Jolo	*Philippines*	83	B1
Jonesboro	*United States*	98	B3
Jönköping	*Sweden*	29	G8
Jonquière	*Canada*	93	S7
Joplin	*United States*	98	B3
Jordan	*Middle East*	54	C4
Jordan	*Middle East*	54	C6
Jos	*Nigeria*	63	F2
Jos Plateau	*Nigeria*	63	F3
Joseph Bonaparte Gulf	*Australia*	86	E2
Jotunheimen	*Norway*	29	D6
Juan de Nova (Réunion)	*South Africa*	67	G3
Jubaland	*Somalia*	65	G3
Juist	*Germany*	34	B3
Juiz de Fora	*Brazil*	109	J8
Jukagirskoye Ploskogorye	*Russia*	73	T3
Juliana Top	*Surinam*	109	F3
Jülich	*Germany*	35	B6
Junction	*United States*	101	G2
Julische Alpen	*Slovakia / Italy*	43	J4
Junagadh	*India*	53	K5
Junea	*United States*	92	E5
Juneau	*Alaska*	100	L4
Jungfrau	*Switzerland*	42	C4
Junin	*Argentina*	110	J5
Jura	*United Kingdom*	36	G6
Jura	*France / Switzerland*	42	A4
Juruá	*South America*	108	D5
Juventud (Isla de Pinos)	*Caribbean*	105	H4
Juzar Qarqannah	*Tunisia*	59	H1
Juzhny Ural	*Russia*	71	K7
Jyväskylä	*Finland*	28	N5

K

Name	Location		Page	Ref.
Kırıkkale	Turkey	•	50	E4
Kızıl Irmak	Turkey	∠	50	F3
Kızılca Dağı	Turkey	▲	50	C5
Ka	Nigeria	∠	63	F2
Ka Lae	United States	≥	101	(2)F5
Kaarta	Mali	⊘	58	D6
Kabinda	Democratic Republic of Congo	•	64	C5
Kabir Kuh	Iran	▲	51	M7
Kabul	Afghanistan	■	53	J3
Kabwe	Zambia	○	66	D2
Kachul	Moldova	•	47	R4
Kadamat	Laccadive Islands (India)		75	B6
Kadan Kyun	Myanmar (Burma)		76	B4
Kaduna	Nigeria	○	63	F2
Kaédi	Mauritania	•	58	C6
Kafue	South Africa	∠	66	D3
Kagoshima	Japan	○	80	F8
Kahler Asten	Germany	▲	27	M3
Kahoolawe	United States		101	(2)E3
Kahramanmaras	Turkey	○	50	G5
Kaifeng	China	•	78	E4
Kaimakchalan	Greece	▲	48	D4
Kaimanawa Mountains	New Zealand	▲	88	E4
Kainji Reservoir	Nigeria	∫	63	E3
Kaipara Harbour	New Zealand	►	88	D3
Kairauan	Tunisia	•	59	G2
Kaiserslautern	Germany	•	35	C7
Kaiwi Channel	United States	►	101	(2)D3
Kajaani	Finland	•	28	P4
Kakinada	India	•	75	D5
Kalahari Desert	South Africa	⊘	66	C4
Kalámai	Greece	•	48	D7
Kálamos	Greece		48	C6
Kalemie	Democratic Republic of Congo	•	64	D5
Kalevala	Russia	•	30	G1
Kálimnos	Greece		49	J8
Kaliningrad	Russia	•	32	K3
Kalispell	United States	•	96	D1
Kalisz	Poland	•	32	H6
Kallavesi	Finland	∫	28	P5
Kallsjön	Sweden	∫	28	G5
Kalmar	Sweden	•	29	J8
Kalpeni	Laccadive Islands (India)		75	B6
Kamaran	Yemen		61	H4
Kamchatskiy Zaliv	Russia	►	73	U5
Kamet	India	▲	74	C2
Kamina	Democratic Republic of Congo	•	64	C5
Kamloops	Canada	•	94	B1
Kampar	Indonesia	∠	82	C2
Kampen	Netherlands	•	27	K2
Kamvoúnia Óri	Greece	▲	48	D5
Kamyshin	Russia	•	30	K4
Kananga	Democratic Republic of Congo	○	64	C5
Kanazawa	Japan	○	81	J5
Kanchenjunga	Nepal / India	▲	74	E3
Kanchipuram	India	•	75	D6
Kandahar	Afghanistan	○	53	J3
Kandalaksha	Russia	•	30	G1
Kandalakshskaya Guba	Russia	►	30	G1
Kandi	Benin	•	63	E2
Kanem	Chad	⊘	60	B5
Kangaroo Island	Australia		87	G7
Kanggye	North Korea	○	79	H2
Kangirsut	Canada	•	93	S4
Kangrinboqê Feng	China	▲	74	D2
Kanin Nos	Russia	•	30	J1
Kankan	Guinea	○	62	C2
Kano	Nigeria	○	63	F2
Kanpur	India	•	74	D3
Kansas	United States	a	97	E3
Kansas City	United States	•	98	B3
Kantaanpaä	Finland	•	29	M6
Kao-Hsiung	Taiwan	•	79	G6
Kaolack	Senegal	•	58	B6
Kap Arkona	Germany	≥	34	J2
Kap Farvel	Greenland	≥	93	Y5
Kapfenberg	Austria	•	43	L3
Kaposvár	Hungary	•	46	E3
Kapuskassing	Canada	•	99	D1
Kara Kum	Turkmenistan	⊘	53	G2
Kara Sea (Karskoye More)	Russia	►	70	L3
Kara-Bogaz-Göl	Turkmenistan	►	71	J9
Karachi	Pakistan	○	53	J5
Karadeniz Bogazi (Bosporus)	Turkey	►	50	C3
Karaganda	Kazakhstan	•	31	Q5
Karaganda	Kazakhstan	○	71	N8
Karaginskiy Zaliv	Russia	►	73	U5
Karakorum	Southern Asia	▲	74	C1
Karakumskiy-kanaal	Turkmenistan	∠	53	H2
Karamay	China	•	71	R8
Karamea Bight	New Zealand	►	89	D5
Karasu Aras Daglari	Turkey	▲	51	K3
Karawanken	Austria / Slovakia	▲	43	K4
Karazhal	Kazakhstan	•	31	Q5
Karbala	Iraq	•	52	D3
Karcag	Hungary	•	46	H2
Kargopol'	Russia	•	30	H2
Karigasniemi	Finland	•	28	L2
Karisimbi	Rwanda	▲	64	D4
Karlik Shan	China	▲	78	A2
Karlovac	Croatia	•	46	C4
Karlovy Vary	Czech Republic	•	35	H6
Karlshamn	Sweden	•	32	D1
Karlskrona	Sweden	•	29	H8
Karlsruhe	Germany	•	35	D7
Karlstad	Sweden	•	29	G7
Karmøy	Norway		29	C7
Karonga	Zambia	•	67	E1
Karonga	Malawi	•	65	E5
Kárpathos	Greece		49	K9
Karskoye More (Kara Sea)	Russia	►	70	L3
Karun	Middle East	∠	55	C1
Kasai	Central Africa	∠	64	B4
Kasama	Zambia	○	64	E6
Kashan	Iran	•	52	F3
Kásos	Greece		49	J9
Kaspiyskiy	Russia	•	31	K5
Kassala	Sudan	○	61	G4
Kassel	Germany	•	35	E5
Kastamonu	Turkey	○	49	R3
Kasumiga-ura	Japan	∫	81	L5
Katakwi	Uganda	•	65	E3
Katanga	Democratic Republic of Congo	⊘	64	C5
Katchall	India		75	F7
Katerini	Greece	•	48	E4
Kathmandu	Nepal	■	74	E3
Kathu	South Africa	•	66	C5
Katowice	Poland	•	33	H7
Katsina	Nigeria	•	63	F2
Kattara Senke	Egypt	⊘	60	D4
Kattegat	Denmark / Sweden	►	29	F8
Kauai	United States	►	100	(2)B1
Kauai Channel	United States	►	100	(2)B2
Kaufleuren	Germany	•	35	F9
Kauhajoki	Finland	•	28	M5
Kaukauveld	South Africa	⊘	66	C3
Kaunas	Lithuania	•	29	M9
Kautokeino	Norway	•	28	M2
Kavála	Greece	•	47	M9
Kavála	Greece	•	48	G4
Kavaratti	Laccadive Islands (India)		75	B6
Kawasaki	Japan	•	81	K6
Kawich Peak	United States	▲	96	C3
Kayes	Mali	•	58	C6
Kayseri	Turkey	○	50	F4
Kazakhstan	Asia	A	71	L8
Kazan'	Russia	•	31	K3
Kazan-Retto (Japan)	Japan	•	84	E3
Kazbek	Georgia	▲	51	L2
Kazhim	Russia	•	31	L2
Kazincbarcika	Hungary	•	46	H1
Kéa	Greece		48	G7
Keban Gölu	Turkey	∫	51	H4
Kebbi	West Africa	∠	59	F6
Kebnekaise	Sweden	▲	28	K3
Kecskemét	Hungary	•	46	G3
Kédainiai	Lithuania	•	32	P2
Kediri	Indonesia	•	82	E4
Keetmanshoop	Namibia	•	66	B5
Kefallonia	Greece	A	48	C6
Keitele	Finland	∫	28	P5
Kelang	Malaysia	•	82	C2
Kem	Russia	•	30	G2
Kemerovo	Russia	○	71	R6
Kemi	Finland	•	28	N4
Kempten	Germany	•	35	F9
Kënet'e Karavastas	Albania	►	48	B3
Kénitra	Morocco	○	58	D2
Kenora	Canada	•	95	H1
Kentucky	United States	a	98	C3
Kenya	Central Africa	A	65	F3
Kep. Bonerate	Indonesia		83	G4
Kep i Gjuhëzës	Albania	≥	48	B4
Kep i Rodonit	Albania	≥	48	B3
Kepe	Russia	•	28	S4
Kepulauan Alor	Indonesia		83	B4
Kepulauan Anambas	Indonesia		82	D2
Kepulauan Aru	Indonesia		83	D4
Kepulauan Asia	Indonesia		83	D2
Kepulauan Ayu	Indonesia		83	D2
Kepulauan Babar	Indonesia		83	C4
Kepulauan Banda	Indonesia		83	C3
Kepulauan Banyak	Indonesia		82	B2
Kepulauan Batu	Indonesia		82	B2
Kepulauan Bonerate	Indonesia		83	B4
Kepulauan Gorong	Indonesia		83	D3
Kepulauan Kai	Indonesia		83	D4
Kepulauan Kangean	Indonesia		82	A4
Kepulauan Karimata	Indonesia		82	D3
Kepulauan Karimunjawa	Indonesia		82	E4
Kepulauan Laut Kecil	Indonesia		82	F4
Kepulauan Leti	Indonesia		83	C4
Kepulauan Lingga	Indonesia		82	C2
Kepulauan Maluku	Indonesia		83	C2
Kepulauan Mapia	Indonesia		83	D2
Kepulauan Mentawai	Indonesia		82	B3
Kepulauan Natuna	Indonesia	a	82	D2
Kepulauan Pagai	Indonesia		82	B3
Kepulauan Riau	Indonesia		82	C2
Kepulauan Salabangka	Indonesia		83	B3
Kepulauan Sangir	Indonesia		83	C2
Kepulauan Sermata	Indonesia		83	C4
Kepulauan Solor	Indonesia		83	B4
Kepulauan Talaud	Indonesia		83	C2
Kepulauan Tanimbar	Indonesia		83	D4
Kepulauan Togian	Indonesia		83	B3
Kepulauan Tukangbesi	Indonesia		83	B4
Kepuluaun Mentawai	Indonesia	a	82	N10
Kercenski Proliv	Russia	►	50	G1
Kerch	Ukraine	•	30	H5
Kerempe Burun	Turkey		49	R2
Keriya He	China	∠	71	Q10
Kérkira (Corfu)	Greece		48	B5
Kermadec Islands	New Zealand		85	J8
Kermadec Trench	Oceania	⊘	85	J9
Kerman	Iran	○	53	G3
Kerulen	Mongolia	∠	78	E1
Kesan	Turkey	•	47	P9
Kettering	United Kingdom	•	26	C2
Key West	United States	•	103	E5
Khabarovsk	Russia	•	72	N7
Khadra	Algeria	•	41	L8
Khalij as Suways	Egypt	►	61	F2
Khalij Hammamat	Tunisia	►	59	H1
Khalij Masirah	Oman	►	53	G6
Khalij Qabis	Tunisia	►	59	H2
Khalij Surt (Gulf of Sirte)	Tunisia	►	60	C1
Khalij Tunis	Tunisia	►	45	E12
Khálki	Greece		49	K8
Khalkis	Greece	•	48	F6
Khánia	Greece	•	48	G9
Khanty Mansiysk	Russia	•	31	P2
Kharabali	Russia	•	31	K5
Kharagpur	India	•	74	E4
Kharit	Saudi Arabia	•	55	D5
Kharkov	Ukraine	•	30	H4
Khartoum (El Khartum)	Sudan	■	61	F4
Khaskovo	Bulgaria	•	48	H3
Khatanga	Russia	∠	72	F2
Khatangskiy Zaliv	Russia	►	72	H2
Khazzon ar Rusayris	Sudan	∫	61	F5
Khemis Miliana	Algeria	•	41	N8
Kherson	Ukraine	•	30	G5
Kheta	Russia	•	72	F2
Khilok	Russia	∠	72	J6
Khios	Greece		48	H6
Khlonótripa	Greece	▲	48	G3
Khokhok Kra	Myanmar (Burma)		76	B4
Khorramabad	Iran	○	52	E3
Khorramshahr	Iran	•	55	C1
Khrebet Cherskogo	Russia	▲	73	P3
Khrebet Dzagdy	Russia	▲	72	M6
Khrebet Dzhugdzhur	Russia	▲	73	P5
Khrebet Dzhungarskiy Alatau	Kazakhstan / China	▲	71	Q8
Khrebet Kobet Dag	Turkmenistan	▲	53	G2
Khrebet Kolymskiy	Russia	▲	73	U4
Khrebet Kopet Dag	Iran	▲	71	K10
Khrebet Kungey Alatau	Kazakhstan	▲	71	P9
Khrebet Pekul'ney	Russia	▲	73	X3
Khrebet Suntar Khayata	Russia	▲	73	P3
Khrebet Tarbagatay	Kazakhstan	▲	71	Q8
Khrebet Turana	Russia	▲	72	N6
Khulna	Bangladesh	•	74	E4
Khvoy	Iran	•	51	L4
Kiantajärvi	Finland	∫	28	Q4
Kidal	Mali	•	59	F5
Kiel	Germany	○	34	F2
Kielce	Poland	•	33	K7
Kieler Bucht	Germany	►	34	F2
Kiev (Kyyiv)	Ukraine	■	30	G4
Kiffi	Mauritania	•	58	C5
Kigali	Rwanda	■	64	E4
Kihnu	Estonia		29	M7
Kii-Suido	Japan	►	80	H7
Kikai-Shima	Japan		79	J5
Kikinda	Yugoslavia	•	46	H4
Kikwit	Democratic Republic of Congo	•	64	B5
Kil-Sanchi	Japan	▲	80	H7
Kilija	Ukraine	•	47	S4
Kilimanjaro	Tanzania	▲	65	F4
Kilkis	Greece	•	47	K8
Killini	Greece	▲	48	E7
Kilpisjärvi	Finland	•	28	L2
Kilttan	Laccadive Islands (India)		75	B6
Kimberley	South Africa	○	66	D5
Kimberley Plateau	Australia	⊘	86	E3
Kimolos	Greece		48	G8
Kinabalu	Malaysia	▲	84	B5
Kindia	Guinea	•	58	C6
Kindu	Democratic Republic of Congo	•	64	D4
King Island	Australia		87	H7
King Leopold Ranges	Australia	▲	86	D3
King Sound	Australia	►	86	D3
King William Island	Canada		92	M3
King's Lynn	United Kingdom	•	26	D2
Kingman	United States	•	96	D3
Kingman	United States		85	K5
Kingston	Jamaica	○	105	J5
Kingston upon Hull	United Kingdom	•	37	N8
Kinka-San	Japan	≥	81	L4
Kinnairds Head	United Kingdom	≥	36	M4
Kinshasa	Democratic Republic of Congo	■	63	H5
Kintyre	United Kingdom		36	H6
Kiparissiakos Kólpos	Greece	►	48	D7
Kipengere Range	Tanzania	▲	65	E5
Kirchheim	Germany	•	35	E8
Kiribati	Oceania		85	J6
Kirishi	Russia	•	31	G3
Kiritimati (Christmas)	Kiribati (Pacific Ocean)		85	L5
Kirkland Lake	Canada	•	99	D1
Kirklareli	Turkey	•	47	Q8
Kirkuk	Iraq	•	52	D2
Kirov	Russia	•	31	K3
Kirovakan	Armenia	•	51	L3
Kirovsk	Russia	•	28	S3
Kiruna	Sweden	•	28	L3

Name	Country		Page	Ref
Kisangani	Democratic Republic of Congo	○	64	D3
Kiska Island	United States		100	(3)B1
Kiskunhalas	Hungary	●	46	G3
Kismaayo	Somalia	●	65	G4
Kisumu	Kenya	○	65	F3
Kit Carson	United States	●	97	F3
Kita-Kyushu	Japan	●	80	F7
Kitami-Sanchi	Japan	▲	81	M1
Kitchener	Canada	●	99	D2
Kithira	Greece		48	E8
Kithnos	Greece		48	G7
Kitimat Ranges	Canada	▲	92	F6
Kitwe-Nkana	Zambia	●	66	D2
Kitzbüheler Alpen	Austria	▲	43	H3
Kiuruvesi	Finland	●	28	P5
Kizlyarskiy Zaliv	Russia	►	51	M1
Kjustendil	Bulgaria	●	47	K7
Kladno	Czech Republic	●	33	D7
Klagenfurt	Austria	●	43	K4
Klaipeda	Lithuania	●	29	L9
Klamath Falls	United States	●	96	B2
Klarälven	Sweden	∫	29	G6
Klatovy	Czech Republic	●	33	C8
Klekovaca	Bosnia-Herzegovina	▲	43	M6
Klerksdorp	South Africa	●	66	D5
Kleve	Germany	●	34	B5
Klodzko	Poland	●	33	F7
Klyuchevskaya Sopka	Russia	▲	73	U5
Knockmealdown Mountains	Ireland	▲	37	E9
Knokke-Heist	Belgium	●	26	F4
Knoxville	United States	●	103	E3
Ko Chang	Thailand		76	C4
Ko Kut	Thailand		76	C4
Ko Phangan	Thailand		76	C5
Ko Phuket	Thailand		76	B5
Ko Samui	Thailand		76	C5
Kobe	Japan	○	80	H6
København (Copenhagen)	Denmark	■	29	F9
Koblenz	Germany	●	35	C6
Kobrin	Belarus	●	29	N10
Koch Island	Canada		93	R3
Kochi	Japan	○	80	G7
Kodiak Island	United States		100	(1)G4
Kodza Balkan	Bulgaria	▲	47	P7
Kofu	Japan	○	81	K6
Kohtla-Järve	Estonia	●	29	P7
Koje	North Korea		80	E6
Kök Shaal Tau	North West Asia	▲	71	P9
Kokand	Uzbekistan	●	71	N9
Kokchetav	Kazakhstan	●	31	P4
Kokkola	Finland	●	28	L5
Koko Nor (Qinghai Hu)	China	∫	78	C3
Koksoak River	Canada	∫	93	S5
Kolding	Denmark	●	34	E1
Kolente	West Africa	∫	62	B3
Kolhapur	India	●	75	B5
Kolin	Czech Republic	●	33	E7
Köln (Cologne)	Germany	●	35	B6
Kolobrzeg	Poland	●	32	E3
Kolomyja	Ukraine	●	47	N1
Kolpasevo	Russia	●	70	Q6
Kólpos Ierisoú	Greece	►	48	F4
Kólpos Kassándras	Greece	►	48	F4
Kólpos Kaválas	Greece	►	48	G4
Kólpos Khanion	Greece	►	48	F9
Kólpos Mirambélou	Greece	►	48	H9
Kólpos Petalión	Greece	►	48	F6
Kólpos Singitikós	Greece	►	48	F4
Kolumadulu Atoll	Maldives		75	B8
Kolyma	Russia	∫	73	T3
Komadugu Gana	Central Africa	∫	60	B5
Komandorskiye Ostrova	Russia		73	R8
Komárno	Slovakia	●	46	E1
Komotini	Greece	●	48	H3
Komsa	Russia	●	72	D4
Komsomol'sk-na-Amure	Russia	●	73	P6
Kömür Burun	Turkey		48	J6
Konar	Southern Asia	∫	74	B2
Kondopoga	Russia	●	30	G2
Kongolo	Democratic Republic of Congo	●	64	D5
Kongsringer	Norway	●	29	F6
Kongur Shan	China	▲	71	P10
Konin	Poland	●	32	H5
Konstanz	Germany	●	35	E9
Konya	Turkey	○	50	E5
Kootenai	Canada	∫	96	C1
Kopaonik	Yugoslavia	▲	46	H6
Kopeysk	Russia	●	31	N3
Korab	Albania	▲	48	C3
Korçë	Albania	●	48	C4
Korcula	Croatia		46	D7
Korea Strait (Taehan-Haehyop)	South Korea / Japan	►	80	D7
Korea Strait (Tsushima-Kaikyo)	South Korea / Japan	►	80	D7
Korhogo	Côte D'Ivoire	●	62	C3
Korinthiakos Kolpos	Greece	►	48	E6
Koritnik	Yugoslavia	▲	46	H7
Koriyama	Japan	●	81	L5
Korkinitskiy Zaliv	Ukraine	►	30	G5
Korla	China	●	71	R9
Kormakiti Burun	Cyprus		46	Q9
Kornat	Croatia		46	C6
Köroglu Daglari	Turkey	▲	50	D3
Köroglu Tepesi	Turkey	▲	50	D3
Kortrijk	Belgium	●	26	G4
Koryakskiy Khrebet	Russia	▲	73	V4
Koryakskiye Nagorye	Russia		112	LL3
Kos	Greece		49	K8

Name	Country		Page	Ref
Koshikizima-Retto	Japan		80	E8
Kosice	Slovakia	●	33	L9
Koslan	Russia	●	31	K2
Kosovska/Mitrovica	Yugoslavia	●	46	H7
Kosrae	Micronesia		84	G5
Kostroma	Russia	●	30	J3
Koszalin	Poland	●	32	F3
Kota	India	●	74	C3
Kota Baharu	Malaysia	●	82	C1
Kota Kinabalu	Malaysia	●	77	F5
Köthen	Germany	●	34	G5
Kotka	Finland	●	29	P6
Kotlas	Russia	●	31	K2
Kotobrzeg	Poland	●	29	H9
Kotovsk	Ukraine	●	47	S2
Kotuy	Russia	∫	72	G2
Kotzebue Sound	United States	►	100	(1)D2
Kouvola	Finland	●	29	P6
Kovdor	Russia	●	30	G1
Kovdozero	Russia	∫	28	S3
Kowloon	China	●	77	E2
Kozáni	Greece	●	48	D4
Kozara	Bosnia-Herzegovina	▲	46	D4
Kozhikode (Calicut)	India	●	75	B6
Kozu-Shima	Japan		81	K6
Kozuf	Macedonia	▲	48	E3
Kraków	Poland	●	33	K7
Kraljevo	Yugoslavia	●	46	H6
Kranj	Slovenia	●	43	K4
Krárnik	Poland	●	33	M7
Krasnodar	Russia	●	30	H5
Krasnosel'kup	Russia	●	31	S1
Krasnovishersk	Russia	●	31	M2
Krasnoyarsk	Russia	○	71	S6
Krefeld	Germany	●	35	B5
Kremenchug	Ukraine	●	30	G5
Kremenchugskoye Vdkhr.	Ukraine	∫	30	G5
Krems a.d. Donau	Austria	●	43	L2
Krimmi	Austria	●	43	G3
Kristiansand	Norway	●	29	D7
Kristianstad	Sweden	●	29	H8
Kristiansund	Norway	●	28	D5
Kriti (Crete)	Greece		48	G9
Krivoy Rog	Ukraine	●	30	G5
Krk	Croatia		46	B4
Krka	Slovakia	∫	43	L5
Kroken	Norway	●	28	H4
Kromeriz	Czech Republic	●	33	G8
Kronotskaya Sopka	Russia	▲	73	U6
Kronotskiy Zaliv	Russia	►	73	U6
Krosno	Poland	●	33	L8
Krotoszyn	Poland	●	32	G6
Krugersdorp	South Africa	●	66	D5
Krung Thep (Bangkok)	Thailand	■	76	C4
Krusevac	Yugoslavia	●	46	J6
Krusné Hory	Czech Republic	▲	33	C7
Kryazh Hara-Tas	Russia	▲	70	V3
Kryazh Polousnyy	Russia	▲	73	Q3
Krymskiye Gory	Ukraine	▲	30	G6
Ksar-el-Boukhari	Algeria	●	41	N9
Kuala Lumpur	Malaysia	■	82	C2
Kuban	Russia	∫	51	H1
Kuching	Malaysia	●	82	E2
Kuchurgan	Ukraine	∫	47	S2
Kücük Menderes	Turkey	∫	50	B4
Kuçukçekmec	Turkey	●	47	R9
Kuczbork	Poland	●	33	H7
Kudus	Indonesia	●	82	E4
Kufstein	Austria	●	43	H3
Kuh-e Bakhun	Iran	▲	55	G3
Kuh-e Biaban	Iran	▲	55	G3
Kuh-e Bul	Iran	▲	55	E1
Kuh-e Davaran	Iran	▲	55	F1
Kuh-e Dinar	Iran	▲	55	D1
Kuh-e Hazaram	Iran	▲	55	G2
Kuh-e Khaiz	Iran	▲	55	D1
Kuh-e Kuhran	Iran	▲	55	H3
Kuh-e Marreh	Iran	▲	55	E2
Kuh-e Masahim	Iran	▲	55	F1
Kuh-e Sahand	Iran	▲	51	M5
Kuh-e Tabask	Iran	▲	55	D2
Kuh-e-Seh Kooj	Iran	▲	55	G2
Kuhha-ye Sabalan	Iran	▲	51	M4
Kuhha-ye Zagros (Zagros Mountains)	Iran	▲	52	F3
Kuhha-ye-Tavalesh	Iran	▲	51	M4
Kuhmo	Finland	●	28	Q4
Kuito	Angola	●	64	B6
Kujuarapik	Canada	●	93	R5
Kul'sary	Kazakhstan	●	31	L5
Kulanoy	Kazakhstan	●	31	M5
Kulmbach	Germany	●	35	G6
Kuma	Russia	∫	51	L1
Kumamoto	Japan	○	80	F7
Kumanovo	Macedonia	●	46	J7
Kumasi	Ghana	○	62	D3
Kumbakonam	India	●	75	C6
Kume-Jima	Japan		79	H5
Kumo	Nigeria	●	63	G2
Kunlun Shan	China	▲	71	Q10
Kunming	China	○	76	C1
Kunsan	South Korea	●	80	D6
Kuopio	Finland	●	28	P5
Kupa	Slovakia / Croatia	∫	43	L5
Kupang	Indonesia	○	83	D1
Kupreanof Island	United States		100	(1)L4
Kurashiki	Japan	●	80	G6
Kurdzhali	Bulgaria	●	47	N8
Kure	Japan	●	80	G6

Name	Country		Page	Ref
Kuresaare	Estonia	●	29	M7
Kurgan	Russia	○	71	M6
Kuril Islands (Kuril'skije Ostrova)	Russia		73	S8
Kuril Trench	Pacific Ocean	►	81	P2
Kuril'skije Ostrova (Kuril Islands)	Russia		73	S8
Kurnool	India	●	75	C5
Kursk	Russia	●	30	H4
Kurski Zaliv	Russia	►	29	L9
Kuru Dagi	Turkey	▲	49	J4
Kuruktag	China	▲	71	R9
Kurume	Japan	●	80	F7
Kus Gölü	Turkey	∫	50	B3
Kusadasi Körfezi	Turkey	►	50	B5
Kushiro	Japan	●	81	N2
Kusnica	Ukraine	●	33	N9
Kustanay	Kazakhstan	○	71	L7
Kütahya	Turkey	●	49	M5
Kutaisi	Georgia	○	51	K2
Kutina	Croatia	●	46	D4
Kuto	Democratic Republic of Congo	●	64	B4
Kuusamo	Finland	●	28	Q3
Kuwait	Middle East	A	55	B2
Kuwait (Al Kuwayt)	Kuwait	■	55	C2
Kuznetskiy Alatau	Russia	▲	71	R7
Kuzomen	Russia	●	30	H1
Kvænangen	Norway	►	28	L1
Kvaløy	Norway		28	J2
Kvarner	Croatia	►	44	J4
Kvarneric	Croatia	►	44	J4
Kwa	Democratic Republic of Congo	●	64	B4
Kwa	West Africa	∫	63	H5
Kwangju	South Korea	○	80	D6
Kwango	Central Africa	∫	64	B5
Kwidzyn	Poland	●	32	H4
Kyklades (Cyclades)	Greece		48	G7
Kyoga-Misaki	Japan		80	H6
Kyonggi-Man	South Korea	►	80	C5
Kyoto	Japan	○	80	H6
Kyrgyzstan	Asia	A	71	N9
Kyushu	Japan		80	F7
Kyushu-Sanchi	Japan	▲	80	F7
Kyustendil	Bulgaria	○	48	E2
Kyyiv (Kiev)	Ukraine	■	30	G4
Kzyl-Orda	Kazakhstan	○	71	M9
Kzyltu	Kazakhstan	●	31	Q4

L

Name	Country		Page	Ref
L.Tiberias (Yam Kinneret)	Israel	∫	54	C4
L'Aquala	Italy	●	44	H6
L'viv	Ukraine	●	30	E5
La Baneza	Spain	●	40	E2
La Chaux de Fonds	Switzerland	●	42	B3
La Coruña	Spain	○	40	B1
La Esmeralda	Venezuela	●	108	D3
La Estrada	Spain	●	40	B2
La Galite	Tunisia		45	C11
La Gran Sabana	Venezuela	▲	108	E2
La Granja	Spain	●	40	G3
La Linea	Spain	●	40	E8
La Palma (Canary Islands)	Spain		58	B3
La Paz	Mexico	●	94	D6
La Paz	Bolivia	●	108	D7
La Pedrera	Colombia	●	108	D4
La Pérouse Strait	Russia / Japan	►	79	L1
La Puebla	Spain	●	41	P5
La Rioja	Argentina	●	110	H4
La Roche-sur-Yon	France	●	39	D7
La Rochelle	France	○	39	D7
La Roda	Spain	●	40	H5
La Serena	Chile	●	110	G4
La Spezia	Italy	●	44	D4
La Tortuga	Central America		108	D1
Laâyoune	Western Sahara	○	58	C3
Laba	Russia	∫	51	J1
Labé	Guinea	●	58	C6
Labe (Elbe)	Germany / Czech Republic	∫	35	K6
Labrador Sea	North America	▲	93	V4
Lac Alaotra	Madagascar	∫	67	H3
Lac Albanel	Canada	∫	93	S6
Lac Caniapiscau	Canada	∫	93	S6
Lac d'Annecy	France	∫	42	B5
Lac de Kossou	Côte D'Ivoire	∫	62	C3
Lac de Lagdo	Cameroon	∫	63	G3
Lac de Neuchâtel	Switzerland	∫	42	B4
Lac Débo	Mali	∫	58	E5
Lac Evans	Canada	∫	93	R6
Lac Faguibine	Mali	∫	58	E5
Lac Fitri	Chad	∫	63	H2
Lac La Martre	Canada	∫	92	H4
Lac la Ronge	Canada	∫	92	L5
Lac Léman(Lake Geneva)	Switzerland / France	∫	42	B4
Lac Mai-Ndombe	Democratic Republic of Congo	∫	63	H5
Lac Minto	Canada	∫	93	R5
Lac Mistassini	Canada	∫	93	R6
Lac Mobutu Sese Seko				
Lac Nantais	Canada	∫	93	S4
Lac Niangay	Mali	∫	58	E5
Lac Rutanzige (Lake Edward)	Democratic Republic of Congo / Uganda	∫	64	E4
Lac Saint-Jean	Canada	∫	93	S7
Lac-au-Gouin	Canada	∫	99	E1
Laccadive Islands	India (Arabian Sea)		75	B6
Lacepede Bay	Australia	►	87	G7
Lacul Brates	Romania	∫	47	R4

Name	Region	Page	Grid
Lingayen Gulf	Philippines	77	F3
Lingen (Ems)	Germany	34	C4
Linköping	Sweden	29	H7
Linosa	Italy	45	G13
Linz	Austria	43	K2
Lipari	Italy	45	K10
Lipetsk	Russia	30	H4
Lipova	Romania	33	L11
Lippe	Germany	34	B5
Lippstadt	Germany	34	D5
Lipsoi	Greece	49	J7
Liria	Spain	41	K5
Lisala	Democratic Republic of Congo	64	C3
Lisbon (Lisboa)	Portugal	40	A6
Lisichansk	Ukraine	30	H5
Lisieux	France	26	D5
Liski	Russia	30	H4
Lithuania	Europe	29	M9
Little Andaman	India	75	F6
Little Inagua	Caribbean	105	K4
Little Karoo	South Africa	66	C6
Little Minch	United Kingdom	36	G4
Little Nicobar	India	75	F7
Little Rock	United States	102	C2
Liuzhou	China	78	D6
Liverpool	United Kingdom	37	K8
Liverpool Bay	United Kingdom	37	K8
Livingstone	Zambia	66	D3
Livingstone Mountains	Tanzania	65	E5
Livorno (Leghorn)	Italy	44	E5
Lizard Point	United Kingdom	37	H12
Ljubisnja	Bosnia-Herzegovina / Yugoslavia	46	F6
Ljubljana	Slovakia	46	B3
Ljungan	Sweden	28	J5
Ljungby	Sweden	29	G8
Ljusdal	Sweden	29	J6
Ljusnan	Sweden	29	J6
Llanes	Spain	40	E8
Lobito	Angola	64	A6
Loch Awe	United Kingdom	36	H5
Loch Ericht	United Kingdom	36	J5
Loch Fyne	United Kingdom	36	H6
Loch Linnhe	United Kingdom	36	H5
Loch Lochy	United Kingdom	36	J5
Loch Lomond	United Kingdom	36	J5
Loch Maree	United Kingdom	36	H4
Loch Morar	United Kingdom	36	H4
Loch Ness	United Kingdom	36	J4
Loch Shiel	United Kingdom	36	H5
Loch Shin	United Kingdom	36	J3
Loch Tay	United Kingdom	36	J5
Lochnager	United Kingdom	36	K5
Lodi	Italy	42	E5
Lódz	Poland	32	J6
Loffa	West Africa	62	B3
Lofoten	Norway	28	G2
Logone	Central Africa	60	C5
Logroño	Spain	41	H2
Logudoro	Sardinia (Italy)	45	C8
Loire	France	38	D6
Lokan tekojärvi	Finland	28	P2
Lokeren	Belgium	27	G3
Loks Land	Canada	93	U4
Lol	Sudan	64	D2
Lol	Central Africa	60	E6
Lolland	Denmark	29	F9
Lom	Bulgaria	47	L6
Loma Mountains	Sierra Leone	62	B3
Lomami	Central Africa	64	C4
Lombok	Indonesia	84	B6
Lomé	Togo	63	E3
Lomza	Poland	32	M4
London	Canada	99	D2
London	United Kingdom	37	N10
Londonderry	United Kingdom	37	E7
Londrina	Brazil	108	G8
Long Beach	United States	100	C2
Long Island	Bahamas	105	K4
Long Island	United States	99	F2
Longpujungan	Indonesia	83	A2
Longs Peak	United States	97	E2
Longuyon	France	27	J5
Longview	United States	102	C2
Lons-le-Saunier	France	39	L7
Lop-Nur	China	71	R9
Lorca	Spain	41	J7
Lord Howe Island	Australia	87	L6
Lorient	France	38	B6
Lörrach	Germany	35	C9
Los Angeles	United States	100	C2
Los Mochis	Mexico	104	C3
Los Roques	Caribbean	105	L6
Losinj	Croatia	46	B5
Lot	France	39	G9
Lough Allen	Ireland	37	F7
Lough Conn	Ireland	37	D7
Lough Corrib	Ireland	37	D8
Lough Derg	Ireland	37	E9
Lough Foyle	United Kingdom / Ireland	37	F6
Lough Mask	Ireland	37	D8
Lough Neagh	United Kingdom	37	G7
Lough Ree	Ireland	37	E8
Lough Swilly	Ireland	37	F6
Louisiade Archipelago	Papua New-Guinea	84	F7
Louisiana	United States	102	C2
Louisville	United States	103	D1
Loukhi	Russia	28	S3
Lovech	Bulgaria	47	M6
Lovozero	Russia	28	T2
Lower Lough Erne	United Kingdom	37	F7
Lower Post	Canada	100	M3
Lowestoft	United Kingdom	26	E2
Lowicz	Poland	32	J5
Loyalty Islands	France	84	G8
Lquria	Italy	45	K8
Luachimo	Central Africa	64	C5
Luanda	Angola	64	A5
Luang Prabang Range	South East Asia	76	C2
Luanginga	South Africa	66	C2
Luangwa	South Africa	66	E2
Luanshya	Zambia	64	D6
Luapula	Central Africa	64	D6
Luarca	Spain	40	D1
Lubang	Philippines	77	F4
Lubango	Angola	66	A3
Lubbock	United States	101	F2
Lübeck	Germany	34	F3
Lübecker Bucht	Germany	34	G2
Lubenec	Czech Republic	35	J6
Lubin	Poland	32	F6
Lublin	Poland	30	E4
Lubumbashi	Democratic Republic of Congo	64	D6
Lucca	Italy	42	F7
Luce Bay	United Kingdom	37	J7
Lucena	Spain	40	F7
Lucenec	Slovakia	33	J9
Lucera	Italy	46	C8
Luckenwalde	Germany	34	J4
Lucknow	India	74	D3
Lüdenscheid	Germany	27	L3
Lüderitz	Namibia	66	B5
Lüderitz Bay	Namibia	66	A5
Ludhiana	India	74	C2
Ludogorsko Plato	Bulgaria	47	P6
Ludvika	Sweden	29	H6
Ludwigshafen	Germany	35	D7
Ludwigslust	Germany	34	G3
Luena	Angola	64	B6
Lufkin	United States	102	C3
Luga	Russia	30	G2
Lugansk	Ukraine	30	H5
Lugnaguillia	Ireland	37	G9
Lugo	Italy	43	G6
Lugo	Spain	40	C1
Lugoj	Romania	46	J4
Lukenie	Democratic Republic of Congo	64	B4
Lulea	Sweden	28	M4
Lüleburgaz	Turkey	49	K3
Lulonga	Democratic Republic of Congo	63	H4
Lulonga	Central Africa	64	B3
Lumajangdong Co	China	74	D2
Lüneburg	Germany	34	F3
Lunéville	France	42	B2
Luoyang	China	78	E3
Lupeni	Romania	47	L4
Lurio	Mozambique	67	F2
Lusaka	Zambia	66	D3
Lusambo	Democratic Republic of Congo	64	C4
Luton	United Kingdom	37	N10
Lützow-Holmbukta	Antarctica	112	(2)J3
Luxembourg	Europe	27	J5
Luxembourg	Luxemburg	27	K5
Luxor	Egypt	52	B4
Luzern	Switzerland	39	M7
Luzon	Philippines	77	G3
Luzon Strait	Philippines	84	C3
Alvila	Spain	40	F4
Lycksele	Sweden	28	K4
Lyme Bay	United Kingdom	37	K11
Lymington	United Kingdom	26	B4
Lyna	Poland	32	K3
Lyngeidet	Norway	28	L2
Lynn Lake	Canada	92	L5
Lyon	France	39	K8
Lyons River	Australia	86	C4

M

Name	Region	Page	Grid
M'banza Congo	Angola	63	G6
Ma'an	Jordan	54	C6
Ma-tsu Lieh-Tao	Taiwan	79	G5
Maalosmadulu Atoll	Maldives	75	B7
Maas	Central Europe	34	B5
Maastricht	Netherlands	27	J4
Macao	South East Asia	77	E2
Macao	South East Asia	77	E2
Macapá	Brazil	109	G3
Macdonnell Ranges	Australia	86	F4
Macedonia	Europe	48	C3
Maceió	Brazil	109	K5
Macgillycuddy's Reeks	Ireland	37	C10
Machilipatnam	India	75	D5
Macina	Mali	62	D2
Macizo Galaico	Spain	40	C3
Mackenzie	United States	100	(1)M2
Mackenzie Bay	Antarctic	112	M3
Mackenzie Bay	Canada	92	D3
Mackenzie Mountains	Canada	100	(1)K3
Mackenzie River	Canada	92	F3
Mâcon	France	39	K7
Macon	United States	103	E3
Macujer	Colombia	108	C3
Macuzari	Mexico	101	D3
Madagascar	Southern Africa	67	G4
Madama	Niger	59	H4
Maddalena	Sardinia	45	D7
Madeira	Portugal	58	B2
Madeira	South America	108	E4
Madeira (Ilhas Selvagens)	Portugal	58	B2
Madison	United States	98	C2
Madras (Chennai)	India	75	D6
Madrid	Spain	40	G4
Madurai	India	75	C7
Madyan	Saudi Arabia	52	C4
Madyan	Russia	73	S5
Maebashi	Japan	81	K5
Mafia	Tanzania	65	G5
Mafikeng	South Africa	66	D5
Magadan	Russia	73	S5
Magdalena	Colombia	108	C2
Magdeburg	Germany	34	G4
Magdelaine Cays	Australia	87	K3
Mageröya	Norway	28	N1
Magnitogorsk	Russia	31	M4
Mahajanga	Madagascar	67	H3
Mahanadi	India	74	D4
Mahé	Seychelles	67	(2)C1
Mahia Peninsula	New Zealand	88	F4
Mahón	Spain	41	Q5
Maidenhead	United Kingdom	26	C3
Maidstone	United Kingdom	26	D3
Maiduguri	Nigeria	63	G2
Main	Germany	35	D6
Maine	United States	99	G1
Mainland (Orkney Islands)	United Kingdom	36	K2
Mainland (Shetland Islands)	United Kingdom	36	M1
Mainz	Germany	35	D7
Maio	Cape Verde	62	(1)B1
Majerten	Somalia	65	H2
Majevica	Bosnia-Herzegovina	46	F5
Makassar Strait	Indonesia	83	A3
Makgadikgadi Pans	Botswana	66	D4
Makhachkala	Russia	51	M2
Makkah (Mecca)	Saudi Arabia	52	D5
Makó	Hungary	46	H3
Makurdi	Nigeria	63	F3
Mala Kapela	Croatia	46	C5
Malabo	Equatorial New Guinea	63	F4
Malacky	Slovakia	43	N2
Málaga	Spain	40	F8
Malaita	Solomon Islands	84	G6
Malakula	Vanuatu	84	G7
Malang	Malaysia	82	E4
Malanje	Angola	63	H6
Mälaren	Sweden	29	J7
Malatya	Turkey	51	H4
Malawi	Southern Africa	67	E2
Malay Reef	Australia	87	J3
Malaysia	Asia	82	C2
Malden	Kiribati	85	L6
Maldives	Indian Ocean	75	B8
Male Atoll	Maldives	75	B8
Malé Karpaty	Slovakia	43	N2
Malegaon	India	53	K5
Malgomaj	Sweden	28	H4
Mali	West Africa	58	E5
Mali Kyun	Myanmar (Burma)	76	B4
Malin Head	Ireland	36	F6
Maljen	Yugoslavia	46	H5
Mallorca	Spain	41	P5
Malmédy	Belgium	27	K4
Malmö	Sweden	29	G9
Malpelo	Colombia	108	A3
Malse	Austria / Czech Republic	43	K2
Malta	United States	97	E1
Malta	Europe	45	J13
Malta Channel	Italy	45	J12
Malvern	United Kingdom	38	C1
Man	Côte D'Ivoire	62	C3
Manado	Indonesia	83	B2
Managua	Nicaragua	105	G6
Manama (Al Manamah)	Bahrain	55	D3
Manaus	Brazil	108	E4
Manchester	United Kingdom	37	L8
Mandal	Norway	29	D7
Mandalay	Myanmar (Burma)	76	B2
Mandalya Körfezi	Turkey	49	K7
Manfredonia	Italy	46	C8
Manga	Niger	59	H6
Mangaia	Cook Islands	85	K8
Mangalore	India	75	B6
Mangareva	French Polynesia	85	N8
Mangin Yoma	Myanmar (Burma)	76	B2
Manicouagan Réservoir	Canada	93	T6
Manihiki	Cook Islands	85	K7
Manila	Philippines	77	G4
Manila Bay	Philippines	77	G4
Manisa	Turkey	50	B4
Manitoba	Canada	92	L6
Manitoulin	Canada	99	D1
Maniwaki	Canada	99	E1
Manjra	India	75	C5
Mankato	United States	98	B2
Mannheim	Germany	35	D7
Manning	Canada	92	H5
Manokwari	Indonesia	83	D3
Manra	Kiribati (Pacific Ocean)	85	J6
Manresa	Spain	41	M3
Mansa	Zambia	66	D2
Mansel Island	Canada	93	Q4
Mansfield	United Kingdom	26	B1

Name	Region		Page	Ref
Mantes-la-Jolie	France	•	26	E5
Mantova	Italy	•	42	F5
Manukau	New Zealand	•	88	E3
Manukau Harbour	New Zealand		88	E3
Manzano Peak	United States	▲	101	E2
Maomao Shan	China	▲	78	C3
Maotou Shan	China	▲	76	C2
Maputo	Mozambique	■	67	E5
Mar Cantábrico	Spain		40	D1
Mar del Plata	Argentina	•	111	K6
Mar Menor	Spain		41	K7
Maraba	Brazil	•	109	H5
Maracaibo	Venezuela	○	108	C1
Maracay	Venezuela	○	108	D1
Maradi	Niger	•	59	G6
Marahuaca	Venezuela	▲	108	D3
Marathon	Canada	•	98	C1
Marbella	Spain	•	40	F8
Marburg	Germany	•	35	D6
March	United Kingdom	•	26	D2
Marchena	Ecuador		108	(1)A1
Mardan	Pakistan	•	53	K3
Mardin Daglari	Turkey		51	J5
Mare Tirreno (Tyrrhenian Sea)	Italy		45	G9
Marettimo	Sardinia		45	F11
Margarita	Central America		108	E1
Marguerite Bay	Antarctica		112	(2)KK3
Maria	French Polynesia		85	L8
Maribor	Slovakia	•	46	C3
Marica	Bulgaria		47	N7
Mariestad	Sweden	•	29	G7
Marijampole	Lithuania	•	29	M9
Marinduque	Philippines		77	G4
Mariupol'	Ukraine	•	30	H5
Marlow	United Kingdom	•	26	D3
Marmande	France	•	39	F9
Marmara	Turkey		50	B3
Marmara Denizi (Sea of Marmara)	Turkey		50	B3
Marmara Gölü	Turkey		49	K6
Marmolada	Italy	▲	44	F2
Marne	France		38	J4
Maro	Chad		59	J5
Maromokotro	Madagascar	▲	67	H2
Marotiri	French Polynesia		85	M8
Maroua	Cameroon	•	64	A1
Marova	Cameroon	•	60	B5
Marquesas Islands	French Polynesia		85	N6
Marquette	United States	•	98	C1
Marradi	Italy	•	43	G6
Marrakech	Morocco	○	58	D2
Marsberg	Germany	•	35	D5
Marseille	France	○	39	L10
Marshall Islands	Oceania	A	84	G4
Martigues	France	•	39	L10
Martin	Slovakia	•	33	H8
Martinique	Caribbean		105	M6
Maryland	United States	a	99	E3
Masan	South Korea	○	80	E6
Masbate	Philippines		77	G4
Maseru	Lesotho	•	66	D5
Mashabih	Saudi Arabia		61	G2
Mashhad	Iran	○	53	G2
Maskovo	Bulgaria	•	47	N8
Mason City	United States	•	92	N8
Masringo	Zimbabwe	•	66	E4
Massa	Italy	•	42	F7
Massachusetts	United States	a	99	F2
Massala	Italy	•	45	G11
Massenya	Chad	•	60	C5
Massif Central	France		39	H8
Massif d'Abo	Chad		60	C3
Massif d'Afafi	Chad		60	C3
Massif de l'Isalo	Madagascar		67	G3
Massif de l'Itremo	Madagascar		67	H4
Massif de l'Ouarsenis	Algeria		41	M9
Massif de Termit	Niger		59	H5
Massif des Bongos	Central African Republic		64	C2
Massif du Chaillu	Gabon		63	G5
Massif du Kapka	Chad		60	D5
Massif du Pelvoux	France		42	B5
Massif du Tamgué	Guinea		62	B2
Massif du Yadé	Central African Republic		63	G3
Matadi	Democratic Republic of Congo	○	64	A5
Matagami	Canada	•	99	E1
Matagorda	United States		102	B4
Matamoros	Mexico	•	104	C3
Mataram	Indonesia	•	82	F4
Mataró	Spain	•	41	N3
Matehula	Mexico	•	101	E4
Mateni	Sierra Leone	•	62	B3
Mathura	India	•	74	C3
Mato Grosso	Brazil		109	F6
Matra	Hungary		33	J10
Matsue	Japan	○	80	G6
Matsumoto	Japan	•	81	K5
Matsuyama	Japan	○	80	G7
Matterhorn	Italy / Switzerland	▲	42	C5
Maturin	Venezuela	○	108	E2
Maubeuge	France	•	27	G4
Maui	United States		101	(2)E3
Maun	Botswana	•	66	C3
Mauna Kea	United States	▲	101	(2)F4
Mauna Loa	United States	▲	101	(2)F4
Mauritania	West Africa	A	58	C5
Mauritius	Indian Ocean	A	67	(1)B2
Mayaguana	Caribbean		105	K4
Mayenne	France		38	E6

Name	Region		Page	Ref
Maykop	Russia	•	30	J6
Maykop	Russia	○	51	J1
Mayotte (France)	Indian Ocean		67	H2
Mazar-e-Sharif	Afghanistan	○	53	J2
Mazatlán	Mexico	•	104	C4
Mazeikiai	Lithuania	•	32	M1
Mbabane	Mozambique	•	67	E5
Mbaiki	Central African Republic	•	63	H4
Mbandaka	Democratic Republic of Congo	○	64	B4
Mbeya	Tanzania	•	65	E5
Mbomou	Central Africa		64	D2
Mbuji-Mayi	Democratic Republic of Congo	○	64	C5
McAlester	United States	•	97	G3
McCamey	United States	•	101	F2
McClintock Channel	Canada		92	L2
McClure Strait	Canada		92	H2
Mcherrah	Algeria		58	E3
Mdennah	Mali / Algeria		58	E4
Meaux	France	•	26	F6
Mecca (Makkah)	Saudi Arabia	•	52	D5
Mechelen	Belgium	•	27	H3
Mecklenburger Bucht	Germany		34	G2
Mecsek	Hungary		33	H11
Medan	Indonesia	•	82	B2
Médéa	Algeria	•	41	N8
Medellin	Colombia	○	108	B2
Medford	United States	•	96	B2
Medgidia	Romania	•	47	R5
Medias	Romania	•	47	M3
Medina (Al Madinah)	Saudi Arabia	•	52	C5
Medina del Campo	Spain	•	40	F3
Medina Gounas	Senegal	•	58	C6
Mediterranean Sea	Europe		39	K11
Medvednica	Croatia		46	C4
Medvezh'yegorsk	Russia	•	30	G2
Meerut	India	•	74	C3
Megísti	Greece		49	M8
Mehran	Iran		55	F3
Meiningen	Germany	•	35	F6
Meißen	Germany	•	35	J5
Meknès	Morocco	○	58	D2
Mekong	South East Asia		76	D4
Melanesia	Oceania		84	F5
Melbourne	United States	•	103	E4
Melbourne	Australia	○	87	H7
Melilla	Spain	•	40	H9
Mellum	Germany		34	D3
Melun	France	•	38	H5
Melville Bay	Australia		87	G2
Melville Hills	Canada		92	G3
Melville Island	Australia		86	F2
Melville Island	Canada		92	J2
Memmert	Germany	•	34	B3
Memphis	United States	•	102	C2
Mende	France	•	39	J9
Mendebo	Ethiopia		65	F2
Mendoza	Argentina	•	110	H5
Menorca	Spain		41	Q5
Mentawai Is.	Indonesia		82	B3
Menton	France	•	42	B7
Meppen	Germany	•	34	C4
Merano/Meran	Italy	•	42	G4
Mercury Islands	New Zealand		88	E3
Mergui Archipelago	Myanmar (Burma)		76	B4
Mérida	Spain	•	40	D6
Merida	Venezuela	○	108	C2
Mérida	Mexico	○	104	G4
Meridian	United States	•	102	D3
Merlitopol	Ukraine	•	30	H5
Merrick	United Kingdom	▲	37	J6
Mersa Fatma	Eritrea	•	61	H5
Merseburg	Germany	•	35	G5
Mersin	Turkey	•	50	F5
Mértola	Portugal	•	40	C7
Merzedes	Uruguay	•	111	K5
Mesa de Yambi	Colombia		108	C3
Meschede	Germany	•	34	D5
Messina	Sicily (Italy)	•	45	K10
Messiniakós Kólpos	Greece		48	E8
Mesuji	Indonesia		82	D3
Meta	South America		108	D2
Metauro	Italy		43	H7
Metz	France	○	38	M4
Meuse	France / Belgium		38	L3
Meuzenti	Chad		59	J5
Mexicali	Mexico	○	104	A2
Mexico	Central America	A	104	C4
Mexico City (Ciudad de Mexico)	Mexico	■	104	D5
Mezen'	Russia	•	30	J1
Mezen	Russia	•	30	J1
Mezenskaya Guba	Russia		30	J1
Mi-Shima	Japan		80	F6
Miami	United States	•	103	E4
Miass	Russia	•	31	M3
Michalovce	Slovakia	•	33	L9
Michigan	United States	a	98	C2
Michipicoten	Canada		93	P7
Micronesia	Oceania		84	F4
Mid-Atlantic Ridge	Atlantic Ocean		106	G2
Middelburg	Netherlands	•	26	G3
Middle Andaman Islands	India		75	F6
Middlesbrough	United Kingdom	•	37	M7
Midland	United States	•	101	F2
Midyan	Saudi Arabia		61	G2
Mielec	Poland	•	33	L7
Mieres	Spain	•	40	E2
Mihaylovgrad	Bulgaria	•	47	L6
Mijares	Spain		41	K4

Name	Region		Page	Ref
Mikkeli	Finland	•	28	P6
Mikonos	Greece		48	H7
Mikun	Russia	•	31	L2
Mikuni-Sammyaku	Japan		81	K5
Mikura-Jima	Japan		81	K7
Miladunmadulu Atoll	Maldives		75	B7
Milan (Milano)	Italy	•	44	D3
Milano (Milan)	Italy	•	44	D3
Mileh Tharthar	Iraq		52	D3
Miles City	United States	•	97	E1
Milford Sound	New Zealand		89	B7
Mill Island	Canada		93	R4
Millau	France	•	39	J9
Mille Lacs	United States		98	B1
Millerova	Russia	•	30	J5
Milos	Greece		48	G8
Milwaukee	United States	•	98	C2
Min Jiang	China		78	F5
Min Shan	China		78	C4
Mina	United States	•	96	C3
Minami-Tori-Shima (Marcus)	Japan		84	F3
Mindanao	Philippines		77	H5
Minden	Germany	•	34	D4
Mindoro	Philippines		77	G4
Mindoro Strait	Philippines		77	G4
Mingechaurskoye Vdkhr.	Azerbaijan		51	M3
Minicoy	Laccadive Islands (India)		75	B7
Minna	Nigeria	•	63	F3
Minneapolis	United States	•	98	B1
Minnesota	United States		98	A1
Minnesota	United States	a	98	A1
Miño	Spain / Portugal		40	C2
Minot	United States	•	97	F1
Minsk	Belarus	■	30	F4
Miranda de Ebro	Spain	•	40	H2
Mirtóon Pélagos	Greece		48	F7
Mirzapur	India	•	74	D3
Miskolc	Hungary	•	46	H1
Misratah	Libya	○	60	C1
Missinipe	Canada	•	92	L5
Mississippi	United States		102	C3
Mississippi	United States	a	102	C3
Mississippi Delta	United States		102	C4
Missoula	United States	•	96	D1
Missouri	United States	a	102	C2
Missouri River	United States		102	C2
Mitchell	United States	•	97	G2
Mitchell River	Australia		87	H3
Mito	Japan	•	81	L5
Mittellandkanal	Germany		34	F4
Miyake-Jima	Japan		81	K6
Miyakonojo	Japan	•	80	F8
Miyazaki	Japan	•	80	F8
Mjøsa	Norway		29	F6
Mladá Boleslav	Czech Republic	•	33	D7
Mljet	Croatia		46	E7
Mo i Rana	Norway	•	28	H3
Moa	West Africa		62	B3
Moa (Banks Island)	Australia		87	H2
Moab	United States	•	97	E3
Mobile	United States	•	102	D2
Moctezuma	Mexico	•	100	D3
Modane	France	•	42	B5
Modena	Italy	•	44	E4
Moers	Germany	•	34	B5
Mogadouro	Portugal	•	40	D4
Mohawk	United States		99	F2
Mohéli	Comoros		65	G6
Möhne	Germany		27	M3
Mojave Desert	United States		100	C2
Mokp'o	South Korea	•	80	C6
Molat	Croatia		46	B5
Molatón	Spain	▲	41	J5
Moldau (Vltava)	Czech Republic		33	D8
Molde	Norway	•	28	D5
Moldova	Europe	A	30	F5
Molfetta	Italy	•	46	D8
Mölln	Germany	•	34	F3
Molokai	United States		101	(2)E2
Molopo	South Africa		66	C5
Molucca Sea	Indonesia		83	C3
Moma	Russia		73	Q3
Mombasa	Kenya	○	65	F4
Momskiy Khrebet	Russia		73	Q3
Møn	Denmark		29	G9
Monaco	Europe	A	39	N10
Monadhliath Mountains	United Kingdom		36	J4
Moncayo	Spain	▲	41	J3
Monchegorsk	Russia	•	30	G1
Mönchengladbach	Germany	•	35	B5
Monclova	Mexico	•	104	D3
Mondego	Portugal		40	C4
Monfalcone	Italy	•	43	J5
Monforte	Spain	•	40	C2
Mongo	Chad	•	60	C5
Mongol Altain Nuruu	Mongolia		78	A1
Mongolia	Asia	A	72	H7
Mongu	Zambia	•	66	C3
Mönh Hayrhan Uul	Mongolia	▲	71	S8
Mono Lake	United States		96	C3
Monopoli	Italy	•	46	E9
Monroe	United States	•	102	C3
Monrovia	Liberia	■	62	B3
Mons	Belgium	○	27	G4
Møns Klint	Denmark		34	H2
Mont Blanc	France / Italy	▲	42	B5
Mont Cameroun	Cameroon	▲	63	F4
Mont du Guèra	Chad	▲	63	H2
Mont Forel	Greenland	▲	112	(1)U3

Mont-de-Marsan	France	39	E10
Montana	United States	97	D1
Montauban	France	39	G9
Montbéliard	France	42	B3
Monte Bello Islands	Australia	86	B4
Monte Carlo	Monaco	44	B5
Monte Cinto	Corsica	44	C6
Monte del Papa	Italy	45	K8
Monte Ferru	Sardinia (Italy)	45	C8
Monte Perdido	Spain	41	L2
Monte Rosa	Italy / Switzerland	42	C5
Monte Rotondo	Corsica	44	D6
Monte Viso	France / Italy	42	C6
Montecristo	Italy	44	E6
Monterey	United States	94	B4
Monterey Bay	United States	96	B3
Monteria	Colombia	108	B2
Monterrey	Mexico	104	E3
Montes Claros	Brazil	109	J7
Montes de León	Spain	40	D2
Montes de Toledo	Spain	40	F5
Montes Universales	Spain	41	J4
Montevideo	Uruguay	111	K5
Montgomery	United States	103	D3
Montluçon	France	39	H7
Montpelier	United States	95	M3
Montpellier	France	39	J10
Montréal	Canada	99	F1
Monts Bagzane	Niger	59	G5
Monts Bambouto	Cameroon	63	F3
Monts d'Arrée	France	38	B5
Monts de la Margeride	France	39	J8
Monts de la Medjerda	Tunisia / Algeria	45	C12
Monts de Tabursuq	Tunisia / Algeria	45	C12
Monts des Ksour	Algeria / Morocco	59	E2
Monts du Forez	France	39	J8
Monts du Velay	France	39	J8
Monts Kundelungu	Democratic Republic of Congo	64	D6
Monts Malimba	Democratic Republic of Congo	64	D5
Monts Mandara	Cameroon	60	B5
Monts Mandara	Mauritania	63	G2
Monts Mandara	Nigeria	64	A1
Monts Mandingues	Mali	58	C6
Monts Marungu	Democratic Republic of Congo / Zambia	64	D5
Monts Mitumba	Democratic Republic of Congo	64	D5
Monts Mugila	Democratic Republic of Congo	64	D5
Monts Nimba	Guinea	62	C3
Monts Notre-Dame	Canada	93	T7
Montserrat	Caribbean	105	M5
Monza	Italy	44	D3
Monzón	Spain	41	L2
Moorhead	United States	97	G1
Moosehead Lake	United States	99	G1
Mopti	Mali	62	D2
Mora	Sweden	29	H6
Mora	Spain	40	G5
Mora	Portugal	40	B6
Morane	French Polynesia	85	N8
Moratuwa	Sri Lanka	75	C7
Moray Firth	United Kingdom	36	K4
More Laptevykh (Laptev Sea)	Russia	72	L2
Morecambe Bay	United Kingdom	37	K8
Morehead	Papua New-Guinea	83	F4
Morella	Spain	41	K4
Moresby Island	Canada	100	(1)L5
Moreton Bay	Australia	87	K5
Moreton Island	Australia	87	K5
Morhange	France	27	K6
Morioka	Japan	81	L4
Morlaix	France	38	B5
Mornington Island	Australia	87	G3
Morocco	North Africa	58	D2
Morogoro	Tanzania	65	F5
Mörön	Mongolia	72	G7
Morón de la Frontera	Spain	40	E7
Moroni	Comoros	65	G6
Morozovst	Russia	30	J5
Morvan	France	38	K6
Moselle	France	27	K6
Moskenesøya	Norway	28	G3
Moskow (Moskva)	Russia	30	H3
Moskva (Moskow)	Russia	30	H3
Moss	Norway	29	F7
Mossoró	Brazil	109	K5
Most	Czech Republic	35	J6
Mostaganem	Algeria	59	F1
Mosty	Belarus	33	P4
Mosul (Al Mawsil)	Iraq	52	D2
Motala	Sweden	29	H7
Motril	Spain	40	G8
Motu One	French Polynesia	85	L7
Mouhoun (Black Volta)	West Africa	62	E3
Moulins	France	39	J7
Moulmein	Myanmar (Burma)	76	B3
Moundou	Chad	64	B2
Mount Adams	United States	96	B1
Mount Afo	Philippines	83	C1
Mount Apo	Philippines	77	H5
Mount Ararat (Büyük Agrı Dagı)	Turkey	51	L4
Mount Aspiring	New Zealand	89	C7
Mount Augustus	Australia	86	C4
Mount Blackburn	United States	92	C4
Mount Columbia	Canada	92	H6
Mount Cook	New Zealand	89	C6
Mount Egmont	New Zealand	88	E4
Mount Elbert	United States	97	E3
Mount Essendon	Australia	86	D4
Mount Everest	Nepal / China	74	E3
Mount Graham	United States	100	E2
Mount Halcon	Philippines	77	G4
Mount Hayes	United States	92	B4
Mount Hermon	Lebanon	54	C3
Mount Hood	United States	96	B2
Mount Huxley	New Zealand	89	C7
Mount Islo	United States	112	(1)FF3
Mount Jackson	Antarctica	112	(2)LL2
Mount Kenya / Kirinyaga	Kenya	65	F4
Mount Kiangarow	Australia	87	K5
Mount Kirkpatrick	Antarctica	112	(2)X1
Mount Kosciusko	Australia	87	J7
Mount Liebig	Australia	86	F4
Mount Logan	United States	100	(1)J3
Mount McKinley	United States	100	(1)G3
Mount Meharry	Australia	86	C4
Mount Menzies	Antarctica	112	(2)M2
Mount Minto	Antarctica	112	(2)X2
Mount Murchison	New Zealand	89	D6
Mount Ossa	Australia	87	J8
Mount Owen	New Zealand	89	E5
Mount Pinatubo	Philippines	77	G3
Mount Pulog	Philippines	77	G3
Mount Rainer	United States	96	B1
Mount Richmond	New Zealand	89	E5
Mount Roberts	Australia	87	K5
Mount Robson	Canada	92	H6
Mount Shasta	United States	96	B2
Mount Sneffels	United States	97	E3
Mount Suckling	Papua New-Guinea	87	J1
Mount Travers	New Zealand	89	E6
Mount Troodos (Olympus)	Cyprus	49	Q10
Mount Victoria	Myanmar (Burma)	76	A2
Mount Waddington	Canada	92	F6
Mount Whitney	United States	96	C3
Mount Woodroffe	Australia	86	F5
Mount Ziel	Australia	86	F4
Mount's Bay	United Kingdom	37	H12
Mountains of Connemara	Ireland	37	D8
Mourne Mountains	United Kingdom	37	G7
Mouth of the Shannon	Ireland	37	C9
Mouths of the Niger	Atlantic Ocean	63	F4
Mouydir	Algeria	59	F4
Moyale	Ethiopia / Kenya	65	F3
Mozambique	Southern Africa	67	E3
Mozambique Channel	Mozambique	57	G8
Mrtú	Colombia	108	C3
Mt. Stanley	Uganda	64	E3
Mt. Ward	New Zealand	89	C6
Mtwara	Tanzania	67	G2
Muchinga Mountains	Zambia	64	E6
Mudan Jiang	China	79	H2
Mudanjiang	China	79	H2
Mudurnu	Turkey	49	N4
Mufulira	Zambia	64	D6
Mugodzhary	Kazakhstan	71	K8
Muhu	Estonia	29	M7
Mukachevo	Ukraine	47	K1
Mukawwar	Sudan	61	G3
Mulaku Atoll	Maldives	75	B8
Mulanje Mountains	South Africa	67	F3
Mulde	Germany	34	H5
Mulegé	Mexico	94	D5
Mulgrave Island	Australia	87	H2
Mulhacén	Spain	40	G7
Mülhausen	Germany	345	F5
Mülheim	Germany	35	C5
Mulhouse	France	38	M6
Mull	United Kingdom	36	G5
Multan	Pakistan	53	K3
Mumbai (Bombay)	India	75	B5
Muna	Russia	72	L3
München (Munich)	Germany	35	G8
Münden	Germany	35	E5
Munifah	Saudi Arabia	55	C3
Münster	Germany	34	C5
Muntii Apuseni	Romania	47	K3
Muntii Harghita	Romania	47	P3
Munzur Silselesi	Turkey	51	H4
Muonio	Finland	28	M3
Muonio älv	Sweden	28	M2
Muoniojoki	Finland	28	M2
Muqayshit	United Arab Emirates	55	E4
Muqdisho (Mogadishu)	Somalia	65	H3
Mur	Austria / Slovakia	43	L4
Mura	Austria / Slovakia	43	M4
Murashi	Russia	31	K3
Murat	Turkey	51	J4
Murat Dagı	Turkey	49	M6
Murcia	Spain	41	K6
Mures	Romania	33	L11
Murgab	Turkmenistan / Afghanistan	53	H2
Müritz	Germany	34	H3
Murmansk	Russia	70	E4
Muroran	Japan	81	L2
Muros	Spain	40	B2
Muroto-Zaki	Japan	80	H7
Murray River	Australia	87	G6
Mururoa	French Polynesia	85	M8
Mus-Haja	Russia	73	Q4
Musala	Bulgaria	47	L7
Musgrave Ranges	Australia	86	F5
Musoma	Tanzania	65	E4
Musqat (Muscat)	Oman	55	H5
Musselburgh	Scotland	36	K6
Musu-Dan	North Korea	80	E3
Mutsu-Wan	Japan	81	L3
Muyezerskiy	Russia	28	S5
Muzaffarnagar	India	74	C3
Muzaffarpur	India	74	E3
Muztag	China	74	E1
Muztagata	China	71	P10
Mwali (Mohéli)	Comoros	67	G2
Mwanza	Tanzania	65	E4
Mweelrea	Ireland	37	D8
Mwene-Ditu	Democratic Republic of Congo	64	C5
My Tho	Vietnam	76	D4
Myanmar (Burma)	Southern Asia	74	F4
Mymensingh	Bangladesh	74	F4
Myrdalsjökull	Iceland	28	(1)D3
Mys Aniva	Russia	73	Q7
Mys Chaplino	Russia	73	Z4
Mys Chelyuskin	Russia	70	V2
Mys Govena	Russia	73	V5
Mys Kanin Nos	Russia	70	G4
Mys Lopatka	Russia	73	T6
Mys Meganom	Ukraine	30	H6
Mys Navarin	Russia	73	X4
Mys Olyutorskiy	Russia	73	W5
Mys Sarych	Ukraine	50	E1
Mys Shelogskiy	Russia	73	V2
Mys Svatoy Nos	Russia	73	P2
Mys Svyatoy Nos	Russia	30	J1
Mys Tarkhankut	Ukraine	30	G5
Mys Taygonos	Russia	73	T4
Mys Terpeniya	Russia	73	Q7
Mys Tolstoy	Russia	73	T5
Mys Yelizavety	Russia	73	Q6
Mysore	India	75	C6
Myvatn	Iceland	28	(1)E2
Mzuzu	Malawi	65	E6
Mzuzu	Zambia	67	E2

N

N'Djamena	Chad	63	H2
N.W.Christmas Island Ridge	Oceania	85	K4
Naberezhnyye Chelny	Russia	31	L3
Nabeul	Tunisia	45	E12
Nabire	Indonesia	83	E3
Nabulus	Israel	54	C4
Nacala	Mozambique	67	G2
Nadiad	India	74	B4
Nadym	Russia	31	Q1
Næstved	Denmark	29	F9
Nagano	Japan	81	K5
Nagaoka	Japan	81	K5
Nagasaki	Japan	80	E7
Nagercoil	India	75	C7
Nagoya	Japan	81	J6
Nagpur	India	74	C4
Nagykanizsa	Hungary	46	E3
Nagykörös	Hungary	33	J10
Naha	Japan	79	H5
Nahr Al' Asi	Turkey / Syria / Lebanon	50	G6
Nahr an Nil (Nile)	Africa	61	F2
Nairobi	Kenya	65	F4
Najd	Saudi Arabia	52	D4
Nakambé (White Volta)	West Africa	62	D2
Nakano-Shima	Japan	80	G6
Nakhodka	Russia	72	N8
Nakuru	Kenya	65	F4
Nal'chik	Russia	51	K2
Nam Co	China	74	F2
Namakzar-e Shahdad	Iran	55	H1
Namangan	Uzbekistan	71	N9
Namib Desert	Namibia	66	A3
Namibe	Angola	66	A3
Namibia	Southern Africa	66	B4
Namous	Algeria	59	E2
Nampula	Mozambique	67	F3
Namsos	Norway	28	F4
Namur	Belgium	38	K3
Nan Hai (South China Sea)	China	78	F6
Nan Ling	China	78	E5
Nanatsu-Jima	Japan	81	J5
Nanchang	China	78	F5
Nancowry	India	75	F7
Nancy	France	38	M5
Nanded	India	75	C5
Nanga Parbat	Pakistan	74	B1
Nangnim-Sanmaek	North Korea	80	D3
Nanjing	China	79	F4
Nanning	China	78	D6
Nanpan Jiang	China	76	C2
Nantes	France	38	D6
Nanumea	Tuvalu	84	H6
Nanuque	Brazil	109	J7
Nanyang	China	78	E4
Napier	New Zealand	88	F4
Naples	United States	103	E4
Naples (Napoli)	Italy	45	J8
Napoli (Naples)	Italy	45	J8
Nar'yan-Mar	Russia	31	L1
Narbonne	France	39	J10
Nardo	Italy	45	N8
Nares Strait	United States	112	(1)Y1
Narew	Poland	32	L4
Narmada	India	74	B4
Narsarsuaq	Greenland	93	X4
Narvik	Norway	28	J2
Naryn	Kyrgyzstan	71	P9

Name	Region	Page	Grid
Nashville	United States	102	D2
Nasik	India	74	B4
Naskov	Denmark	34	G2
Nassau	Cook Islands	85	K7
Nassau	Bahamas	103	F3
Nassau	Bahamas	103	F4
Natal	Brazil	109	K5
Natchez	United States	102	C3
Natitingou	Benin	63	E2
Nauru	Nauru	84	G5
Nauru	Oceania	84	G6
Navajo Lake	United States	101	E1
Navoi	Uzbekistan	71	M9
Navojoa	Mexico	100	D3
Náxos	Greece	48	H7
Nazca	Peru	108	C6
Nazca Ridge	Pacific Ocean	107	C6
Nazilli	Turkey	49	L7
Ndola	Zambia	64	D6
Nebit Dag	Turkmenistan	53	F2
Neblina	Venezuela / Brazil	108	D3
Nebraska	United States	97	F2
Nebrodi	Sicily (Italy)	45	J11
Neckar	Germany	35	E7
Neder-Rijn	Netherlands	27	J3
Neftekamsk	Russia	31	L3
Neger	Israel	52	B3
Negev	Israel	54	B6
Negro	South America	111	K5
Negros	Philippines	77	G5
Neiße	Poland / Germany	33	D7
Neiva	Colombia	108	B3
Nellore	India	75	D6
Nelson	New Zealand	89	E5
Nelson River	Canada	92	N5
Neman	Lithuania / Belarus	29	N10
Nëmërckë	Albania	48	C4
Nemunas	Russia / Lithuania / Belarus	29	M9
Nen Jiang	China	79	G1
Nene	United Kingdom	37	P9
Nens	Lithuania	32	P3
Nepal	Southern Asia	74	D3
Nequén	Argentina	110	H6
Neretva	Bosnia-Herzegovina	44	M5
Nerva	Spain	40	D7
Neskaupstadur	Iceland	28	G2
Netanya	Israel	54	B4
Netherlands	Europe	27	H2
Netherlands Antilles	Caribbean	105	L6
Nettiling Lake	Canada	93	T3
Nettuno	Italy	45	G7
Neubrandenburg	Germany	34	J3
Neuchâtel	Switzerland	38	M6
Neufchâteau	France	42	A2
Neumünster	Germany	34	E2
Neusiedler See	Austria	43	M2
Neuss	Germany	35	B5
Neustrelitz	Germany	34	J3
Neuwerk	Germany	34	D3
Neuwied	Germany	35	C6
Nevada	United States	96	C3
Nevado de Ampato	Peru	108	C7
Nevado de Illampu	Bolivia	108	D7
Nevado de Sajama	Bolivia	108	D7
Nevado Palomani	Bolivia / Peru	108	D6
Nevers	France	39	J7
New Britain	Papua New-Guinea	84	E6
New Brunswick	Canada	93	T7
New Caledonia	France	84	G7
New Delhi	India	74	C3
New Georgia	Solomon Islands	84	F6
New Hampshire	United States	99	F2
New Hanover	Papua New Guinea	84	F5
New Iberia	United States	102	C3
New Ireland	Papua New Guinea	84	F6
New Jersey	United States	99	F3
New Mexico	United States	101	D2
New Orleans	United States	102	C3
New Plymouth	New Zealand	88	E4
New Siberian Islands	Russia	73	P1
New South Wales	Australia	87	H6
New York	United States	99	F2
New York	United States	99	E2
New Zealand	New Zealand	88	B4
New Guinea	South East Asia	83	E4
New-Ulm	Germany	35	F8
Newark	United States	99	F8
Newcastle	Australia	87	K6
Newcastle Creek	Australia	86	F3
Newcastle upon Tyne	United Kingdom	37	M6
Newfoundland	Canada	93	V7
Newfoundland	Canada	93	U5
Newport	United Kingdom	37	L10
Neyriz	Iran	55	F2
Ngangla Ringco	China	74	D2
Nganglong Kangri	China	74	D2
Nganze Co	China	74	E2
Ngaoundéré	Cameroon	63	G3
Nha Trang	Vietnam	76	D4
Niagara Falls	United States	99	E2
Niamey	Niger	63	E2
Nias	Indonesia	76	B6
Nicaragua	Central America	105	G6
Nice	France	39	N10
Nicobar Islands	India	76	A5
Nicosia (Levkósia)	Cyprus	49	R9
Niedere Tauern	Austria	43	K3
Nienburg	Germany	34	E4
Niger	West Africa	63	F3
Niger	West Africa	59	G5
Nigeria	West Africa	63	F3
Niigata	Japan	81	K5
Niihau	United States	100	(2)A2
Nijmegen	Netherlands	27	J3
Nikol'skoye	Russia	30	K3
Nikolayevsk-na-Amure	Russia	73	Q6
Niksic	Yugoslavia	46	F7
Nilande Atoll	Maldives	75	B8
Nile	Africa	52	B4
Nile (Nahr an Nil)	Africa	61	F2
Nîmes	France	39	K10
Nin-Jimi	Japan	81	K6
Ningbo	China	79	G5
Ningjing Shan	China	74	G2
Niobrara	United States	97	F2
Niort	France	39	E7
Nis	Yugoslavia	46	J6
Nishino-Shima	Japan	80	G5
Niteroi	Brazil	111	N3
Nitra	Slovakia	33	H9
Niue	New Zealand	85	K8
Nizamabad	India	75	C5
Nizh Pesa	Russia	31	K1
Nizhneangarsk	Russia	72	H5
Nizhneudinsk	Russia	72	F6
Nizhnevartovsk	Russia	70	P5
Nizhniy Novgorod	Russia	30	J3
Nizhniy Tagil	Russia	70	L6
Nizhniy Tunguska	Russia	72	H4
Nizke Tatry	Slovakia	33	J8
Njazidja (Grande Comore)	Comoros	67	G2
Nkongsamba	Cameroon	63	G3
Nobeoka	Japan	80	F7
Nogales	United States	94	D5
Nogales	Mexico	100	C2
Nomoi Islands	Micronesia	84	F5
Noordfriese Eilanden	Germany	34	C2
Nord-Ostsee-Kanal	Germany	34	E2
Nordenham	Germany	34	D3
Norderney	Germany	34	C3
Nordfjorden	Norway	29	C6
Nordfold	Norway	28	H3
Nordhausen	Germany	34	F5
Nordhom	Germany	34	C4
Nordkapp	Norway	28	P1
Nordkinn	Norway	28	P1
Nordoostpolder	Netherlands	27	J2
Nordre Strømfjord	Greenland	93	V3
Nordstrand	Germany	34	D2
Norfolk	United States	103	F1
Noril'sk	Russia	70	R4
Norra Kvarken	Sweden	28	K5
Norrköping	Sweden	29	J7
North Andaman	India	75	F6
North Bay	Canada	99	E1
North Belcher Islands	Canada	93	Q5
North Cape	New Zealand	88	D2
North Carolina	United States	103	E2
North Channel	United Kingdom / Ireland	37	H7
North Dakota	United States	97	F1
North Downs	United Kingdom	37	N10
North East Pacific Basin	Oceania	85	M4
North Foreland	United Kingdom	26	E3
North Island	New Zealand	88	D3
North Korea	North Korea	72	M8
North Korea	South East Asia	79	H3
North Minch	United Kingdom	36	G4
North Platte	United States	94	F3
North Ronaldsay	United Kingdom	36	L2
North Saskatchewan River	Canada	92	J6
North Sea	Europe	37	N3
North Sentinel	India	75	F6
North Siberian Plain (Severo-Sibirskaya Nizmennost)	Russia	70	S3
North Stradbroke Island	Australia	87	K5
North Taranaki Bight	New Zealand	88	E4
North Uist	United Kingdom	36	F4
North West Cape	Australia	86	B4
North West Highlands	United Kingdom	36	H5
Northampton	United Kingdom	37	N9
Northern Mariana Islands(U.S.)	Pacific Ocean	84	F4
Northern Territory	Australia	86	F4
Northern-Ireland	United Kingdom	37	F7
Northwest Territories	Canada	92	J4
Norton Sound	United States	100	(1)D3
Norva	Estonia	29	M8
Norway	Europe	28	E5
Norwegian Sea	Norway	28	B4
Norwich	United Kingdom	37	Q9
Nos Emine	Bulgaria	47	Q7
Nos Kaliakra	Bulgaria	47	R6
Nosy Bé	Madagascar	67	H2
Nosy-Mitsio	Madagascar	67	H2
Nottingham	United Kingdom	37	M9
Nottingham Island	Canada	93	R4
Nouâdhibou	Western Sahara	58	B4
Nouakchott	Mauritania	58	B5
Nouvelle Calédonie	France	84	G8
Nova Gradiska	Croatia	46	E4
Nova Scotia	Canada	93	U8
Novapolock	Belarus	30	F3
Novara	Italy	44	C3
Novaya Zemlya	Russia	70	J3
Nové Zámky	Slovakia	33	H10
Novgorod	Russia	30	G3
Novi Ligure	Italy	42	D6
Novi Pazar	Yugoslavia	46	H6
Novi Sad	Yugoslavia	46	G4
Novigrad	Croatia	43	J5
Novogrudok	Belarus	29	N10
Novokuznetsk	Russia	71	R7
Novorossiysk	Russia	30	H6
Novorybnaya	Russia	72	H2
Novoshakhtinsk	Russia	30	H5
Novosibirsk	Russia	71	Q6
Novouzensk	Russia	31	K4
Novvy Port	Russia	31	Q1
Novy Jicin	Czech Republic	33	H8
Novy Vasyugan	Russia	31	R3
Nowy Sącz	Poland	32	K8
Nowy Targ	Poland	32	K8
Noyon	France	26	F5
Nu River (Salween)	South East Asia	78	B6
Nubian Desert (As Sahra' an Nubiyah)	Sudan	61	F3
Nueltin Lake	Canada	92	M5
Nueva Rosita	Mexico	101	E3
Nuevo Casas Grandes	Mexico	101	D2
Nuevo Laredo	Mexico	104	D3
Nugal	Somalia	65	H2
Nugget Point	New Zealand	89	C8
Nuku Hiva	French Polynesia	85	M6
Nukunonu	Tokelau	85	J6
Nukus	Uzbekistan	71	L9
Nullarbor Plain	Australia	86	E6
Nulu'erhu Shan	China	79	F2
Numazu	Japan	81	K6
Nunivak Island	United States	100	(1)D3
Nuoro	Italy	45	D8
Nürnberg	Germany	35	G7
Nyainqêntanglha Feng	China	74	F2
Nyainqêntanglha Shan	China	74	F2
Nyala	Sudan	60	E5
Nyda	Russia	31	Q1
Nyiregyháza	Hungary	46	J2
Nykøbing	Denmark	34	H2
Nyköping	Sweden	29	J7
Nyon	Switzerland	42	B4
Nysa	Poland	32	G7
Nyudo-Zaki	Japan	81	K4
Nzérékoré	Guinea	62	C3
Nzwani (Anjouan)	Comoros	67	G2

O

Name	Region	Page	Grid
O-luan-pi	Taiwan	79	G6
O-Shima	Japan	81	K3
O-Shima	Japan	81	K6
Oachita Mountains	United States	98	A4
Oahu	United States	101	(2)D2
Oakland	United States	96	B3
Oaxaca de Juárez	Mexico	104	E5
Ob	Russia	70	Q6
Obando	Colombia	108	D3
Oberhausen	Germany	34	B5
Oberpfälzer Wald	Germany	35	H7
Obihiro	Japan	81	M2
Obo	Central African Republic	64	D2
Obrovac	Croatia	46	C5
Obskaya Guba	Russia	70	N4
Odda	Norway	29	D6
Odense	Denmark	29	E9
Odenwald	Germany	35	D7
Oder	Germany / Poland	34	K4
Oderhaff	Germany / Poland	29	H10
Odessa	United States	101	F2
Odessa	Ukraine	30	G5
Odienné	Côte D'Ivoire	62	C3
Odorheiu Secuisc	Romania	47	N3
Odra	Poland	32	D5
Offenbach am Main	Germany	35	D6
Offenburg	Germany	35	C8
Ogaden	Ethiopia	65	G2
Ogaki	Japan	81	J6
Ogasawara-Shoto(Japan)	Japan	84	E3
Ogbomosho	Nigeria	63	E3
Ogden	United States	96	D2
Oglio	Italy	42	F5
Ogo	Somalia	65	H2
Ogoki	Canada	95	J1
Ogosta	Bulgaria	47	L6
Ogražden	Greece	48	H3
Ogražden Belasica	Bulgaria / Macedonia / Greece	48	E3
Ogre	Latvia	29	N8
Ohio	United States	98	D2
Ohio River	United States	99	D3
Ohre	Germany / Czech Republic	35	J6
Ohrid	Macedonia	48	C3
Ohridsko Ezero	Macedonia / Albania	48	C3
Oise	France	38	H4
Oita	Japan	80	F7
Oka	Russia	30	J3
Okaba	Indonesia	83	E4
Okanogan	United States	96	C1
Okara	Pakistan	53	K3
Okavango	South Africa	66	C3
Okavango Swamp	Botswana	66	C3
Okayama	Japan	80	H6
Okazaki	Japan	81	J6
Okha	Russia	73	Q6
Oki-Shoto	Japan	80	G5
Okinawa-Shoto	Japan	79	H5
Okinoerabu-Shima	Japan	79	H5
Oklahoma	United States	102	B2

Name	Country / Region	Page	Grid
Oklahoma City	United States	102	B2
Oktjobrskoye	Russia	31	P2
Okushiri-To	Japan	81	K2
Öland	Sweden	29	J8
Olavarria	Argentina	110	A4
Ólbia	Sardinia (Italy)	45	D8
Old Head of Kinsale	Ireland	37	E10
Oldenburg	Germany	34	D3
Olenëk	Russia	72	L2
Olenëkskiy Zaliv	Russia	72	K2
Olib	Croatia	46	B5
Olite	Spain	41	J2
Olomouc	Czech Republic	33	G8
Olongapo	Philippines	77	F4
Olsztyn	Poland	30	E4
Olsztyn	Poland	29	L10
Olt	Romania	47	M5
Olten	Switzerland	38	N6
Oltenita	Romania	47	P5
Olympia	United States	96	B1
Olympus (Ólimbos)	Greece	48	E4
Ólimbos (Olympus)	Greece	48	E4
Olympus (Mount Troodos)	Cyprus	49	Q10
Olyutorskiy Zaliv	Russia	73	V6
Omaha	United States	98	A2
Oman	Middle East	53	F6
Omdurman (Umm Durman)	Sudan	61	F4
Omineca Mountains	Canada	92	E5
Ommanney Bay	Canada	92	L2
Omolon	Russia	73	T3
Omsk	Russia	71	N6
Omuramba Omatako	South Africa	66	B3
Omuta	Japan	80	F7
Onega	Russia	30	H2
Ontario	Canada	93	P6
Oost-Alpen	Austria	43	G3
Oostende (Ostend)	Belgium	26	F3
Oosterschelde	Netherlands	27	H3
Opava	Czech Republic	33	G8
Opole	Poland	33	G7
Oppda	Norway	29	E5
Oradea	Romania	46	J2
Oran	Algeria	59	E1
Orange	France	39	K9
Orange/Oranje	South Africa	66	B5
Orango	Guinea-Bissau	62	A2
Orayská priehradni nádrz	Slovakia	33	J8
Orcadas	South Atlantic Ocean	112	(2)A3
Örebro	Sweden	29	H7
Oregon	United States	96	B2
Orel	Russia	30	H4
Orenburg	Russia	71	K7
Orense	Spain	40	C2
Orford Ness	United Kingdom	26	E2
Orgeyev	Moldova	47	R2
Orihuela	Spain	41	K6
Orillia	Canada	99	E2
Orinoco	South America	108	D2
Cristano	Italy	45	C9
Orivesi	Finland	28	Q5
Orkney Islands	United Kingdom	36	L2
Orlando	United States	103	E4
Orléans	France	38	H6
Órmos Vistonias	Greece	48	G4
Örnsköldsvik	Sweden	28	K5
Crocué	Colombia	108	C3
Orona	Kiribati (Pacific Ocean)	85	J6
Cronsay	United Kingdom	36	L2
Oroshàza	Hungary	46	H3
Orsha	Belarus	30	G4
Orsk	Russia	31	M4
Ortles	Italy	44	E2
Crumíyeh	Iran	52	E2
Cruru	Bolivia	108	D7
Crust	Sweden	29	F7
Osaka	Japan	79	K4
Osaka-Wan	Japan	80	H6
Ose-Zaki	Japan	80	E7
Osh	Kyrgyzstan	71	N9
Oshawa	Canada	99	E2
Oshmyany	Belarus	29	N9
Oshogbo	Nigeria	63	E3
Osijek	Croatia	46	F4
Oskarshamn	Sweden	29	J8
Oskélanéo	Canada	99	F1
Oslo	Norway	29	F7
Oslofjord	Norway	29	F7
Osmaniye	Turkey	50	G5
Osnabrück	Germany	34	D4
Osogovske Planine	Bulgaria / Macedonia	48	E2
Osprey Reef	Australia	87	J2
Osrtov Moscny	Russia	29	P6
Oss	Netherlands	27	J3
Ossa	Greece	48	E5
Ostashkov	Russia	30	G3
Ostend (Oostende)	Belgium	26	F3
Östersund	Sweden	28	H5
Ostfriesische-Inseln	Germany	34	B3
Ostrava	Czech Republic	33	H8
Ostrelka	Poland	29	L10
Ostróda	Poland	32	J4
Ostroleka	Poland	32	L4
Ostrov Anzhu	Russia	73	P1
Ostrov Arkticheskogo Instituta	Russia	70	P2
Ostrov Ayon	Russia	73	V3
Ostrov Belyy	Russia	70	M3
Ostrov Beringa	Russia	73	V6
Ostrov Bol'shoy Begichev	Russia	70	W3
Ostrov Bollyakhovsky	Russia	73	Q2
Ostrov Chechen	Russia	51	M2
Ostrov Faddeyevskiy	Russia	73	Q1
Ostrov Iturup / Etorofu-To	Russia	73	R8
Ostrov Karaginskiy	Russia	73	U5
Ostrov Kolguyev	Russia	70	H4
Ostrov Kotel'nyy	Russia	73	P1
Ostrov Kunashir / Kunashiri-To	Russia	73	Q8
Ostrov Maly Lyakhovskiy	Russia	73	Q2
Ostrov Mednyy	Russia	73	V6
Ostrov Novaya Sibir	Russia	73	R1
Ostrov Oleniy	Russia	70	P3
Ostrov Onekotan	Russia	73	S6
Ostrov Paramushir	Russia	73	S6
Ostrov Peschanyy	Russia	72	K2
Ostrov Shumshu	Russia	73	T6
Ostrov Sibiryakova	Russia	70	P3
Ostrov Stolbovoy	Russia	72	N2
Ostrov Urup	Russia	73	R7
Ostrov Vaygach	Russia	70	K3
Ostrov Vrangelya (Wrangel)	Russia	73	Y2
Ostrova Izvestiy	Russia	70	P2
Ostrova Medvezh'i	Russia	73	U2
Ostrova Sakhalin	Russia	73	Q6
Ostrova Shantarskiye	Russia	73	P6
Ostrów Wielkopolski	Poland	32	G6
Osumi-Shoto	Japan	80	E8
Otaru	Japan	81	L2
Otnes	Norway	29	F6
Otok	Croatia	46	B6
Otsu	Japan	81	J6
Otta	Norway	29	E6
Ottawa	Canada	93	R7
Otwock	Poland	32	L5
Ötztaler Alpen	Austria	42	F4
Ou-Sammyaku	Japan	81	L4
Ouachita Mountains	United States	102	C3
Ouaddai	Chad	60	C5
Ouagadougou	Burkina Faso	62	D2
Ouargla	Algeria	59	G2
Ouarzazate	Morocco	58	D2
Oued Djedi	Algeria	59	F2
Oued el Ma	Mauritania	58	D4
Oued Moulouya	Morocco	58	E2
Oued Rheris	Morocco	58	E2
Oued Sous	Morocco	58	D2
Ouésso	Congo	64	B3
Oujda	Morocco	59	E2
Oulu	Finland	28	N4
Oulujärvi	Finland	28	P4
Oulujoki	Finland	28	P4
Ouse	United Kingdom	37	P9
Outer Hebrides	United Kingdom	36	F4
Oviedo	Spain	40	E1
Owando	Congo	64	B4
Oxford	United Kingdom	37	M10
Özarfjöroar	Iceland	28	(1)E1
Ozark Plateau	United States	102	C2
Ozero Baykal (Lake Baikal)	Russia	72	H6
Ozero Beloye	Russia	30	H2
Ozero Il'men'	Russia	30	G3
Ozero Imandra	Russia	30	G1
Ozero Issyk Kul'	Kyrgyzstan	71	P9
Ozero Khanka (Lake Khanka)	China / Russia	79	J1
Ozero Kitay	Ukraine	47	S4
Ozero Onezhskoye (Lake Onega)	Russia	30	H2
Ozero Sevan	Armenia	51	L3
Ozero Taymyr	Russia	70	U3
Ozero Tengiz	Kazakhstan	71	M7
Ozero Umbozero	Russia	28	T3
Ozero Verhni Kujto	Russia	28	R4
Ozero Yalpug	Ukraine	47	R4
Ozero Zaysan	Kazakhstan	71	Q8

P

Name	Country / Region	Page	Grid
P'yongyang	North Korea	80	C4
P'eng Hu Lieh-Tao	Taiwan	77	F2
Paarl	South Africa	66	B6
Pabianice	Poland	32	J6
Pacific Ocean	Pacific Ocean	69	U9
Padang	Indonesia	82	C3
Paderborn	Germany	34	D5
Padova	Italy	44	F3
Padre	United States	102	B4
Paducah	United States	102	D2
Paektu-San	North Korea	80	E3
Paengnyong-Do	South Korea	80	C5
Pag	Croatia	46	B5
Pagai Selatan	Indonesia	82	B3
Pagai Utara	Indonesia	82	B3
Pagan	Northern Mariana Islands / U.S.A.	84	E4
Pagasitikós Kólpos	Greece	48	E5
Pagatan	Indonesia	83	A3
Page	United States	96	D3
Pahang	Malaysia	76	C6
Páhnes	Greece	48	F9
Päijänne	Finland	29	N6
Paikü Co	China	74	E3
Pajala	Sweden	28	M3
Pakistan	Southern Asia	53	J4
Paks	Hungary	33	H11
Palagruza	Croatia	46	D7
Palana	Russia	73	T5
Palau	Palau	84	D5
Palau	Oceania	84	D5
Palau Breuech	Indonesia	82	A1
Palawan	Philippines	77	F5
Palembang	Indonesia	82	C3
Palencia	Spain	40	F2
Palermo	Sicily (Italy)	45	H10
Paljavaam	Russia	73	W3
Palk Strait	India / Sri Lanka	75	C7
Pallasovka	Russia	31	K4
Palma	Spain	41	N5
Palmerston	Cook Islands	85	K7
Palmerston North	New Zealand	88	E5
Palmira	Colombia	108	B3
Palmyra Atoll	United States	85	K5
Palu	Indonesia	83	A3
Pamir	Tajikistan	71	N10
Pamlico Sound	United States	103	F2
Pampa del Tamarugal	Chile	110	H2
Pampas	Argentina	110	H6
Pamplona	Spain	41	J2
Panamá	Central America	105	H7
Panama City	United States	103	D3
Panama City	Panama	108	B2
Panama-Canal (Canal de Panama)	Panama	105	J7
Panay	Philippines	77	G4
Panevézys	Lithuania	29	N9
Pangutaran	Philippines	83	A1
Pantanal	Brazil	109	F7
Pantelleria	Italy	45	G12
Pantoja	Peru	108	B4
Pápa	Hungary	46	E2
Papakura	New Zealand	88	E3
Papenburg	Germany	34	C3
Papua New-Guinea	Oceania	84	E6
Papuk	Croatia	46	E4
Paraguay	South America	110	J3
Paraguay	South America	111	K3
Parakou	Benin	63	E2
Paramaribo	Surinam	109	F2
Paramo Frontino	Colombia	108	B2
Paraná	Argentina	110	J5
Paraná	South America	111	L3
Parc National de la Salonga	Democratic Republic of Congo	64	C4
Parchim	Germany	34	G3
Parczew	Poland	32	M6
Pardubice	Czech Republic	33	E7
Paris	United States	102	C3
Paris	France	38	H5
Parma	Italy	44	E4
Parnaíba	Brazil	109	J4
Parnassos (Liákoura)	Greece	48	E6
Párnon Óros	Greece	48	E7
Parnu	Estonia	29	N7
Páros	Greece	48	G7
Parpaillon	France	42	B6
Pasman	Croatia	46	C6
Passau	Germany	35	J8
Pasto	Colombia	108	B3
Pastora Peak	United States	101	E1
Patagonia	Argentina	110	G7
Pátmos	Greece	48	J7
Patna	India	74	E3
Patomskoye Nagorye	Russia	72	K5
Pátrai	Greece	48	D6
Patuca	Honduras	105	G5
Pau	France	39	E10
Paulatuk	Canada	92	G3
Pavia	Italy	42	E5
Pavlodar	Kazakhstan	71	P7
Paxoi	Greece	48	B5
Pazardzhik	Bulgaria	47	M7
Pazartası Burun	Turkey	50	D3
Peace River	Canada	92	J5
Pec	Yugoslavia	46	H7
Pechora	Russia	31	M1
Pechorskoye More	Russia	70	J4
Pecos	United States	101	F2
Pecos River	United States	101	F2
Pécs	Hungary	33	H11
Pedreiras	Brazil	109	J4
Pedro Juan Caballero	Paraguay	109	F8
Peene	Germany	34	J3
Peer	Belgium	27	J3
Peera Peera Poolanna Lake	Australia	87	G5
Pegasus Bay	New Zealand	89	E6
Pegu	Myanmar (Burma)	76	B3
Pegu Yoma	Myanmar (Burma)	76	B2
Pegunungan Iran	Malaysia / Indonesia	77	E6
Pegunungan Jayawijaya	South East Asia	83	E3
Pegunungan Maoke	South East Asia	83	E3
Pegunungan Sudirman	South East Asia	83	E3
Pegunungan van Rees	South East Asia	83	E3
Pekalongan	Indonesia	82	D4
Pekanbaru	Indonesia	82	C2
Pélagos	Greece	48	F5
Pelinaion	Greece	48	J6
Peljesac	Croatia	46	E7
Pellg i Drinit	Albania	48	B3
Pellworm	Germany	34	D2
Pelly Mountains	Canada	92	E4
Pelotas	Brazil	111	L5
Pematangsiantar	Indonesia	82	B2
Pemba	Mozambique	67	G2
Pemba	Tanzania	65	G5
Pemba	Mozambique	65	G6
Peña Trevinca	Spain	40	D2
Peña Ubiña	Spain	40	E1
Pend Orielle	United States	96	C1
Pendik	Turkey	49	M4
Pendleton	United States	96	C1

Name	Location		Page	Grid
Peniche	Portugal	•	40	A5
Peninsular Malaysia	Malaysia		76	C6
Penner	India		75	C6
Pennines	United Kingdom		37	L7
Pennsylvania	United States	a	99	E2
Penny Highlands	Canada		93	T3
Penrhyn	Cook Islands		85	L6
Pensacola	United States	•	102	D3
Pentenwell Lake	United States		98	C2
Penticton	Canada	•	96	C1
Pentland Firth	United Kingdom		36	K3
Penza	Russia	•	30	J4
Penzhinskaya Guba	Russia		73	U4
Peoria	United States	•	98	C2
Pergunungan Natuna	Malaysia		82	F2
Périgueux	France	•	39	f8
Peristéri	Greece	▲	48	D5
Perm	Russia	•	31	M3
Pernik	Bulgaria	•	47	L7
Perpignan	France	○	39	J11
Perth	Australia	○	86	C6
Pertuis Breton	France		39	D7
Pertuis d'Antioche	France		39	D7
Peru	South America	A	108	B5
Peru-Chile Trench	Pacific Ocean		106	D5
Perugia	Italy	•	44	G5
Pesaro	Italy	•	43	H7
Pescara	Italy	•	44	J6
Peshawar	Pakistan	○	53	K3
Peshkopia	Albania	•	46	H8
Peter I. Island	Antarctica	•	112(2)	JJ3
Peterborough	United Kingdom	•	26	C2
Petermann Ranges	Australia		86	E4
Petermanns Bjerg	Greenland	▲	112	(1)T2
Petites Pyrénées	France		41	M1
Petre Bay	New Zealand		89	B2
Petrila	Romania	•	47	L4
Petrolina	Brazil	•	109	J5
Petropavlovsk	Kazakhstan	•	31	P4
Petropavlovsk-Kamchatskiy	Russia	•	73	T6
Petrozavodsk	Russia	•	30	G2
Pevek	Russia	•	73	W3
Pfälzer Wald	Germany		35	C7
Pforzheim	Germany	•	35	D8
Phanom Dang Raek	South East Asia		76	C4
Philadelphia	United States	•	99	E3
Philippines	South East Asia	A	77	G5
Phnom Penh	Cambodia	■	76	D4
Phoenix	United States	○	100	D2
Phoenix Island	Kiribati (Pacific Ocean)		85	J6
Phou Bia	Laos	▲	76	C3
Piacenza	Italy	•	44	D3
Pianosa	Italy		44	K6
Piatra Neamt	Romania	•	47	P3
Piave	Italy		44	G3
Pic Boby	Madagascar	▲	67	H4
Pic d'Ánie	France	▲	41	K2
Pic Toussíde	Chad	▲	60	C3
Picacho del Centinela	Mexico	▲	101	E3
Pico (Azores)	Portugal		58	(1)B2
Pico Bolivar	Venezuela	▲	108	C2
Pico de Almanzor	Spain	▲	40	E4
Pico de Teide	Canary Islands	▲	58	B3
Picos de Europa	Spain		40	E1
Pidurutalagala	Sri Lanka	▲	75	D7
Piedras Negras	Mexico	•	101	E3
Pielinen	Finland		28	Q5
Pierre	United States	•	97	F2
Pietermaritzburg	South Africa	○	66	E5
Pietersburg	South Africa	•	66	D4
Pik Aborigen	Russia	▲	73	R4
Pik Kommunizma	Tajikistan	▲	53	K2
Pik Pobedy	China	▲	71	P9
Pīla	Poland	•	32	F4
Pilica	Poland		32	K6
Pilsen (Plzen)	Czech Republic	•	33	C8
Pinang	Malaysia		82	C1
Pinar	Spain	▲	40	E8
Pinar del Rio	Cuba	○	105	H4
Pindos Oros	Greece		48	D5
Pine Island Bay	Antarctica		112(2)	GG2
Pinerolo	Italy	•	42	C6
Pingvallavatn	Iceland		28	(1)C2
Pingxiang	China	•	78	E5
Pinneberg	Germany	•	34	E3
Pinta	Ecuador		108	(1)A1
Piombino	Italy	•	44	E6
Pireás	Greece	•	48	F6
Pirin	Bulgaria		48	F3
Pirineos (Pyrénées)	France / Spain		41	K2
Pirmasens	Germany	•	35	C7
Pirna	Germany	•	35	J6
Pirot	Yugoslavia	•	47	K6
Pisa	Italy	•	44	E5
Pisek	Czech Republic	•	33	D8
Pistilfjördur	Iceland		28	(1)F1
Pitcairn Islands	Pacific Ocean		85	P8
Pite älv	Sweden		28	L4
Piteå	Sweden	•	28	L4
Pitesti	Romania	•	47	M5
Pitkjaranta	Russia	•	30	G2
Pitt Island	New Zealand		89	(1)B2
Pitt Strait	New Zealand		89	B2
Pittsburgh	United States	•	99	E2
Piura	Peru	•	108	A5
Pjörsá	Iceland		28	(1)D2
Placentia Bay	Canada		93	W7
Plackovica	Macedonia		48	E3
Planalto de Mato Grosso	Brazil	•	106	F5

Name	Location		Page	Grid
Planalto do Bié	Angola		66	B2
Planalto do Brasil				
(Brazilian Highlands)	Brazil		109	J7
Plasencia	Spain	•	40	D4
Plateau du Bemaraha	Madagascar		67	G3
Plateau du Djado	Niger		60	B3
Plateau du Tademaït	Algeria		59	F3
Plateaux Batéké	Congo		64	A4
Plateaux Batéké	Congo		63	G5
Platte	Seychelles		67	(2) C2
Platte River	United States		97	F2
Plauer See	Germany		34	H3
Plaven	Germany	•	35	G6
Plesetsk	Russia	•	30	J2
Pleven	Bulgaria	•	47	M6
Plituice	Croatia	•	44	K4
Pljesevica	Bosnia-Herzegovina /			
	Croatia		46	C5
Pljevlja	Yugoslavia	•	46	G6
Plock	Poland	•	32	J5
Plöckenstein / Plechy	Germany / Austria /			
	Czech Republic	▲	35	J8
Ploiesti	Romania	○	47	P5
Plöner See	Germany		34	F2
Plovdiv	Bulgaria	•	47	M7
Plymouth	United Kingdom	•	37	K11
Plymouth Sound	United Kingdom		37	A3
Plzen (Pilsen)	Czech Republic	•	33	C8
Po	Italy		44	E4
Pobeda	Russia	▲	112	(1)A3
Pocatello	United States	•	96	D2
Podgorica	Yugoslavia	•	46	G7
Podgorica	Yugoslavia	•	48	B2
Podkamennaya Tunguska	Russia		72	E4
Poel	Germany	•	34	G2
Poggonsi	Italy	•	42	G7
Pogórze Karpackie	Poland		33	J8
Pohnpei	Micronesia		84	F5
Pohorje	Slovakia		46	C3
Point Conception	United States		100	B2
Point Culver	Australia		86	E6
Point d'Entrecasteaux	Australia		86	B7
Point Lay	Alaska	•	100	(1)E2
Pointe de Barfleur	France		26	B5
Pointe de Grave	France		39	D8
Pointe de l'Est	Canada		93	U7
Pointe de la Coubre	France		39	D8
Pointe de Penmarch	France		38	A6
Pointe du Raz	France		38	A5
Pointe Noire	Congo	○	63	G5
Poitiers	France	•	39	F7
Pojezierze				
Wielkopolsko-Kujawskie	Poland		32	F5
Pokhvistnevo	Russia	•	31	L4
Pola de Siero	Spain	•	40	E1
Poland	Europe	A	32	F5
Polatli	Turkey	•	49	Q5
Polillo Islands	Philippines		77	G4
Poluostrov Rybachiy	Russia		28	S1
Polyarny Ural	Russia		31	N1
Polynesia	Oceania		85	J6
Pommersche Bucht	Germany / Poland		34	K2
Pomorskiy Proliv	Russia		31	K1
Ponferrada	Spain	•	40	D2
Ponoy	Russia		30	J1
Pont-Audemer	France		26	D5
Ponta Albina	Angola		66	A3
Ponta da Baleia	Brazil		109	K7
Ponta da Barra	Mozambique		67	F4
Ponta da Barra Falsa	Mozambique		67	F4
Pontevedra	Spain	•	40	B2
Pontianak	Indonesia	•	82	D3
Pontivy	France	•	38	C5
Ponza	Italy	•	45	H8
Pool-Plateau	Antarctica		112	(2)LL1
Poole	United Kingdom	•	37	L11
Poona (Pune)	India	•	75	B5
Poprad	Slovakia	•	33	K8
Porcupine River	United States/Canada		92	C3
Pordenono	Italy	•	43	H5
Pori	Finland	•	29	L6
Pórisvatn	Iceland		28	(1)D2
Porpoise Bay	Antarctica	•	112	(2)T3
Porsangen	Norway		28	N1
Porsuk Baraji	Turkey		49	N5
Port Alberni	Canada	•	96	B1
Port Angeles	United States	•	96	B1
Port Arthur	United States	•	102	C4
Port Elizabeth	South Africa	•	66	D6
Port Gentil	Gabon	○	63	F5
Port Harcourt	Nigeria	○	63	F4
Port Moresby	Papua New Guinea	•	84	E6
Port of Spain	Trinidad and Tobago	○	105	M6
Port Phillip Bay	Australia		87	H7
Port Said (Bûr Sa'îd)	Egypt	•	61	F1
Port Sudan (Bur Sudan)	Sudan	○	61	G4
Port-au-Prince	Haiti	○	105	K5
Port-Louis	Mauritius	■	67	(1) B2
Portalegre	Portugal	•	40	C5
Portales	United States	•	101	F2
Porthmós Kafiréos	Greece		48	G7
Portimão	Portugal	•	40	B7
Portland	United States	•	99	F2
Portland (Oreg.)	United States	•	96	B1
Portland Bill (ME.)	United Kingdom		37	L11
Porto	Portugal	•	40	B3
Pôrto Alegre	Brazil	○	111	L5
Porto Santo (Madeira)	Portugal	•	58	B2
Pôrto Velho	Brazil	•	108	E5

Name	Location		Page	Grid
Porto-Novo	Benin	■	63	E3
Portsmouth	United Kingdom	•	37	N11
Porttipahdan Tekojärvi	Finland		28	N2
Portugal	Europe	A	40	B6
Posadas	Argentina	•	111	K4
Potenza	Italy	•	45	K8
Potes	Spain	•	40	F1
Potosí	Bolivia	•	108	D7
Potsdam	Germany	○	34	H4
Poverty Bay	New Zealand		88	G4
Poyang Hu	China		78	F5
Poza Rica de Hidalgo	Mexico	•	104	E4
Pozarevac	Yugoslavia	•	46	J5
Poznan	Poland	•	32	F5
Pozoblanco	Spain	•	40	F6
Pra	West Africa		62	D3
Prague (Praha)	Czech Republic	■	33	D7
Praha (Prague)	Czech Republic	■	33	D7
Praia	Cape Verde	■	62	A5
Praslin	Seychelles		67	(2) C1
Prato	Italy	•	44	F5
Pratomagno	Italy	▲	43	G7
Pregel	Russia		32	K3
Premuda	Croatia		46	B5
Prenj	Bosnia-Herzegovina		46	E6
Preparis North Channel	South East Asia		76	A3
Presa V. Carranza	Mexico		101	E3
Prescott	United States	•	100	D2
Presidio	United States	•	101	F3
Presov	Slovakia	•	33	L8
Prest'ány	Slovakia	•	33	G9
Preston	United Kingdom	•	37	K8
Pretoria	South Africa	■	66	D5
Pretov	Czech Republic	•	33	G8
Pribram	Czech Republic	•	33	C8
Pridz Bay	Antarctica		112	(2)N3
Priego	Spain	•	41	H4
Prijedor	Bosnia Hersogovina	•	46	D5
Prikaspiyskaya Nizmennost	Kazakhstan		71	H8
Prilep	Macedonia	•	48	D3
Primorsko-Akhtarsk	Russia	•	30	H5
Prince Albert	Canada	•	92	K6
Prince Albert Sound	Canada		92	H2
Prince Charles Island	Canada		93	R3
Prince Edward Island	Canada		93	U7
Prince Edward Island (P.E.)	Canada	a	93	U7
Prince George	Canada	•	92	G6
Prince of Wales Island	United States		100	(1)L4
Prince of Wales Island	Australia		87	H2
Prince of Wales Island	Canada		92	L2
Prince Rupert	Canada	•	92	E6
Princess Charlotte Bay	Australia		87	H2
Principe	São Tomé and Príncipe		63	F4
Pripyat	Belarus		30	F4
Pristina	Yugoslavia	•	48	D2
Privas	France	•	39	K9
Prizren	Yugoslavia	•	48	C2
Probilov Islands	United States		100	(1)D4
Professor van				
Blommesteen Meer	Surinam		109	F3
Profitis Ilías	Greece	▲	48	E8
Prokop'yevsk	Russia	•	71	Q7
Proliv Dmitriya Lapteva	Russia		73	P2
Proliv Karskiye Vorota	Russia		70	K3
Proliv Longa	Russia		73	X3
Proliv Sannikova	Russia		73	P2
Proliv Vil'kitskogo	Russia		70	U2
Providence	Seychelles		67	(2) B2
Providence	United States	○	99	F2
Providencia	Caribbean	•	105	H6
Provins	France	•	38	J5
Provo	United States	•	97	D2
Prüm	Germany	•	35	B6
Prusk'ów	Poland	•	32	K5
Prut	Europe		47	R3
Psará	Greece		48	H6
Pskov	Russia	•	30	F3
Pskovskoye Ozero (Lake Peipus)	Russia		30	F3
Pucallpa	Peru	○	108	C5
Pudasjärvi	Finland	○	28	P4
Puebla de Zaragoza	Mexico	○	104	E5
Pueblo	United States	•	97	F3
Puente-Genil	Spain	•	40	F7
Puerto Montt	Chile	•	110	G7
Puerto Penasco	Mexico	•	100	D2
Puerto Rico	Caribbean	•	105	L5
Puertollano	Spain	•	40	F6
Puig Mayor	Spain	▲	41	N5
Pukapuka	French Polynesia		85	N7
Pula	Croatia	•	43	J6
Pulau Adi	Indonesia		83	D3
Pulau Ambon	Indonesia		83	C3
Pulau Bacan	Indonesia		83	C3
Pulau Bali	Indonesia		82	F4
Pulau Banggi	Malaysia		77	F5
Pulau Bangka	Indonesia		82	D3
Pulau Belitung	Indonesia		82	D3
Pulau Biak	Indonesia		83	E3
Pulau Bintan	Indonesia		82	C2
Pulau Breueh	Indonesia		76	A5
Pulau Buru	Indonesia		83	C3
Pulau Buton	Indonesia		83	B4
Pulau Damar	Indonesia		83	C4
Pulau Dolak	Indonesia		83	E4
Pulau Enggano	Indonesia		82	C4
Pulau Flores	Indonesia		83	B4
Pulau Kabaena	Indonesia		83	B4
Pulau Karakelong	Indonesia		83	C2
Pulau Kobroor	Indonesia		83	D4

Name	Country	Page	Grid
Rockford	United States	98	C2
Rockglen	Canada	96	E1
Rocky Mountains	United States/ Canada	92	E5
Ródhos (Rhodes)	Greece	49	L8
Rodopi	Bulgaria / Greece	48	F3
Roes Welcome Sound	Canada	93	P4
Roeselare	Belgium	26	G4
Rohtak	India	74	C3
Roja	Latvia	29	M8
Rolla	United States	98	B3
Roman	Romania	47	P3
Roman-Kos	Ukraine	50	F1
Romania	Europe	47	L4
Rome	United States	96	C2
Rome (Roma)	Italy	44	G7
Rømø	Denmark	29	E9
Rona	United Kingdom	36	H2
Roncagua	Chile	110	G5
Ronco	Italy	43	H6
Rønne	Denmark	32	D2
Ronne Ice Shelf	Antarctica	112	LL1
Ronneby	Sweden	32	E1
Roraima	Venezuela/Brazil	108	E2
Rosario	Argentina	110	J5
Rose	American Samoa	85	K7
Rosemary Bank	United Kingdom	36	C2
Rosenheim	Germany	35	H9
Rosiori de Vede	Romania	47	M5
Roskilde	Denmark	32	B2
Ross Ice Shelf	Antarctica	112	(2)Z2
Ross Sea	Antarctica	112	(2)Z2
Rossan Point	Ireland	37	D7
Rossano	Italy	45	L9
Rossnava	Slovakia	33	K9
Rossosh	Russia	30	H4
Rostock	Germany	34	H2
Rostov-na-Donu	Russia	30	H5
Roswell	United States	101	F2
Rota	Northern Mariana Islands, U.S.A.	84	E4
Rotenburg	Germany	34	E3
Rothaargebirge	Germany	35	D5
Roti	Indonesia	86	D2
Rottenburg	Germany	35	D8
Rotterdam	Netherlands	27	H3
Rottumerplaat	Netherlands	34	B3
Rotuma	Fiji	84	H7
Rotura	New Zealand	88	F4
Roubaix	France	38	J3
Rouen	France	38	G4
Rousay	United Kingdom	36	K2
Rovaniemi	Finland	30	F2
Rovaniemi	Finland	28	P3
Rovereto	Italy	42	G5
Rovigo	Italy	43	G5
Rovno	Ukraine	30	F4
Rowley Island	Canada	93	Q3
Royal Canal	Ireland	37	G8
Royal Tunbridge Wells	United Kingdom	26	D3
Royan	France	39	D8
Roztocze	Poland	33	M7
Rsita	Romania	46	K5
Rt Kamenjak	Croatia	43	J6
Rt Savudrija	Croatia	43	J5
Ruacana Falls	Namibia / Angola	66	A3
Ruapehu	New Zealand	88	E4
Ruapuke Island	New Zealand	89	C8
Rub al Khali	Saudi Arabia	52	E6
Rubtsovsk	Russia	71	Q7
Rudnyy	Kazakhstan	31	N4
Rugby	United Kingdom	26	B2
Rügen	Germany	34	J2
Rugles	France	26	D6
Ruhnu	Estonia	29	M8
Ruhr	Germany	27	L3
Rumbek	Sudan	64	D2
Rundu	Namibia	66	B3
Ruo Shui	China	78	C2
Rur	Germany	35	B5
Rurutu	French Polynesia	85	L8
Ruse	Bulgaria	47	N6
Russia	Russia	32	K3
Russia	Asia	30	J3
Rustavi	Georgia	51	L3
Rutland	India	75	F6
Ruvuma (Rovuma)	Tanzania	67	F2
Ruvuma/Rovuma	Central Africa	65	F6
Ruzomberok	Slovakia	33	J8
Rwanda	Central Africa	64	D4
Ryazan	Russia	30	H4
Rybinskoye Vdkhr.	Russia	30	H3
Rybnik	Poland	33	H7
Rybnitsa	Moldova	47	R2
Rypin	Poland	32	J4
Ryukyu Islands (Ryukyu-Shoto)	Japan	79	G6
Ryukyu-Shoto (Ryukyu Islands)	Japan	79	G6
Rzeszów	Poland	33	M7
Rzhev	Russia	30	G3

S

Name	Country	Page	Grid
's Hertogenbosch/Den Bosch	Netherlands	27	J3
S.Sandwich Islands	South Atlantic Ocean	112	(2)C4
Sivas	Turkey	50	G4
's-Gravenhage (Den Haag) (The Hague)	Netherlands	38	J1
Sa'idabad	Iran	55	F2
Saale	Germany	35	G6

Name	Country	Page	Grid
Saalfeld	Germany	35	G6
Saarbrücken	Germany	35	C7
Saaremaa	Estonia	29	M7
Sabac	Yugoslavia	46	G5
Sabadell	Spain	41	N3
Sabah	Malaysia	77	F5
Sabha	Libya	59	H3
Sabi	South Africa	67	E4
Sabkhat al Bardawil	Egypt	54	A5
Sabkhat Ghuzayyil	Libya	60	C2
Sabkhat Shunayn	Libya	60	D1
Sabkhat Tawurgha	Libya	60	B1
Sable Island	Canada	93	V8
Sabzevar	Iran	71	K11
Sachs Harbour	Canada	92	G2
Sack	Ukraine	33	N6
Sacramento	United States	96	B3
Sadd el Aali	Egypt	52	B4
Sado	Portugal	40	B6
Sado-Shima	Japan	81	K4
Safi	Morocco	58	D2
Safid Kuh	Afghanistan	53	H3
Safonovo	Russia	31	K1
Saga	Japan	80	E7
Sagami-Nada	Japan	81	K6
Sagar	India	74	C4
Sagiz	Kazakhstan	31	L5
Sagres	Portugal	40	B7
Saguia el-Hamra	Western Sahara	58	C3
Sagunto	Spain	41	K5
Sahagún	Spain	40	E2
Sahara	Africa	58	D4
Sahara-Atlas	Algeria	59	F2
Saharanpur	India	74	C2
Sahel	West Africa	62	C1
Sahiwal	Pakistan	53	K3
Sahra at Tih	Egypt	54	A6
Sahra' Bayyudah	Sudan	61	F4
Sahra Marzuq	Libya	60	B3
Sahra' Rabyanah	Libya	60	C2
Sahyadri / Western Ghats	India	75	B5
Saigon (Ho Chi Minh)	Vietnam	76	D4
Saimaa	Finland	30	F2
Saint Jérôme	Canada	99	F1
Saint Lawrence River	Canada	99	G1
Saint Lô	France	26	B5
Saint Paul	United States	98	B2
Saint Pierre	Seychelles	(2) 67	A2
Saint-Brieuc	France	38	C5
Saint-Denis	South Africa	67	(1) B2
Saint-Denis	France	38	H4
Saint-Dié	France	38	M5
Saint-Dizier	France	38	K5
Saint-Étienne	France	39	K8
Saint-Gaudens	France	39	F10
Saint-Nazaire	France	38	C6
Saint-Omer	France	26	F4
Saintes	France	39	E8
Saipan	Northern Mariana Islands, U.S.A	84	E4
Sajó	Hungary	33	K9
Sakai	Japan	80	H6
Sakar	Bulgaria	48	J3
Sakarya	Turkey	50	E4
Sakata	Japan	81	K4
Saki	Nigeria	63	E3
Sakishima-Gunto	Japan	79	G5
Sal	Cape Verde	62	(1)B1
Sal'sk	Russia	30	J5
Salamanca	Spain	40	E3
Salar de Atacama	Chile	110	H3
Salar de Uyuni	Bolivia	110	H3
Salas de los Infantes	Spain	40	G2
Salavat	Russia	31	M4
Salda Gölü	Turkey	49	M7
Saldanha	South Africa	66	B6
Saldus	Latvia	29	M8
Salé	Morocco	58	D2
Salekhard	Russia	31	P1
Salem	United States	96	B2
Salem	India	75	C6
Salerno	Italy	45	J8
Salina	Italy	45	J10
Salinas	United States	96	B3
Salinta	Romania	33	L11
Salisbury	United Kingdom	26	B3
Salisbury Island	Canada	93	R4
Salisbury Plain	United Kingdom	37	L10
Salla	Finland	28	Q3
Salmon	United States	96	D1
Salon-de-Provence	France	39	L10
Saloniki (Thessaloniki)	Greece	48	E4
Salor	Spain	40	D5
Salt Lake City	United States	96	D2
Salta	Argentina	110	H3
Saltillo	Mexico	101	F3
Salton Sea	United States	100	B2
Salvador	Brazil	109	K6
Salween (Nu Jiang)	South East Asia	78	B6
Salyótarján	Hungary	33	J9
Salzach	Germany / Austria	35	H9
Salzburg	Austria	43	J3
Salzgitter	Germany	34	F4
Salzwedel	Germany	34	G4
Samar	Philippines	77	H4
Samara	Russia	31	L4
Samarinda	Indonesia	82	F3
Samarkand	Uzbekistan	71	M10
Sambor	Ukraine	33	N8

Name	Country	Page	Grid
Samburg	Russia	31	R1
Samokov	Bulgaria	48	F2
Sámos	Greece	49	J7
Samothráki	Greece	48	H4
Samsun	Turkey	50	G3
San'a'	Yemen	52	D6
San Andrés	Caribbean	105	H6
San Angelo	United States	101	F2
San Antonio	United States	101	G3
San Carlos de Bariloche	Argentina	110	G7
San Clemente	United States	100	C2
San Cristóbal	Ecuador	108	(1)B2
San Cristóbal	Solomon Islands	84	G7
San Cristóbal	Venezuela	108	C2
San Diego	United States	100	C2
San Doná di Piave	Italy	43	H5
San Francisco	United States	96	B3
San Joaquin Valley	United States	100	B1
San Jose	United States	96	B3
San José	Costa Rica	108	A2
San José	Mexico	104	B3
San Juan	Argentina	110	H5
San Juan	United States	101	E1
San Juan	Puerto Rico	105	L5
San Juan Basin	United States	101	E1
San Julián	Argentina	110	H8
San Luis Obispo	United States	100	B1
San Luis Obispo Bay	United States	100	B1
San Luis Potosi	Mexico	101	F4
San Luis Rio Colorado	Mexico	100	C2
San Luis Valley	United States	97	D3
San Marino	Europe	44	G5
San Miguel de Tucuman	Argentina	110	H4
San Nicolas	United States	100	C2
San Pablo	Philippines	77	G4
San Pedro Sula	Honduras	104	G5
San Pietro	Sardinia	45	C9
San Rafael	Argentina	110	H5
San Remo	Italy	42	C7
San Salvador	Ecuador	108	(1)A2
San Salvador	El Salvador	104	F6
San Salvador	Bahamas	105	K4
San Sebastián	Spain	41	H1
San Severo	Italy	46	C8
San-Pédro	Côte D'Ivoire	62	C3
Sanaga	West Africa	63	G4
Sanandaj	Iran	52	E2
Sand	Norway	29	D7
Sandakan	Malaysia	82	F1
Sandanski	Bulgaria	47	L8
Sanday	United Kingdom	36	L2
Sandefjord	Norway	29	E7
Sanderson	United States	101	F2
Sandy Cape	Australia	87	K4
Sangerhausen	Germany	35	G5
Sangli	India	75	B5
Sanhago del Estero	Argentina	110	J4
Sankt	Austria	43	L2
Sankt Pölten	Austria	46	C1
Sankt Wendel	Germany	35	C7
Sankt-Peterburg (St. Petersburg)	Russia	30	G2
Sankuru	Democratic Republic of Congo	64	C4
Sanlúcar de Barrameda	Spain	40	D8
Sanok	Poland	33	M8
Santa Ana	United States	104	A2
Santa Barbara	United States	100	C2
Santa Catalina	United States	100	C2
Santa Cruz	United States	100	C2
Santa Cruz	Bolivia	108	E7
Santa Cruz	Ecuador	108	(1)A2
Santa Cruz de Tenerife	Canary Islands	58	B3
Santa Cruz Islands	Solomon Islands	84	G7
Santa Fe	United States	101	E1
Santa Fé	Argentina	110	J5
Santa Isabel	Solomon Islands	84	F6
Santa Luzia	Cape Verde	62	(1)B1
Santa Maria	United States	94	B5
Santa Maria	Brazil	111	L4
Santa Maria	Ecuador	108	(1)A2
Santa Maria (Azores)	Portugal	58	(1)B2
Santa Marta	Colombia	108	C1
Santa Rosa	United States	96	B3
Santa Rosa	Argentina	110	J6
Santa Rosa	United States	100	B2
Santander	Spain	40	F1
Santarém	Portugal	40	B5
Santarém	Brazil	109	G4
Santiago	Chile	110	G5
Santiago de Compostela	Spain	40	B2
Santiago de Cuba	Cuba	105	J4
Santo Antão	Cape Verde	62	(1)A1
Santos	Brazil	111	M3
São Jorge (Azoress)	Portugal	58	(1)B2
São José do Rio Prêto	Brazil	109	H8
São Luís	Brazil	109	J4
São Miguel (Azores)	Portugal	58	(1)B2
São Nicolau	Cape Verde	62	(1)B1
São Paulo	Brazil	111	M3
São Tiago	Cape Verde	62	(1)B2
São Tomé	São Tomé and Príncipe	63	F4
São Tomé and Príncipe	West Africa	63	F4
São Vicente	Cape Verde	62	(1)A1
Saône	France	39	K7
Saoura	Algeria	59	E3
Sapiéntza	Greece	48	D8
Sapporo	Japan	81	L2
Sarır Tibesti	Libya	60	C3
Sariyer	Turkey	49	L3

Name	Region	Page	Grid
Sarajevo	Bosnia-Herzegovina	46	F6
Saramati	Myanmar (Burma)	76	B1
Sarangani Islands	Philippines	83	B1
Saransk	Russia	30	K4
Saratov	Russia	30	K4
Sarawak	Malaysia	77	E6
Sardegna (Sardinia)	Italy	24	E3
Sardinia	Sardinia	45	C9
Sarektjåkkå	Sweden	28	J3
Sargasso Sea	Central America	105	L3
Sargodha	Pakistan	53	K3
Sarh	Chad	60	C6
Sarigan	Northern Mariana Islands, U.S.A.	84	E4
Sarine	Switzerland	42	C4
Sarinena	Spain	41	K3
Sarir Kalanshiyu	Libya	60	D2
Sariyer	Turkey	47	R8
Sark	United Kingdom	37	L12
Sarnia	Canada	98	D2
Saronikós Kólpos	Greece	48	F7
Saros Körfezi	Turkey	50	B3
Sarasoto	United States	103	E4
Sarrebourg	France	38	N5
Sarreguemines	France	27	L5
Sarykamys	Kazakhstan	31	L5
Sarykamyshkoye Ozero	Turkmenistan / Uzbekistan	71	K9
Sasebo	Japan	80	E7
Saskatchewan	Canada	92	K6
Saskatoon	Canada	92	K6
Saßnitz	Germany	34	J2
Sassandra	West Africa	62	C3
Sassari	Sardinia (Italy)	45	C8
Sassuolo	Italy	42	F6
Sata-Misaki	Japan	80	F8
Satu Mare	Romania	47	K2
Saudi Arabia	Middle East	52	D4
Saül	French Guyana	109	G3
Sault Saint Marie	Canada	98	D1
Saumur	France	38	E6
Saurimo	Angola	64	C5
Sava	Croatia	46	C4
Sava	Europe	43	K4
Savaii	Western Samoa	85	J7
Savannah	United States	103	E3
Savannah River	United States	103	E3
Save	South Africa	67	E4
Savoie	France	39	M8
Savolinna	Finland	28	Q6
Savona	Italy	42	D6
Sawu	Indonesia	86	D2
Sawu Sea	Indonesia	83	B4
Sayn-Sand	Mongolia	72	J8
Sázava	Czech Republic	33	E8
Scafell Pike	United Kingdom	37	K7
Scapa Flow	United Kingdom	36	K3
Schaalsee	Germany	34	F3
Schaffhausen	Switzerland	42	D3
Scharhörn	Germany	34	D3
Schawäbisch Hau	Germany	35	E7
Schefferville	Canada	93	T5
Scheibbs	Austria	43	L2
Schelde	Belgium	27	H3
Schiermonnikoog	Netherlands	27	J1
Schio	Italy	42	G5
Schladming	Austria	43	J3
Schleiden	Germany	35	B6
Schleswig	Germany	34	E2
Schruns	Austria	42	E3
Schwabach	Germany	35	G7
Schwäbische Alb	Germany	35	D8
Schwandorf	Germany	35	H7
Schwarzwald	Germany	35	D9
Schwedt	Germany	34	K3
Schweinfurt	Germany	35	F6
Schwerin	Germany	34	G3
Schweriner See	Germany	34	G3
Sciassa	Italy	45	K11
Scotia Ridge	Atlantic Ocean	107	F9
Scotland	United Kingdom	36	H5
Scott Island	Antarctica	112	(2)Z3
Sea of Azov	Ukraine	30	H5
Sea of Japan	East Asia	80	H4
Sea of Japan (Tong-Hae / Nippon-Kai)	South East Asia	79	J2
Sea of Marmara (Marmara Denizi)	Turkey	50	B3
Sea of Ochotsk (Hok-Kai)	East Asia	81	M1
Sea of the Hebrides	United Kingdom	36	F5
Seal Point	South Africa	66	C6
Seattle	United States	96	B1
Seaward Kaikoura Range	New Zealand	89	E6
Sebkha Azzel Matti	Algeria	59	F3
Sebkha de Timimoun	Algeria	59	F3
Sebkha de Tindouf	Algeria	58	D3
Sebkha Mekherrhane	Algeria	59	F3
Sebkhet Oumm ed Droûs Guebli	Mauritania	58	C4
Sebkhet Oumm ed Droûs Telli	Mauritania	58	C4
Sebkra du Ndaghamcha	Mauritania	58	B5
Secretary Island	New Zealand	89	B7
Sedan	France	27	H5
Sedano	Spain	40	G2
Segezha	Russia	30	G2
Ségou	Mali	58	D6
Segovia	Spain	40	F4
Segre	Spain	41	L3
Seguam Island	United States	100	(3)D1
Séguéla	Côte D'Ivoire	62	C3
Segura	Spain	41	J6
Seiland	Norway	28	M1
Seine	France	38	J5
Sekondi-Takoradi	Ghana	62	D4
Selat Balabac	Malaysia / Philippines	77	F5
Selat Mentawai	Asia	82	B3
Selecka Planina	Macedonia	48	D3
Selenter See	Germany	34	F2
Selfoss	Iceland	28	C3
Selkirk Mountains	United States/ Canada	92	H7
Selma	United States	102	D3
Selsey Bill	United Kingdom	38	E3
Selwyn Lake	Canada	92	L4
Selwyn Mountains	Canada	92	E4
Semarang	Indonesia	82	E4
Semipalatinsk	Kazakhstan	71	P7
Sendai	Japan	81	L4
Sendai-Wan	Japan	81	L4
Senegal	Mauritania	58	C5
Senigallia	Italy	42	J7
Senj	Croatia	46	B5
Senja	Norway	28	J2
Senkaku-Gunto	Japan	79	G5
Sens	France	38	H5
Senta	Yugoslavia	46	H4
Seoul (Soul)	South Korea	80	D5
Sept-Îles	Canada	93	T6
Sepúlveda	Spain	40	G3
Seram (Ceram)	Indonesia	83	C3
Sérifos	Greece	48	G7
Serov	Russia	31	N3
Serowe	Botswana	66	D4
Serra da Estrela	Portugal	40	C4
Serra da Mantiqueira	Brazil	111	M3
Serra da Neve	Angola	66	A2
Serra da Nogueira	Portugal	40	D3
Serra de Maracaju	Brazil	111	K3
Serra de Monchique	Portugal	40	B7
Serra do Espanhaço	Brazil	106	G5
Serra do Gerês	Spain	40	C3
Serra do Mar	Brazil	111	L4
Serra do Marão	Portugal	40	C3
Serra do Mogadouro	Portugal	40	D3
Serra dos Parecis	Brazil	108	E5
Serra Geral	Brazil	111	L4
Serra Geral do Paraná	Brazil	109	H6
Serra Namuli	Mozambique	67	F3
Sérrai	Greece	47	L8
Sérrai	Greece	48	F3
Serranía de Cuenca	Spain	41	H4
Sète	France	39	J10
Sétif	Algeria	59	G1
Setit	North East Africa	61	G5
Seto Naikai	Japan	80	G6
Sètubal	Portugal	40	B6
Sevastopol'	Ukraine	30	G6
Severn	United Kingdom	37	L10
Severnaya Dvina	Russia	30	J2
Severnaya Zemlya	Russia	70	S1
Severnyy Ural	Russia	31	M2
Severo-Sibirskaya Nizmennost (North Siberian Plain)	Russia	70	S3
Severodvinsk	Russia	30	H2
Sevier Lake	United States	96	D3
Sevilla	Spain	40	E7
Sèvre	France	39	E7
Seychelles	Indian Ocean	67	(2)A2
Sfax	Tunisia	59	H2
Sfîntu Gheorghe	Romania	47	N4
Shiraz	Iran	52	F4
Sha'ib Nisah	Saudi Arabia	55	B4
Shakhty	Russia	30	J5
Shakotan-Misaki	Japan	81	K2
Shaluli Shan	China	78	B4
Shanghai	China	79	G4
Shanghang	China	77	F1
Shannon	Ireland	37	E9
Shantou	China	78	F6
Shaoguan	China	78	E5
Shaoxing	China	79	G4
Shaoyang	China	78	E5
Shaqra	Saudi Arabia	55	A4
Shark Bay	Australia	86	B5
Shark Reef	Australia	87	J2
Sharya	Russia	30	J3
Shashe	South Africa	66	D4
Shashi	China	78	E4
Shatt al Arab	Middle East	55	B1
Shawinigan	Canada	99	F1
Sheffield	United Kingdom	37	M8
Shelikof Strait	United States	100	(1)F4
Shelter Point	New Zealand	89	C8
Shenyang	China	79	G2
Sherbro Island	Sierra Leone	62	B3
Sherbrooke	Canada	99	F1
Sheridan	United States	94	E3
Shetland Islands	United Kingdom	36	N1
Sheykh Sho'eyb	Iran	55	E2
Shib Kuh	Iran	55	D2
Shibushi-Wan	Japan	80	F8
Shijiazhuang	China	78	G3
Shikoku	Japan	80	G7
Shikoku-Sanchi	Japan	80	G7
Shikotan-To	Russia	73	R8
Shikotsu-Ko	Japan	81	L2
Shilega	Russia	30	J2
Shiliguri	India	74	L3
Shilla	India	74	C2
Shillong	India	76	A1
Shimoga	India	75	C6
Shimonoseki	Japan	80	F6
Shinyanga	Tanzania	65	E4
Shiono-Misaki	Japan	80	H7
Shirane-San	Japan	79	K3
Shiretoko-Misaki	Japan	81	N1
Shiriya-Zaki	Japan	81	L3
Shizuoka	Japan	81	K6
Shkodër	Albania	48	B2
Shoshoni	United States	97	E2
Shreveport	United States	102	C3
Shubar-Kuduk	Kazakhstan	31	M5
Shul	Middle East	55	D1
Shule He	China	78	B2
Shumen	Bulgaria	47	P6
Shur	Iran	55	E2
Sialkot	Pakistan	53	K3
Siargao	Philippines	77	H5
Siauliai	Lithuania	29	M9
Sibenik	Croatia	46	C6
Siberia	Russia	70	Q4
Sibiu	Romania	47	M4
Sibut	Central African Republic	63	H3
Sibuyan	Philippines	77	G4
Sibuyan Sea	Philippines	77	G4
Sicilia (Sicily)	Italy	45	H11
Sicilian Channel	Italy	45	F11
Sicily (Sicilia)	Italy	45	H11
Sidi Aissa	Algeria	41	P9
Sidorovosk	Russia	31	S1
Siedlce	Poland	32	M5
Siegen	Germany	35	D6
Siena	Italy	44	F5
Sierra de Alcaraz	Spain	41	H6
Sierra de Almijara	Spain	40	F8
Sierra de Aracena	Spain	40	C7
Sierra de Gata	Spain	40	D4
Sierra de Gredos	Spain	40	E4
Sierra de Guadarrama	Spain	40	F4
Sierra de Gúdar	Spain	41	K4
Sierra de la Peña	Spain	41	J2
Sierra de Taibilla	Spain	41	H7
Sierra Leone	West Africa	62	B3
Sierra Madre	Mexico	104	F5
Sierra Madre Occidental	Mexico	104	C3
Sierra Madre Oriental	Mexico	104	D4
Sierra Mojada	Mexico	101	F3
Sierra Morena	Spain	40	E6
Sierra Nevada	Spain	40	G8
Sierra Nevada	United States	96	C3
Sierras de Córdoba	Argentina	110	H5
Sifnos	Greece	48	G8
Sig	Algeria	41	K9
Sighetu Marmatiei	Romania	47	L2
Sighisoara	Romania	47	M3
Signy Island	South Atlantic Ocean	112	(2)A3
Sikhote-Alin	Russia	72	N8
Sikinos	Greece	48	G8
Silhouette	Seychelles	67	(2) B1
Siling Co	China	74	E2
Silistra	Bulgaria	47	Q5
Siljan	Sweden	29	H6
Silka	Russia	72	K6
Silvretta Gruppe	Austria / Switzerland	42	F4
Simbirsk	Russia	31	K4
Simferopol'	Ukraine	30	G6
Simi	Greece	49	K8
Simmern	Germany	35	C7
Simpson Desert	Australia	87	G5
Simrishamn	Sweden	29	H9
Sinai	Egypt	54	A6
Sindelfingen Böblingen	Germany	35	E8
Sines	Portugal	40	B7
Singapore	Asia	82	C2
Singen	Germany	35	D9
Singkawang	Indonesia	82	D2
Sinj	Croatia	46	D6
Sinjavina	Yugoslavia	46	G7
Sinop Burun	Turkey	50	F3
Sinsheim	Germany	35	D7
Sintana	Romania	33	C11
Sinuiju	North Korea	80	C3
Sion	Switzerland	39	N7
Sioux City	United States	98	A2
Sioux Falls	United States	94	G3
Sir Bani Yas	United Arab Emirates	55	E4
Sir Edward Pellew Group	Australia	87	G3
Siracusa (Syracuse)	Sicily (Italy)	45	K11
Siros	Greece	48	G7
Sisak	Croatia	46	D4
Sistema Central	Spain	40	D4
Sistema Penibético	Spain	40	E8
Sistemas Béticos	Spain	40	E8
Sittwe	Myanmar (Burma)	76	A2
Siwalik Range	Nepal / India	74	D3
Sjælland	Denmark	29	F9
Sjasstroj	Russia	30	G2
Skadarsko Jezero	Yugoslavia	46	G7
Skagen	Denmark	29	F8
Skagerrak	Norway / Denmark	29	D8
Skaidi	Norway	28	N1
Skarsvåg	Norway	28	N1
Skeena Mountains	Canada	92	E5
Skegness	United Kingdom	26	D1
Skellefte älv	Sweden	28	K4
Skellefteå	Sweden	28	L4
Skhiza	Greece	48	D8
Skíathos	Greece	48	F5
Skien	Norway	29	E7
Skierniewic	Poland	32	K6

Skiftet Kihti	*Finland*	29	L7
Skikda	*Algeria*	59	G1
Skiros	*Greece*	48	G6
Skjálfandafljöt	*Iceland*	28	(1)E2
Skjálfandi	*Iceland*	28	(1)E1
Skópelos	*Greece*	48	F5
Skopje	*Macedonia*	48	D2
Skye	*United Kingdom*	36	G4
Slagelse	*Denmark*	34	G1
Slantsy	*Russia*	30	F3
Slatina	*Romania*	47	M5
Slavkoje	*Ukraine*	33	N9
Slavonski Brod	*Croatia*	46	F4
Slavskoje	*Ukraine*	47	L1
Slavyansk	*Ukraine*	30	H5
Slievefelim Mountains	*Ireland*	37	E9
Sligo	*Ireland*	37	E7
Sliven	*Bulgaria*	47	P7
Slobozia	*Romania*	47	Q6
Slomim	*Belarus*	29	N10
Slovakia	*Europe*	33	H9
Slovenia	*Europe*	43	K5
Slyne Head	*Ireland*	37	C8
Smålandsfarvandet	*Denmark*	34	G1
Smallingerland	*Netherlands*	27	K1
Smallwood Réservoir	*Canada*	93	U6
Smederevo	*Yugoslavia*	46	H5
Smoky Hills	*United States*	102	B2
Smøla	*Norway*	28	D5
Smolensk	*Russia*	30	G4
Smolikas	*Greece*	48	C4
Smolyan	*Bulgaria*	47	M8
Smyrna (Izmir)	*Turkey*	50	B4
Snake River	*United States*	96	C1
Snåsavatn	*Norway*	28	F4
Sneek	*Netherlands*	27	J1
Snezka	*Czech Republic / Poland*	33	E7
Snowdon	*United Kingdom*	37	J9
Snowdonia	*United Kingdom*	37	J9
Sobaek-Sanmaek	*South Korea*	80	D6
Sobat	*Central Africa*	61	F6
Sochi (Soci)	*Russia*	51	H2
Soci (Sochi)	*Russia*	51	H2
Society Islands	*French Polynesia*	85	L7
Socorro	*United States*	101	E2
Socotra	*Yemen*	53	F7
Sodankylä	*Finland*	28	P3
Södehamn	*Sweden*	29	J6
Södra Kvarken	*Sweden / Finland*	29	K6
Sofia (Sofiya)	*Bulgaria*	47	L7
Sofiya (Sofia)	*Bulgaria*	47	L7
Sofporog	*Russia*	28	R4
Sogamoso	*Colombia*	108	C2
Sognefjorden	*Norway*	29	C6
Sohâg	*Egypt*	61	F2
Sohuksan	*South Korea*	80	C6
Soissons	*France*	26	G5
Sojoson-Man	*North Korea / China*	80	C4
Söke	*Turkey*	49	K7
Sokolov	*Czech Republic*	33	B7
Sokolov Podlaski	*Poland*	29	M10
Sokoto	*West Africa*	63	E2
Sokoto	*Nigeria*	63	F2
Solapur	*India*	75	C5
Solihull	*United Kingdom*	26	B2
Solimões	*South America*	108	D4
Solingen	*Germany*	35	C5
Sollefteå	*Sweden*	28	J5
Solomon Islands	*Oceania*	84	G6
Solta	*Croatia*	46	D6
Soltau	*Germany*	34	E4
Solunska	*Macedonia*	48	D3
Solway Firth	*United Kingdom*	37	K7
Solwezi	*Zambia*	64	D6
Somalia	*Central Africa*	65	H3
Sombar	*Yugoslavia*	46	G4
Somerset	*United States*	103	E2
Somerset Island	*Canada*	92	M2
Somes	*Hungary / Romania*	47	L2
Somme	*France*	38	H3
Son	*India*	74	D4
Sønderborg	*Denmark*	29	E9
Söndre Strømfjord	*Greenland*	93	V3
Sondrio	*Italy*	42	E4
Songea	*Tanzania*	65	F6
Songera	*Tanzania*	76	F2
Songhua Hu	*China*	79	H2
Songhua Jiang	*China*	79	H1
Songkhla	*Thailand*	76	C5
Sonneberg	*Germany*	35	G6
Sonsorol Islands	*Palau*	83	D1
Sont	*Denmark / Sweden*	29	G9
Sopka Shiveluch	*Russia*	73	U5
Sopron	*Hungary*	46	D2
Sora	*Italy*	44	H7
Soria	*Spain*	41	H3
Soroki	*Moldova*	47	R1
Sørøya	*Norway*	28	L1
Sorraia	*Portugal*	40	B5
Sorsele	*Sweden*	28	J4
Sort	*Spain*	41	M2
Sortavala	*Russia*	28	R6
Sosnow	*Poland*	33	J7
Sotra	*Norway*	29	C6
Souk Ahras	*Tunisia*	45	B12
Soul (Seoul)	*South Korea*	80	D5
Soumussalmi	*Finland*	28	Q4
Sound of Jura	*United Kingdom*	36	H6
Sound of Raasay	*United Kingdom*	36	G4
Sound of Sleat	*United Kingdom*	36	G5
Sousse	*Tunisia*	59	H1
South Africa	*South Africa*	66	C6
South Andaman	*India*	75	F6
South Aulatsivik Island	*Canada*	93	U5
South Australia	*Australia*	86	F5
South Bend	*United States*	98	C2
South Carolina	*United States*	103	E3
South China Sea (Nan Hai)	*China*	78	F6
South Dakota	*United States*	97	F2
South Downs	*United Kingdom*	37	N11
South East Cape	*Australia*	87	J8
South Georgia	*South Atlantic Ocean*	111	P9
South Island	*New Zealand*	89	B7
South Korea	*South East Asia*	79	H3
South Orkney Islands	*South Atlantic Ocean*	112	(2)A4
South Ronaldsay	*United Kingdom*	36	L3
South Taranaki Bight	*New Zealand*	88	D4
South Uist	*United Kingdom*	36	F4
South West Pacific Basin	*Oceania*	85	L9
Southampton	*United Kingdom*	37	M10
Southampton Island	*Canada*	93	Q4
Southend-on-Sea	*United Kingdom*	37	P10
Southern Alps	*New Zealand*	89	B7
Southern Ocean	*Australia*	86	E7
Southern Uplands	*United Kingdom*	36	J6
Southwest Cape	*New Zealand*	89	B8
Soutpansberg	*South Africa*	66	D4
Sovetsk	*Russia*	32	L2
Sovetskaya-Gaven	*Russia*	73	Q7
Sovetskiy	*Russia*	31	N2
Soya-Misaki	*Japan*	79	L1
Spain	*Europe*	40	F5
Spargi	*Sardinia (Italy)*	45	D7
Spencer Gulf	*Australia*	87	G6
Spenser Mountains	*New Zealand*	89	D6
Sperrin Mountains	*United Kingdom*	37	F7
Spessart	*Germany*	35	E7
Spey	*United Kingdom*	36	K4
Spiekeroog	*Germany*	34	C3
Spitsbergen	*Norway*	112	M1
Split	*Croatia*	46	D6
Spokane	*United States*	96	C1
Spree	*Germany*	34	K5
Springfield (Oreg.)	*United States*	96	B2
Springfield (Ill.)	*United States*	98	C3
Springfield (MO.)	*United States*	98	B3
Springs	*South Africa*	66	D5
Spurn Head	*United Kingdom*	37	P8
Srinagar	*India*	53	L3
Sredinnyy Khrebet	*Russia*	73	T6
Sredna Gora	*Bulgaria*	48	G2
Srednerusskaya Vozvysennost	*Russia*	30	G4
Srednesibirskoye Ploskogorye (Central Siberian Plain)	*Russia*	72	F4
Sredniy Ural	*Russia*	31	M4
Sremska Mitrovica	*Yugoslavia*	46	G5
Sri Lanka	*Indian Ocean*	75	D7
St. Alban's Head	*United Kingdom*	38	C3
St. Catherine's Point	*United Kingdom*	26	B4
St. David's Head	*United Kingdom*	37	H10
St. Elias Mountains	*United States*	100	(1)K3
St.Gallen	*Switzerland*	42	E3
St. George's Channel	*United Kingdom*	37	G10
St.Helena	*Atlantic Ocean*	57	C7
St. Helena Bay	*South Africa*	66	B6
St.Helier	*United Kingdom*	38	C4
St. John	*United States*	99	G1
St. John's	*Canada*	93	W7
St. John's	*United States*	103	E3
St. Kilda	*United Kingdom*	36	E4
St. Kitts-Nevis	*Caribbean*	105	M5
St. Lawrence Island	*United States*	100	(1)C3
St. Lawrence Seaway	*Canada*	99	F1
St. Louis	*Senegal*	58	B5
St. Louis	*United States*	98	B3
St. Lucia	*Caribbean*	105	M6
St. Malo	*France*	38	D5
St. Matthew	*United States*	100	(1)C3
St. Maurice	*Canada*	99	F1
St. Paul	*United States*	98	B2
St. Petersburg	*United States*	103	E4
St. Petersburg (Sankt-Peterburg)	*Russia*	30	G3
St.-Pierre and Miquelon	*North Alantic Ocean*	93	V7
St.-Quentin	*France*	26	G5
St. Vincent and The Grenadines	*Caribbean*	105	M6
Stade	*Germany*	29	E10
Stadskanaal	*Netherlands*	27	K2
Stalawa Wola	*Poland*	33	M7
Stanke Dimitrov	*Bulgaria*	47	L7
Stanley	*Falkland Islands*	111	K9
Stanovoy Khrebet	*Russia*	72	K6
Stanovoye Nagorye	*Russia*	72	J5
Stara Planina	*Yugoslavia / Bulgaria*	47	K6
Stara Zagora	*Bulgaria*	47	N7
Starachowice	*Poland*	32	L6
Staraya Russa	*Russia*	30	G3
Starbuck	*Kiribati (Pacific Ocean)*	85	L6
Stargad Szczecinski	*Poland*	32	E4
Starnberger Sea	*Germany*	35	G9
Start Point	*United Kingdom*	37	K11
Stassfurt	*Germany*	34	G5
Stavanger	*Norway*	29	C7
Stavropol'	*Russia*	30	J5
Stavropol'skaya Vozvyshennost	*Russia*	30	J5
Stefansson Island	*Canada*	92	K2
Steigerwald	*Germany*	35	F7
Stellenboch	*South Africa*	66	B6
Stendal	*Germany*	34	G4
Stenó Andikithiron	*Greece*	48	F9
Stenó Elafónissou	*Greece*	48	E8
Stenó Mikonou	*Greece*	48	H7
Stenó Tinou	*Greece*	48	G7
Stenón Karpathou	*Greece*	49	K8
Stenón Kithnou	*Greece*	48	G7
Stenón Serifou	*Greece*	48	G7
Sterling	*United States*	97	F2
Sterlitamak	*Russia*	31	M4
Stettiner Haff	*Germany / Poland*	34	K3
Stevenage	*United Kingdom*	26	B3
Stewart Island	*New Zealand*	89	B8
Steyr	*Austria*	43	K2
Stip	*Macedonia*	48	E3
Stockholm	*Sweden*	29	K7
Stockholms	*Sweden / Finland*	29	K7
Stockport	*United Kingdom*	37	L8
Stockton	*United States*	96	B3
Stockton Plateau	*United States*	101	F2
Stoke-on-Trent	*United Kingdom*	37	L8
Stora Lulevatten	*Sweden*	28	K3
Storavan	*Sweden*	28	K4
Stord	*Norway*	29	C7
Store Bælt	*Denmark*	29	F9
Storsjön	*Sweden*	28	H5
Storuman	*Sweden*	28	J4
Storuman	*Sweden*	28	J4
Stour	*United Kingdom*	38	F1
Strait of Belle Isle	*Canada*	93	S6
Strait of Bonifacio	*Europe*	45	C7
Strait of Canso	*Canada*	93	U7
Strait of Dover	*United Kingdom / France*	26	E4
Strait of Georgia	*Canada*	96	B1
Strait of Gibraltar	*Spain / Morocco*	40	D9
Strait of Hormuz	*Middle East*	55	F3
Strait of Juan de Fuca	*North America*	96	B1
Strait of Malacca	*Asia*	82	B2
Strait of Messina	*Italy*	45	K10
Strait of Otranto	*Italy*	45	N8
Straits of Florida	*United States*	103	E5
Stralsund	*Germany*	34	J2
Strasbourg	*France*	38	N5
Straubing	*Germany*	35	H8
Straumsjøen	*Norway*	28	H2
Streaky Bay	*Australia*	86	F6
Strimon	*Bulgaria / Greece*	48	F3
Strimonikós Kólpos	*Greece*	48	F4
Strogard Gdanski	*Poland*	32	H4
Stromboli	*Italy*	45	K10
Stronsay	*United Kingdom*	36	L2
Struma	*Turkey / Greece*	47	L8
Strumica	*Macedonia*	47	K8
Stry	*Ukraine*	33	N8
Stryn	*Norway*	29	D6
Stubaier Alps	*Austria*	42	G3
Stubbenkammer	*Germany*	34	J2
Stupsk	*Poland*	32	G3
Sturt Stony Desert	*Australia*	87	G5
Stuttgart	*Germany*	35	E8
Stykkishólmur	*Iceland*	28	B2
Styr	*Ukraine*	30	F4
Subbético	*Spain*	41	H6
Subotica	*Yugoslavia*	46	G3
Suceava	*Romania*	47	P2
Suchona	*Russia*	30	J2
Suchumi (Sukhumi)	*Georgia*	51	J2
Sucre	*Bolivia*	108	D7
Sudan	*West Africa*	62	D2
Sudan	*Central Africa*	60	E4
Sudbury	*Canada*	99	D1
Sudety Krkonose (Sudeten)	*Poland*	33	E7
Sudkarpaten	*Romania*	47	K4
Suez (As Suways)	*Egypt*	61	F1
Suez Canal	*Egypt*	61	F1
Suhar	*Oman*	55	G4
Suippes	*France*	27	H5
Sukhumi (Suchumi)	*Georgia*	51	J2
Sukkur	*Pakistan*	53	J4
Sula	*Norway*	29	C6
Sulaiman Range	*Southern Asia*	74	A2
Sulawesi (Célebes)	*Indonesia*	83	A3
Sulitjelma	*Norway*	28	J3
Sullana	*Peru*	108	A4
Sultan Daglari	*Turkey*	50	D4
Sulu Archipelago	*Philippines*	77	F6
Sulu Sea	*South East Asia*	77	F5
Sulzberger Bay	*Antarctica*	112	(2)BB2
Sumatera (Sumatra)	*Indonesia*	82	C3
Sumatra (Sumatera)	*Indonesia*	82	C3
Sumava	*Czech Republic*	33	C8
Sumba	*Indonesia*	86	C1
Sumbawanga	*Tanzania*	64	E5
Sumburgh Head	*United Kingdom*	36	M2
Sumgait	*Azerbaijan*	52	E1
Sumperk	*Czech Republic*	33	F8
Sumy	*Ukraine*	30	G4
Sunda Strait	*Asia*	82	D4
Sunderland	*United Kingdom*	37	M7
Sündiken Daglari	*Turkey*	50	D3
Sundsvall	*Sweden*	29	J5
Sup'ung-Chosuji	*North Korea*	80	C3
Superior	*Canada*	95	H2
Superior	*United States*	92	N7
Superior Upland	*United States*	98	B1
Süphan Dagı	*Turkey*	51	K4
Surabaya	*Indonesia*	82	E4
Surakarta	*Malaysia*	82	E4
Surat	*India*	74	B4
Surgut	*Russia*	70	N5

Name	Country / Region		Page	Grid
Surgutkiha	Russia	•	72	D4
Surinam	South America	A	109	F2
Surt (Sirte)	Libya	•	60	C1
Suruga-Wan	Japan	►	81	K6
Susac	Croatia	°	46	D7
Susice	Czech Republic	•	35	J7
Sutlej	Southern Asia	⌒	74	C2
Suursaari	Russia	°	29	P6
Suva Planina	Yugoslavia	▲	46	K6
Suvadiva Atoll	Maldives	°	75	B8
Suwalki	Poland	•	32	M3
Suwon	South Korea	•	80	D5
Suzhou	China	•	79	G4
Svalbard	Norway	a	112	P1
Sveg	Sweden	•	29	H5
Svendborg	Denmark	•	34	F1
Sverdrup Islands	Canada	°	112	(1)CC2
Svetac	Croatia	°	46	C7
Svetlyy	Russia	•	31	N4
Svetozarevo	Yugoslavia	•	46	J6
Svíahnúkar	Iceland	▲	28	(1)E2
Svilaja	Croatia	▲	46	D6
Swain Reefs	Australia	°	87	K4
Swakopmund	Namibia	•	66	A4
Swan	Caribbean	°	105	H5
Swansea	United Kingdom	•	37	J10
Swaziland	Southern Africa	A	67	E5
Sweden	Europe	A	28	H5
Swidnica	Poland	•	33	F7
Swidwin	Poland	•	32	E4
Swindon	United Kingdom	•	26	C3
Swinoujscie	Poland	•	32	D4
Switzerland	Europe	A	42	C4
Sydney	Australia	○	87	K6
Syktyvkar	Russia	○	70	J5
Sylt	Germany	°	34	D2
Syracuse	United States	•	99	E2
Syracuse (Siracusa)	Sicily (Italy)	•	45	K11
Syrdar'ya	Kazakhstan	⌒	71	M9
Syria	Middle East	A	54	D2
Syrian Desert (Badiet esh Sham)	Syria	⌀	54	E3
Syzran'	Russia	•	71	H7
Szczecin	Poland	•	32	D4
Szczecinek	Poland	•	32	F4
Szcztno	Poland	•	32	K4
Szeged	Hungary	○	33	K11
Székesfehérvár	Hungary	•	46	F2
Szekzárd	Hungary	•	46	F3
Szentes	Hungary	•	46	H3
Szómbathely	Hungary	•	46	D2

T

Name	Country / Region		Page	Grid
T'ai-nan	Taiwan	•	79	F6
T'ai-pei	Taiwan	■	79	G5
Ta'izz	Yemen	•	61	H5
Tablas	Philippines	°	77	G4
Table Cape	New Zealand	°	88	G4
Tábor	Czech Republic	•	33	D8
Tabora	Tanzania	○	65	E4
Tábris (Tabriz)	Iran	○	51	M4
Tabriz (Tābris)	Iran	○	51	M4
Tabuaeran	Kiribati (Pacific Ocean)	°	85	L5
Tachov	Czech Republic	•	33	B8
Tacloban	Philippines	•	77	H4
Tacoma	United States	•	96	B1
Tadzjikistan	Asia	A	53	J2
Taebaek-Sanmaek	North Korea / South Korea	▲	80	D4
Taegu	South Korea	○	80	E6
Taehan-Haehyop / (Korea Strait)	South Korea / Japan	►	80	D7
Taehuksan	South Korea	°	80	C6
Taejon	North Korea	○	80	D5
Tafahi	Tonga	A	85	J7
Taganrog	Russia	•	30	H5
Tagaytay City	Philippines	•	77	F4
Tagliamento	Italy	⌒	44	G3
Tahat	Algeria	▲	59	G4
Tahiti	French Polynesia	°	85	M7
Tahoua	Niger	•	59	G6
Tahtali Daglari	Turkey	▲	50	F5
Tai Hu	China	⌀	79	G4
Taibai Shan	China	▲	78	D4
Tainan	Taiwan	•	77	G2
Taipeh	Taiwan	■	77	G2
Taiwan	South East Asia	A	77	G2
Taiwan Strait	Taiwan / China	►	79	F6
Taiyetos	Greece	▲	48	E7
Taiyuan	China	○	78	E3
Tajo	Spain	⌒	40	G4
Tajrish	Iran	•	52	F2
Takamatsu	Japan	○	80	G6
Takaoka	Japan	•	81	J5
Takijuq Lake	Canada	⌀	92	J3
Takla Lake	Canada	⌀	92	F5
Tal'at Musá	Lebanon / Syria	▲	54	D2
Talak	Niger	⌀	59	F5
Talavera de la Reina	Spain	•	40	F5
Talca	Chile	•	110	G6
Talcahuano	Chile	•	110	G6
Taldy-Kurgan	Kazakhstan	○	71	P8
Talisayan	Malaysia	°	82	F2
Tallahassee	United States	○	103	E3
Tallinn	Estonia	■	29	N7
Tamale	Ghana	°	62	D3
Tamanrasset	Algeria	•	59	G4
Tamar	United Kingdom	⌒	38	A3
Tambacounda	Senegal	•	58	C6
Tambov	Russia	•	30	J4
Tambre	Spain	•	40	B2
Tâmega	Spain / Portugal	⌒	40	C3
Tammerfors (Tampere)	Finland	•	29	M6
Tampa	United States	•	103	E4
Tampere (Tammerfors)	Finland	•	29	M6
Tampico	Mexico	•	104	E4
Tamsweg	Austria	•	43	J3
Tan-Tan	Morocco	•	58	C3
Tana	Kenya	⌒	65	F4
Tana	Norway / Finland	•	28	P1
Tana Bru	Norway	•	28	Q1
Tanafjord	Norway	►	28	Q1
Tanami Desert	Australia	⌀	86	F3
Tanca	Peru	•	108	C7
Tanega-Shima	Japan	°	80	F8
Tanezrouft	Algeria	⌀	59	E4
Tanezrouft-Tan-Ahenet	Algeria	⌀	59	F4
Tanga	Tanzania	•	65	F5
Tanggula (Dangla) Shan	China	▲	74	E2
Tanggula Shan	China	▲	74	F2
Tangier	Morocco	○	58	D1
Tangra Yumco	China	⌀	74	E2
Tanimbar Islands	Indonesia	°	84	D6
Tanjung Cina	Indonesia	≥	82	C4
Tanjung Deyong	Indonesia	≥	83	E4
Tanjung Guhakolak	Indonesia	≥	82	C4
Tanjung Libobo	Indonesia	≥	83	C3
Tanjung Mengkalihat	Indonesia	≥	83	A2
Tanjung Pangkalsiang	Indonesia	≥	83	B3
Tanjung Perkam	Indonesia	≥	83	E3
Tanjung Selatan	Indonesia	≥	82	E3
Tanjung Sopi	Indonesia	≥	83	C2
Tanjung Vals	Indonesia	≥	83	E4
Tannu Ola	Mongolia / Russia	▲	71	S7
Tanta	Egypt	•	61	F1
Tanzania	Central Africa	A	65	E5
Taoudenni	Mali	•	58	E4
Tapa	Estonia	•	29	N7
Tapajós	South America	⌒	109	F4
Tappi-Zaki	Japan	°	81	K3
Tapul	Philippines	°	83	B1
Tara	Russia	•	31	Q3
Tara	Yugoslavia	⌒	46	G6
Tara	Yugoslavia	▲	46	G6
Tarábulus (Tripoli)	Libya	■	60	B1
Taranto	Italy	•	45	M8
Tararua Range	New Zealand	▲	88	E5
Tarasa	India	°	75	F7
Tarawa	Kiribati (Pacific Ocean)	▲	84	H5
Tarbagataj	Kazakhstan	▲	71	Q8
Tarbes	France	○	41	L1
Tarija	Bolivia	•	109	E8
Tarim Basin	China	⌀	71	Q10
Tarim He	China	⌒	71	Q9
Tarko-Sale	Russia	•	31	R2
Tarn	France	⌒	39	G10
Tärnaby	Sweden	•	28	H4
Tarnobrzeg	Poland	•	33	L7
Tarnow	Poland	•	33	L7
Taroudannt	Morocco	•	58	D2
Tarragona	Spain	•	41	M3
Tarrasa	Spain	•	41	M3
Tarso Emisu	Chad	▲	60	C3
Tarsus	Turkey	•	50	F5
Tartagul	Argentina	•	109	E8
Tartu	Estonia	•	29	P7
Tartus	Syrius	•	54	C2
Tarut	Saudi Arabia	°	55	D3
Tashauz	Turkmenistan	○	71	K9
Tashkent	Uzbekistan	■	71	M9
Tasikmalaya	Indonesia	•	82	D4
Tåsinge	Denmark	°	34	F2
Tasman Bay	New Zealand	►	88	D5
Tasman Sea	Australia	▬	87	K7
Tasmania	Australia	a	87	J8
Tassili-N'ajjer	Algeria	▲	59	G3
Tassili-Oua-n-Ahaggar	Algeria	⌀	59	F4
Tata Mailau	Indonesia	▲	83	C4
Tatabánya	Hungary	•	46	F2
Tatarbunary	Ukraine	•	47	S4
Tatarskiy Proliv	Russia	►	73	Q7
Tathlina Lake	Canada	⌀	92	H4
Tatry	Poland / Slovakia	▲	33	J8
Taunus	Germany	▲	35	D6
Taurage	Lithuania	•	32	M2
Tauranga	New Zealand	•	88	F3
Tauroa Point	New Zealand	►	88	D2
Tauyskaya Guba	Russia	►	73	R5
Tavda	Russia	•	31	P3
Tavda	Russia	⌒	31	N3
Tavoy	Myanmar (Burma)	•	76	B4
Tawau	Malaysia	•	77	F6
Tawitawi	Philippines	°	83	A2
Tay	United Kingdom	⌒	36	K5
Taza	Morocco	•	58	E2
Tbilisi (Tiflis)	Georgia	■	51	L3
Tczew	Poland	•	32	H3
Tecer Daglari	Turkey	▲	50	G4
Tecuci	Romania	•	47	Q4
Tedzhen	Turkmenistan / Afghanistan	⌒	53	H2
Tees	United Kingdom	⌒	37	L7
Tegucigalpa	Honduras	■	105	G6
Teheran (Tehran)	Iran	●	52	E2
Tehi-n-Isser	Algeria	▲	59	G3
Tehran (Teheran)	Iran	•	52	E2
Tejô	Spain / Portugal	⌒	40	B5
Teke Burun	Turkey	≥	48	J6
Tekirdag	Turkey	○	49	K3
Tekke Burun	Turkey	≥	48	H4
Tel Aviv-Yafo (Jaffa)	Israel	•	54	B4
Telukan Darvel	Malaysia	►	77	F6
Telukan Labuk	Malaysia	►	77	F5
Telukbetung	Indonesia	•	82	D4
Temirtau	Kazakhstan	•	31	Q4
Temple	United States	•	101	G2
Temuco	Chile	•	110	G6
Ten Degree Channel	Andaman Islands and Nicobar	►	75	F7
Tenali	India	•	75	C5
Ténéré	Niger	⌀	59	G5
Ténéré du Tafassasset	Niger	⌀	59	G4
Tenerife (Canary Islands)	Spain	°	58	B3
Ténès	Algeria	•	41	M8
Tennessee	United States	a	98	C3
Tennessee River	United States	⌒	98	C4
Tepic	Mexico	•	94	F7
Tepic	Mexico	○	104	D4
Teplice	Czech Republic	•	35	J6
Teramo	Italy	•	44	H6
Terceira (Azores)	Portugal	°	58	(1)B2
Teresina	Brazil	○	109	J5
Terminillo	Italy	▲	44	H6
Terneuzen	Netherlands	•	27	G3
Terni	Italy	•	44	G6
Ternopol'	Ukraine	•	30	F5
Tersakan Gölü	Turkey	⌒	49	Q6
Terschelling	Netherlands	°	27	J1
Teruel	Spain	○	41	J4
Teseney	Eritrea	•	61	G4
Tessiner Alps	Switzerland / Italy	▲	44	C2
Testa del Gargano	Croatia	≥	46	D8
Tétouan	Morocco	○	58	D1
Tetovo	Macedonia	•	48	D2
Teutoburger Wald	Germany	⌀	34	D4
Tevriz	Russia	•	31	Q3
Texakana	United States	•	102	C3
Texas	United States	a	102	B3
Texel	Netherlands	°	27	H1
Thabana Ntlenyana	Lesotho	▲	66	D5
Thailand	South East Asia	A	76	C3
Thames	United Kingdom	⌒	37	P10
Thanjavur	India	•	75	C6
Thásos	Greece	°	48	G4
The Black Sugarloaf	Australia	▲	87	K6
The Cheviot	United Kingdom	▲	36	L6
The Dalles	United States	•	96	B1
The Everglades	United States	⌀	103	E4
The Gulf	Middle East	►	55	C2
The Hague ('s-Gravenhage) (Den Haag)	Netherlands	○	38	J1
The Needles	United Kingdom	≥	26	B4
The Round Mountain	Australia	▲	87	K6
The Solent	United Kingdom	►	37	M11
The Wash	United Kingdom	►	37	P8
The Weald	United Kingdom	▲	37	N10
Themiet el Had	Algeria	•	41	N9
Thermaikós Kólpos	Greece	►	48	E4
Thessaloniki (Saloniki)	Greece	•	48	E4
Thiès	Senegal	•	58	B6
Thiladunmathi Atoll	Maldives	°	75	B7
Thionville	France	•	27	K5
Thira (Santorini)	Greece	°	48	G8
Thompson	Canada	•	92	M5
Thomson River	Australia	⌒	87	H4
Thonon-les-Bains	France	•	42	B4
Thrakikó Pélagos	Greece	►	48	G4
Three Kings Islands	New Zealand	°	88	C2
Thun	Switzerland	•	39	N7
Thunder Bay	Canada	•	93	P7
Thuner See	Switzerland	⌀	42	C4
Thüringer Wald	Germany	⌀	35	F6
Ti-n-Toumma	Niger	⌀	59	H5
Tianjin	China	○	78	F3
Tiber Reservoir	United States	⌀	96	D1
Tibesti	Chad	▲	60	C3
Tibet	China	⌀	74	D2
Tiburón	Mexico	°	104	B3
Tidjika	Mauritania	•	58	C5
Tiel	Netherlands	•	27	J3
Tien Shan	China	▲	71	Q9
Tienen	Belgium	•	27	H4
Tietê	Brazil	⌒	111	L3
Tiflis (Tbilisi)	Georgia	■	51	L3
Tighina	Moldova	•	47	S3
Tigris (Dicle)	Middle East	⌒	55	B1
Tihamat Ash Sham	Saudi Arabia	▲	52	D5
Tijuana	Mexico	•	104	A2
Tikhoreck	Russia	•	30	J5
Tikhvin	Russia	•	31	G3
Tiksi	Russia	•	72	M2
Tilburg	Netherlands	•	27	J3
Tillanchang	India	°	75	F7
Tilos	Greece	°	49	K8
Timanskiy Kryazh	Russia	▲	70	H5
Timaru	New Zealand	•	89	D7
Timimoun	Algeria	•	59	F3
Timisoara	Romania	○	46	J4
Timmins	Canada	•	93	Q7
Timor	Indonesia	A	84	C6
Timor Sea	South East Asia	▬	83	C5
Tinaca Point	Philippines	≥	77	G5
Tindouf	Algeria	•	58	D3
Tinée	France	⌒	42	C6
Tingsryd	Sweden	•	32	D1
Tinos	Greece	°	48	H7
Tirana (Tiranë)	Albania	■	48	B3
Tiranë (Tirana)	Albania	■	48	B3

Name	Region	Page	Grid
Tiraspol'	Moldova	47	S3
Tiraz Mountains	Namibia	66	B5
Tiree	United Kingdom	36	F5
Tirgoviste	Romania	47	N5
Tirgu Jiu	Romania	47	L4
Tirgu Mures	Romania	47	M3
Tirnaveni	Romania	47	M3
Tirunelveli	India	75	C7
Tisza	Europe	46	H2
Titov Veles	Macedonia	48	D3
Titov vrh	Macedonia	48	C3
Titovo Uzice	Yugoslavia	46	G6
Tizi Ouzou	Algeria	59	F1
Tjeukemeer	Netherlands	27	J2
Tjörn	Sweden	29	F8
Toamasina	Madagascar	67	J3
Toba & Kakar Ranges	Pakistan	53	J3
Tobago	Central America	108	E1
Tobi	Palau	83	D2
Tobol'sk	Russia	31	P3
Tobseda	Russia	31	L1
Todoga-Saki	Japan	81	M4
Togo	West Africa	62	E3
Toi-Misaki	Japan	80	F8
Tok-To (Take-Shima)	South Korea / Japan	80	G5
Tokara-Retto	Japan	84	D2
Tokelau	New Zealand	85	J4
Tokuno-Shima	Japan	79	H5
Tokushima	Japan	80	H7
Tokyo	Japan	81	K6
Tokyo-Wan	Japan	81	K6
Tol'yatti	Russia	71	H7
Tôlanaro	Madagascar	67	H4
Toledo	Spain	40	G5
Toledo	United States	98	D2
Toledo Bend Reservoir	United States	102	C3
Toliara	Madagascar	67	G4
Tolmezo	Italy	43	J4
Toluca de Lerdo	Mexico	104	D5
Tomaszów Mazowiecki	Poland	32	K6
Tombouctou	Mali	58	E5
Tomelloso	Spain	40	G5
Tomkinson Ranges	Australia	86	E6
Tomsk	Russia	71	R6
Tong-Hae / Nippon-Kai (Sea of Japan)	South East Asia	79	J2
Tonga	Oceania	85	J7
Tonga Islands	Tonga	85	J8
Tonga Trench	Oceania	85	J8
Tongatapu Group	Tonga	85	J8
Tonghua	China	80	C3
Tongjoson-Man	North Korea	80	D4
Tonle Sap	Cambodia	76	C4
Tonopah	United States	96	C3
Tooele	United States	96	D2
Topeka	United States	98	A3
Topozero	Russia	28	R4
Tori-Shima (Japan)	Japan	84	E3
Torino (Turin)	Italy	44	B3
Törmänen	Finland	28	P2
Tormes	Spain	40	E3
Torne älv	Sweden	28	L3
Torne träsk	Sweden	28	K2
Tornio	Finland	28	N4
Tornionjoki	Finland	28	N3
Toronto	Canada	93	Q8
Toros Daglari	Turkey	50	E5
Torquay	United Kingdom	37	K11
Torrelavega	Spain	40	F1
Torreón	Mexico	104	D3
Torres Strait	Australia	87	H2
Tortona	Italy	42	D6
Tortosa	Spain	41	L4
Torun	Poland	32	H4
Torysa	Slovakia	46	J1
Torzhok	Russia	30	G3
Tot'ma	Russia	30	J3
Tottori	Japan	80	H6
Tougan	Burkina Faso	62	D2
Touîl	Algeria	59	F1
Toul	France	42	A2
Toulon	France	39	M10
Toulouse	France	39	G10
Tourcoing	France	38	H3
Tournai	Belgium	26	G4
Tours	France	38	F6
Townsville	Australia	87	J3
Toyama	Japan	81	J5
Toyama-Wan	Japan	81	J5
Toyohashi	Japan	81	J6
Tozeur	Tunisia	59	G2
Trablous (Tripoli)	Lebanon	54	C2
Trabzon	Turkey	51	H3
Trail	Canada	96	C1
Trapani	Italy	45	G11
Traunsee	Austria	43	J3
Traunstein	Germany	33	B10
Traverse City	United States	98	C2
Trebic	Czech Republic	33	E8
Tregosse Islets	Australia	87	K3
Trelew	Argentina	110	H7
Trelleborg	Sweden	32	C2
Tremiti	Italy	46	C7
Trencin	Slovakia	33	H9
Trent	United Kingdom	37	M9
Trento	Italy	44	F2
Trenton	United States	99	F2
Treviso	Italy	43	H5
Trier	Germany	35	B7
Trieste	Italy	44	H3
Triglav	Slovakia	46	A3
Trikkala	Greece	48	D5
Trinec	Czech Republic	33	H8
Trinidad	United States	97	F3
Trinidad	Bolivia	109	F2
Trinidad	Central America	108	E1
Trinidad and Tobago	Caribbean	105	N6
Trinity Bay	Canada	93	W7
Tripoli (Tarábulus)	Libya	59	H2
Tripoli (Trablous)	Lebanon	54	C2
Tristan Da Cunha	Atlantic Ocean	57	B9
Trivandrum	India	75	C7
Trnava	Slovakia	43	N2
Trofors	Norway	28	G4
Troitsko-Pechorsk	Russia	31	M2
Tromso	Norway	28	K2
Trona	United States	100	C1
Trondheim	Norway	28	F5
Trondheimsfjorden	Norway	28	F5
Trout Lake	Canada	92	G4
Troyan	Bulgaria	47	M7
Troyes	France	38	K5
Trujillo	Peru	108	B5
Trung Phan	South East Asia	76	D3
Trutnov	Czech Republic	33	E7
Trysilelva	Norway	29	G6
Tsaris Mountains	Namibia	66	B4
Tshuapa	Central Africa	64	C4
Tsiafajavona	Madagascar	67	H3
Tsimlyanskoye Vdkhr.	Russia	30	J5
Tsu	Japan	81	J6
Tsuchiura	Japan	81	L5
Tsugaru-Kaikyo	Japan	81	L3
Tsumeb	Namibia	66	B3
Tsuruoka	Japan	81	K4
Tsushima	Japan	80	E6
Tsushima-Kaikyo (Korea Strait)	South Korea / Japan	80	D7
Tuamotu Archipelago	French Polynesia	85	M7
Tubruq	Libya	60	D1
Tubuai	French Polynesia	85	M8
Tubuai Islands	French Polynesia	85	L8
Tucson	United States	101	D2
Tucuruí	Brazil	109	H4
Tudela	Spain	41	J2
Tula	Russia	30	H4
Tulcea	Romania	47	R4
Tuloma	Russia	28	R2
Tulsa	United States	102	B2
Tumaco	Colombia	108	B3
Tundzha	Bulgaria	47	P7
Tunis	Tunisia	59	H1
Tunisia	North Africa	59	G2
Tununak	Alaska	100	D3
Tuostakh	Russia	73	P3
Tura	Russia	72	G4
Turda	Romania	47	L3
Turgay	Kazakhstan	31	N5
Turgayskaya Stolovaya Strana	Russia	31	N4
Turgovishte	Bulgaria	47	P6
Turhout	Belgium	27	H3
Turia	Spain	41	K5
Turimiquire	Venezuela	108	E2
Turin (Torino)	Italy	44	B3
Turkey	Europe	50	F4
Turkmenistan	Asia	53	G2
Turks and Caicos Islands	Caribbean	105	K4
Turku / Åbo	Finland	29	L6
Turnu Magurele	Romania	47	M6
Turquino	Cuba	105	J4
Turtle Island	Australia	87	K3
Tuticorin	India	75	C7
Tuttlingen	Germany	35	D9
Tutuila	American Samoa	85	K7
Tuul Gol	Mongolia	72	H7
Tuvalu	Oceania	84	H6
Tuxtla Gutiérrez	Mexico	104	F5
Tuz Gölü	Turkey	50	E4
Tuzla	Bosnia Herzegovina	46	F5
Tver'	Russia	30	H3
Tweed	United Kingdom	36	L6
Twilight Cove	Australia	86	E6
Twin Falls	United States	96	D2
Twin Islands	Canada	93	Q6
Two Thumb Range	New Zealand	89	D6
Tyan' Shan	China	71	Q9
Tychy	Poland	33	J7
Tyler	United States	102	C3
Tyne	United Kingdom	37	M7
Tyrifjorden	Norway	29	E6
Tyrrhenian Sea (Mare Tirreno)	Italy	45	G9
Tyumen	Russia	31	P3

U

Name	Region	Page	Grid
Uaupés	Brazil	108	D4
Ubangi	Central Africa	64	B2
Ubangi Chari	Central African Republic	64	B2
Ube	Japan	80	F7
Uberaba	Brazil	111	M2
Uberlândia	Brazil	109	H7
Uchiura-Wan	Japan	81	L2
Udachny	Russia	72	G4
Udaipur	India	74	B4
Uddevalla	Sweden	29	F7
Uddjaur	Sweden	28	K3
Udine	Italy	44	H2
Udskaya Guba	Russia	73	P5
Uecker	Germany	34	K3
Ueda	Japan	81	K5
Ufa	Russia	31	M4
Uganda	Central Africa	65	E3
Ugljan	Croatia	46	C5
Uherské Hradiste	Czech Republic	33	G8
Uíge	Angola	63	H6
Uji-Gunto	Japan	80	E8
Ujjain	India	74	C4
Ujung Pandang	Indonesia	83	A4
Ukhta	Russia	31	L2
Ukiah	United States	96	B3
Ukmerge	Lithuania	32	P2
Ukraine	Europe	30	G5
Ulaanbaator	Mongolia	72	H7
Ulan Ul Hu	China	74	F1
Ulan-Ude	Russia	72	H6
Ulhasnagar	India	74	B5
Ullung Do	South Korea	79	J3
Ulm	Germany	35	F8
Ulsan	South Korea	80	E6
Ulubat Gölü	Turkey	50	C3
Uludag	Turkey	50	C3
Uluguru Mountains	Tanzania	65	F5
Ulutau	Kazakhstan	31	P5
Ulya	Russia	73	Q5
Umba	Russia	28	T3
Ume älv	Sweden	28	K4
Umeå	Sweden	28	K5
Umm As Samim	Oman	53	G5
Umm Durman (Omdurman)	Sudan	61	F4
Umnak Island	United States	100	(1)D5
Umtata	South Africa	66	D6
Una	Croatia	44	L3
Unalaska Island	United States	100	(1)D5
Ungava Bay	Canada	93	T5
Unije	Croatia	46	B5
Unimak Island	United States	100	(1)E5
United Arab Emirates	Middle East	55	E5
United Kingdom	Europe	36	M5
United States	North America	94	E4
Unst	United Kingdom	36	N1
Unza	Russia	30	J3
Upington	South Africa	66	C5
Upolu	Western Samoa	85	J7
Upper Lough Erne	United Kingdom	37	F7
Uppsala	Sweden	29	K7
Ural	Kazakhstan	31	L4
Ural'sk	Kazakhstan	31	L4
Ural'skiy Khrebet Ural Mountains	Russia	71	K7
Uranium City	Canada	92	K5
Uray	Russia	31	N2
Urbino	Italy	43	H7
Urfa	Turkey	51	H5
Urfa Yaylâsi	Turkey	51	H5
Urgench	Uzbekistan	71	L9
Uritskiv	Kazakhstan	31	P4
Uruapan del Progreso	Mexico	104	D5
Uruguaiana	Brazil	111	L3
Uruguay	Uruguay	111	K5
Uruguay	South America	111	K5
Ürümqi	China	71	R9
Uryupinsk	Russia	30	J4
Usak	Turkey	49	M6
Usambara Mountains	Tanzania	65	F4
Usedom	Germany / Poland	34	J3
Usetin	Czech Republic	33	G8
Ushuaia	Argentina	110	H9
Usinsk	Russia	31	M1
Ussel	France	39	H8
Ussuri	Russia	72	N7
Ussuriysk	Russia	80	G1
Ust'-Nera	Russia	73	Q4
Ust-Ilimsk	Russia	72	G5
Ust-Isil'ma	Russia	31	L1
Ust-kamchatsk	Russia	73	U5
Usti nad Labem	Czech Republic	35	K6
Ustica	Italy	45	H10
Usumacinta	Guatemala	104	F5
Utah	United States	96	D3
Utah Lake	United States	96	D2
Utena	Lithuania	29	N9
Utrecht	Netherlands	27	J2
Utrera	Spain	40	E7
Utsjoki	Finland	28	P2
Utsunomiya	Japan	81	K5
Uvéa	Wallis and Futuna	85	J7
Uvira	Democratic Republic of Congo	64	D4
Uvs Nuur	Mongolia	71	S7
Uyo	Nigeria	63	F3
Uzbekistan	Asia	71	L9
Uzgorod	Poland	33	M9
Uzhgorod	Ukraine	47	K1
Uzungwa Range	Tanzania	65	F5
Uzunköprü	Turkey	47	P8

V

Name	Region	Page	Grid
Vaal	South Africa	66	D5
Vaasa	Finland	28	L5
Vác	Hungary	46	G2
Vadehavet	Denmark	34	D1
Vadodara	India	53	K5
Vadsø	Norway	28	Q1
Vågsfjorden	Norway	28	J2
Váh (Vág)	Slovakia	33	H10
Val-d'Or	Canada	99	E1

Name	Location	Page	Grid
Valdagno	Italy	42	G5
Valdepenas	Spain	40	G6
Valdivia	Chile	110	G6
Valdosta	United States	103	E3
Valence	France	39	K9
Valencia	Spain	41	K5
Valenciennes	France	26	G4
Valentine	United States	97	F2
Valga	Estonia	29	P8
Valjevo	Yugoslavia	46	G5
Vall de Uxó	Spain	41	K5
Valladolid	Spain	40	F3
Valle	Norway	29	D7
Vallée de l'Azaouak	Mali / Niger	59	F5
Vallée du Tilemsi	Mali	59	F5
Valletta	Malta	45	J13
Valli di Comacchio	Italy	43	H6
Valmiera	Latvia	29	N8
Valparaíso	Chile	110	G5
Valuyki	Russia	30	H4
Van	Turkey	51	K4
Van Diemen Gulf	Australia	86	F2
Van Gölü	Turkey	51	K4
Vancouver	Canada	92	G7
Vancouver Island	Canada	92	F7
Vänern	Sweden	29	G7
Vänersborg	Sweden	29	G7
Vanna	Norway	28	K1
Vannes	France	38	C6
Vansittart Island	Canada	93	Q3
Vanua Levu	Fiji	84	H7
Vanuatu	Oceania	84	G2
Var	France	42	B6
Varanasi	India	74	D3
Varangerfjord	Norway	28	Q1
Varazdin	Croatia	46	D3
Varberg	Sweden	29	G8
Vardar	Macedonia	48	D3
Varese	Italy	42	D5
Varkous	Finland	28	Q5
Varna	Bulgaria	47	R6
Värnamo	Sweden	29	G8
Varniai	Lithuania	32	M2
Vasa Barris	Brazil	109	K6
Vaskaganish	Canada	93	R6
Västerås	Sweden	29	J7
Västervik	Sweden	29	J8
Vasto	Italy	44	J6
Vatican City	Europe	44	G7
Vatnajökull	Iceland	28	(1)E2
Vättern	Sweden	29	H7
Vaubecourt	France	27	J6
Vaucouleurs	France	42	A2
Växjö	Sweden	29	H8
Vega	Norway	28	F4
Vejle	Denmark	29	E9
Vel'sk	Russia	30	J2
Velebit	Croatia	46	C5
Velez	Bosnia-Herzegovina	46	F6
Vélez-Málaga	Spain	40	F8
Velika Kapela	Croatia	46	B4
Velikaya	Russia	73	W4
Velikiye-Luki	Russia	30	G3
Veliko Turnovo	Bulgaria	47	N6
Velingrad	Bulgaria	47	M7
Velino	Italy	44	H6
Vellore	India	75	C6
Veluwemeer	Netherlands	27	J2
Velzen	Germany	34	F4
Venezia (Venice)	Italy	44	G3
Venezuela	South America	108	D2
Venice (Venezia)	Italy	44	G3
Venraij	Netherlands	27	J3
Ventimiglia	Italy	39	N10
Ventotene	Italy	45	H8
Ventspils	Latvia	29	L8
Venus Bay	Australia	87	H7
Veracruz Llave	Mexico	104	E5
Verbania	Italy	42	D5
Vercelli	Italy	42	D5
Verdon	France	42	B7
Verdun	France	27	J5
Vereeniging	South Africa	66	D5
Verhovina	Ukraine	47	M1
Verhoyanskiy Khrebet	Russia	72	M3
Vermont	United States	99	F2
Vernon	France	26	E5
Vernon	United States	101	G2
Véroia	Greece	48	E4
Verona	Italy	44	E3
Versailles	France	38	G5
Verviers	Belgium	27	J4
Vesoul	France	38	L6
Vestbygd	Norway	28	D7
Vesterålen	Norway	28	H2
Vestfjorden	Norway	28	H2
Vestvågøy	Norway	28	G2
Vesuvio	Italy	45	J8
Veszprém	Hungary	46	E2
Vetlanda	Sweden	29	G8
Vézère	France	39	G8
Viana de Castelo	Portugal	40	B3
Viangchan (Vientiane)	Laos	76	C3
Viareggio	Italy	42	F7
Viborg	Denmark	29	E8
Vic	Spain	41	N3
Vicenza	Italy	44	F3
Vichy	France	39	J7
Victoria	Canada	96	B1
Victoria	United States	101	G3
Victoria	Australia	87	H7
Victoria	China	77	E2
Victoria	Canada	92	G7
Victoria	Papua New-Guinea	84	E6
Victoria de Durango	Mexico	104	D4
Victoria Falls	South Africa	66	D3
Victoria Island	Canada	92	K2
Victoria Nile	Uganda	65	E3
Victoria Strait	Canada	92	L3
Vidal	United States	100	D2
Vidin	Bulgaria	47	K6
Viedma	Argentina	110	J7
Vienna (Wien)	Austria	43	M2
Vienne	France	38	F6
Vientiane (Viangchan)	Laos	76	C3
Vierwaldstätter See	Switzerland	42	D3
Vierzon	France	38	H6
Vietnam	South East Asia	76	C2
Vigevano	Italy	42	D5
Vigo	Spain	40	B2
Vihena	Brazil	108	E6
Viitasaari	Finland	28	N5
Vijayawada	India	75	C5
Vik	Iceland	28	D3
Vikhren	Bulgaria	47	L8
Vikna	Norway	28	F4
Vila Real	Portugal	40	C3
Vilaine	France	38	D6
Vilanova i la Geltrú	Spain	41	M3
Viliya	Northern Europe	32	P3
Viljandi	Estonia	29	N7
Villablino	Spain	40	D2
Villach	Austria	43	J4
Villagarcia de Arosa	Spain	40	B2
Villahermosa	Mexico	104	F5
Villalba	Spain	40	C1
Villefranche-sur-Saône	France	39	K7
Villena	Spain	41	K6
Vilnius	Lithuania	29	N9
Vilyuy	Russia	72	K4
Vilyuyskoye Vdkhr.	Russia	72	J4
Vinaroz	Spain	41	L4
Vindelälven	Sweden	28	K4
Vindhya Range	India	74	C4
Vinkovci	Croatia	46	F4
Vinnitsa	Ukraine	30	F5
Vinson Massif	Antarctica	112	(2)JJ2
Vir	Croatia	46	C5
Vire	France	26	C6
Virful Moldoveanu	Romania	47	M4
Virful Pietrosul	Romania	30	E5
Virgin Islands (UK)	Caribbean	105	M5
Virgin Islands (US)	Caribbean	105	L5
Virginia	United States	99	E3
Virginia Beach	United States	99	E3
Virovitica	Croatia	46	E4
Virrat	Finland	28	M5
Virton	Belgium	27	J5
Virtul Peleaga	Romania	47	K4
Vis	Croatia	46	D6
Visayan Sea	Philippines	77	G4
Visby	Sweden	29	K8
Viscount Melville Sound	Canada	92	J2
Viseu	Portugal	40	C4
Vishakhapatnam	India	75	D5
Vistula (Wisla)	Poland	32	L6
Vitebsk	Belarus	30	G3
Viterbo	Italy	44	G6
Viti Levu	Fiji	84	H7
Vitön	Northern Europe	112	(1)N2
Vitoria	Spain	40	H2
Vitória	Brazil	111	N3
Vitorog	Bosnia-Herzegovina	46	D5
Vittel	France	42	A2
Vittorio Veneto	Italy	43	H5
Vivero	Spain	40	C1
Vjaz'ma	Russia	30	G3
Vladikavkaz	Russia	51	L2
Vladimir	Russia	30	J3
Vladivostok	Russia	80	F2
Vlasic	Yugoslavia	46	G5
Vlasic	Bosnia-Herzegovina	46	E5
Vlieland	Netherlands	27	H1
Vlorë	Albania	48	B4
Vltava (Moldau)	Czech Republic	33	D8
Vltave	Czech Republic	35	K6
Vogelsberg	Germany	35	E6
Voghera	Italy	42	E5
Volcán Baru	Panama / Costa Rica	108	A2
Volcan Corcovado	Chile	110	G7
Volcan Cotopaxi	Ecuador	108	B4
Volcan Domuyo	Argentina	110	G6
Volcan Irazu	Costa Rica	105	H6
Volcan Lanin	Chile / Argentina	110	G6
Volcán Tajumulco	Guatemala	104	F6
Volga	Russia	31	K4
Volgodonst	Russia	30	J5
Volgograd	Russia	30	J5
Vologda	Russia	30	H3
Vólos	Greece	48	F5
Volzhskiy	Russia	30	J5
Vorderrhein	Switzerland	42	D4
Vories Sporádes (Sporades)	Greece	48	F6
Vorkuta	Russia	70	L4
Vormsi	Estonia	29	M7
Voronezh	Russia	30	H4
Voru	Estonia	29	P8
Vosges	France	38	M6
Vostochnyy Sayan	Russia	72	F6
Vostocno-Sibirskoye More (East Siberian Sea)	Russia	73	T2
Vostok	Kiribati (Pacific Ocean)	85	L7
Vranica	Bosnia-Herzegovina	46	E5
Vranje	Yugoslavia	48	D2
Vratsa	Bulgaria	47	L6
Vrbas	Bosnia-Herzegovina	46	N6
Vrbovsko	Croatia	46	C4
Vrsac	Yugoslavia	46	J4
Vukovar	Croatia	46	F4
Vuktyl'	Russia	31	M2
Vulcano	Italy	45	K10
Vyatka	Russia	112	L4
Vyborg	Russia	30	F2
Vyshniy-Volochek	Russia	30	G3
Vytegra	Russia	30	H2
Vyvenka	Russia	73	V4

W

Name	Location	Page	Grid
Wa	Ghana	62	D3
Waal	Netherlands	27	J3
Wabash	United States	102	D2
Wabe Shebele	Ethiopia / Somalia	65	G2
Waco	United States	102	B3
Waconda	United States	98	A3
Wadi al Batin	Middle East	55	B2
Wadi ash Shati	Libya	60	B2
Wad Medani	Sudan	61	F5
Waddeneilanden	Netherlands	27	H1
Waddenzee	Netherlands	27	J1
Wadi al Arish	Egypt	54	A6
Wadi al 'Inab	Saudi Arabia / Jordan	54	D6
Wadi Ba'ir	Saudi Arabia / Jordan	54	E5
Wadi Halfa	Sudan	61	F3
Wadi Jabjabah	Sudan	61	F3
Wadi Sirhan	Saudi Arabia / Jordan	54	E5
Wadi Watir	Egypt	54	B7
Wahat Jalu	Libya	60	D2
Waigeo	Indonesia	83	D2
Waitaki River	New Zealand	89	D7
Wakasa-Wan	Japan	80	H6
Wakayama	Japan	80	H6
Wake	United States	84	G3
Waku-Kungo	Angola	64	B5
Walbrzych	Poland	33	F7
Wales	Alaska	100	D2
Wales	United Kingdom	37	J9
Wales Island	Canada	93	P3
Wallis and Futuna	France (Pacific Ocean)	85	J7
Walliser Alps	Switzerland	42	C4
Walsall	United Kingdom	26	B2
Walvis Bay	Namibia	66	A4
Wanganui	New Zealand	88	E4
Wanganui	New Zealand	88	E4
Wangerooge	Germany	34	C3
Wangpan Yang	China	79	G4
Wanxian	China	78	D4
Warangal	India	75	C5
Warburton Range	Australia	86	E5
Warnow	Germany	34	G3
Warsaw (Warszawa)	Poland	32	L5
Warszawa (Warsaw)	Poland	32	L5
Warta	Poland	32	F5
Wasatch Range	United States	97	D3
Washington	United States	96	B1
Washington	United States	99	E3
Washington D.C.	United States	99	E3
Wasserkuppe	Germany	35	E6
Waterberg Plateau	Namibia	66	B3
Watertown (SD.)	United States	97	F2
Watertown (N.Y.)	United States	99	E2
Watson Lake	Canada	92	F4
Watton	United Kingdom	26	D2
Wausau	United States	98	C1
Wear	United Kingdom	37	L7
Webi Shabelle	Ethiopia / Somalia	65	H3
Weddell Sea	Antarctica	112	(2)A2
Weert	Netherlands	27	J3
Wei He	China	78	D4
Weiden	Germany	35	H7
Weima	Germany	35	G5
Weinheim	Germany	35	D7
Weisse Elster	Germany / Czech Republic	35	H5
Weissenfels	Germany	35	G5
Weitra	Austria	43	K2
Welkom	South Africa	66	D5
Welland	United Kingdom	37	N9
Wellesley Islands	Australia	87	G3
Wellington	New Zealand	89	E5
Wells	United States	96	D2
Wels	Austria	43	K2
Wenatchee	United States	96	B1
Wenman	Ecuador	108	(1)A1
Wenzhou	China	79	G5
Werra	Germany	35	E7
Wertheim	Germany	35	E7
Wesel	Germany	27	K3
Weser	Germany	34	E3
Weserbergland	Germany	34	E5
Wessel Islands	Australia	87	G2
West Alps	France	42	B6
West Cape	New Zealand	84	G10
West Falkland	South Atlantic Ocean	111	J9
West Siberian Plain	Russia	70	N5
West Virginia	United States	99	D3
Western Australia	Australia	86	D5
Western Sahara (Morocco)	West Africa	58	C4

World Physical, Pacific Projection